Transfer Pricing Developments Around the World 2022

Transfer Pricing Developments Around the World 2022

Edited by

Michael Lang
Raffaele Petruzzi

Wolters Kluwer

Published by:
Kluwer Law International B.V.
PO Box 316
2400 AH Alphen aan den Rijn
The Netherlands
E-mail: lrs-sales@wolterskluwer.com
Website: www.wolterskluwer.com/en/solutions/kluwerlawinternational

Sold and distributed by:
Wolters Kluwer Legal & Regulatory U.S.
7201 McKinney Circle
Frederick, MD 21704
United States of America
E-mail: customer.service@wolterskluwer.com

ISBN 978-94-035-4603-2

e-Book: ISBN 978-94-035-4623-0
web-PDF: ISBN 978-94-035-4633-9

Editors

Michael Lang holds a chair in tax law with special emphasis on international tax law. He is Director of the LL.M. Program in International Tax Law and Head of the Institute for Austrian and International Tax Law. The research group at the Institute is jointly led by Josef Schuch, Claus Staringer, Michael Lang, Caroline Spies, Georg Kofler and Alexander Rust, and consists of more than thirty-five researchers. Their fields of specialization are International and European Tax Law and Business Tax Law. Michael Lang is also the Chairman of the Academic Committee of the European Association of Tax Law Professors (EATLP) and has been visiting professor at Sorbonne University, France; NYU, U.S.; Georgetown Law School, U.S.; the University of Florida, U.S.; University of Sao Paulo, Brazil; Peking University; and other academic institutions. He is Member of the Editorial Board of the *World Tax Journal*, one of the Editors-in-Chief of the *Bulletin of International Taxation*. In his research, he focuses on ECJ case law and tax treaty law.

Raffaele Petruzzi, LL.M., is the Managing Director of the WU Transfer Pricing Center at the Institute for Austrian and International Tax Law at WU (Vienna University of Economics and Business), Austria and an international tax advisor specializing in international tax and transfer pricing at Baker McKenzie, where is part of the EMEA Transfer Pricing Group and is the Head of the Austria Transfer Pricing Group.
Raffaele has gained extensive experience in dealing with topics related to international tax and transfer pricing for many years, from both a professional and an academic side. He is a frequent speaker in international conferences and lecturer of numerous courses all over the world, as well as author of many publications. Finally, among others, he is a member of the United Nations Subcommittee on Transfer Pricing, of the International Fiscal Association (IFA), and of Transfer Pricing Economists for Development (TPED). Raffaele holds a Ph.D. in International Business Taxation at WU, an LL.M. in International Tax Law at WU, and an M.Sc. in Business Administration and Law at Bocconi University, Italy.

Contributors

Önder Albayrak is the Head of Transfer Pricing and Head of Tax for a global biopharmaceutical company providing healthcare solutions in more than 170 countries. Following his career at a Big4 firm, he moved in 2006 to industry to work at a NASDAQ-listed biotechnology company which got acquired in 2011 by a global pharmaceutical company. With the acquisition, he pursued his career in various regional and global corporate tax and transfer pricing roles.

During his twenty+ years of experience in international taxation, he advised and supported corporate, regional and local management, operations, finance and legal teams on international corporate taxation and transfer pricing matters such as intangible assets planning, supply chain and transfer pricing structuring, business expansions and restructurings, post-merger integrations, tax and transfer pricing controversy and negotiations with tax administrations.

Önder Albayrak holds an LL.M. in Dutch and International Tax Law from the University of Utrecht, the Netherlands and appears from time to time as guest speaker and lecturer at conferences and courses.

Mukesh Butani is Founder and Managing Partner of BMR Legal Advocates, a boutique law firm. With specialization in domestic corporate international tax and transfer pricing, he has over three decades of experience in advising multinationals and Indian conglomerates on a wide range of matters relating to FDI policy, business reorganizations, cross-border tax structuring, tax controversy and regulatory policy. He is an acknowledged expert with several landmark judgments to his credit in the areas of international tax policy, controversy and advocacy. He has deposed as Expert Witness on contentious cross-border tax treaty and TP matters in foreign jurisdictions. Mukesh is a qualified Chartered Accountant and holds a Bachelor's in Commerce and Law, and practices as an Advocate before various Tribunals, High Courts and the Supreme Court of India. He has been consistently ranked as Leading Individual (*Legal 500*), Elite Practitioner (*Asialaw Profiles*), Litigation Star (*Benchmark Litigation*), Band 1 Lawyer (*Chamber & Partners*) and Thought Leader (*Who's Who Legal*).

Stefaan De Baets is a senior counsel in the transfer pricing team of PwC Belgium since 1 January 2016, where he is responsible for avoiding and settlement of transfer pricing controversy, further development of the transfer pricing market, and promoting the key presence of PwC on that market as well as delivering contributions to the development of transfer pricing policies. From 1 April 2011 to 31 December 2015, he was a transfer pricing advisor at the OECD in Paris, France. Until he joined the OECD, Stefaan worked for the Federal Public Service of Finances in Belgium, mostly on transfer pricing and international tax, for more than twenty years. He was a delegate for Belgium to OECD Working Party 6 (transfer pricing) from March 1996 to March 2011 and to the Joint Transfer Pricing Forum from March 2003 to March 2011. Stefaan is a guest lecturer on international taxation at the University of Lausanne, Switzerland, the Ecole des Mines (France) and Catholic University of Leuven, Belgium. He is a regular guest speaker or panelist at international tax events.

Gianni De Robertis is the Chief Economist, Head of Transfer Pricing and Economic Consulting Services of Studio Associato (a KPMG international affiliate in Italy) and GTPS Leader for the KPMG EMA Region. Gianni has provided assistance for more than twenty years to multinational companies operating in Europe, America and the Asia Pacific regions. His main areas of expertise include the economics of international taxation, intra-firm trade (economic, fiscal and management aspects), value chain and IP analyses, pricing analysis and management.

Clive Jie-A-Joen is a Ph.D. economist and Master of Business Valuation with a specialism in transfer pricing, and counsel within the Financial Markets practice group of Simmons & Simmons. He designs, implements, documents and defends transfer pricing policies for multinational enterprises. Clive has more than two decades of experience working on the pricing of related party transactions, such as financial transactions and transfers of intangibles, for clients in various industries. Clive is part of a team focussing on controversy management of transfer pricing and dispute resolution and on avoidance of double taxation, considering both the quantitative and procedural angles of the tax and transfer pricing issues on the table. Clive is also an university lecturer on transfer pricing at the Erasmus School of Law and a Board member of the Transfer Pricing section of the Dutch Association of Tax Advisors. He is recognized as leader in TP in Legal Media's Transfer Pricing Guide and rated as highly regarded in World TP.

Seema Kejriwal is a partner in the firm BMR Legal Advocates, specializing in corporate international tax and transfer pricing with nearly two decades of experience in advising *Fortune 500* multinationals and large Indian business houses on a wide range of international tax and transfer pricing matters. Seema is a Commerce graduate from the University of Mumbai, India and is a qualified Chartered Accountant. She has worked with Big 4 firms and was seconded to U.S. transfer pricing practice of the firm. Besides her contributions to public policy initiatives of the firm, she regularly speaks at global seminars and contributes to research papers and columns on tax and transfer pricing policy which find mention in leading academic publications such as Vienna University, Kluwers, Bloomberg, and Tax Notes.

Dorottya Kovács is a Senior Transfer Pricing Associate at PwC Austria and a Research and Teaching Associate in the WU Transfer Pricing Center at the Institute for Austrian and International Tax Law at WU (Vienna University of Economics and Business), Austria. Dorottya has also gained practical experience in international tax and transfer pricing while working at the Tax Department of Sberbank Europe (Vienna) and at Bella Beratung (Mönchof). Her main responsibilities included *inter alia* global transfer pricing documentation, consolidation of country-by-country reports, calculation of head office charges, group tax risks monitoring and reporting, development of tax methodologies and procedures, tax communications on projects and transfer pricing audit defense. Dorottya is a Doctoral Candidate in Economics and Social Sciences at the WU (Vienna University of Economics and Business).

Yasmin Lawson is a PwC – Research Project Associate at the Institute for Austrian and International Tax Law at WU (Vienna University of Economics and Business), Austria. Yasmin is currently working in research at the institute while also gaining practical experience in domestic and international tax law at PwC. Her main focus is on cross-border restructurings and transactions from a tax perspective, but she also does research in the areas of mandatory disclosure rules and cryptocurrencies. Yasmin is a Doctoral Candidate in Law at the WU (Vienna University of Economics and Business), Austria.

Marc M. Levey is Senior Counsel in the New York office of Baker & McKenzie. He has over forty years of experience in international taxation and is a nationally recognized expert in his field, particularly in structuring and defending transfer pricing strategies. He has frequently been acknowledged by Euromoney as one of the "World's Leading Tax Advisors," included in its "Best of the Best" global tax experts. Mr. Levey's practice focuses on transfer pricing and cross-border transactions; tax controversies and litigation; general corporate, international and partnership taxation, and restructuring multinational company's global operations. He has also worked extensively in various capacities with not-for-profit organizations. Mr. Levey served as the past Chair of the firm's Global Transfer Pricing Steering Committee. Mr. Levey previously served as Tax Attorney with the International Tax Ruling Group of the National Office of the IRS from 1975 to 1977. He acted as Senior Trial Attorney with the Tax Division of the U.S. Department of Justice from 1977 to 1981.

Carlos Mallen has more than fifteen years of experience in transfer pricing consultancy and documentation, as well as two years of experience in tax automations. Throughout his career, Carlos has focused on financial modeling and has developed several technological solutions for the business units he has worked for. Carlos is constantly working with clients to develop End-To-End (E2E) tools that reduce the time needed to comply with transfer pricing obligations and monitor transfer pricing policies.

Carlos is currently a director in PwC Mexico's Transfer Pricing business unit. Carlos has a strong programming background, as well as outstanding research and analytical skills, which allow him to develop technological solutions from scratch. Additionally, Carlos holds a position as a Digital Accelerator in PwC Mexico. In his role as a Digital Accelerator, Carlos helps other business units increase their digital services offering and boost the adoption of new technologies.

From March 2019 to March 2021, Carlos was a director in PwC Mexico's Tax Reporting & Strategy business, where he acquired a deeper understanding of taxes and helped clients with transfer pricing and tax automations, in areas such as value-added tax and payroll, among others. From January to November 2015, Carlos was seconded as a transfer pricing manager to the New York office of PwC USA, where he assisted leading European clients in the commercial banking industry.

Carlos has a Bachelor of Science in Economics from Instituto Tecnológico Autónomo de México, Mexico, a diploma in Corporate Finance from Universidad Iberoamericana, Mexico and a course in data science from the University of California, Berkeley.

Marta Milewska holds a Ph.D. in Financial Science and she is a Transfer Pricing Partner in PricewaterhouseCoopers' Mexico City office. Over her fifteen years plus career in transfer pricing, she has advised companies on how to best navigate the ever-evolving international business landscape. She has helped multinationals with the planning and execution of efficient international operational structuring and with the design and implementation of their global transfer pricing policies. Her experience covers nearly all areas of intercompany dealings, with principal focus on licensing transactions, transfers of intangibles, financial services dealings, and services arrangements. In particular, she has performed projects in the consumer goods, pharmaceuticals, mining, heavy and industrial equipment industries. She has also been involved in resolving controversial issues with tax authorities in audit defense environments. Marta has authored numerous publications on the economics of transfer pricing dedicated to impact of behavioral economics on transfer pricing, transfer pricing in resource-dependent developing countries, as well as a series of articles on value creation and second-brand strategies for the *International Transfer Pricing Journal*, *International Tax Review*, *Financier Worldwide*, *Tax Notes International*, and *Puntos Finos*. Marta is also a frequent speaker at transfer pricing, conferences and training workshops. Marta is part of Transfer Pricing Economists for Development, a think tank aimed at promoting the development and sharing of business economics knowledge in transfer pricing as an enabler of development of emerging economies and developing countries.

Anh Nguyen is a senior manager in KPMG's Economic and Valuation Services (EVS) practice in Chicago. Anh has more than ten years of experience providing transfer pricing (TP) services across various industries, including industrial goods, food and beverages, real estates, telecommunication, and business services. Anh works on a variety of TP-related issues, including documentation and planning, and tax controversy engagements.

Prita Subramanian is Principal with the Economic and Valuation Services group of the Washington National Tax (WNT) practice at KPMG. As a senior transfer pricing economist, Prita supports a variety of transfer pricing engagements, including litigation support, audits, planning and documentation studies. Prita has extensive experience with transfer pricing for intangibles, in particular in the life sciences and technology sectors. Prita serves as WNT's technical transfer pricing lead for the life sciences industry. Prita routinely contributes to KPMG's thought leadership on transfer pricing issues and is an active participant in drafting KPMG's comment letters to the OECD. She is a member of KPMG's transfer pricing Quality Review Process team, which is responsible for overseeing quality control for all KPMG US transfer pricing engagements. Prita has also served as a national technical resource for FAS 123r/ASC 718 stock-based compensation valuation. Prita has a Ph.D. in Economics from Princeton University, U.S.

Monique van Herksen is a partner specializing in transfer pricing, dispute resolution and related international tax issues. Her practice includes advising multinational enterprises on handling global tax audits and risk assessment related to transfer pricing, permanent establishment exposure and business restructurings in the jurisdictions where they do business. Monique personally handles audit settlements, advance pricing agreements and competent authority requests calling on her previous experience of leading a "Big 4" accountancy firm's global transfer pricing controversy team and of working with the US Internal Revenue Service APA team. Monique also advises the United Nation's Tax Committee. She serves as expert on the transfer pricing subcommittee and assists the United Nations' Financing for Development Office with training and preparing training materials for tax authorities in developing countries, trains tax inspectors for organizations such as the Inter-American Center of Tax administrations (CIAT) and the African Tax Authorities Forum (ATAF). She has been teaching transfer pricing at leading universities and professional institutions for over twenty years. She is a Dutch and U.S. trained lawyer with an LL.M. in Trade & Banking (American University, U.S.) and an LL.M. in Taxation (Georgetown University, U.S.), admitted to the Bar in the Netherlands and the Commonwealth of Virginia. She has published over 185 articles to date on transfer pricing and related topics.

Jean-Philippe Van West is a professor at the Vrije Universiteit Brussel, Belgium and senior counsel in international tax with PwC Belgium, as well as the author of various publications on international and EU tax law.

Isabel Verlinden is a Brussels-based partner who has been active in global roles at PwC since 2014. She is serving the world's most successful and admired companies as a Corporate Strategy consultant focusing on Transfer Pricing. In this role she helps clients navigate through transformation and disruption that mark today's volatile geopolitical climate. She gathered first-hand knowledge of the tax challenges faced by companies operating across the globe based on over thirty years of experience working for PwC (and its legacy Firms) in Brussels and Washington, DC. She is an active writer for international tax and business periodicals. She has (co-) authored over 150 articles and books to date. Isabel teaches International Tax/Transfer Pricing at various academic institutions across the globe.

Scott Wilkie is Distinguished Professor of Practice at Osgoode Hall Law School, York University, Canada and also Senior Counsel at the law firm Blake, Cassels & Graydon LLP. He has widely published and has lectured and taught in many areas of taxation, notably international taxation and tax policy. He is also a codirector of the Osgoode Hall Law School Professional LL.M. in Tax Law and teaches a course in trade and tax policy called WTO and Tax Policy at the Vienna University of Economics and Business, Vienna, Austria, in the LL.M. program in international tax law. Professor Wilkie is the most recent former vice-chair of the Permanent Scientific Committee of the International Fiscal Association, and formerly has served as president of the Canadian branch of the International Fiscal Association, a governor and chair of the Canadian Tax Foundation, Chair of the Tax Section of the Canadian Bar Association (CBA), joint chair of the Joint Committee on Taxation of the CBA and the Canadian Institute of Chartered Accountants (now Canadian Professional Accountants), and cochair of the Tax Committee of the American Bar Association Section of International Law.

Summary of Contents

Table of Contents

Preface

Transfer pricing is currently one of the most relevant and challenging topics in the international tax environment. It is under constant development around the globe, and the years 2021-2022 have certainly been no different in this regard. The intense work of international organizations has provided new guidance on transfer pricing topics with several projects.

The global legislative framework on transfer pricing has undergone several relevant changes during the past year in the wake of international guidelines. The year 2021 has witnessed uncertainty spreading from several directions: renewed discussions on Pillar One and Two, political tensions, trade frictions, and international discussions on digital services taxes. Covid-19 and digitization continued to present new challenges for the international community.

The Organisation for Economic Co-operation and Development continued working on the Pillar One and Pillar Two proposals and, as part of the ongoing work of the OECD/G20 Inclusive Framework on Base Erosion and Profit Shifting, invited public comments on proposed changes to the commentaries on Article 9 and related articles of the OECD Model Tax Convention. Meanwhile, the United Nations updated its Transfer Pricing Manual and worked on its solution to address issues related to the digitalization of the economy.

The European Commission published a Communication titled Business Taxation for the 21st Century, which sets out the Commission's vision to provide a fair and sustainable EU business tax system. Some of the proposed projects may impact the European Union's transfer pricing framework. The Commission also published guidelines on the ETACA (European Trust and Cooperation Approach), a non-legislative project that focuses on cooperative compliance in the EU as concerns TP risks of large MNEs. Further, several important cases dealing with transfer pricing and state aid matters were decided by the respective decision-making bodies. Finally, after years of debate, the EU adopted a directive introducing Public Country-by-Country Reporting obligations for large MNEs. In addition to these measures, international developments are changing the EU landscape, as the EC has announced plans to implement the Inclusive Framework's Two Pillar solution.

Not only the EU but also developing countries and emerging economies will be impacted by Pillars One and Two. Further, the update to the UN Transfer Pricing Manual will certainly have a large impact on developing countries and emerging economies. In this continuous international development, many countries have amended and updated their domestic guidance in 2021.

In the United States, major transfer pricing developments during the past year stem mainly from recent cases and the seeming trend of decisions being more favorable to the IRS, as the *Coca-Cola* Case, the *Medtronic* Case and the *Amgen* Case. Moreover, the question of the validity of APAs during the Covid-19 pandemic which was already an issue in 2020 remains unresolved. New public statements and guidance in this area have meanwhile been developed.

Furthermore, this book also covers issues such as the practical question of the long-term impacts of the COVID-19 pandemic, as well as the more theoretical, but fundamental, issue of transfer pricing and substance. Additional chapters analyze the interplay of transfer pricing and restructurings and the ever more relevant topic of new technologies.

The WU Transfer Pricing Center at the Institute for Austrian and International Tax Law is conducting research projects to analyze the transfer pricing topics mentioned above and their global impacts. The current research is based on eight topic-based papers that have been drafted by well-renowned international experts on transfer pricing. The results of this work were presented and discussed at the fifth 'Global Transfer Pricing Conference: Transfer Pricing Developments around the World' in February 2022 organized by the Transfer Pricing Center at WU Vienna University of Economics and Business. This book is aimed at academics, practitioners (including the business community and advisory firms), international organizations, and government officials who are tax and transfer pricing experts as well as CEOs and CFOs who are interested in this topic. The book provides an in-depth analysis of the topics described above and the global impacts and suggestions for future solutions to any issues that are raised.

The editors would like to express their sincere thanks to the authors who made it possible to provide this ambitious work. Many thanks are forwarded to Kluwer Law International B.V. for supporting and cooperating with this publication project. Last, but not least, the editors would like to thank Yasmin Lawson and Dorottya Kovács for their precious support and Jenny Hill for providing linguistic support to the authors during the publishing process.

Prof. Dr. Dr. hc. Michael Lang
Dr. Raffaele Petruzzi, LL.M.

CHAPTER 1

Global Transfer Pricing Developments

Dorottya Kovács & Yasmin Lawson

1 INTRODUCTION

The global legislative framework on transfer pricing has undergone several relevant changes in 2021 in the wake of international guidelines. The Organisation for Economic Co-operation and Development (OECD) and the Inclusive Framework on Base Erosion and Profit Shifting (BEPS and the IF) continued to provide various guidelines on specific transfer pricing issues that could ensure effective implementation of the BEPS

Action Plan.[1] In early 2022, the OECD issued its latest Transfer Pricing Guidelines which included among others the 2020 Financial Transactions Guideline (TPGFT).[2] Meanwhile the United Nations (UN) has also updated its Practical Manual on Transfer Pricing in Developing Countries.[3] The European Union (EU) has continued to initiate measures for ensuring tax transparency and harmonization among its Member States. On June 1, 2021, a political agreement on the proposed directive on public country-by-country reporting (CbCR)[4] was reached which is one of the most discussed transfer pricing news of 2021.

With respect to the recent developments in country-specific transfer pricing legislation, guidelines, and jurisprudence, 2021 was a very active year in terms of new administrative or even legal guidance and case law. Many countries have amended their domestic frameworks, bringing them closer to the OECD Guidance but mainly trying to provide the taxpayers with as much clarity as possible. Of course, this was also accompanied by new documentation requirements, which—as will be discussed below—can be a significant burden for taxpayers. As COVID-19 is still reshaping the international framework, the need for legal certainty is also reflected in the ever-increasing demand for APAs and MAPs. This chapter will provide an overview of the most relevant domestic guidance and changes to the legal framework.

This chapter will examine the above developments in detail. Section 2 will describe the developments under the work of the international organizations and the EU, and section 3 will look into the influence of these developments on country-specific transfer pricing legislation and jurisprudence.

2 RECENT DEVELOPMENTS ON THE WORK OF INTERNATIONAL ORGANIZATIONS

2.1 Transfer Pricing Developments at the OECD

The OECD and its updated Transfer Pricing Guidelines for Multinational Enterprises and Tax Administrations continue to lead as the main source of guidance for transfer pricing schemes around the world. The updated OECD Guidelines' major goal is still to provide guidance on the application of the "arm's length principle," but it also includes

1. OECD, Aligning Transfer Pricing Outcomes with Value Creation, Actions 8-10, 2015 Final Reports, OECD/G20 Base Erosion and Profit Shifting Project (Paris: OECD Publishing, 2015).
2. OECD Transfer Pricing Guidelines for Multinational Enterprises and Tax Administrations 2022, https://www.oecd.org/tax/transfer-pricing/oecd-transfer-pricing-guidelines-for-multinational-enterprises-and-tax-administrations-20769717.htm.
3. United Nations, Practical Manual on Transfer Pricing for Developing Countries (updated in October 2020). *See* https://www.un.org/development/desa/financing/sites/www.un.org.development.desa.financing/files/2020-10/CRP40%20Transfer%20Pricing%20Manual%20Combined%20compressed.pdf.
4. European Parliament and European Council, Proposal for a directive of the European Parliament and of the Council amending Directive 2013/34/EU as regards disclosure of income tax information by certain undertakings and branches (June 9, 2021), COM (2016)0198- C8-0146/2016-2016/0107(COD).

among others the help for tax administrations on the application of the approach to hard-to-value intangibles (HTVI), as well as the new transfer pricing guidance on financial transactions. To further help the work of tax administrations, the OECD Forum on Tax Administration (FTA) released its International Compliance Assurance Programme (ICAP) which is a voluntary risk assessment and assurance project. A significant step was reached regarding the two-pillar solution to address the taxation challenges arising from the digitalization of the economy in 2021 since the OECD/G20 Inclusive Framework on BEPS has presented a Statement which has been discussed and by now agreed to by 137 member jurisdictions. In 2021, the OECD also released the updated transfer pricing country profiles for 63 countries, which included new information on the transfer pricing treatment of financial transactions and the application of the Authorised OECD Approach (AOA) to attribute profits to permanent establishments. The updated profiles are reflecting the current transfer pricing legislation and practices of countries' jurisdictions.

The OECD/G20 Inclusive Framework on Base Erosion and Profit Shifting (IF) has agreed on a two-pillar solution to address the tax challenges arising from the digitalization of the economy as digitalization has already posed significant challenges to the current tax landscape and continues to do so. Therefore, addressing the digitalized economy's tax challenges remained a priority on the OECD's agenda in 2021.[5]

A program of work on Pillar One and Pillar Two was adopted in May 2019 and later endorsed by the G20 in June 2019. As part of the work program, the OECD was mandated to carry out an economic analysis and impact assessment of the Pillar One and Pillar Two proposals. In July 2020, the G20 mandated the IF to produce reports on the Blueprints of Pillar One and Pillar Two by the G20 Finance Ministers meeting in October 2020. Indeed, on October 8-9, 2020, the IF approved a package consisting of reports on Pillar One and Pillar Two Blueprints that explore alternatives in relation to the design of a global minimum tax that tackles the remaining BEPS issues.[6] On November 4, 2021, OECD/G20 Inclusive Framework on BEPS has presented a Statement which has been discussed and by now agreed to by 137 member jurisdictions.[7]

Pillar One addresses the allocation of taxing rights between jurisdictions and describes new profit allocation and nexus rules based on the concepts of "significant

5. OECD, Addressing the Tax Challenges of the Digitalisation of the Economy—Policy Note, approved by the Inclusive Framework on BEPS on 23 January 2019 OECD/G20 Base Erosion and Profit Shifting Project, available at https://www.oecd.org/tax/beps/policy-note-beps-inclusive-framework-addressing-tax-challenges-digitalisation.pdf. For a detailed description of Pillar One and Pillar Two, refer to M. Lang, R. Petruzzi, Transfer Pricing Development around the World, (2020). Kluwer Law International BV, the Netherlands.
6. OECD (2020), Tax Challenges Arising from Digitalisation—Report on Pillar One Blueprint: Inclusive Framework on BEPS, OECD/G20 Base Erosion and Profit Shifting Project, OECD Publishing, Paris, https://doi.org/10.1787/beba0634-en. OECD (2020), Tax Challenges Arising from Digitalisation—Report on Pillar Two Blueprint: Inclusive Framework on BEPS, OECD/G20 Base Erosion and Profit Shifting Project, OECD Publishing, Paris, https://doi.org/10.1787/abb4c3d1-en.
7. OECD/G20 Base Erosion and Profit Shifting Project, Statement on a Two-Pillar Solution to Address the Tax Challenges Arising from the Digitalisation of the Economy, October 8, 2021, available at https://www.oecd.org/tax/beps/statement-on-a-two-pillar-solution-to-address-the-tax-challenges-arising-from-the-digitalisation-of-the-economy-october-2021.pdf.

economic presence" as well as the exploitation of "user participation" and "marketing intangibles" in a jurisdiction. Within the scope of Pillar One are multinational enterprises (MNEs) with global turnover above EUR 20 billion and profitability above 10% (i.e., profit before tax/revenue), contingent on successful implementation including of tax certainty on Amount A, with the relevant review beginning seven years after the agreement comes into force, and the review being completed in no more than one year.[8] Based on the 2021 Statement, there will be a new special purpose nexus rule permitting the allocation of Amount A to a market jurisdiction when the in scope MNE derives at least EUR 1 million in revenue from that jurisdiction. For smaller jurisdictions with GDP lower than EUR 40 billion, the nexus will be set at EUR 250,000. With Amount B the application of the arm's-length principle to marketing and distribution activities will be simplified and streamlined, with a particular focus on the needs of low capacity countries. This work will be completed by the end of 2022. No newly enacted Digital Services Taxes or other relevant similar measures will be imposed on any company from October 8, 2021, and until the earlier of December 31, 2023—*see* on DSTs that are already in force in section 3.2. The MLC through which Amount A is implemented will be developed and opened for signature in 2022, with Amount A coming into effect in 2023.[9]

Pillar Two is the development of a coordinated set of rules to address ongoing risks from structures that allow MNEs to shift profit to jurisdictions where they are subject to no or very low taxation.[10] Pillar Two consists of two interlocking domestic rules: (i) an Income Inclusion Rule (IIR), which imposes top-up tax on a parent entity in respect of the low taxed income of a constituent entity; and (ii) an Undertaxed Payment Rule (UTPR), which denies deductions or requires an equivalent adjustment to the extent the low-tax income of a constituent entity is not subject to tax under an IIR; and a treaty-based rule (the Subject to Tax Rule (STTR)) that allows source jurisdictions to impose limited source taxation on certain related party payments subject to tax below a minimum rate. The minimum tax rate used for purposes of the IIR and UTPR will be 15% and 9% for the minimum rate for the STTR. To ensure that the administration of the GloBE rules is as targeted as possible and to avoid compliance and administrative costs that are disproportionate to the policy objectives, the OECD implementation

8. OECD, Addressing the Tax Challenges of the Digitalisation of the Economy—Policy Note, approved by the Inclusive Framework on BEPS on 23 January 2019 OECD/G20 Base Erosion and Profit Shifting Project, available at https://www.oecd.org/tax/beps/policy-note-beps-inclusive-framework-addressing-tax-challenges-digitalisation.pdf. For a detailed description of Pillar One and Pillar Two, refer to M. Lang, R. Petruzzi, Transfer Pricing Development around the World (2020). Kluwer Law International BV, the Netherlands.
9. OECD/G20 Base Erosion and Profit Shifting Project, Statement on a Two-Pillar Solution to Address the Tax Challenges Arising from the Digitalisation of the Economy, October 8, 2021, available at https://www.oecd.org/tax/beps/statement-on-a-two-pillar-solution-to-address-the-tax-challenges-arising-from-the-digitalisation-of-the-economy-october-2021.pdf.
10. OECD, Addressing the Tax Challenges of the Digitalisation of the Economy—Policy Note, approved by the Inclusive Framework on BEPS on 23 January 2019 OECD/G20 Base Erosion and Profit Shifting Project, available at https://www.oecd.org/tax/beps/policy-note-beps-inclusive-framework-addressing-tax-challenges-digitalisation.pdf. For a detailed description of Pillar One and Pillar Two, please refer to M. Lang, R. Petruzzi, Transfer Pricing Development around the World (2020). Kluwer Law International BV, the Netherlands.

framework will include safe harbors and/or other mechanisms. It is agreed that Pillar Two will apply a minimum rate on a jurisdictional basis. In that context, consideration will be given to the conditions under which the US GILTI regime will coexist with the GloBE rules, to ensure a level playing field. Pillar Two should be brought into law in 2022, to be effective in 2023, with the UTPR coming into effect in 2024.[11] While these international agreements are not legally binding, the broad consensus as represented by the agreement of 137 members does indicate that the international community is prepared to transpose the GloBE rules into domestic law.[12]

On February 18, 2021, the FTA released a new handbook for the ICAP which is a handbook for tax administrations and MNE groups. The FTA, created in 2002, is a unique body bringing together Commissioners from 53 advanced and emerging tax administrations from across the globe, including all OECD and G20 members. The FTA member administrations raise over EUR 12.2 trillion a year to fund public services and to deliver government objectives. Its vision is to create a forum through which Commissioners can identify, discuss and influence relevant international trends and develop new ideas to increase the fairness, efficiency and effectiveness of tax administration, reducing burdens and improving tax compliance and tax certainty.[13] The ICAP[14] is a voluntary risk assessment and assurance program designed to facilitate open and cooperative multilateral engagement between MNEs that are willing to engage actively and transparently and tax administrations in jurisdictions where the MNE groups have business activities. The new handbook contains information on the process for ICAP reflecting the experience and feedback of tax administrations and MNE groups that participated in two pilots for the program, commencing in 2018 and 2019. It also includes a detailed description of each stage of the ICAP process, the documentation and information an MNE group participating in ICAP will provide, the level of comfort they may achieve as a result of participation in the program, and a comparison of ICAP with other possible routes to greater tax certainty.[15] According to an OECD media release, ICAP will now be run as a full program, open to all 53 FTA member tax administrations. When this chapter was written, 23 countries' tax administrations have already joined the program.

In 2021, the OECD also invited public input on proposed changes to Commentaries in the OECD Model Tax Convention on Article 9 and on related articles realized on March 29, 2021. Many organizations including the WU Transfer Pricing Center at the

11. OECD/G20 Base Erosion and Profit Shifting Project, Statement on a Two-Pillar Solution to Address the Tax Challenges Arising from the Digitalisation of the Economy, October 8, 2021, available at https://www.oecd.org/tax/beps/statement-on-a-two-pillar-solution-to-address-the-tax-challenges-arising-from-the-digitalisation-of-the-economy-october-2021.pdf.
12. On the legal character of the GloBE proposal *see* V. Bendlinger, Die OECD Model Rules für ein globales Mindestbesteuerungsregime, SWI 2022, 2 (3 et seq.).
13. OECD Forum on Tax Administration https://www.oecd.org/tax/forum-on-tax-administration/.
14. OECD International Compliance Assurance Programme (ICAP) https://www.oecd.org/tax/forum-on-tax-administration/international-compliance-assurance-programme.htm.
15. International Compliance Assurance Programme: Handbook for tax administrations and MNE groups https://www.oecd.org/tax/forum-on-tax-administration/publications-and-products/international-compliance-assurance-programme-handbook-for-tax-administrations-and-mne-groups.htm.

Institute for Austrian and International Tax Law at WU (Vienna University of Economics and Business) have provided their input to help and improve the project of the OECD.[16]

In early 2022, the OECD released its updated Transfer Pricing Guidelines for Multinational Enterprises and Tax Administrations.[17] The latest edition is mainly a consolidated version of a number of reports resulting from the OECD/G20 Base Erosion and Profit Shifting (BEPS) Project; however, it also includes some related changes for consistency. The 2022 Guidelines intercorporate the revised guidance on the application of the transactional profit method and the guidance for tax administrations on the application of the approach to HTVI, both approved by the OECD/G20 Inclusive Framework on BEPS on June 4, 2018, as well as the new transfer pricing guidance on financial transactions approved on January 20, 2020.[18] The revised guidance on the transactional profit split method[19] is intended to clarify when a profit split method is the most appropriate method and how the method should be applied, including the determination of the relevant profits to be split and the appropriate profit-splitting factors. The revised guidance also includes several examples illustrating the concepts discussed. The Guidance for Tax Administrations on the Application of the Approach to Hard-to-Value Intangibles[20] aims to reach a common understanding on how to apply adjustments for HTVI, and as a result, the guidance is intended to improve consistency and mitigate the risk of economic double taxation. The guidance consists of three main parts: (i) an outline of principles underlying the application of the HTVI approach; (ii) a number of examples clarifying the application of the HTVI approach; and (iii) specifics on the interaction between the HTVI approach and access to the mutual agreement procedure. The Transfer Pricing Guidance on Financial Transactions[21] covers the accurate delineation of financial transactions with respect to capital structures of multinational enterprises, and it also addresses specific issues related to the pricing of financial transactions such as treasury functions, intragroup loans, cash pooling, hedging, guarantees, and captive insurance.

16. https://www.oecd.org/tax/treaties/oecd-invites-public-input-on-proposed-changes-to-commentaries-in-the-oecd-model-tax-convention-on-article-9-and-on-related-articles.htm.
17. OECD Transfer Pricing Guidelines for Multinational Enterprises and Tax Administrations 2022, https://www.oecd.org/tax/transfer-pricing/oecd-transfer-pricing-guidelines-for-multinational-enterprises-and-tax-administrations-20769717.htm.
18. OECD Transfer Pricing Guidelines for Multinational Enterprises and Tax Administrations 2022, https://www.oecd.org/tax/transfer-pricing/oecd-transfer-pricing-guidelines-for-multinational-enterprises-and-tax-administrations-20769717.htm.
19. Revised Guidance on the Application of the Transactional Profit Split Method—BEPS Action 10 https://www.oecd.org/tax/transfer-pricing/revised-guidance-on-the-application-of-the-transactional-profit-split-method-beps-action-10.htm.
20. Guidance for Tax Administrations on the Application of the Approach to Hard-to-Value Intangibles—BEPS Action 8 https://www.oecd.org/tax/transfer-pricing/guidance-for-tax-administrations-on-the-application-of-the-approach-to-hard-to-value-intangibles-beps-action-8.htm.
21. Transfer Pricing Guidance on Financial Transactions: Inclusive Framework on BEPS: Actions 4, 8-10 https://www.oecd.org/tax/transfer-pricing/transfer-pricing-guidance-on-financial-transactions-inclusive-framework-on-beps-actions-4-8-10.htm.

Based on the OECD work, MNEs should understand and analyze the implications of the development for each jurisdiction in which they operate. They should review the amendments to the OECD TP Guidelines with respect to their global operations and their current transfer pricing policies and approaches. Increased scrutiny is likely to be expected by tax authorities from OECD member countries and non-OECD member countries on the application of the concepts reflected in the amendments of the OECD Guidelines and developments to cross-border intercompany transactions.

2.2 Transfer Pricing Developments at the European Union

In 2021, the EU has continued moving forward with its goal to ensure tax transparency and harmonization among its Member States. Among others, the European Parliament has approved, the important and long-awaited development, the amendment to the EU Accounting Directive that will impose additional reporting requirements on large multinational enterprises. The new rules—commonly referred to as the public country-by-country report—expect certain MNEs to publicly disclose tax-related information in the form of a CbCR.

Only two days after the GloBE Model Rules were published, the European Commission presented a proposal for a directive implementing the globe within the European Union.[22] Such a directive was already announced in the Commissions Communication "Business Taxation for the 21st Century."[23]

The proposal follows the international agreement and sets out how the principles of the 15% effective tax rate should be applied in practice within the EU and transposed into the domestic legal frameworks of the Member States. It includes a common set of rules on how to calculate this effective tax rate so that it is properly and consistently applied across the EU. The Executive Vice President for an Economy that Works for People, Valdis Dombrovskis, said: "By moving quickly to align with the far reaching OECD agreement, Europe is playing its full part in creating a fairer global system for corporate taxation. This is particularly important at a time when we need to increase public financing for fair sustainable growth and investment and meet public financing needs too—both for tackling the pandemic's aftermath and driving forward the green and digital transitions. Putting the OECD agreement on minimum effective taxation into EU law will be vital for fighting tax avoidance and evasion while preventing a 'race to the bottom' with unhealthy tax competition between countries. It is a major step forward for our fair taxation agenda."[24]

The proposed rules will apply to any large group, both domestic and international, with a parent company or a subsidiary situated in any EU Member State. If the minimum effective rate is not imposed by the country where a low taxed company is based, there are provisions for the Member State of the parent company to apply a "top-up" tax. The proposal also ensures effective taxation in situations where the

22. Available at https://ec.europa.eu/taxation_customs/system/files/2021-12/COM_2021_823_1_EN_ACT_part1_v11.pdf.
23. Available at https://eur-lex.europa.eu/legal-content/EN/TXT/?uri=CELEX%3A52021DC0251.
24. Available at https://ec.europa.eu/commission/commissioners/2019-2024/dombrovskis_en.

parent company is situated outside the EU in a low-tax country.[25] A departure from the OECD framework is the inclusion of purely domestic groups, presumably to avoid the discrimination of cross-border circumstances.[26]

In line with the global agreement, the proposal also provides for certain exceptions to reduce the impact on groups carrying out real economic activities; therefore, some companies will be able to exclude an amount of income equal to 5% of the value of tangible assets and 5% of payroll. The rules also provide for an exclusion of minimal amounts of profit, to reduce the compliance burden in low-risk situations. This means that when the average profit and revenues of a multinational group in a jurisdiction are below certain minimum thresholds, then that income is not taken into account in the calculation of the rate.[27]

The question still remains if this transposition is actually in line with the EU competences and the European fundamental freedoms and will certainly be a main issue of discussion for months and maybe years to come.[28]

The EU Commission will also make a proposal on the reallocation of taxing rights in 2022, once the technical aspects of the multilateral convention are agreed. The tax agenda is complementary to, but broader than just the elements covered by the OECD agreement. By the end of 2023, the Commission will also publish a new framework for business taxation in the EU, which will reduce the administrative burden for businesses working across Member States, remove tax obstacles and create a more business-friendly environment in the Single Market.[29]

After many years of discussion, political agreement on the proposed directive on public country-by-country reporting (CbCR) was reached on June 1, 2021, as the result of a trialogue between the Council, the Parliament and the Commission.[30] Country-by-country reports have to contain income tax information (including type of activity, number of employees and taxes paid), separately for each Member State and each third country included in the list of noncooperative countries and territories for tax purposes. This country-by-country report must be made publicly available free of charge within twelve months after the end of the business year (usually on the company's website). Only companies (with a registered office, subsidiary or permanent establishment in the EU) that have achieved a consolidated total turnover of more than EUR 750 million in each of the last two consecutive financial years are affected. The disclosure of information that would weaken the economic position of the company can be

25. OECD/G20 Inclusive Framework on BEPS agreement on a Two Pillar Solution to Address the Tax Challenges Arising from the Digitalisation of the Economy.
26. V. Bendlinger, Die OECD Model Rules für ein globales Mindestbesteuerungsregime, SWI 2022, 2 (4).
27. OECD/G20 Inclusive Framework on BEPS agreement on a Two Pillar Solution to Address the Tax Challenges Arising from the Digitalisation of the Economy.
28. V. Bendlinger, Die OECD Model Rules für ein globales Mindestbesteuerungsregime, SWI 2022, 2 (5) with further references.
29. OECD/G20 Inclusive Framework on BEPS agreement on a Two Pillar Solution to Address the Tax Challenges Arising from the Digitalisation of the Economy.
30. European Parliament and European Council, Proposal for a directive of the European Parliament and of the Council amending Directive 2013/34/EU as regards disclosure of income tax information by certain undertakings and branches (June 9, 2021), COM (2016)0198-C8-0146/2016-2016/0107(COD).

postponed for up to five years if this postponement is justified in the report. This exception does not apply to information regarding noncooperative third countries.[31]

The Parliament adopted the proposed directive on November 11, 2021, according to Article 50 iVm 294 TFEU also by majority vote.[32] The directive was published in the OJ on December 1, 2021, and entered into force on December 21. The Member States now have to transpose Public CbCr into national law by June 22, 2023. This means that at the latest, for financial years starting in 2025 (cf. Article 48g Public-CbCR-RL), depending on the national implementation already from 2023, income tax information (including, e.g., type of activity, number of employees and taxes paid), separately for each Member State and each third country on the "black list" (and, if applicable, on the "gray list," *see* section 2.2 for more details), on the company's website. The legal basis chosen was again criticized by Ireland, Croatia, Luxembourg, Malta, Sweden, the Czech Republic, Hungary and Cyprus in a joint statement,[33] so the risk of a challenge before the ECJ by one or more of the outvoted Member States therefore appears to remain unchanged.[34] Such action is possible within a period of just under three months from publication in the OJ.[35]

Not only for the public but also for the tax administration, the Public CbCR will result in more information: The breakdown into individual tax jurisdictions and also data on smaller subsidiaries, for example, were not part of the previous CbCR.[36]

The EU Council adopted Directive 2011/16 in relation to cross-border tax arrangements, which is commonly known as DAC6 (Directive on Administrative Cooperation).[37] The Directive has been in force since June 25, 2018, and it aims for transparency and fairness in taxation. In a nutshell, the Directive demands that tax support with the implementation of advice given to MNEs, meeting certain predefined hallmarks, should be disclosed within thirty days of the fact. On March 25, 2021, with the publication of DAC7,[38] another episode was added to the EU administrative cooperation. DAC7 addresses three different topics, namely, the extension of the scope of the EU automatic information exchange to include data on sellers through digital platform operators; multilateral audits; and the presence of officials from one MS in another one.

31. K. Spies, V. Hellebrandt, Y. Lawson, Steuerrechtliche Entwicklungen auf EU-Ebene, ÖStZ 2021, 609 (609).
32. Position of the Council at First Reading with view to the adoption of Directive of the European Parliament and of the Council amending Directive 2013/34/EU as regards disclosure of income tax information by certain undertakings and branches (September 15, 2021) 9722/21—2016/0107(COD).
33. Statement by Croatia and Statement by Cyprus, the Czech Republic, Hungary, Ireland, Luxembourg, Malta and Sweden, 11832/21 ADD 1, 2016/0107(COD).
34. *See* K. Spies, Y. Lawson, Steuerrechtliche Entwicklungen auf EU-Ebene, ÖStZ 2021, 694 (695).
35. Article 263 AEUV, Article 50 VerfO EuGH und Article 101 § 1 sowie Article 102 VerfO EuG.
36. T. Bornemann, E. Eberhartinger, Die Initiative der EU zum öffentlichen Country-by-Country Reporting, RWZ 2017, 391; A. Langer, "Public" Country-by-Country-Reporting in der EU, AVR 2021, 19; C. Sommer, S. Litterscheid, Das Public Country-by-Country Reporting in der EU, IWB 2021, 370.
37. Council Directive (EU) 2018/822 of 25 May 2018 amending Directive 2011/16/EU as regards mandatory automatic exchange of information in the field of taxation in relation to reportable cross-border arrangements, OJ L 139/1, June 5, 2018.
38. OJ of the EU, L 104/1, Council Directive (EU) 2021/514 of 22 March 2021 amending Directive 2011/16/EU on administrative cooperation in the field of taxation.

The so-called DAC8[39] should cover the exchange of information with respect to cryptocurrencies and the harmonization of penalties, but no proposal for the Directive has been published yet.[40]

In July 2020, the European Commission (EC) announced plans to introduce an EU cooperative compliance program based on greater cooperation, trust, and transparency among tax administrations.[41] The EC has published guidelines on the European Trust and Cooperation Approach (ETACA),[42] a voluntary pilot project on cooperative compliance within the EU specifically focusing on TP risks for large multinationals. ETACA provides a clear EU framework for a preventive dialog between tax administrations and large multinational enterprises, therefore supports companies in reducing tax compliance costs and avoid double taxation. The ETACA Pilot Project was set to start in March 2022. The project will run alongside the International Compliance Assurance Project (ICAP)[43] and multiple domestic cooperative compliance programs. While the scope of ETACA is limited to large multinationals, a separate trial was also announced for small- and medium-sized enterprises (SMEs) on June 23, 2021.[44]

The year 2021 was again a busy year with many significant TP state aid cases. The *Amazon*[45] case is just one of many disputes between the European Commission and multinational companies that raises fundamental questions about transfer pricing and in particular the arm's-length principle. Some multinational companies, including Amazon, have won significant court cases on TP in 2021, while the courts have ruled against companies such Engie[46] over EU state aid claims.[47] TP state aid cases always serve as examples for MNEs with similar arrangements as many of the significant cases will set a precedent for future treatment of multinational companies. Concerning tax controversy, transfer pricing is arguably one of the most relevant and challenging topics in international taxation.

Chapter 2 of this volume will take a closer look at the mentioned EU developments and each transfer pricing case related to the EU Commission's investigation and the Court's Decision delivered in 2021 as well as practical transfer pricing aspects.

---

39. Annex to the Communication from the Commission to the European Parliament and the Council—An Action plan for fair and simple taxation supporting the recovery strategy, COM(2020) 312 final, p. 2.
40. *See* more details in Chapter 2.
41. European Commission: Package for fair and simple taxation https://ec.europa.eu/taxation_customs/package-fair-and-simple-taxation_en.
42. *See* Guidelines European trust and cooperation approach—ETACA https://ec.europa.eu/taxation_customs/document/download/1e2d7158-f083-4e68-9ece-b96ce02668c9_en.
43. *See* Transfer Pricing Developments at the OECD at p. 4.
44. *See* https://ec.europa.eu/taxation_customs/news/eu-cooperative-compliance-programme-2021-06-23_en.
45. Cases T-816/17 and T-318/18.
46. Cases T-516/18 and T-525/18.
47. J. White, The Biggest TP Cases of 2021 so far and *see* Chapter 1 for more details.

2.3 Transfer Pricing Developments at the United Nations

In addition to the OECD Transfer Pricing Guidelines for Multinational Enterprises and Tax Administrations, the UN Manual embodies as the principal source of guidance for transfer pricing regimes, especially for emerging economies and developing countries. Regarding the UN, the main news of the year 2021 was its updated Practical Manual on Transfer Pricing for Developing Countries.

The United Nations released its latest (third) edition of its practical manual on transfer pricing for developing countries on April 27, 2021. The manual consists of 645 pages, and it provides a detailed guidance and various country-specific issues on transfer pricing. The need for a UN Transfer Pricing Manual was born out of the demand expressed by developing countries for clearer guidance on the application of transfer pricing analyses.[48]

The manual consist of four parts, Part A provides an overview of multinational enterprises, their operation and structure, and the management of their transfer pricing function, and Part B addresses the arm's-length principle, comparability analyses, transfer pricing methods, and policy considerations for certain types of arrangements and transactions. Part C focuses on designing transfer pricing legislation and implementing regulations, documentation requirements, assessing risk, conducting audits, and dispute resolution, and Part D looks at country practices in selected developing countries. The 2021 edition includes sections on the leading emerging markets of Brazil, China, India, Mexico, and South Africa. The 2021 edition also adds a new country practices profile for Kenya.[49]

The new content on intragroup financial transactions is included under Part B in Chapter 9. It includes information on common types of intragroup financial transactions, how country tax policies affect multinational enterprise financing decisions, and the application of the arm's-length principle to intragroup loans. Part B also features new content on centralized procurement functions in sections 5.6 through 5.13. The chapter explains that most multinationals operate some form of centralized procurement function, but that the underlying activities and their economic substance can vary widely. The guidance is intended to help developing countries identify features of substantive arrangements versus those lacking economic substance.[50]

The OECD Manual adds new content on financial transactions, centralized procurement functions, and country practices. The 2021 edition of the manual, which replaces the second edition published in 2017, also updates guidance on profit splits and comparability issues and makes other revisions and organizational changes. The manual is especially intended to help policymakers and tax administrations in developing countries tackle transfer pricing issues to avoid double taxation and resolve disputes. The new edition of UN Manual is drafted by a UN subcommittee whose

48. A. Padwalkar, The 2021 UN Transfer Pricing Manual—A Step in the Right Direction. Transfer Pricing International (TPI), 5 (2021), 204-207.
49. D. Connolly, UN Updates Transfer Pricing Manual for Developing Countries.
50. A. Padwalkar, The 2021 UN Transfer Pricing Manual—A Step in the Right Direction. Transfer Pricing International (TPI), 5 (2021), 204-207.

members include various government policy and tax officials, as well as representatives of the private sector, academia, and nongovernmental organizations. It introduces a new organizational numbering system for paragraphs, but it still follows the four-part, lettered layout of previous editions.[51]

The guidance between the OECD and UN with regards to transfer pricing is different on topics such as intangibles, financial transactions, transfer pricing methods, and PSM in particular, risk control framework, comparability factors, and effective use of country-by-country reports. The adoption of BEPS measures by countries in the OECD and UN guidelines and manual have brought the two guidances closer. Moreover, the UN Manual stresses that the documentation requirement should be roughly consistent between the countries and the two guidances in order to reduce the compliance burden to the MNEs. The 2021 Manual provides extensive guidance on issues and topics not covered by earlier versions. Some of them even differ from the OECD Guidelines and country-specific practices, but tax administrations have to harmoniously apply and interpret them in order to avoid double taxation problems. To sum up, both the OECD Guidelines and the UN Manual share the same goal of addressing current transfer pricing issues due to the rapid digitalization of the economy and the prolonged nature of the COVID-19 pandemic. In addition to the common goal, the updated UN Manual, as well as the earlier version, aims to help developing countries and addresses their country-specific issues, which analyses are not complete or even entirely missing from the OECD Transfer Pricing Guidelines.

For detailed information about the work of the UN on the Practical Manual on Transfer Pricing for Developing Countries, refer to Chapter 4.

2.4 Other Organizations

The year 2021 was not a groundbreaking year when it comes to TP developments among other international organizations.

In September 2019, the Platform for Collaboration on Tax (PCT), a joint initiative of the International Monetary Fund (IMF), the OECD, the UN and the World Bank Group (WBG), published a draft version of its Practical Toolkit to Support the Successful Implementation by Developing Countries of Effective Transfer Pricing Documentation Requirements.[52] On January 19, 2021, the final version of the "Practical Toolkit to Support the Successful Implementation by Developing Countries of Effective Transfer Pricing Documentation Requirements" was released and serves as guidance on implementing transfer pricing documentation requirements for developing countries.[53] The

51. D. Connolly, UN Updates Transfer Pricing Manual for Developing Countries.
52. Practical Toolkit to Support the Successful Implementation by Developing Countries of Effective Transfer Pricing Documentation Requirements, https://www.oecd.org/tax/practical-toolkit-to-support-the-successful-implementation-by-developing-countries-of-effective-transfer-pricing-documentation-requirements.htm.
53. Platform for Collaboration on Tax. PCT Progress Report 2020, p. 19. https://www.tax-platform.org/sites/pct/files/publications/Platform-for-Collaboration-on-Tax-PCT-Progress-Report-2020.pdf, accessed January 6, 2021.

toolkit assembles essential information on transfer pricing documentation and analyses policy choices and legislative solutions. Examples and practices from over thirty countries and additional approaches to transfer pricing documentation can be found also in the toolkit. The document aims to help countries implement effective transfer pricing documentation requirements in order to protect their tax bases, reduce profit shifting and raise much-needed revenues for the recovery phase. The new version is the fourth toolkit published by the PCT to help countries address challenges in international taxation.[54]

3 RECENT DEVELOPMENTS IN COUNTRY-SPECIFIC TRANSFER PRICING LEGISLATION, GUIDELINES, AND JURISPRUDENCE

While 2021 saw no real paradigm shifts in any domestic transfer pricing approach, many countries have adapted and changed their local legal frameworks and administrative guidance in an effort to make their national TP requirements more clear and approachable. Even though there was not as much case law as in some other years, some impactful decisions by various courts have been made.

This section summarizes critical recent developments in country-specific transfer pricing legislation, administrative guidelines, and case law. These developments have been broadly identified in relation to the following topics:

- ALP and transfer pricing methods
- Digitalization of the economy
- Intangibles
- Documentation
- CbC reporting
- Dispute resolution
- Significant domestic case law.

3.1 Arm's-Length Principle and Transfer Pricing Methods

Despite the OECD Transfer Pricing Guidelines 2017 (OECD Guidelines)[55] having been issued in 2017 already, countries around the globe are still in the middle of the process of changing their domestic practice and issuing administrative guidelines to more closely follow these international standards. While taxpayers have strived toward adapting their TP structures as quickly as possible to match as closely as possible the new OECD Guidelines, the mismatch between domestic practice and the OECD's

54. Platform for Collaboration on Tax's new toolkit helps countries implement effective transfer pricing documentation requirements, https://www.oecd.org/tax/platform-for-collaboration-on-tax-new-toolkit-helps-countries-implement-effective-transfer-pricing-documentation-requirements.htm.
55. OECD, Transfer Pricing Guidelines for Multinational Enterprises and Tax Administrations 2017, OECD Publishing, Paris, https://doi.org/10.1787/tpg-2017-en.

approach has made this transition difficult. Additionally, past transactions from before the new Guidance was published continue to be scrutinized by tax authorities and courts.

With international guidance, the domestic tax authorities and courts are striving toward applying the transfer pricing methods, and more specifically the ALP, coherently and predictably.[56] Court decisions play an important part, as they can confirm or correct the decisions of tax authorities and lawmakers.

At least some amount of legal certainty as regards company's past transactions was confirmed in several court decisions[57] in 2021. In June 2021, the Court of Appeal of Ghent, Belgium, issued a decision siding with the taxpayer.[58] The Belgian tax authorities had partly applied the DEMPE concept from the 2017 version of OECD Guidelines in assessing the taxpayer's transfer pricing for a transaction from 2009. This retroactive application was ruled to be in conflict with the principle of legal certainty and thus unlawful.[59] The Finnish Supreme Administrative Court explicitly stated that material from 2018 could not be used to examine a set of circumstances from 2009 to 2011.[60]

In 2021, several court decisions confirmed that the taxpayer's approach was in conformity with the arm's-length principle.[61] This as well provides the taxpayer with legal certainty. In *Malaysia v. Ensco Gerudi Malaysia*, for example, the court held that,[62] first, the payments were not artificial. Second, and more importantly, it stated that the taxpayers have the freedom to structure their arrangements in such a way that they make use of tax advantages provided for by the legislator, as long as the activities are commercially and economically realistic. In a judgment from October 2021, the Kenya Tax Appeal Court ruled in favor of the taxpayer,[63] holding that the KRA had rejected the method on wholly arbitrary grounds.[64] Also in 2021, Canada's Supreme Court blocked Cameco's appeal.[65] Still, the Canadian budget from April 19 does address concerns about TP loopholes that the *Cameco* case highlighted. This means

56. On the ALP a substance in general, *see* Chapter 6.
57. For example, though on purely domestic law, *India v. Engineering Analysis Centre of Excellence Private Limited*, March 2021, Supreme Court, Case No 8733-8734 OF 2018.
58. *Belgium v. "Uniclick B.V.,"* June 8, 2021, Court of Appeal, Case No 2016/AR/455.
59. *See* on this decision B. Markey, R. Devroye "Back to the Future?"—Belgian Court Rules That DEMPE Concept Cannot Be Applied Retroactively, September 13, 2021, Kluwer tax blog, available at http://kluwertaxblog.com/2021/09/13/back-to-the-future-belgian-court-rules-that-dempe-concept-cannot-be-applied-retroactively/ (December 21, 2021).
60. *Finland v. A Oyj*, May 21, 2021, Supreme Administrative Court, Case No. KHO:2021:66; crit.: M. Raunio, M. Urpilainen, Case SAC 2021:66 on Group Internal Financing—Supreme Administrative Court Provides Lessons on How the OECD Transfer Pricing Guidelines Should and Should Not Be Used, International Transfer Pricing of Journal 28(5) (2021); Journal Articles & Opinion Pieces IBFD (accessed December 22, 2021).
61. *See* Chapter 4 on India's faceless audit system.
62. *Malaysia v. Ensco Gerudi*, June 2016, High Court, Case No. 14-11-08-2014.
63. *Kenya v. PE of Man Diesel*, August 2021, High Court of Kenya, Income Tax Appeal No. E125 OF 2020.
64. *See* Chapter 4 for a critical evaluation of this judgment.
65. *Canada v. Cameco Corp.*, February 18, 2021, Supreme Court, Case No. 39368.

that despite this case being decided in favor of the taxpayer, changes to Canadian TP practice will still have to be looked at in the future.[66]

In 2021, several countries adapted their local application of the transfer pricing methods, or more specifically the ALP. Some of the more extensive changes will be discussed in this chapter, though other countries like Singapore[67] have also amended, clarified or provided additional guidance on the application of the ALP domestically.

In July, Germany issued the Administrative Principles of Transfer Pricing (AP TP)[68] with the goal to much more closely align the domestic interpretation of the ALP to the international standards. Central to this new publication is Chapter II on the OECD Guidelines and their attachment to the letter. In the future, these Guidelines can be used by the German tax administration in examining transfer pricing schemes. This is the first time the German authorities have explicitly referred to the OECD's Guidelines as relevant for national practice (though it has to be noted that this publication by the tax authorities itself is not legally binding). These Guidelines impact the interpretation of the ALP in other contexts domestically,[69] which means that the German practice concerning the ALP will now be harmonized very closely with the OECD's approach.[70] However, in some aspects, the AP TP does deviate from the OECD Guidelines, e.g., for intercompany financing transactions. What is worth mentioning is that by attaching the Guidelines to the AP TP, the reference is static. Should the OECD change the content of the Guidelines, this would only have an effect on German national practice if the publication issued by the German tax authorities also novates the AP TP.[71] This memo followed Germany's "Act to Modernise the Relief from Withholding Tax and the Certification of Capital Gains Tax,"[72] which removed the hierarchy of preferred TP methods formerly followed by the German tax administration and contained new TP rules related to intangible assets.

A welcome step toward more legal certainty was the Finance Bill 2021[73] in Ireland. In 2019, section 835E TCA 1997 entered into force.[74] This rule in essence disapplied transfer pricing rules for certain non-trading Ireland-to-Ireland transactions. While being an important exception for domestic non-arm's-length transactions, this rule

66. L. Reeves, The Top Transfer Pricing Cases of Q3 2021. International Tax Review (2021) (October 14, 2021).
67. In detail on the changes in Singapore: A. Bose, U. Alvarez, Updated E-Tax Guide on Singapore Transfer Pricing Guidelines, International Transfer Pricing of Journal 29, 1 (2022); Journal Articles & Opinion Pieces IBFD (accessed December 22, 2021); Singapore tax authorities issue revised TP guidelines, Crowe Singapore; S. Saravan; S. Varadharajan. International Tax Review; London (September 3, 2021).
68. BMF, Schreiben vom 14. Juli 2021, IV B 5, S 1341/19/100117:001.
69. A. Saliger, L. Wrgowske, S. Greil, Die neuen Verwaltungsgrundsätze Verrechnungspreise, IStR 2021, 571 (571).
70. X. Ditz, S.-E. Bärsch, C. Engelen, C. Quilitzsch, Die neuen Verwaltungsgrundsätze Verrechnungspreise, DStR 2021, 2817 (2817).
71. A. Saliger, L. Wrgowske, S. Greil, Die neuen Verwaltungsgrundsätze Verrechnungspreise, IStR 2021, 573.
72. Gesetz zur Modernisierung der Entlastung von Abzugsteuern und der Bescheinigung der Kapitalertragsteuer (Abzugsteuerentlastungsmodernisierungsgesetz—AbzStEntModG) BGBl 2021/I/28, August 8, 2021, p. 1259.
73. Finance Bill 2021, No. 132c of 2021, December 15, 2021.
74. Finance Act 2019, No. 45 of 2019, December 22, 2019.

presented taxpayers with difficulties in determining the scope and effect of the provision. After a failed attempt to amend this provision in 2020,[75] the Finance Bill 2021 has taken a more radical step: This bill will repeal and replace section 835E completely. The general principle is that the exemption will apply where both supplies and acquirer are (or would be, as no actual remuneration has to be paid) within the charge to Irish tax on their profits if the main purpose is not the avoidance of tax and the arrangement was entered into for bona fide commercial reasons (anti-avoidance safeguards).

3.2 Taxation of the Digital Economy

At the time of writing this chapter, more than thirty countries have implemented some kind of direct tax on digital services, with this trend moving from Europe to Asia and Africa[76] (e.g., Argentina, Austria, Costa Rica, Finland, France, Greece, Hong Kong, Hungary, India, Indonesia, Israel, Italy, Kenya, Malaysia, Mexico, Nigeria, Pakistan, Paraguay, Poland, Portugal, Sierra Leone, Slovakia, Singapore, Spain, Taiwan, Tunisia, Turkey, Ukraine, UK, Uruguay, Vietnam, and Zimbabwe). Several other countries have at this time announced plans for taxes on digital services (e.g., Belgium, Brazil, the Czech Republic, and Thailand). The trend toward more domestic digital service taxes gained momentum, with a marked increase of such taxes in the last couple of years. For example, more than ten digital service taxes were enacted in 2021 before an agreement on Pillar One was reached, with several more announced. In 2020 thirteen such laws entered into force.[77]

The adoption of the two-pillar solution, *see* on this in chapter 1.2.1., seems to have now at least dampened this move away from international toward national solutions. This can be seen quite clearly than examining the EU efforts regarding the implementation of a digital service tax. Already in 2018 a directive implementing a digital levy was proposed by the European Commission.[78] Even though this proposal was not adopted in the Council, the apparent standstill on an international level led to the EU pursuing its own path toward the taxation of digital services. Several EU countries implemented domestic DSTs, among them in particular Austria, France, Italy, Spain and the UK. In 2020, the Executive Vice President Dombrovskis announced at the informal Economic and Financial Affairs Council of the European Union (ECOFIN) press conference that the EU will move ahead with a digital tax proposal in the first half

75. Finance Act 2020, No. 26 of 2020, December 19, 2020; S.I. No. 294/2021—Finance Act 2020 (Section 13) (Commencement) Order 2021, June 25, 2021.
76. J. Whitem, C.C. Matthias, MNEs Struggling with Multiple Transfer Pricing Challenges in 2021, International Tax Review (February 4, 2021).
77. https://tax.kpmg.us/content/dam/tax/en/pdfs/2021/digitalized-economy-taxation-developm ents-summary.pdf (December 16, 2021).
78. Proposal for a Council Directive laying down rules relating to the corporate taxation of a significant digital presence (March 21, 2018) COM(2018) 147 final.

of 2021.[79] This was then postponed, but in August 2021 Commissioner Hahn announced an EU proposal for a digital tax for Autumn of 2021, irrespective of the results of the OECD meeting in October.[80] As in this meeting 136 OECD Member States historically agreed on the two-pillar solution and thus an international approach of how to tax the digital economy; this announced EU levy was now tabled indefinitely. Instead, on December 22, 2021, a proposal for a directive to implement the Pillars was presented,[81] *see* on this section 2.2 and Chapter 2 of this book.

But also other international relations have been impacted by this deal. When Austria and other (EU) countries implemented domestic DSTs, the US threatened to implement retaliatory tariffs on certain products from these jurisdictions (Austria, India, Italy, Spain, Turkey, and the United Kingdom) of up to 25%.[82] Immediately after the enactment of these tariffs, the US suspended them until November 29, 2021, to have more time to complete the OECD negotiations and come to a multilateral agreement.[83] On October 21, 2021, the "Joint statement from the United Kingdom, Austria, France, Italy, Spain and the United States regarding a compromise on a transitional approach to existing unilateral measures during the interim period before Pillar One is in effect" (joint statement) was issued. In this joint statement, Austria, France, Italy, Spain, and the United Kingdom committed to withdrawing their DST rules once Pillar One takes effect. DST liabilities that exceed an amount equivalent to the tax due under Pillar One in the first full year of Pillar One implementation enters into force, or December 31, 2023, will be able to be credited against the tax liability arising from the introduction of Amount A under Pillar One. In return, the US will terminate the tariffs and will not impose any new trade actions until the end of the interim period with respect to the existing DSTs imposed by the countries participating in the joint statement.

3.3 Intangibles

The year 2021 actually—though very subtly—marks an international paradigm change of how intangible assets shall be treated. In Action 5, the agreement on the modified nexus approach for IP regimes, June 30, 2021, was fixed as the abolition date for old

79. S.S. Johnston, EU Will Respect New OECD Deadline for Reaching Global Tax Deal, Tax Notes Int'l 2020, p. 427.
80. *Bloomberg* (https://news.bloomberglaw.com/tech-and-telecom-law/budget-commissioner-defends-eu-digital-tax-delay-amid-concerns), *The Parliament Magazine* (https://www.theparliamentmagazine.eu/news/article/hahn-v.-budg-on-the-eus-own-resources) und *Orbitax* (https://www.orbitax.com/news/archive.php/European-Commission-to-Propose-47510) (September 7, 2021).
81. Proposal for a Council Directive on ensuring a global minimum level of taxation for multinational groups in the Union, COM(2021) 823 final.
82. Find the Section 301 Investigations against the six European countries under https://ustr.gov/issue-areas/enforcement/section-301-investigations/section-301-digital-services-taxes, *see* on the decision, e.g., K. Kubik, Update: Österreichs Digitalsteuer diskriminiert US-Gesellschaften, AVR 1/2021, p. 24.
83. USTR Announces, and Immediately Suspends, Tariffs in Section 301 Digital Services Taxes, Investigations, Press Release, United States Trade Representative (June 2, 2021), available at https://ustr.gov/about-us/policy-offices/press-office/press-releases/2021/june/ustr-announces-and-immediately-suspends-tariffs-section-301-digital-services-taxes-investigations.

regimes that are considered inconsistent with the nexus approach.[84] This means that domestic old or transitional provisions have expired or will fundamentally change in June 2021. Examples of this are France's regime, the UK's patent box regime[85] or the PID regime in Belgium.[86]

The Austrian tax authorities updated their administrative guidelines on transfer pricing (VPR 2021)[87] and adapted them to include changes made to the OECD Guidelines in 2017 while also taking into account Austrian specificities. These Guidelines are not legally binding but significantly influence domestic practice of the tax administration as well as of practitioners and taxpayers. In particular, Chapter VI of the OECD Guidelines on intangibles, including the DEMPE concept,[88] was adopted into the domestic practice.[89] The intention of this was to ensure and facilitate the domestic application of the international standards.[90] Germany also, in an update to the Foreign Tax Code, included both the new definition of intangibles and the DEMPE concept.[91] Outside of the EU, Ghana[92] and Australia also adapted their local guidance toward including the DEMPE concept. With its Practical Compliance Guidance (PCG)[93] from May 19, 2021, the Australian Taxation Office released new guidance also implementing the DEMPE concept while aiming for consistency with the domestic legal framework.

Case law on intangibles from 2021 was rather limited and mostly focused on the appropriate arm's-length pricing of transaction, e.g., *Italy v. Vibac S.p.A*[94] or *Ukraine v. PJSP Gals-K.*[95] More fundamental was the decision by a Belgian court, which was already mentioned above, that held that the DEMPE criteria could only be applied to evaluate facts that took place after the DEMPE concept was introduced. This means that domestic changes that transpose the DEMPE concept into domestic law are very important for taxpayers, as this will frequently also be the point in time in which their activities in that country will be measured by the DEMPE criteria (though of course this may not be the case in countries with a lesser standard of legal certainty). The European Commission in 2021 did not prevail in the *Amazon*[96] case. This case, while

84. OECD, Action 5: the Agreement on the modified nexus approach for IP regimes (2015) p. 4.
85. J. Henshall, D. Griese, P. Henderson, S. Austin, United Kingdom, in: B. Heidecke, M.C. Hübscher, R. Schmidtke, M. Schmitt (eds.), Intangibles in the World of Transfer Pricing (2021) p. 619.
86. A. Gaublomme, M. Panina, A. Schaffers, Belgium, in: B. Heidecke, M.C. Hübscher, R. Schmidtke, M. Schmitt (eds.), Intangibles in the World of Transfer Pricing (2021) p. 405
87. Richtlinie des BMF vom 07.10.2021, 2021-0.586.616, BMF-AV Nr. 140/2021.
88. VPR 2021 Rz 140.
89. B. Wenzel, Die Umsetzung des DEMPE-Konzepts in den VPR 2021, TPI 2021, 197 (197).
90. VPR 2021 Rz 3.
91. Gesetz über die Besteuerung bei Auslandsbeziehungen vom 8. September 1972 (BGBl. I S. 1713), das zuletzt durch Artikel 6 des Gesetzes vom 25.6.2021 (BGBl. I S. 2050) geändert worden ist.
92. Transfer Pricing Regulations 2020 (L.I.2412).
93. ATO, Draft Practical Compliance Guideline, PCG 2021/D4.
94. *Italy v. Vibac S.p.A.*, January 21, 2021, Corte di Cassazione, Case No 1232/2021.
95. *Ukraine v. PJSP Gals-K*, July 5, 2021, Supreme Administrative Court, Case No 620/1767/19.
96. *European Commission v. Amazon and Luxembourg*, May 12, 2021, State Aid–European General Court, Case Nos. T-816/17 and T-318/18.

regarding the treatment of intangible assets, was really about a State Aid Issue, namely if Luxembourg granted preferential treatment to Amazon or not.[97]

Also in 2021, the UN published the third edition of the Guide to Transfer Pricing Issues, whose main focus lies on the application of the arm's-length principle—where it emphasizes the significance of intangible assets—and the implementation of a legal framework for transfer pricing audits in developing countries. While the Action 5 deadline thus marks the end of an old regime, this new UN Manual marks a new step toward international harmonization and more legal certainty for taxpayers. It is to be expected that the next years will bring further changes in the practice of countries and stakeholders.

3.4 Documentation

The increasing importance of documentation for TP was visible in the activities of various jurisdictions also in 2021. New formal and material requirements were introduced and accompanied by strict enforcement consequences. Some of these new rules shall be presented in this chapter,[98] to provide some insight into current international trends. That the compliance with documentation requirements is extremely important for the taxpayers was shown in several court cases in which the income of the taxpayer was increased by the tax authorities by significant amounts (nearly USD 9 million in *Denmark v. "Advisory business ApS"*[99]) or could be determined on a discretionary basis (*Denmark v. Tetra Pak Processing Systems A/S*[100]). These two Danish cases should communicate a clear warning to the taxpayers: Denmark has tightened the filing requirements for the local and the master files starting with January 2021,[101] and these decisions confirm that a failure to comply might lead to harsh consequences.

Other jurisdictions have also tightened the screws on their domestic documentation requirements. The Italian tax authorities have published a circular letter,[102] which contains the obligation of a digital signature with the time stamp when filing the master file and the local file. This letter clarifies several aspects of the new regulations on transfer pricing documentation[103] which were issued on November 23, 2020;[104] it, e.g., confirms the possibility for small- and medium-sized enterprises, i.e., companies with

97. *See* Chapter 3.
98. *See also* Chapter 4.
99. *Denmark v. "Advisory business ApS,"* June 29, 2021, High Court, Case No SKM2021.335.OLR.
100. *Denmark v. Tetra Pak Processing Systems A/S*, April 26, 2021, Supreme Court, Case No BS-19502/2020-HJR.
101. (L28/2020) on December 3, 2020.
102. The final version was published on November 26, 2021, Italian Revenue Agency, Circular 15/E.
103. Administrative Provision n. 360494, November 23, 2020; on this provision *see, e.g.*, S. Versino, Italy Issues New Guidance on Transfer Pricing Documentation: New Requirements to Avoid Penalties and (Some) Simplification, Kluwer international tax blog, March 12, 2021, available at http://kluwertaxblog.com/2021/03/12/italy-issues-new-guidance-on-transfer-pricing-documentation-new-requirements-to-avoid-penalties-and-some-simplification/#_ftn3 (December 22, 2021).
104. A. Valentem, F. Vincenti, Clarification on TP Documentation in Italy Starts Moving Forward, ITR, October 20, 2021.

an annual turnover of less than USD 50 million, not to update certain elements in the local file for up to three years or that the documentation must be presented in Italian, except for the master file, which can be prepared in English. While the content of this letter reaffirms Italy's alignment with the OECD as regards TP documentation, the strict formal requirements (electronic signature) do represent an additional hurdle.[105] In Malaysia, since January 2021, it is mandatory for companies undertaking related party transactions to submit a TPD to the IRB on time. Upon request, the taxpayer now has to produce appropriate documentation within fourteen days instead of thirty days. Also introduced were penalties for companies who fail to comply with this documentation requirement.[106] New transfer pricing regulations have entered into force in Poland on January 1, 2021, which imposed additional documenting obligations on the taxpayer, in particular as regards transactions with or in which are in certain ways involved territories or countries applying harmful tax competition. These stricter rules are also accompanied by an exemption for transaction between domestic entities. Other countries have introduced new documentation requirements for specific MNEs or sectors.[107] The Bulgarian tax administration has focused on transfer pricing in the last couple of years. In 2019, Bulgaria introduced a new transfer pricing documentation requirement, for which the first deadline was June 30, 2021. Additionally, multinational groups of companies are required to prepare a master file by June 30, 2022.[108]

Other countries, while not reducing the burden for the taxpayer, are trying to provide clearer guidance and to make compliance easier or at least more unambiguous. The Mexican tax reform proposal (Economic Package for fiscal year 2022) strives to clarify the current "patchwork" that is the application of the transfer pricing rules in Mexico. The broadly employed use of averages is to be reduced to specific industries, where the results are affected by business cycles and the profits cannot be appropriately assessed solely by a fiscal year. Additionally, documentation requirements will be adapted, e.g., regarding the content of the analysis of functions, assets and risks, with the intent to give greater emphasis to profit sharing methods.[109] In the future, taxpayers will also have to disclose the adjustment formulas used to eliminate differences between the analyzed entity and the proposed comparables. Other changes relate to TP informative returns.[110] In Argentina, Resolution 5010/2021[111] has amended the thresholds for

105. F. Vincenti, A. Valente, Italy Releases Circular on TP Documentation Rules, ITR, December 9, 2021.
106. Section 113B Finance Act 2020 changing the Income Tax Act, 1967 ("ITA").
107. E.g., Senegal for banks and financial institutions, insurance and reinsurance companies, as well as all other financial institutions holding accounts; December 2, 2020, on the Finance Law for 2021 (new point 9 added to Article 31 of the General Tax Code).
108. Amendments to the Bulgarian Tax and Social Insurance Procedure Code, August 13, 2019.
109. J.A. Rojas, Facing the tightening of the screws on TP documentation in Mexico. *International Tax Review* (October 22, 2021).
110. J.A. Rojas, Mexican Government Proposes New TP Rules, *International Tax Review* 2021 (September 27, 2021).
111. Issued by the AFIP (Administración Federal de Ingresos Públicos, Federal Tax Authority); published in the Official Gazette of June 18, 2021.

mandatory filing of transfer pricing documentation and introduced a Simplified Compliance Regime.[112]

3.5 CbC Reporting

On October 18, 2021, the fourth annual peer review of the CbC report was published.[113] The peer review of the Action 13 Minimum Standard proceeded in stages with four annual reviews in 2017, 2018, 2019 and 2020. The peer-review process focused on three critical elements of the minimum standard and covered 132 jurisdictions:

(1) the domestic legal and administrative framework;
(2) the exchange of information (EOI) framework; and
(3) measures in place to ensure the confidentiality and appropriate use of CbC reports.

This review is again a positive sign for the status of implementation of CbC reporting. Over hundred jurisdictions now have a domestic legal framework for CbC reporting in place, with even more in various stages of implementing such legislation, though some have reported difficulties due to COVID-19. This review covers in detail the status of CbC reporting in the covered jurisdictions and contains general or specific recommendations as regards the domestic legal or administrative framework of many or the examined countries. The peer review of the Action 13 Minimum Standard is an annual process; therefore, work will continue to monitor the implementation and operation of CbC reporting by IF members and highlight progress made by jurisdictions to address the recommendations that are made.[114]

One of the countries that introduced CbC reporting obligations in 2021 was Kenya. Kenya, as part of a far-reaching reform in 2021,[115] has now introduced CbC reporting requirements for ultimate parent entities of multinational enterprises. Such ultimate parent entities (meaning entities that are not controlled by another entity and own/control an MNE group with tax residency in Kenya) now have to submit CbC reports.

3.6 Dispute Resolution

With the increasing complexity of the international environment for multinational actors, the demand for APAs is also increasing. APAs are, as the Court in Coca-Cola also stressed, binding agreements which provide legal certainty for the taxpayer and

112. In detail on this *see* E.O. Meloni, Resolution 5010/2021 on Transfer Pricing Reporting Obligations in COVID-19 Times, International Transfer Pricing of Journal 28(6) (2021); Journal Articles & Opinion Pieces IBFD (accessed January 10, 2022).
113. https://www.oecd.org/tax/country-by-country-reporting-compilation-of-2021-peer-review-reports-73dc97a6-en.htm.
114. https://www.oecd-ilibrary.org/docserver/fa6d31d7-en.pdf?expires = 1609957040&id = id&accname = guest&checksum = 16B0401B0E068915B2257C59207EB3D7
115. Finance Act, 2021, Kenya Gazette Supplement No. 128 (Acts No. 8) p. 139.

establish "genuine interests grounded on a binding contract."[116] Despite the ongoing COVID-19 pandemic, current APAs, and even APAs from before this radical change in circumstance, provide taxpayers with some security in their TP activities.[117] Because of this, many jurisdictions are issuing legislation of administrative guidance to make APA proceedings more accessible and efficient for both the taxpayer and the tax authorities. China,[118] for example, has published simplified procedures for advance pricing agreements (APA) in July of 2021,[119] with the goal of encouraging more enterprises to apply for such simplified unilateral APAs. In a decree from June,[120] China also simplified the procedure to apply for bi- or multilateral APAs—a very welcome step toward more legal certainty for international players.[121]

Vietnam, while not simplifying the procedure, has attempted to make APAs more easily accessible by issuing new and quite detailed guidance in August 2021.[122] Only one year prior, in December 2020, Vietnam issued Decree 126,[123] which was the first time guidance on APAs was provided, despite the government having had promoted the APA program since its inception in Vietnam in 2013.[124] For practice, the main change of the new APA process consists of the now no longer compulsory consultation stage. This stage used to be very arduous and limited the number of official applications made.[125] This might also be the next step for the Maledives, where the possibility of applying for an APA is completely new and was introduced only in March 2021.[126] This legislative act even includes the opportunity for a retroactive effect of an APA, though the details of this option are still quite unclear.[127]

Singapore, on the other hand, has limited which application will be considered for an APA/a MAP. In the future, such applications, in which the transaction is not carried out for bona fide commercial reasons, or of which the main purpose is the avoidance or

116. *The Coca-Cola Co. v. Commissioner*, No. 31183-15 (2021) p. 7; *see* in detail on the recent Coca-Cola judgment in Chapter 3 of this book.
117. Explicitly Mr. John Hughes, Director of the IRS APMA program, available at https://www.taxathand.com/article/18868/United-States/2021/Managing-transfer-pricing-risks-with-advance-pricing-agreements#_ftn3 (December 22, 2021); Businesses continue to find certainty on TP through APA procedures; L. Reeves, International Tax Review; London (Sep. 30, 2021); *see* also on Mexico Growth of advanced pricing agreements in Mexico R. Barbieri, R. Cruz, International Tax Review; London (May 5, 2021).
118. *See* in detail Chapter III.
119. Announcement of State Administration of Taxation on matters concerning the application of simple procedures for unilateral advance pricing arrangements.
120. June 24, 2021, the Ministry of Finance (MoF) of Chinese Taipei (Tai Tsai Ji No. 11024508100)
121. L. Hsu and J.R. Shie, Income Adjustments for Cross-Border Bilateral or Multilateral Advance Pricing Arrangements, 28 Intl. Transfer Pricing J. 6 (2021), Journal Articles & Opinion Pieces IBFD (accessed January 10, 2022).
122. Circular 45/2021/TT-BTC, June 18, 2021.
123. Law on Tax Administration and Decree 126/2020/ND-CP (Decree 126), December 5, 2020.
124. Circular 201/2013/TT-BTC.
125. T. Ha, Vietnam's new transfer pricing APA regulations—some hurdles but still promising, MNE Tax, August 30, 2021.
126. Advance Pricing Arrangement Regulation Number 2021/R-42.
127. Z. Zahir, Maledives publishes advance pricing arrangement regulations, MNE Tax, April 22, 2021; Z. Zahir, Advance Pricing Agreements to bring tax, transfer pricing certainty in Maldives, TP News, May 28, 2021.

reduction of tax, or when request concerns a related party transaction that is undergoing audit or investigation, will not be accepted by the IRAS. This applies also if the ALP documentation does not meet the standards.[128]

And while not yet in force, the South African Revenue Service (SARS) has in December 2021 published a proposal for the introduction of an advance pricing agreement program in South Africa.[129] This proposal not only sets out the legal framework but also covers the implementation process itself. Envisioned is a pilot project which will only accept bilateral applications and "should allow the SARS APA unit to learn from other jurisdictions and expand capacity in the APA space."[130] Also worth mentioning is that the APA unit will, at least in the beginning stages, not be completely separate from the transfer pricing unit.[131]

3.7 Significant Domestic Case Law

Despite the ongoing COVID-19 pandemic, 2021 saw many significant TP cases decided. Several large companies, such as Amazon and Cameco saw cases decided in their favor, while the courts ruled against Nike over EU state aid claims. It can be expected that the next years will be even busier for the courts, when the predicted wave of audits following the pandemic will lead to a rise in TP disputes.[132]

In addition to the cases mentioned above, the following countries issued decisions that are significant for domestic practice and can also be of interest from an international perspective:[133]

- Argentina
  - *Argentina v. Malteria Pampa SA*, October 6, 2021, Federal Administrative Court, Case No. TF 35123-A.
  - *Australia v. CUB Australia Holding Pty Ltd*, September 21, 2021, Federal Court of Australia, Case No. FCAFC 171.
  - *Argentina v. Molinos Río de la Plata S.A.*, September 2, 2021, Supreme Court, Case No. CAF 1351/2014/1/RH1.
- Australia
  - *Australia v. Glencore*, May 20, 2021, High Court, Case No. [2021] HCATrans 098.

128. IRAS, 6th Edition Transfer Pricing Guidelines, August 10, 2021; detailed in A. Bose, U. Alvarez, Updated E-Tax Guide on Singapore Transfer Pricing Guidelines, 29 Intl. Transfer Pricing J. 1 (2022), Journal Articles & Opinion Pieces IBFD (accessed December 22, 2021).
129. SARS, 10.12.21, Proposed Model for Establishing an Advance Pricing Agreement Programme in South Africa and Release of Draft Legislation.
130. SARS, 10.12.21, Proposed Model for Establishing an Advance Pricing Agreement Programme in South Africa and Release of Draft Legislation, p. 1.
131. SARS, 10.12.21, Proposed Model for Establishing an Advance Pricing Agreement Programme in South Africa and Release of Draft Legislation, p. 1.
132. Significant US Case Law will be discussed in Chapter 3.
133. *See* for most cases https://tpcases.com/.

- Belgium
  - *Belgium v. ENGIE CC cv*, January 29, 2021, Supreme Court, Case No. F.18.0140.N.
- Canada
  - *Canada v. Loblaw Financial Holdings Inc.*, December 3, 2021, Supreme Court, Case No. 2021 SCC 51.
  - *Canada v. Alta Energy Luxembourg S.A.R.L.*, November 26, 2021, Supreme Court, Case No. 2021 SCC 49.
  - *Canada v. Bank of Nova Scotia*, October 20, 2021, Tax Court, Case No. 2021 TCC 70.
- Chile
  - *Chile v. Avery Dennison Chile S.A.*, March 31, 2021, Tax Court, Case No. RUT°96.721.090-0.
- The Czech Republic
  - *Czech Republic v. LCN GROUP s.r.o.*, July 23, 2021, Supreme Administrative Court, Case No. 2 Afs 148/2020, 37.
  - *Czech Republic v. STARCOM INTERNATIONAL s.r.o.*, February 4, 2021, Regional Court, Case No. 25Af 18/2019, 118.
- Denmark
  - *Denmark v. Takeda A/S and NTC Parent S.a.r.l.*, November 25, 2021, High Court, Cases No. B-2942-12 and B-171-13.
  - *Denmark v. "Fashion Seller A/S,"* November 8, 2021, High Court, Case No. SKM2021.582.OLR.
  - *Denmark v. NETAPP ApS and TDC A/S*, May 3, 2021, High Court, Cases B-1980-12 and B-2173-12.
  - *Denmark v. "H Borrower and Lender A/S,"* January 18, 2021, Tax Tribunal, Case No. SKM2021.33.LSR.
- EU
  - *European Commission v. Belgium*, September 16, 2021, The European Court of Justice, Case No. C-337/19 P.
  - *The European Commission v. Nike and the Netherlands*, July 14, 2021, European Court of Justice Case No. T-648/19.
  - *European Commission v. Luxembourg and Engie*, May 12, 2021, EU General Court, Case Nos. T-516/18 and T-525/1.
- Finland
  - *Finland v. A Oy*, September 13, 2021, Supreme Administrative Court, Case No. KHO:2021:127.
  - *Finland v. A Oy*, June 2, 2021, Supreme Administrative Court, Case No. KHO:2021:73.
- France
  - *France v. (SAS) SKF Holding France*, October 4, 2021, Conseil d'Etat, Case No. 443133.
  - *France v. SMAP*, March 2, 2021, Administrative Court of Appeal, Case No. 19VE01161.

  - *France Genefinance (Interga)*, July 19, 2021, Conseil d'Etat, Case No. 434268.
  - *France v. SA Compagnie Gervais Danone*, June 22, 2021, CAA, Case No. 19VE0315.
  - *France v. SARL Elie Saab France*, June 17, 2021, Conseil d'État, Case No. 433985.
  - *France v. SARL SRN Métal*, May 27, 2021, CAA, Case No. 19NC03729.
  - *France v. SARL Cosi Immobilier*, April 1, 2021, CAA de LYON, Case No. 19LY00527.
  - *France v. SMAP*, March 2, 2021, Administrative Court of Appeal, Case No. 19VE01161.
  - *France v. Bluestar Silicones France*, February 9, 2021, Supreme Administrative Court (CAA), Case No. 16VE00352.
  - *France v. Société Générale S.A.*, February 9, 2021, Administrative Court of Appeal, Case No. 16VE00352.
- Germany
  - *Germany v. Lender GmbH*, June 17, 2021, Bundesfinanzhof, Case No. IR 4/17.
  - *Germany v. "G-Corp GmbH,"* June 9, 2021, Bundesfinanzhof, Case No. I R 32/17.
  - *Germany v. Lender GmbH*, May 18, 2021, Bundesfinanzhof, Case No. I R 62/17.
  - *Germany v. A… GmbH*, March 4, 2021, Bundesverfassungsgericht, Case No. 2 BvR 1161/19
- Greece
  - *Greece v. X Ltd.*, May 28, 2021, Court, Case No. 1674.
- India
  - *India v. Times Infotainment Media Ltd*, August 30, 2021, Income Tax Appellate Tribunal - Mumbai, TIA No 298/Mum/2014.
  - *India v. Concentrix Services & Optum Global Solutions Netherlands B.V.*, March 22, 2021, High Court, Case No. 9051/2020 and 2302/2021.
  - *India v. Engineering Analysis Centre of Excellence Private Limited*, March 2, 2021, Supreme Court, Case No. 8733-8734 OF 2018.
- Israel
  - *Israel v. Sephira & Offek Ltd and Israel Daniel Amram*, August 16, 2021, Jerusalem District Court, Case No. 2995-03-17.
- Italy
  - *Italy v. Felofin S.p.A.*, November 23, 2021, High Court, Case No. 36093/2021.
  - *Italy v. Pompea S.p.A.*, October 12, 2021, Supreme Court, Case No. 27636/2021.
  - *Italy v. NEOPOST ITALIA s.r.l. (QUADIENT ITALY s.r.l.)*, September 16, 2021, Supreme Court, Case No. 25025/2021.
  - *Italy v. TMC Italia SpA*, June 30, 2021, Supreme Court, Case No. 18436/2021.

  - *Italy v. GI Group S.p.A.*, May 20, 2021, Supreme Court, Case No. 13850/2021.
  - *Italy v. "Fruit old s.a.s,"* March 2021, Supreme Court, Case No. 8176, R.G.N. 8952/2013, 2021-25.
  - *Italy v. E.I S.r.l.*, February 12, 2021, Administrative Court, Case No. 12/02/2021 n. 546.
  - *Italy v. "Plastic Pipes s.p.a.,"* January 12, 2021, Supreme Court, Case 230-2021.
- Kenya
  - *the Appellant v. the Commissioner of Customs and Border Control,* October 29, 2021, Kenya Tax Appeal Tribunal, Case No. 340 of 2020.
- Luxemburg
  - *Luxembourg v. "Lux PPL SARL,"* July 13, 2021, Administrative Tribunal, Case No. 43264.
- Netherlands
  - *Netherlands v. Lender [X] B.V.*, July 16, 2021, Supreme Court, Case No. ECLI:NL:2021:1152.
  - *Netherlands v. X B.V.*, July 9, 2021, Supreme Court, Case No. ECLI:NL:2021:1102.
  - *Netherlands v. "Related Party B.V.,"* July 1, 2021, District Court, Case No. ECLI:NL:RBGEL:2021:3382.
  - *Netherlands v. Lender B.V.*, March 6, 2021, Supreme Court, Case No. ECLI:NL:GHAMS:2021:724.
  - *Netherlands v. "Share Owner/Lender,"* February 26, 2021, Supreme Court (Preliminary ruling by the Advocate General), Case No. 20/01884.
- Norway
  - *Norway v. New Wave Norway AS*, March 19, 2021, Court of Appeal, Case No. LB-2020-10664.
  - *Norway v. Petrolia Noco AS*, March 19, 2021, Court of Appeal, Case No. LB-2020-5842.
  - *Norway v. "Distributor A AS,"* March 15, 2021, Tax Board, Case No. 01-NS 131/2017.
- Panama
  - *Panama v. "Pharma Distributor S.A.,"* July 9, 2021, Administrative Tax Court, Case No. TAT-RF-066.
- Peru
  - *Peru v. Telefonica*, February 20, 2021, Supreme Court, Case No. 210/2021.
- Philippines
  - *Philippines v. Snowy Owl Energy Inc*, March 13, 2021, Tax Court, CTA CASE No. 9618.
- Poland
  - *Poland v. R.B.P. (P.) Sp. z o.o.*., August 12, 2021, Supreme Administrative Court, Case No. II FSK 3830/18.

  - *Poland v. A S.A.*, June 30, 2021, Provincial Administrative Court, Case No. I SA/Gl 1649/20.
  - *Poland v. Q. F. sp. z o.o.*, January 15, 2021, Supreme Administrative Court, Case No. II FSK 2514.
- Russia
  - *Russia v. PJSC Vimpelcom-Communications*, May 31, 2021, Arbitration Court of Moscow, Case No. A40-36350/21-140-102.
- South Africa
  - *South Africa v. Levi Strauss SA (PTY) LTD*, April 7, 2021, Supreme Court of Appeal, Case No. (509/2019) [2021] ZASCA 32.
  - *South Africa v. ABSA bank*, March 11, 2021, High Court, Case No. 2019/21825.
  - *South Africa v. ABC (PTY) LTD*, January 7, 2021, Tax Court of Johannesburg, Case No. IT 14305.
- Spain
  - *Spain v. Varian Medical Systems Iberica S.L.*, October 13, 2021, Audiencia Nacional, Case No. SAN 4241/2021, ECLI:ES:AN:2021:4241.
  - *Spain v. Comeresa Prensa S.L.U.*, September 23, 2021, Audiencia Nacional, Case No. SAN 3857/2021, ECLI:ES:AN:2021:3857.
  - *Spain v. SGL Carbon Holding*, September 22, 2021, Tribunal Supremo, Case No. 1151/2021 ECLI:EN:TS:2021:3572
  - *Spain v. EPSON IBÉRICA S.A.U.*, March 18, 2021, Supreme Court, Case No. 390:2021.
  - *Spain v. DIGITEX INFORMÁTICA S.L.*, February 12, 2021, National Court, Case No. 2021:629.
  - *Spain v. BIOMERIEUX ESPAÑA SA*, February 7, 2021, National Court, Case No. 2021:416.
- St. Vincent & the Grenadines
  - *St. Vincent & the Grenadines v. Unicomer (St. Vincent) Ltd.*, April 29, 2021, Supreme Court, Case No. SVGHCV2019/0001.
- Sweden
  - *Sweden v. TELE2 AB*, January 4, 2021, Administrative Court, Case No. 13259-19 and 19892-19.
- Switzerland
  - *Switzerland v. "A SA,"* July 29, 2021, Federal Supreme Court, Case No. 2C_80/2021.
  - *Switzerland v. "Contractual Seller SA,"* January 14, 2021, Federal Supreme Court, Case No. 2C_498/2020.
- Ukraine
  - *Ukraine v. PJSP Gals-K*, July 5, 2021, Supreme Administrative Court, Case No. 620/1767/19.
  - *Ukraine v. PJSC "Azot,"* January 21, 2021, Supreme Administrative Court, Case No. 826/17841/17.
- United Kingdom

- *UK v. GE Capital*, April 14, 2021, Court of Appeal, Case No. [2020] EWHC 1716.

4 CONCLUSIONS AND INSIGHTS

After 2020 being colored heavily by the impact of the COVID-19 epidemic, the 2021 transfer pricing world is impacted most significantly by the agreement of 137 countries to the Pillar One and Pillar Two proposal. This enormous shift in international tax policy will certainly impact the discussion for many years to come, as with this final proposal, questions of implementation and the actual impact on MNEs will become more and more pressing. In 2021, the global legislative framework has undergone several relevant transfer pricing changes. Besides the Pillar Two solutions, the OECD issued its updated Transfer Pricing Guidelines which incorporate the revised guidance on the application of the transactional profit method and the guidance for tax administrations on the application of the approach to HTVI, as well as the new transfer pricing guidance on financial transactions. The updated OECD Guidelines' main aim is still to provide guidance on the application of the "arm's length principle," but it helps MNEs and tax administrations in specific transfer pricing cases as well. In 2021, the FTA also released a new handbook for the ICAP in order to increase the fairness, efficiency and effectiveness of tax administration, reducing burdens and improving tax compliance and tax certainty.[134]

In 2021, the EU has continued to ensure tax transparency and harmonization among its Member States. One of the most important developments of the year is the public CbC reporting. On June 1, 2021, the European Parliament has approved the amendment to the EU Accounting Directive that will expect certain MNEs to publicly disclose tax-related information in the form of a CbCR. In 2020, the EC has announced plans to introduce an EU cooperative compliance program for tax administrations, and while the scope of ETACA is limited to large multinationals, a separate trial was also announced for SMEs on June 23, 2021. The year brought again several significant TP state aid cases; the *Amazon* and the *Engie* cases are just two of the many disputes between the European Commission and multinational companies. Most of these cases will set a precedent for future treatment of multinational companies.[135]

On April 27, the UN has also updated its Practical Manual on Transfer Pricing in Developing Countries. The manual provides a detailed and clearer guidance on the application of the transfer pricing analyses and helps developing countries in various country-specific issues.[136] Equipping the tax administrations to deal fairly and effectively with transfer pricing issues presents significant challenges particularly for developing countries. Therefore, the demand for further developments provided by

134. D. Kovacs, Y. Lawson, WU Global Transfer Pricing Conference 2022—Global Transfer Pricing Developments around the Globe, ITPJ 4 (2022) pt. 2.1.
135. D. Kovacs, Y. Lawson, WU Global Transfer Pricing Conference 2022—Global Transfer Pricing Developments around the Globe, ITPJ 4 (2022) pt. 2.2.
136. D. Kovacs, Y. Lawson, WU Global Transfer Pricing Conference 2022—Global Transfer Pricing Developments around the Globe, ITPJ 4 (2022) pt. 2.3.

international organizations to help MNEs and tax administrations in their transfer pricing challenges stays high.

The arm's-length principle again kept administrations and courts busy. While in 2021 cases on the ALP were frequently decided in the taxpayer's favor, the need for more clarity and more detailed guidance is still occupying all stakeholders. Several countries have updated or published completely new guidance on the application of the ALP. We will see if this will indeed lead to the desired effect of more legal certainty in the next years. This interplays with the introduction of the DEMPE concept into the domestic guidance of several countries that took place in 2021.[137]

The agreement on Pillar One is truly a shift in paradigm and does pose many questions, in particular regarding the efforts of an ever-growing number of countries to introduce DSTs. At least for some countries, which have signed an agreement with the US, the new Pillar One era does bring about the end of domestic efforts to tax the digital economy.

Another "hot topic" of 2021 was documentation requirements. Denmark, Italy, Malaysia and Poland, to name just a few, have introduced new documentation requirements or penalties should the requirements not be met. International actors will have to be very careful in the future to meet each country's specific requirements and deadlines or else risk painful penalties. Maybe Mexico's or Argentina's approach of simplifying the guidelines or introducing a simplified procedure could be an approach to follow. It will be interesting to follow the experience of the respective tax administrations and taxpayers to assess whether this could indeed be a model for other countries.

In the face of all of these hurdles and insecurities, APAs and MAPs are very much a sought after tool by taxpayers to ensure some sense of legal certainty into their activities.[138] Countries are feeling this positive attitude of taxpayers and are adapting their guidance to make the proceedings more easily available. A next step, and certainly an area that will bring about new issues and debates in the coming years, is the one of multilateral APAs, as, e.g., the US has already announced.[139]

One of the fundamental conclusions that can be drawn when reviewing the transfer pricing developments in specific countries is the need for international cooperation, knowledge-sharing and assistance. Poland's initiative of furthering cooperation with five "leaders" in TP[140] is a positive example of this, while the disappointing result of some efforts by tax administrations to challenge the taxpayer's transactions[141] shows that there is still quite some way to go.[142]

137. For a discussion of DEMPE, substance and the ALP, refer to Chapter 6 and D. Kovacs, Y. Lawson, WU Global Transfer Pricing Conference 2022—Global Transfer Pricing Developments around the Globe, ITPJ 4 (2022) pt. 4.2.
138. *See* on this also Chapter 4.
139. D. Kovacs, Y. Lawson, WU Global Transfer Pricing Conference 2022—Global Transfer Pricing Developments around the Globe, ITPJ 4 (2022) pt. 3.3.
140. Poland—Poland Launches "Strengthening Transfer Pricing Legal System Against Tax Evasive Behaviour" Project (November 29, 2021), News IBFD.
141. *See* above, also Chapter 3.
142. D. Kovacs, Y. Lawson, WU Global Transfer Pricing Conference 2022—Global Transfer Pricing Developments around the Globe, ITPJ 4 (2022) pt. 3.2.

While major changes are certainly coming, the small ones might impact the day-to-day practice of taxpayers even more. Many countries, and this chapter could only touch on some, have changed and adapted their domestic legal frameworks and administrative guidance this year. With a move toward digitization, transparency and clarity, the international community seems to be on the right track. While the next chapters will deal with uncertainties, difficulties and open questions, we can still see that TP is a current issue, an issue that is moving, changing and adapting, and which might be greatly impacted by discussions such as the ones in this book or the Global Transfer Pricing Conference 2021.

CHAPTER 2

Transfer Pricing Developments in the European Union

Isabel Verlinden, Jean-Philippe Van West & Stefaan De Baets

---

1 INTRODUCTION

What a ride it was once again on the international tax and transfer pricing (TP) rollercoaster. The size of our chapter almost doubled compared to last year which means a few things. First, with its kind invitation to write again, the WU Vienna evidences the strength of our relationship and hence the benefit for practitioners and academia to jointly address international tax conundrums as part of a multi-stakeholder debate. Second, at this pace we will hit the 1,000 pages mark in less than five years from now. It is tempting to speculate about whether the trust in the international tax architecture will be restored by then. Third, a book of such size has attributes of a lethal weapon when left loosely on a bookshelf. Talking weapons ... *The Economist* expects "unknown unknowns" stemming from global tax reform and a bonanza awaiting tax advisers.[1] According to the *Oxford Learner's Dictionary* a bonanza is "a situation in which people can make a lot of money or be very successful." Contrary to what is known to our grandparents as one of the longest-running western series, "bonanza" has nothing to do per se with flexing muscles and gunshots. However, international institutions and governments are sharpening their knives when enacting (draft) rules destined to fund massive budgetary needs. Politicians go the extra mile in their quest to build up political capital founded on the mantra of "tax fairness." Those crafting these rules are working relentlessly to *get things done* and that deserves praise. The tax system can better serve today's needs than based on what the League of Nations came up with about a century ago. As stated by Paul Polman and Andrew Winston in their book *Net Positive*, there is great momentum "to transform the image of taxes as costs to minimize to thinking of them as an investment in our health, well-being, and society."[2] Many of our clients unambiguously live up to these messages and are not sure whether they should engage or rather refrain from taking part in the debate (or trying to do so). One never knows how this will be perceived.

1. The Economist, "To Tax or Not to Tax," Special Report Business and the State, January 15, 2022, p. 11.
2. P. Polman and A. Winston, "Net Positive: How Courageous Companies Thrive by Giving More Than They Take," Harvard Business Review Press, 2021, p. 195.

As we will illustrate, quite some regulatory requirements (that will likely be) imposed on companies these days are ordinarily draconic. One may wonder whether the ghost of Al Capone, eventually (only) caught for tax evasion, glimmers through in the debate, particularly his famous quote "You can get more with a nice word and a gun than you can with a nice word."

Looking at the list of topics that will be covered under this chapter, the least one could say is that the European Commission (EC) has been burning the midnight oil. Driven by the evolutions at the level of the OECD/Inclusive Framework (IF), the Commission has followed suit with the publication of a draft directive on a global minimum level of taxation (the EU GloBE Directive) at the verge of the winter holiday season almost together with a draft directive on the abusive use of shell entities.

The policies of the EU can be centered around two axes: *fair taxation* and *transparency*. Several initiatives can be mentioned under the former such as its first mover role in the Global Anti-Base Erosion rules (GloBE rules), or Anti-Tax Avoidance Directive 3 (ATAD 3) on shell companies, but also other projects that are in the pipeline for 2022 such as the Debt Equity Bias Reduction Allowance (DEBRA). Yet other projects such as Business in Europe: Framework for Income Taxation (BEFIT) may take a bit longer to bloom. With respect to transparency, 2021 was the first year of reporting under the Directive of Administrative Cooperation 6 (DAC6) next to the publication of "DAC7" and progressing work on "DAC8." The directive on public country-by-country reporting (PCbCR)—an accounting directive by the way—was published by year-end as well.

Finally, amidst an amalgam of corporate citizenship-related developments, the issue of environmental taxation under the green deal (Fit for 55) is also on the table of the EC.

Despite many at the time of writing (still) being "grounded" in working from home mode, please fasten your seat belts, set your table in the upright position, and get ready for takeoff!

2 THE EU ROADMAP

On May 18, 2021, the EC published its Communication on Business Taxation for the twenty-first century[3] as a roadmap to set its ambitious and comprehensive tax agenda: enabling fair and sustainable growth and ensuring effective taxation.

It was clear that the EC committed to implement the global agreements that were negotiated at the level of the OECD/Inclusive Framework (IF).[4] The roadmap suggested that "in order to ensure [Pillar One] consistent implementation in all EU Member States, including those that are not Members of the OECD and do not participate in the IF, the Commission will propose a Directive for the implementation of Pillar One in the EU."[5] With regard to Pillar Two, also with the aim of consistent application and

3. Communication from the Commission to the European Parliament and the Council, Business Taxation for the 21st Century, COM (2021) 251 Final, https://eur-lex.europa.eu/legal-content/EN/TXT/PDF/?uri=CELEX:52021DC0251&from=EN.
4. *See* Chapter 1, "Global Transfer Pricing Evolutions."
5. *Supra* n. 3, p. 8.

compatibility with EU law, the EC indicated that the "principal method for implementing [...] will be an EU directive that will reflect the OECD Model Rules with the necessary adjustments."[6] At the same time, the EC indicated that the directive could have implications for existing or pending EU directives and initiatives such as the Anti-Tax Avoidance Directives (ATAD) (in particular with regard to CFC rules), and the interest and royalty directive.[7]

Several commentators already indicated that Pillar Two measures should be carefully transposed as they could conflict with the EU fundamental freedoms, in particular the freedom of establishment.[8,9]

The roadmap indicated going beyond the OECD agreements on Pillar One and Two. One step is improving public transparency on the taxes that large economic actors pay, in particular because of the growing demand from citizens and civil society. The EC will therefore elaborate by 2022 a proposal on the annual publication of the effective corporate tax rate of certain large companies active in the EU, based on the Pillar Two calculations.[10] Another initiative mentioned in the roadmap is the fight against the abusive use of shell companies.[11]

Together with the roadmap, the EC published a recommendation on the tax treatment of losses during the COVID-19 crisis.[12] EU Member States (MSs) should allow loss carry back for businesses to at least the previous fiscal year. This period can be extended to allow carry back to set off losses of the years 2020 and 2021 against taxed profits in 2017 to 2019. The amount of losses to be carried back is limited to 3 million EUR per loss-making fiscal year. It is important to emphasize that the recommendation is not binding upon EU MSs.

Another initiative relates to the contradiction between deductibility of interest through debt financing versus the nondeductibility of costs related to equity financing. This may fuel appetite for excessive debt financing. The EC therefore intends drafting a directive by the first quarter of 2022, under the formal name of the Debt Equity Bias Reduction Allowance (DEBRA).[13]

Last but not least, the EC announced that it will propose a new framework for income taxation: BEFIT, a "makeover" of the Common Consolidated Corporate Tax Base (CCCTB). This proposal will be tabled by 2023.[14]

Several of the initiatives announced in the roadmap are discussed further in this contribution.

6. *See* section 3 for a further discussion on the Pillar Two draft directive.
7. *Supra* n. 3, p. 8.
8. *See*, for example, L. De Broe and M. Massant, "Are the OECD / G20 Pillar Two GloBE-Rules Compliant with the Fundamental Freedoms?," *EC Tax Review* (Volume 30) 2021, p. 86 and C. De Pietro, "The GloBE Income Inclusion Rule and Its Global Character: Complexities Underlying Its Fully Effective Application," *EC Tax Review* 2021, (Volume 30) Nos. 5&6, p. 220.
9. A further discussion on the issue of conflict with the EU fundamental freedoms falls outside the scope of this contribution.
10. *Supra* n. 3, p. 9.
11. *See* section 5 for a further discussion on the ATAD 3 draft directive.
12. Commission Recommendation (EU) 2021/801 of May 18, 2021 on the tax treatment of losses during the COVID-19 crises, Official Journal of the European Union, L 179/10 of 20.2.2021.
13. *Supra* n. 3, p. 11 and section 7.
14. *Supra* n. 3, p. 11 and section 4.

3 THE EU GLoBE DIRECTIVE

The OECD/IF published the Model Rules on Pillar Two on December 20, 2021.[15] Two days later, on December 22, 2021, the EC published its proposal of directive introducing the Model Rules on Pillar Two at EU level (EU GloBE Directive).[16] This part of the international tax reform was nicely gift-wrapped under the Christmas tree.

In short, the EU GloBE Directive provides for the application within the EU of a set of rules to ensure a minimum effective level of taxation of 15% for large multinational enterprises (i.e., with a combined group turnover of at least 750 million) by means of two interacting rules:

(1) an income inclusion rule (IIR) imposing a top-up tax (TPT) on an ultimate parent entity (UPE) in respect of the low-taxed income of constituent entities, and
(2) an undertaxed payment rule (UTPR), to be applied as a "backstop" to the extent the low-tax income of a constituent entity is not subject to tax under an IIR, imposing a top-up tax for a jurisdiction in proportion to an allocation two-factor formula based on the value of tangible assets in the jurisdiction and number of employees in the jurisdiction. No explicit reference is made in the EU GloBE Directive on how the UTPR top-up tax will be levied.

In short, under the IIR, the ultimate parent entity (UPE) of an MNE is primarily responsible for collecting the TPT. In other words, the jurisdiction of the UPE will collect the TPT. The TPT is the difference between the 15% GloBE tax rate and the effective tax rate (ETR) applied in a certain jurisdiction on the so-called GloBE income. The GloBE income is calculated on the basis of consolidated financial statements principles on a jurisdiction-by-jurisdiction basis, with some adjustments. In calculating the TPT, the substance-based income exclusion must be considered. This carve-out is a percentage of the carrying value of tangible assets (8%, declining to 5% over a period of 10 years) and payroll (10%, declining to 5% over a period of 10 years). The TPT will be calculated on the so-called GloBE income, reduced with the substance-based carve-out.

Under the UTPR, where TPT remains after the IIR has been applied, the GloBE adjustment can be achieved in the manner each jurisdiction decides, e.g., denial of a deduction, an additional tax, a reduction in any allowance for equity, or deemed income (reversing a related party expense). The total UTPR amount is allocated among implementing jurisdictions under a formula that is based on the relative proportion of

15. OECD (2021), Tax Challenges Arising from the Digitalisation of the Economy—Global Anti-Base Erosion Model Rules (Pillar Two): Inclusive Framework on BEPS, OECD, Paris, https://www.oecd.org/tax/beps/tax-challenges-arising-from-the-digitalisation-of-theeconomy-Global-anti-base-erosion-model-rules-pillar-two.htm. A discussion of the Model Rules can be found under Chapter 1.
16. Proposal for a Council Directive on ensuring a global minimum level of taxation for multinational groups in the Union, COM(2021) 823 final, 22.12.2021.

employees and tangible assets in each jurisdiction. Importantly, under this formula, there is no requirement that an entity in a UTPR jurisdiction actually makes deductible payments to a low-taxed affiliate.

This is one of the projects that France as Chair of the European Council has set as a priority.[17] It is cited as one of three elements to put in place for a "fairer, effective taxation," as indicated in the French Presidency Program.[18] The ambition is to have the process finalized before France hands over the baton to the Czech Republic at the end of June 2022.

At the same time of publication of the EU GloBE Directive, the EC also launched a feedback consultation procedure which ran until March 1, 2022.[19] The feedback will be summarized and used in feeding the legislative debate.

The EU GloBE Directive is at most places a copy-paste of the Model Rules as elaborated by the OECD/IF. This section discusses only some of the most important variations in the proposal for a directive compared to the OECD/IF Model Rules.

As indicated in section 2 on the EU roadmap, the Pillar Two measures could conflict with the EU fundamental freedoms. Therefore, some specific approaches were introduced to avoid infringement.[20] This relates in particular to the extension of the scope to large-scale domestic groups.[21] The explanatory memorandum indicates that the EU GloBE Directive uses the optionality to require a minimum tax of 15% not only for foreign subsidiaries but also for all constituent entities resident or permanent establishments (PEs) situated in that MS.

According to Article 10 of the EU GloBE Directive, MSs have the option to apply a domestic top-up tax on its eligible entities: the top-up tax is charged and collected in the jurisdiction with an ETR of less than 15%, instead of collecting the additional tax at the level of the UPE. The parent entity that applies the IIR must give a credit for the domestic top-up tax in calculating the top-up tax for the low-taxed jurisdiction.[22] Entities located in a MS that has opted to implement IIR and UTPR equivalent rules in its internal tax system must pay the top-up tax (if any) to the MS. Some flexibility is allowed in the technical implementation of the domestic top-up tax. The EU GloBE Directive provides that such a domestic top-up tax system should ensure the minimum effective taxation *"in the same, or in an equivalent manner, to the IIR and UTPR of this Directive."*[23] The EU GloBE Directive defines a qualified domestic top-up tax therefore as follows:

17. J. Comte, "French EU Council Presidency Prioritizes CBAM, Minimum Taxation," *Tax Notes Today International*, December 14, 2021.
18. "Recovery, Strength and a Sense of Belonging—Program for the French Presidency of the Council of the European Union," p. 28. https://presidence-francaise.consilium.europa.eu/media/qh4cg0qq/en_programme-pfue-v1-2.pdf.
19. *See* https://ec.europa.eu/info/law/better-regulation/have-your-say/initiatives/13327-Minimum-level-of-taxation-for-large-multinational-groups_en.
20. *Supra* n. 16, p. 3.
21. *Supra* n. 16, pp. 6 and 69.
22. *Supra* n. 16, pp. 8 and 28.
23. *Supra* n. 16, pp. 16 and 28-29.

A top-up tax that is implemented in the domestic law of a jurisdiction and that:

(a) provides for the determination of the excess profits of the constituent entities located in that jurisdiction in accordance with the rules laid down in this Directive and the application of the minimum tax rate to those excess profits for the jurisdiction and the constituent entities in accordance with the rules laid down in this Directive; and
(b) is implemented and administered in a way that is consistent with the rules laid down in this Directive and does not allow the jurisdiction to provide any benefits that are related to those rules.[24]

The explanatory memorandum makes a reference to the Commentary to the Model Rules which were not yet available at the time of publication of the proposal of directive (or of this contribution).[25] The OECD Model Rules only provide that the country which applies the income inclusion rule should take into account only the ETR of foreign constituent entities as defined in the Model Rules. Those who would suspect the EC to have the powers of a clairvoyant may rest assured the truth is much less of the obscure or witchcraft. Indeed, the EC participates in the development of the Model Rules and hence sits around the (virtual) table when discussing them at the level of the OECD/IF. What is in the proposal of the directive is simply unveiling one element of possible options that will likely be elaborated upon in the Commentary on the Model Rules.

The EU GloBE Directive mentions in its explanatory memorandum that in practice the ATAD CFC rules will apply first. Additional taxes paid under a CFC regime will be considered and will be attributed to the relevant low-taxed entity in determining its jurisdictional effective tax rate (ETR). Changes to the ATAD are not necessary, at least not according to the EC.[26] The EU GloBE Directive is also used to introduce changes in the interest and royalty directive, in particular with regard to introducing a condition that interest payments are exempted from withholding tax only when such interest is subject to tax in the destination state. This can still give rise to some discussion between MSs as some of them want to set a minimum tax as a condition for exemption of withholding tax.[27]

The EU GloBE Directive will be accompanied by an Annex listing the foreign legal frameworks that are assessed as equivalent to a qualified IIR.[28] The draft Annex to the EU GloBE Directive currently mentions one country (the United States of America), albeit between square brackets as an indication—at least to the authors—that the assessment of the US approach is not final yet. The EU GloBE Directive also indicates that the Union may conclude bilateral agreements with the countries mentioned in the Annex for simplifying the reporting procedures.[29]

24. *Supra* n. 16, p. 22.
25. *Ibid.*
26. *Supra* n. 16, p. 2.
27. *Ibid.*
28. ANNEX to the Proposal for a Council Directive on ensuring a global minimum level of taxation for multinational groups in the Union {SWD(2021) 580 final}, https://data.consilium.europa.eu/doc/document/ST-15294-2021-ADD-2/en/pdf.
29. *Supra* n. 16, p. 71.

On the basis of Article 115 of the Treaty on the Functioning of the EU (TFEU), the EU GloBE Directive requires unanimity among the twenty-seven MSs.[30] It provides that MSs should transpose the directive by December 31, 2022. It is intended to be implemented with regard to the IIR from January 1, 2023, and with regard to the UTPR from January 1, 2024.[31] This is in line with the October 8, 2021, OECD/IF Statement on the two-pillar approach.[32] If all goes well that is because there is a risk of some cracks in the unanimity as some countries question the proposed timetable.[33] According to Mr. Benjamin Angel, director of direct taxation at the EC's Directorate General for Taxation and Customs Union, MSs that would not meet the 15% minimum ETR threshold have three options to implement the EU GloBE Directive. The first one is to increase the corporate tax rate to at least 15%. The second is to increase the corporate tax rate to at least 15% for companies in the scope of the measure (i.e., with a combined group turnover of more than EUR 750 million). Finally, the third option would be not to increase the corporate tax rate, but with the consequence that the jurisdiction of the UPE collects the top-up tax.[34]

Particularly interesting to TP practitioners is that both the OECD Model Rules and the EU GloBE Directive indicate that the intragroup transactions between group members in different countries should be consistent with the arm's-length principle (ALP).[35] The authors wonder how this approach will be made consistent with the plan to introduce the formulaic approach under BEFIT.[36] Once BEFIT is adopted, this could very well lead to the obligation of multiple calculations for ultimately determining the tax obligations of the multinational enterprise (MNE):

- an arm's-length approach for determining the obligations under Pillar Two;[37]
- a formulaic approach for determining the tax obligations under BEFIT; and finally
- (probable) convergence calculations between the two calculations.

The authors look with anticipation to the commentaries on the Model Rules and how they might influence the EU GloBE Directive. A point that may command particular reflection is whether the Treaty on the Functioning of the EU (TFEU) allows adopting

30. On the basis of Article 115 TFEU, the Council shall act unanimously. Article 114, § 2 TFEU provides that the ordinary legislative procedure between European Parliament and Council is not applicable to fiscal provisions.
31. *Ibid.*
32. OECD/IF, Statement on a Two-Pillar Solution to Address the Tax Challenges Arising from the Digitalisation of the Economy, October 8, 2021, p. 5.
33. B. Smith-Meyer, "Europe's Veto Threatens to Stall Global Tax reform," *Politico*, January 18, 2022 and S. Paez, "EU Finance Ministers Concerned about Pillar 2 Adoption Timeline," *Tax Notes Today International*, January 19, 2022.
34. Panel hosted by Union des Entreprises Luxembourgeoises on January 11, 2022. Coverage by Tax Notes Today International, January 12, 2022, EU Member States will have Flexibility in Implementing Pillar Two.
35. *Supra* n. 15, p. 16, and *supra* n. 16, p. 35.
36. BEFIT is discussed in section 4.
37. *Infra*. section 14 captures some reflections on the future of the ALP.

a directive that leads to a minimum tax, in particular, if the minimum tax would not enhance trade and free movement in the EU.[38]

4 CCCTB BECOMES BEFIT

"*Business in Europe—Framework for Income Taxation,*" or "*BEFIT*" for short, is the most prominent initiative included in the communication on business taxation in the twenty-first century addressed in section 2. It aims to introduce a corporate tax system for the Single Market based on a common tax base and allocate profits between different MSs based on a formula, also known as "formulary apportionment." This means that all profits made by a multinational company across different European MSs are aggregated and subsequently allocated based on a formula. The latter will take into consideration the value of the MNE's assets, labor (personnel and salaries) and the turnover (sales by destination) in the MS where it does business. Incidentally, intangible assets are also recognized in the asset factor. However, the communication does not elaborate on the weight that will be applied to the respective factors in the formula.

BEFIT builds upon the EC's previous proposals to implement a CCCTB. With this "rebranding," the EC likely hopes to bring a new genie to the bottle to crystallize its aspiration to take away the need for companies operating in different MSs having to comply with 27 different sets of national tax rules. The idea is to set up a tax system at European level where companies can determine their tax base using a uniform set of rules, resulting in a more streamlined administration.

BEFIT also builds on the ongoing work within the OECD to redesign the international tax system based on Pillar One and Pillar Two addressed in sections 6 and 3, respectively. In other words, the EC likely sees the ongoing developments on Pillar One and Pillar Two as a catalyst for reinvigorating the stalled CCCTB initiatives. The introduction of BEFIT means that the proposals made under the CCCTB will be withdrawn.

In the communication on business taxation in the twenty-first century, the EC mentions it is aiming to draw up a proposal on BEFIT by 2023.

5 SHELL ENTITIES[39]

Immediately next to the EU GloBE Directive, the EC has delivered another—expected—proposal for a directive on December 22, 2021. This proposal for a directive to fight against the misuse of shell companies[40] is also referred to as the ATAD 3 Directive (or Unshell Directive). The text should be transposed by MSs before

38. *See*, for example, J. Becker and J. Englisch, "Implementing an International Effective Minimum Tax in the EU" and *supra* n. 8.
39. The authors would like to thank Francesca Vittoria Bella, Associate at PwC Belgium for the research and support in drafting this section.
40. Proposal for a Council Directive laying down rules to prevent the misuse of shell entities for tax purposes and amending Directive 2011/16/EU, COM(2021) 565 final, 22.12.2021

June 30, 2023, and become effective from January 1, 2024, at the latest. At the same time as the publication of the ATAD 3 Directive, the EC launched a feedback consultation procedure on the said directive which ran until March 7, 2022.[41]

The ATAD 3 Directive can be seen as the next step to introduce rules regarding "economic substance" in certain offshore jurisdictions. The text focuses on the appropriate levels of employees, premises, functions performed, active bank accounts and risks assumed to assess the economic substance at the level of an entity in a given MS. It is certainly another episode in the EC series on transparency, next to the different DACs[42] (which this ATAD 3 Directive also modifies), and the PCbCR.[43]

The ATAD 3 Directive indicates that it would apply to all "undertakings" that are considered tax resident and are eligible to receive a tax residency certificate in a MS. By the term "undertaking," the ATAD 3 Directive aims "any entity engaged in an economic activity, regardless of its legal form, that is a tax resident in a Member State."[44] It means that the text applies not only to legal entities but also to all kinds of legal arrangements, including partnerships and associations, as long as they are a tax resident in a MS.

In order to identify whether a potential risk of abuse exists, the ATAD 3 Directive establishes a "gateway test" to assess the potential tax avoidance risk and to give a first overview of the economic substance at the level of the undertaking.

The undertaking will not meet the gateway requirement and will be considered as a potential shell entity if the following three indicative criteria are met:[45]

(1) more than 75% of the revenues accruing to the undertaking in the preceding two tax years is relevant income. Such relevant income is generally passive income such as royalties, interests, dividends and also crypto-assets are included;
(2) the undertaking is engaged in cross-border activity, i.e.:
    - more than 60% of the book value of the undertaking's assets are immovable property or movable property (not being cash, shares or securities) held for private purposes and with a book value of more than EUR 1 million in the preceding two years;
    - at least 60% of the undertaking's relevant income is earned or paid out via cross-border transactions;
(3) in the preceding two years, the undertaking outsources the processing related to day-to-day administration and decision-making on significant functions.

If these three criteria are met, the undertaking is regarded as a risk entity and it is subject to specific reporting requirements.

41. *See* https://ec.europa.eu/info/law/better-regulation/have-your-say/initiatives/12999-Tax-avoidance-fighting-the-use-of-shell-entities-and-arrangements-for-tax-purposes_en.
42. *See* section 9.
43. *See* section 8.
44. *Supra* n. 40, p. 23.
45. *Supra* n. 40, p. 25.

The following items are considered relevant income for purposes of the ATAD 3 Directive:[46]

- interest (or other income generated from financial assets, including crypto-assets);
- royalties (or other income generated from intangible property or tradable permits);
- dividends and income from the disposal of shares;
- financial leasing;
- income from immovable property;
- income from movable property, other than cash, shares or securities, held for private purposes and with a book value of more than one million euros;
- income from insurance, banking and other financial activities;
- income from services which the undertaking has outsourced to other associated enterprises.

The reader will observe that in particular interest, royalties, income from immovable property and income from services are high on the radar as particularly vulnerable to deemed artificial profit shifting.

As this gateway test works as a sort of filter to determine the existence of a risk, the ATAD 3 Directive establishes a list of criteria that, if met, generate a presumption of low risk. In fact, if an entity meets one of the following criteria, there is no reporting obligation:[47]

- companies which have a transferable security admitted to trading or listed on a regulated market or multilateral trading facility as defined under Directive 2014/65/EU;[48]
- regulated financial undertakings;[49]
- holding companies holding shares in operational businesses in the same MS, while their beneficial owners are also resident for tax purposes in the same MS;
- holding companies resident for tax purposes in the same MS as the undertaking's shareholder(s) or the UPE, as defined for country-by-country reporting purposes;
- undertakings with at least five own full-time equivalent employees or members of staff exclusively carrying out the activities generating the relevant income.

If the gateway test determines that the entity is potentially a "shell company," the undertaking is required to report certain information. The information to be reported

46. *Supra* n. 40, p. 24.
47. *Supra* n. 40, p. 26.
48. Directive 2014/65/EU of the European Parliament and of the Council of May 15, 2014 on markets in financial instruments and amending Directive 2002/92/EC and Directive 2011/61/EU, Official Journal EU L 173/349 of 12.06.2014.
49. *Supra* n. 40, p. 26. The proposal for a Directive contains an exhaustive list of what should be considered regulated financial undertakings.

consists of specific elements indicating a minimum level of economic substance that must be documented and duly proven by the undertaking. The following information should be included in or accompany the annual tax return:[50]

- the existence of own premises or premises available for the exclusive use of the undertaking;
- the existence of at least one own and active bank account in the EU;
- the presence of at least one director resident close to the undertaking and dedicated to its activities or, alternatively, a majority of the undertaking's full-time employees that are engaged with its core income-generating activities being resident close to the undertaking.

Concerning this third and last point, it is quite surprising to the authors that one of the criteria taken into account is reliance on geographical proximity to the undertaking of one director or the majority of full-time employees. The authors wonder whether the current mantra of "working from anywhere" has escaped from the EC's radar.[51]

Further to the items above, the undertaking must accompany its tax return with the following information:[52]

- address and type of premises;
- amount of gross revenue and type thereof;
- amount of business expenses and type thereof;
- type of business activities performed to generate the relevant income;
- the number of directors, their qualifications, authorizations and place of residence for tax purposes or the number of full-time equivalent employees performing the business activities that generate the relevant income and their qualifications, their place of residence for tax purposes;
- outsourced business activities; and
- bank account number, any mandates granted to access the bank account and to use or issue payment instructions and evidence of the account's activity.

Once the undertaking has submitted all the minimum economic substance indicators, the information will be reviewed, and the tax authority will decide whether the entity should be regarded as a "shell." The undertaking that has correctly submitted all the documentation required and has duly proven that all the minimum substance indicators are met shall be presumed not to be a shell entity. In case the undertaking cannot back up all the indicators mentioned above with sufficient evidence, the entity is presumed not to have the minimum substance required and shall be considered a shell entity.[53]

However, it is possible to rebut such presumption by demonstrating that there is no misuse of the entity concerned for tax purposes. The additional evidence to be provided

50. *Supra* n. 40, p. 28.
51. This contribution does not address the potential risk of PE and profit allocation to the location of home working or working from anywhere.
52. *Supra* n. 40, p. 29.
53. *Supra* n. 40, pp. 29-30.

should notably include a document explaining that the establishment of the undertaking does not merely respond to a tax purpose but can be explained by a certain commercial rationale, in-depth information about the employee profiles, and concrete evidence that decision-making concerning the activity generating the relevant income is taking place in the MS of the undertaking.[54]

To reduce the administrative compliance burden, an undertaking may request an exemption if it proves that no tax benefit resulted from its interposition for its beneficial owner or for the group as a whole. Such exemption can be extended for a period of five years.

The ATAD 3 Directive thus recognizes that the establishment of a low substance entity is not per se abusive. It is considered an abusive practice if such an undertaking is used for tax avoidance or evasion purposes. This approach is likely a result of the written public consultation held earlier in 2021 embodied in thirty-two questions.[55] In some cases, undertakings indeed do not fulfil the conditions to pass the minimum substance test or cannot duly provide documentary evidence to prove that they meet all the minimum substance indicators. However, this undertaking does not create any tax advantage in favor of its beneficial owner(s) or of the group. Despite this recognition, the authors still consider the proposal for a Directive to be overly broad.

If the entity can prove that its establishment can be justified for a purpose other than a taxation benefit, the MS can grant an exemption from having to undergo the minimum substance test or having to prove the minimum substance indicators. The tax authorities do not have to prove that the shell entity has no substance; the presumed shell entity has to prove that it has substance or justify its existence. *Guilty until proven innocent*? For example, a regional holding company, situated in a MS, has a staff of two full-time employees on its payroll. The sole activity of the regional holding company consists of holding shares in the operational companies situated across the EU. This holding structure is seen very frequently and can be considered not to be construed for tax avoidance purposes, but rather for an efficient management of the shareholdings. Nevertheless, the holding company needs to deliver adequate information and can be put under higher scrutiny because it will pass the gateway tests. Hence, such holding structures will be looked upon as potentially tax dangerous.

If the minimum substance requirements are not met and the undertaking qualifies to be a shell entity under the ATAD 3 Directive, multiple consequences arise:[56]

- incorporation of the relevant income in the MS of the shareholder of the shell entity (with credit of the tax paid by the shell entity);
- denial of double tax relief;
- denial of tax advantages;
- increased audit risk;

54. *Supra* n. 40, p. 30.
55. Public consultation on Tax avoidance—fighting the use of shell entities and arrangements for tax purposes, June 4-August 27, 2021, https://ec.europa.eu/info/law/better-regulation/have-your-say/initiatives/12999-Tax-avoidance-fighting-the-use-of-shell-entities-and-arrangements-for-tax-purposes/public-consultation_en.
56. *Supra* n. 40, *see*, for example, pp. 31, 32 and 36.

- denial of a tax resident certificate;
- automatic disclosure of information about the shell entity to MS tax authorities;
- possible administrative monetary sanctions of at least 5% of the undertaking's turnover of the relevant tax year.

The ATAD 3 Directive has also a major impact on Directive 2011/16/EU on Administrative Cooperation (DAC) and will amend it consequently. The ATAD 3 Directive sets out new obligations for MSs in terms of both timing and content of the information to be shared.

The MSs shall automatically exchange the data received by the undertaking via a central directory within thirty days from the date of:

- the reception of information related to shell companies in the tax return;
- the certificate that an undertaking has rebutted the presumption of a lack of minimum substance;
- the certificate indicating the entity is exempted;
- the date of audit of a shell entity.

Along with the information received from the entity, the MS should notably include in the information to be exchanged the undertaking's tax identification number (TIN) as well as the VAT number, where available, the identification of the undertaking's shareholders and its beneficial owner(s), the other MSs concerned, other persons in the MS likely to be affected, and declaration and summary of evidence that the substance requirement has been met.[57]

Sanctions will be provided for noncompliant entities, for example, if the minimum substance report was not timely submitted. As already indicated above, the sanction will include in any case an administrative sanction of at least a (draconian) 5% of the undertaking's turnover.

As indicated in the beginning of this section, this is another episode in the transparency journey the EC embarked upon, adding another line of administrative complexity for both tax authorities and multinational enterprises.

Rather than addressing the thirty-two questions in the public consultation one-by-one, PwC's network of Member Firms (PwC) suggested the EC to take stock of the variety of entities and arrangements currently in use, to then determine whether the particular use of those entities and arrangements would violate existing tax policy objectives. Only in the affirmative case, it could then determine whether the existing anti-avoidance rules, including ATAD I and ATAD II, BEPS and the MLI (notably the principal purpose test and the limitation on benefits test), and judicially developed anti-avoidance doctrines, would be robust enough to address the particular use. If and to the extent that would not be the case, the introduction of further specific anti-avoidance rules should be considered.

57. *Supra* n. 40, pp. 33 and 34.

The authors' plea for "meaningful" transparency has probably never been so prominent. Anchoring control over risk, i.e., the actual delineation or—in vulgarizing terms—"finding the real deal" should be the compass. This serves as the criterion rather than the geographic proximity and qualification of people, bank accounts and the like, totally detached from the context that TP practitioners adhere to when following the OECD's TP guidance as a beacon.

6 THE STORY OF A DIGITAL LEVY, PILLAR ONE AND EU OWN RESOURCES[58]

Own resources of the EU are as important as they are sensitive in the current (hopefully) post-pandemic geopolitical tense context. Indeed, the EC and EU are known for launching ambitious projects. Spending is one thing, financing it is another, and usually the more difficult part.

As a reminder, under the Next Generation EU project,[59] the Council mandated the EC to reform its own resources system by supplementing the traditional own resources (mainly customs duties, sugar levies, percentage of VAT, and resources based on the gross national income of MS).[60]

On December 18, 2020, a political agreement was reached on the Recovery and Resilience Facility (RRF) between the European Parliament (EP) and the Council of the EU (the Council). The EC welcomed this political agreement as a key instrument at the heart of the Next Generation EU project. It was supposed to make EUR 672.5 billion available to support the reforms and investments undertaken by the MS.[61]

One part of the plan was to increase the own resources of the EU, including by means of the introduction of a "European digital levy." The EC phrased it as follows:

> A digital tax would build on OECD work on corporate taxation of a significant digital presence; the Commission actively supports the discussions led by the OECD and the G20 and stands ready to act if no global agreement is reached. A digital tax applied on companies with a turnover above EUR 750 million could generate up to EUR 1.3 billion per year for the EU budget.[62]

The digital levy intended introducing a 0.3% to 0.5% digital tax on goods and services sold online by companies in the EU. The companies concerned must have an

58. The authors would like to thank Soufian Wielemans, Associate at PwC Belgium, for the research and support in drafting this section.
59. *See* https://ec.europa.eu/info/strategy/eu-budget/long-term-eu-budget/2021-2027/whats-new_en, accessed January 11, 2022.
60. European Commission, EU Budget own resources, https://ec.europa.eu/info/strategy/eu-budget /long-term-eu-budget/eu-budget-2014-2020/revenue/own-resources_en, accessed December 14, 2020.
61. European Commission, Press release of the EC, Commission welcomes political agreement on Recovery and Resilience Facility, https://ec.europa.eu/commission/presscorner/detail/en/IP_20_2397, accessed December 21, 2020.
62. Communication from the Commission to the European Parliament, the European Council, the Council, the European Economic and Social Committee and the Committee of the Regions, COM(2020) 442 Final, 27.5.2020, https://eur-lex.europa.eu/legal-content/EN/TXT/PDF/?uri=CELEX:52020DC0442&from=EN, accessed December 14, 2020.

annual revenue of (at least) EUR 250 million. The *ratio legis* of this levy was to help pay back the bloc's funding of the EUR 750 billion recovery fund and to ensure a fair contribution of the digital sector.[63]

And then came the IF Statement of October 8, 2021. The reason for dropping the digital levy was the IF Statement that existing Digital Services Taxes (DST) and similar measures should be repealed and that no new DST or similar measures may be introduced between the date of the October 2021 statement and December 31, 2023, or the entry into force of the Multilateral Agreement (implementing Pillar One),[64,65] whichever is earlier. The EU digital levy will remain dead unless Pillar One fails to win the approval needed to enter into force.[66]

The fate of the digital levy remains somewhat unclear. To sharpen the suspense, according to a no-named EC-official, the digital levy that was first suspended is now due to be removed permanently from the EU's legislative agenda.[67] For the authors, however, it would not come as a surprise that the digital levy would be given the kiss of life one way or another; certainly, should no final agreement be reached on the Multilateral Convention implementing Pillar One. One may doubt though whether the frog then turns into a handsome prince or instead is resuscitated under a less attractive embodiment.

On December 22, 2021, the Commission proposed to establish the next generation of own resources for the EU budget and presented three new sources of revenue:

(1) the first is based on revenue from the Emissions Trading Scheme (ETS): the EC proposes that in future, 25 % of the revenue from EU emissions trading end up in the EU budget. Revenues for the EU budget are estimated at around EUR 12 billion per year on average over 2026-2030 (EUR 9 billion on average between 2023 and 2030);[68]

(2) the second is based on the resources generated by the proposed EU carbon border adjustment mechanism (CBAM): the Commission proposes to allocate to the EU budget 75 % of the revenues generated by the carbon border adjustment mechanism. Revenues for the EU budget are estimated at around EUR 1 billion per year on average over 2026-2030 (EUR 0.5 billion on average between 2023 and 2030). CBAM is not expected to generate revenue in the transitional period from 2023 to 2025;[69]

63. Communication from the Commission to the European Parliament and the Council, Business Taxation for the 21st Century, COM(2021) 251 final, 18.5.2021.
64. *See* Chapter 1 for a discussion on Pillar One.
65. OECD/G20 Base Erosion and Profit Shifting Project, Statement on a Two-Pillar Solution to Address the Tax Challenges Arising from the Digitalisation of the Economy, October 8, 2021.
66. M. Thompson, "EU Digital Tax to Be Scrapped for Good, Official Confirms," *Law 360*, December 14, 2021.
67. *Ibid.*
68. Communication from the Commission to the European Parliament, the European Council, the Council, the European Economic and Social Committee and the Committee of the Regions, COM(2021) 566 Final, 22.12.2021.
69. *Ibid.*

(3) the third is based on the share of residual profits of MNEs that will be reallocated to EU MSs (the so-called Amount A under Pillar One) under the recent OECD/G20 agreement on tax sharing.[70]

According to the Commission, over time, between 2026 and 2030, these new sources of revenue should generate on average up to EUR 17 billion per year for the EU budget.

We will focus on the third resource, which is directly related to the reform of the international corporate tax framework.

On October 8, 2021, the OECD/G20 IF agreed on a reform of the international tax framework: a two-pillar solution to tackle tax avoidance and aims at ensuring that profits are taxed where economic activity and value creation occur.[71]

Pillar One will reallocate the right to tax a share of "residual profits" from the world's largest MNEs (global turnover of EUR 20 billion—possibly lowered to EUR 10 billion after seven years—and profitability of 10%) to participating countries worldwide (Amount A). Indeed, Pillar One would ensure that 25% of those residual profits (that exceeds 10% of consolidated net profitability) earned by the largest MNEs would be allocated to the countries in which they have consumers so that those "market countries" may tax them. The EC proposes an own resource equivalent to 15% of the eligible share of the residual profits of in-scope companies that are reallocated under this system to EU MS.

The EC has committed to propose a Directive in 2022, once the details of the OECD/G20 IF agreement on Pillar One are finalized.

Of course, this decision is not unanimous, and some states, such as Hungary and Estonia, have already expressed their reservations should the EU put through its intention to use Pillar One revenues as own EU resources.[72] Any action that gives the EU powers similar to those of a traditional state may indicate (a hint toward) infringement of sovereignty.

On the other hand, it is not impossible that Pillar One will never see the light of day. Indeed, several major outstanding issues will need to be tackled. It is still necessary, among others, to identify the surrendering entities to determine the source jurisdictions and to set out (unambiguous) rules on mandatory and binding dispute avoidance and resolution mechanisms. Also, it seems that the interactions between EU fundamental rights (e.g., free movement of capital and services) and Pillar One may command further consideration. All of these points remain on the pending list and cannot be left unaddressed.

Yet to incorporate the proposed new own resources in the EU budget, the EU needs to amend two key pieces of legislation:

70. *Ibid.*
71. *Supra* n. 63.
72. M. Thompson, "OECD Pillar One Replaces Digital Tax in EU Budget, Draft Says," *Law 360*, December 16, 2021.

(1) the Commission proposes to amend the Own Resources Decision[73] to add the three proposed new resources to the existing ones;
(2) the Commission also puts forward a targeted amendment of the regulation on the current long-term EU budget 2021-2027 (the Multiannual Financial Framework).

The Own Resources Decision needs to be approved unanimously by the Council after consulting the EP. The decision can enter into force once approved by all EU countries in line with their constitutional requirements. The Multiannual Financial Framework Regulation needs to be adopted unanimously by the Council after obtaining the consent of the EP.

The new own resources are therefore genuinely a challenge for the EU, though one that cannot afford to fail and hence is expected to obtain the strongest political support.

7 DEBT EQUITY BIAS REDUCTION ALLOWANCE[74]

DEBRA aims to encourage companies to finance their investments through equity contributions rather than debt.

It was unveiled in the communication "Business Taxation for the 21st Century"[75] in which the EC announced a proposal to address the "debt-equity bias" in corporate taxation.

In most European tax regimes, there is an asymmetry of tax treatment leading companies to prefer loan financing investment over debt financing. Indeed, interest payments on debt are generally tax-deductible, thus reducing the tax base.[76] However, the costs associated with equity financing are not (generally) deductible. This is what DEBRA will try to mitigate hence in derogation of what is dictated under the Capital Asset Pricing Model.

The tax-induced debt-equity bias is said to contribute to an excessive accumulation of debt for nonfinancial corporations. Excessive debt levels make companies vulnerable to unforeseen changes in the business environment and increase their risk of insolvency.

The problem is that within the Single Market, excessive insolvencies (and all that this entails—e.g., restructuring, social costs, mass layoffs) and financial instability have the potential to spread to other MSs and affect the EU as a whole.[77]

In addition, an unprecedented health crisis and a framework for transition to a greener and more digitalized economy require huge investments. For a quick and

73. Council Decision (EU, Euratom) 2020/2053 of December 14, 2020 on the system of own resources of the European Union, OJ L 424, 15.12.2020, p. 1.
74. The authors would like to thank Soufian Wielemans, Associate at PwC Belgium, for the research and support in drafting this section.
75. *Supra* n. 4, p. 11.
76. Commission, Inception impact assessment, Ref. Ares(2021)3879996, June 14, 2021.
77. The European Business Initiative on Taxation, *Debt equity bias reduction allowance—Public consultation*, October 7, 2021, https://www.ebit-businesstax.com/papers/ec-public-consultation-questionnaire-debra-2021.aspx.

healthy recovery, equity financing is important. Companies with a strong capital structure are less vulnerable to shocks and therefore more willing to make investments or take on risks.[78] Ultimately, this could have a positive effect on competitiveness, growth and employment.[79]

It should be noted that six MSs[80] have already introduced legislation to mitigate this tax-induced debt/investment mismatch.

The EC is therefore studying the different ways in which the system could be designed and implemented, as well as the options available to achieve this objective. The common feature of the different measures is that they all provide for a tax allowance on equity. Of course, the Commission is also looking at the different rules it could put in place to prevent the tax relief from being used to divert it from its main purpose.

Input from stakeholders on DEBRA was requested. A public consultation was held from July 1, 2021, to October 7, 2021.[81] PwC indicated in its submission that enhancing equity investment in corporate income taxes is important to achieve more tax neutrality and to stimulate companies to build buffers for any next crisis. PwC also indicated, however, that further limitations of interest deductions are likely to have adverse consequences. Further, careful consideration is needed on the question of how an allowance for corporate equity might coexist not only with other—recent—measures, including interest limitation (EBITDA and ATAD) and anti-hybrid rules (ATAD), but also with a future corporate income tax (BEFIT) system for the EU.

At this stage, no proposal for a Directive has been published yet. According to the Communication of the EC on Business Taxation in the twenty-first century, the EC plans to publish a proposal for a directive in the first half of 2022.[82]

8 PUBLIC COUNTRY-BY-COUNTRY REPORTING

Unanimity within the EU bloc is not absolute, at least when creativity and imagination reign. An accounting directive serves as a helpful instrument.

On November 11, 2021, the European Parliament adopted the Directive on PCbCR.[83] This concludes the procedure on the introduction of specific European transparency rules and requires certain European or non-European multinational groups or stand-alone undertakings to publicly disclose certain financial data.

The PCbCR Directive provides that multinational enterprises or stand-alone undertakings with a total consolidated revenue of EUR 750 million over the last two consecutive financial years should make certain (tax) information public.

78. *Supra* n. 76.
79. *Ibid.*
80. Belgium; Cyprus; Italy; Malta; Poland and Portugal.
81. *See* https://ec.europa.eu/info/law/better-regulation/have-your-say/initiatives/12995-Debt-equity-bias-reduction-allowance-DEBRA-_en.
82. *Ibid.* and *supra* n. 4, p. 11.
83. Directive (EU) 2021/2101 of the European Parliament and of the Council of November 24, 2021 amending Directive 2013/34/EU as regards disclosure of income tax information by certain undertakings and branches, OJ L 429/1 of December 1, 2021.

In principle, reporting should be done by the UPE. However, for groups which carry out activities within the EU solely via subsidiaries or branches, the responsibility to publish the information and make it accessible lies with those subsidiaries and branches. If the information is not available or the UPE does not provide all the required information, the subsidiaries and branches should publish the information they have, accompanied by a statement specifying that their UPE has not made the necessary information available. As mentioned before, the authors believe in "meaningful" transparency. Although one could probably empathize with some sanctioning of deficient companies, TP practitioners tend to be very well aware of the fact that not all MNEs operate truly centrally. Obtaining information often requires more than just pushing a button or two.

The required information should be published no later than twelve months after the balance sheet date of the year concerned on:

- the website of the UPE (or stand-alone undertaking);
- the subsidiary or branch' website; or
- the website of the enterprise which opened the branch or under certain conditions on the website of a related enterprise.

The information to be disclosed under the PCbCR Directive includes:

- the name of the ultimate parent or stand-alone undertaking, the financial year concerned and the currency used, and, where applicable, a list of all the subsidiary undertakings;
- a brief description of the nature of the activities;
- the number of employees on a full-time equivalent basis;
- revenue which includes:
    - (i) the sum of the net turnover, other operating income, income from participating interests, excluding dividends received from affiliated undertakings, income from other investments and loans forming part of the fixed assets, any other interest receivable and similar income; or
    - (ii) the income as defined by or within the meaning of the financial reporting framework on the basis of which financial statements are prepared excluding value adjustments and dividends received from affiliated undertakings;
- the amount of profit or loss before income tax;
- the amount of income tax accrued during the relevant financial year which is the current tax expense recognized on taxable profits or losses of the financial year by undertakings and branches in the relevant tax jurisdiction;
- the amount of income tax paid on cash basis which is the amount of income tax paid (including withholding tax paid by other undertakings) during the relevant financial year by undertakings and branches in the relevant tax jurisdiction; and
- the amount of accumulated earnings at the end of the relevant financial year.

In order to reduce the administrative burden, the PCbCR Directive provides that MSs should allow the information published under the "OECD CbCR"[84] to be accepted under the PCbCR.

The PCbCR Directive provides for a combination of aggregation and disaggregation of the information. The information must be disclosed on a disaggregated basis, that is, on a country-by-country basis for:

- each MS;
- countries that are mentioned in Annex 1 (blacklist) of the Council conclusions[85] on the revised EU list of noncooperative jurisdictions for tax purposes from their meeting of October 5, 2021 (these blacklisted countries are currently: American Samoa, Fiji, Guam, Palau, Panama, Samoa, Trinidad and Tobago, US Virgin Islands, Vanuatu);
- countries that are mentioned in Annex 2 (grey list) of the Council conclusions, if the country is on the list for two consecutive years (currently: Botswana, Jordan, Thailand and Turkey).[86]

The information related to the rest of the world's countries may be disclosed on an aggregated basis.

MSs may allow (but are not obliged to) for one or more specific items of information to be temporarily omitted from the report if their disclosure would be seriously prejudicial to the commercial position of the MNE. Any omission must be clearly indicated in the report together with a duly reasoned explanation. MSs must ensure that all such omitted information is made public in a later report on income tax information no later than five years after the date of its original omission. No omissions are allowed for blacklisted or relevant grey-listed countries.

When the financial accounts are audited, they should contain a statement by the statutory auditor, for the financial year preceding the financial year for which the statements under audit were prepared, whether a PCbCR should have been drawn up. The PCbCR itself does not need to be audited.

The directive entered into force on December 21, 2021, and has a maximum transposition period of eighteen months. The first PCbCR will be for the first financial year which begins two and a half years after the date of entry into force of the directive. At the very latest—that is if MSs only transpose the directive by the very end of the transposition period, the first PCbCR is likely to be the financial year that starts on or after June 2024. Countries may transpose the PCbCR Directive sooner with a corresponding earlier first reporting period.

84. OECD (2015), Transfer Pricing Documentation and Country-by-Country Reporting, Action 13—2015 Final Report, OECD/G20 Base Erosion and Profit Shifting Project, OECD Publishing, Paris, http://dx.doi.org/10.1787/9789264241480-en.
85. *See* https://www.consilium.europa.eu/media/52208/st12519-en21.pdf for the latest list of 2021. This list is updated twice a year in principle.
86. Situation as per January 1, 2022.

Probably thanks to its labeling as an accounting directive, approval through qualified majority was possible hence avoiding the need for massaging discontented countries.[87]

9 THE DIRECTIVE ON ADMINISTRATIVE COOPERATION (DAC)

9.1 Directive on Administrative Cooperation # 6 (DAC6)[88]

The DAC6[89] and the three hallmarks which relate in particular to TP (Hallmark E) were briefly discussed in the previous version of the TP Developments Around the World.[90] These specific hallmarks include: (E.1) the use of unilateral safe harbors, (E.2) transfers of hard-to-value intangibles (HTVI), and (E.3) business restructurings with a substantial impact on the EBIT level post-restructuring.

Several MSs opted in 2020 for deferral of the reporting deadlines due to the COVID-19 pandemic. The deferral brought the deadline for the first DAC6 Reporting for those MSs that opted in to January 2021. This meant that something carrying the attributes of a reporting avalanche by taxpayers and intermediaries was seen in early 2021. After approximately one year of experience, practice has shown that the TP hallmarks, and in particular hallmarks E.2 and E.3, have taken a prominent place under the DAC6 reporting.[91] For example, Hallmark E.2 is listed second in the ranking of the most frequent hallmarks.[92]

It follows from the preamble of DAC6 that it has been drafted "along the lines" of OECD BEPS Action 12, which should then serve as a source of inspiration and illustration for the interpretation of the various hallmarks and concepts included in the directive.[93] Recital 13 of the preamble of DAC6 states explicitly that MS could use the work of the OECD as a source of illustration and interpretation in order to ensure consistency of application across MS.[94] A clear link was consequently established with the work of the OECD. However, despite this, the authors see important differences and inconsistencies in the way MSs interpret DAC6.

Regarding HTVI, the OECD Transfer Pricing Guidelines (TPG) recognize the difficulty of an *ex ante* analysis and valuation, and provides that "the tax administration

87. J. Comte, "EU Ambassadors Approve Public CbC Reporting Deal," *Tax Notes Today International*, October 6, 2021.
88. The authors would like to thank Mesude Nur Kiliç, Associate at PwC Belgium, for the research and support performed in drafting this section.
89. Council Directive (EU) 2018/822 of May 25, 2018 amending Directive 2011/16/EU as regards mandatory automatic exchange of information in the field of taxation in relation to reportable cross-border arrangements, OJ L 139/1, June 5, 2018.
90. *See also Transfer Pricing Developments Around the World 2020*, p. 49 and *Transfer Pricing Developments Around the World 2021*, pp. 68-69.
91. Own practice and measurement.
92. Response of the Deputy Prime Minister and Minister of Finance Vincent Van Petegem to the Parliamentary question # 692 of Representative Steven Matheï, QRVA 55 071 of December 6, 2021, p. 191.
93. D. Weber and J. Steenbergen, "The (Absence of) Member State Autonomy in the Interpretation of DAC6: A Call for EU Guidance (2021)," *EC Tax Review*, 2021 (Volume 30), No. 5, p. 258.
94. *Supra* n. 89, Recital 13.

can consider ex post outcomes as presumptive evidence about the appropriateness of the ex-ante pricing arrangements."[95] Although the DAC6 defines HTVI in line with the OECD TPG, the only element that is available for DAC6 reporting purposes is an *ex ante* analysis. The same applies to business restructurings, where although it is possible to anticipate beforehand based on projections, a complete analysis can only be made *ex post*. Consequently, the requirement to make an *ex ante* analysis for both these hallmarks, which require the taxpayers and intermediaries to make difficult decisions, raises the question of whether they are fit for purpose. One may wonder indeed at what opportunity cost compliance comes in the combat against tax abuse.

The authors fully understand that DAC6 was developed to identify potentially aggressive tax structures.[96] In light of the very broad definition of an HTVI under DAC6, and absent the *ex post* approach as discussed in the OECD TPG, any transfer of (rights in) an intangible could be considered to become reportable under DAC6. This leads to uncertainty and controversy in a couple of years' time when tax authorities will be reviewing the information gathered under DAC6. The authors are convinced that this controversy could be avoided if more and clearer guidance on when the transfer should be reported would be made available. The same could be said about hallmark E3. In practice, and because MSs take a different approach in determining the EBIT and the three year period, the application of this hallmark also leads to uncertainty and potential controversy.

9.2 Directive on Administrative Cooperation # 7 (DAC7)

With the publication of DAC7 on March 25, 2021, in the *Official Journal of the EU* (OJ),[97] another episode is added to the EU administrative cooperation. It is plausible to say that DAC7 addresses three different topics. One concerns the extension of the scope of the EU automatic information exchange to include data on sellers through digital platform operators. The second topic addresses multilateral audits. The third one concerns the presence of officials from one MS in another one.[98]

9.2.1 Platform Operators

A platform is defined as any software (including a website or a part thereof) and (mobile) applications allowing sellers to be connected to other users for the purpose of directly or indirectly carrying out an in-scope activity.[99] The directive is applicable to

95. OECD Transfer Pricing Guidelines for Multinational Enterprises and Tax Administrations, July 2017, § 6.192.
96. *Supra* n. 89, Recital 2.
97. OJ of the EU, L 104/1, Council Directive (EU) 2021/514 of March 22, 2021 amending Directive 2011/16/EU on administrative cooperation in the field of taxation.
98. *See also Transfer Pricing Developments Around the World 2021*, pp. 69-72.
99. *Supra* n. 97, Annex, § A.1.

platform operators that perform commercial activities in the EU and is hence extended to nonresident platforms (non-incorporated, managed, or without a PE in the EU).[100]

The reporting under DAC7 is organized as a three-step approach:[101]

(1) Obligation on the reporting platform operators to collect and verify the information in line with due diligence procedures.
(2) Report information on the reportable sellers that use the platform.
(3) Communicate the reported information to the competent authority (CA) of the MS where the reportable seller is a resident or to the CA of the MS where the immovable property is located.

The relevant activities performed through the platform that are within the scope of the DAC7 are also broad:[102]

- the rental of immovable property;
- the provision of personal services (which is described as services involving time- or task-based work performed by one or more individuals that act either independently or on behalf of an entity, carried out at the request of a user either online or physically offline after having been facilitated via a platform);
- the sale of goods;
- the rental of any mode of transport.

The directive is also assorted with several administrative measures. For example, a platform operator that is not incorporated, managed, or having a PE in a MS must register in the MS where it commences its operations (unless it is already registered for VAT purposes). The platform must collect, verify, and have the required information available by December 31 of the reportable period and communicate the information through a one-stop-shop one month later. Records have to be kept for a period of five to seven years. As usual, the directive provides that the MS must introduce effective proportionate and dissuasive penalties. MSs should transpose this part of the directive by December 31, 2022, with an application as from January 1, 2023, for platform operators.

9.2.2 Joint Audits and Simultaneous Controls

Simultaneous controls are already covered under Article 12 of the DAC. A simultaneous control is a tax inspection for which each MS that is involved simultaneously audits, in its own territory, one or more persons of common or complementary interest to them with a view to exchanging the information that is obtained. A new Article 12A introduces the concept of a "joint audit." A joint audit under the directive is defined as

100. *Supra* n. 97, § 14.
101. *Ibid.*, Annex, sections II, III and IV.
102. *Ibid.*, §18, and Annex § A.8.

an administrative inquiry jointly conducted by the CAs of two or more MSs and linked to one or more persons of common or complementary interest to the CAs of these MS.

The information gathered and exchanged may be used not only for direct tax purposes but also for VAT and other indirect taxes. Such information could also be used for other purposes if the internal law of both (sending and receiving) MSs so allows.[103]

The directive is applicable for joint audits as of January 1, 2024.

9.2.3 *Presence and Participation of Foreign Tax Officials in Audits*

DAC7 has made it clear that, under a joint audit, foreign tax officials are allowed to be present during an audit. Even more, they can effectively take an active part in the audit. According to the DAC7, the role of the foreign tax official includes interviewing individuals and examining records together with the officials of the MS where the activities of the joint audit take place.[104] This approach gives the tax auditors extraterritorial powers and means in their investigations.

Overall, DAC7 appears to broaden public servants' powers. As a corollary, there is the potential to have it serving as a catalyst to boost initiatives in the context of constructive ongoing engagement between tax authorities and taxpayers. Attention to such cooperative compliance-related aspects in the DAC7 remains underwhelming. This seems a missed opportunity to say the least.

9.3 Directive on Administrative Cooperation # 8 (DAC8)

Under the Action plan for fair and simple taxation supporting the recovery strategy (Action plan), the EC already indicated that alternative means of payment and investments are a threat to the progress made on transparency and increase risk for tax evasion.[105] As indicated in last year's publication, this so-called DAC8 should cover the exchange of information with respect to cryptocurrencies and the harmonization of penalties.[106]

The annex to the Action plan provided that a legislative initiative would follow in the form of a Commission proposal for a Council directive amending the DAC in the third quarter of 2021.[107]

---

103. *Ibid.*, § 30.
104. *Ibid.*, Article 12a(3).
105. *See* Communication from the Commission to the European Parliament and the Council—An action plan for fair and simple taxation supporting the recovery strategy, COM(2020) 312 final, 15.7.2020, p. 12. https://ec.europa.eu/taxation_customs/system/files/2020-07/2020_tax_package_tax_action_plan_en.pdf.
106. *See Transfer Pricing Developments Around the World 2021*, pp. 72-73.
107. Annex to the Communication from the Commission to the European Parliament and the Council—An Action plan for fair and simple taxation supporting the recovery strategy, COM(2020) 312 final, p. 2.

In March 2021, a public consultation[108] was launched which addressed two main issues:

- First, the general issues with regard to crypto-assets. This part focused on gathering information regarding the different aspects of the crypto-assets and e-moneys and should inform the EC ultimately to determine whether a directive combating the underreporting of income/revenues generated by crypto-assets and e-money is needed.
- The second part addressed in a more general way the framework on administrative cooperation and reporting obligations. The input on penalties and compliance measures should allow a more precise and common definition of effective, proportionate and dissuasive penalties and compliance measures leading to lessening tax avoidance and potential distortions of the internal market.

The consultation ended on June 2, 2021. No proposal for a directive on DAC8 has been published yet. The authors anticipate that it may see the light still in 2022.

10 EUROPEAN TRUST AND COOPERATION APPROACH (ETACA)

In July 2020, also under the aforementioned Action plan, the EC already announced plans to introduce an EU cooperative compliance framework based on greater cooperation, trust, and transparency among tax administrations.[109]

The EC has now published guidelines on the ETACA,[110] a voluntary pilot project on cooperative compliance within the EU specifically focusing on TP risks for large multinationals (global total consolidated group revenue of more than EUR 750 million and UPE located within the EU). ETACA will function alongside the International Compliance Assurance Project (ICAP) organized at the level of the OECD Forum on Tax Administration (FTA) and multiple domestic cooperative compliance programs. While the scope of ETACA is limited to TP for large multinationals, a separate pilot was also announced for small- and medium-sized enterprises (SMEs) on June 23, 2021.[111]

As with any other cooperative compliance arrangement, ETACA will not offer the legal certainty that a taxpayer may have with unilateral, bilateral or multilateral APAs. Rather, it aims to offer taxpayers some assurance that certain transactions bear a low tax risk given the specific facts and circumstances of the taxpayer. If during their risk review, the tax administrations involved find that there is a low tax risk, they will not

108. The results of the public consultation are available at https://ec.europa.eu/info/law/better-regulation/have-your-say/initiatives/12632-Tax-fraud-evasion-strengthening-rules-on-administrative-cooperation-and-expanding-the-exchange-of-information/public-consultation_en, accessed January 6, 2022.
109. *Supra* n. 105, p. 65.
110. *See* Guidelines European trust and cooperation approach, ETACA https://ec.europa.eu/taxation_customs/document/download/1e2d7158-f083-4e68-9ece-b96ce02668c9_en.
111. *See* https://ec.europa.eu/taxation_customs/news/eu-cooperative-compliance-programme-2021-06-23_en.

anticipate dedicating resources to a further review if the facts and circumstances remain the same.

Access to the ETACA pilot allows eligible taxpayers to explain to the participating tax authorities[112] the relevant data, policy and business/TP models in a proactive, non-adversarial and constructive setting. It also makes it possible for several tax authorities to issue an informed decision on the risk review within a relatively short time frame (target period of maximum thirty-six weeks). Generally speaking, the time frame for this procedure is faster than other available procedures such as bilateral or multilateral APAs. Furthermore, it may reduce the likelihood of audit procedures in the countries concerned, which could in turn reduce the number of disputes in those countries and/or the number of MAP cases.

The program is focused on transactions between European entities. Transactions with related entities outside the EU can be covered if relevant for the participating tax authorities, but assurance can only be provided from the EU tax authorities.

Other eligibility factors to be considered by MNEs before applying include:

- the footprint of the MNE and the volume and materiality of an MNE's covered transactions within the EU;
- the past behavior of the taxpayer in terms of tax compliance (i.e., the taxpayer should not have incurred a serious penalty as a consequence of tax fraud, repeated willful default or repeated gross negligence);
- signs of commitment from the taxpayer to engage cooperatively and transparently throughout the process;
- existence of an internal tax control framework (i.e., a set of processes and internal control procedures ensuring that a company has identified its tax risks and adequately controls and monitors these risks).

In principle, the program focuses on performing a common and multilateral risk assessment of the TP risks for routine transactions in the EU using a one-sided TP method such as for limited risk distribution, contract manufacturing and intragroup services. It is expected, however, that a participating MNE will disclose all relevant intragroup transactions as well as its value chain so that there is a comprehensive understanding of the business and TP policy.

The ETACA guidelines advocate a flexible approach. Although the focus is on routine transactions, ETACA may allow—on a case-by-case basis and subject to acceptance by the relevant tax administrations—that nonroutine transactions (e.g., transactions involving intangibles or business restructurings) may also be included in the risk review process.

The program requires a transparent and cooperative relationship between the MNE and the tax authorities concerned. It applies the one-stop-shop principle: as a rule, the UPE contacts its tax administration which will in principle act as the coordinating tax administration authority alongside the other participating tax administrations. The

112. At the time of writing this contribution (January 2022), the following countries participated in the ETACA project: Austria, Belgium, Denmark, Finland, Germany, Hungary, Italy, Ireland, Luxembourg, Poland, Portugal, the Slovak Republic, and the Netherlands.

UPE may also appoint a "surrogate" coordinating tax administration under certain circumstances.

Like other cooperative compliance arrangements, this arrangement contains an admission phase, a risk assessment phase and an outcome phase.

During the admission phase, the MNE submits a predefined documentation package to the coordinating tax administration. A kick-off meeting is then held to select the participating tax administrations, the transactions to be covered and the relevant period.

During the risk assessment phase, the participating tax authorities endeavor to agree on a common approach to assess the tax risks for the transactions covered. This includes a review of the documentation, a functional analysis and a coherence review of the TP methodology. The review will determine whether the transactions covered represent a low tax risk or not. At the end of the risk assessment phase, the participating tax administrations endeavor to reach a common understanding of the level of tax risk, and give their feedback and their position on their review.

During the outcome phase, the UPE is officially informed of the risk assessment by way of an outcome letter and final summary report signed by all the participating tax administrations. If there are any differences in risk appreciation, taxpayers can expect to receive insights into the underlying reasons.

Taxpayers that receive a "no-low tax risk" outcome can adjust their policy for future years if desired and appropriate. Taxpayers that receive a "low tax risk" outcome can legitimately expect (although this is not always guaranteed) that the low tax risk transactions covered will not lead to further in-depth scrutiny for the period covered and the two subsequent fiscal years if there are no changes to the facts and circumstances.

The entire process is estimated to take between 28 and 36 weeks, so the pilot program is set to be a relatively swift and resource-efficient way of achieving a certain level of multilateral comfort on a company's TP policy.

The authors believe that investing in a cooperative compliance approach is beneficial for both tax administrations and taxpayers. Such an approach may reduce the audit and controversy risk and will ultimately lead to fewer cases entering into MAP. Unfortunately, in all the tax measures presented in the EU during 2021, the ETACA pilot is the only initiative with no overwhelming preponderance of tax authorities' interests but rather one empathizing with the taxpayers' quest for certainty.

11 REVAMPING THE COCG (BUSINESS TAXATION)

Just to set the scene on the Code of Conduct Group (COCG), some history. The COCG was created at the end of the twentieth century (officially on March 9, 1998, to be precise) to combat harmful tax practices. The COCG led to political commitments of MSs (not) undertaking certain actions that could lead to harmful tax practices and created a "soft law" approach. The MSs committed to amend or abolish their harmful tax practices and not to adopt or introduce new ones. This was later extended to promoting good tax governance vis-à-vis third countries. The analysis and subsequent abolishing or modification of existing harmful tax practices within the EU[113] and the creation of the EU list of noncooperative jurisdictions for tax purposes are the main achievements of the COCG.

It was the European Parliament that stood up to air voices that the COCG should reform its working, in particular on noncooperative jurisdictions. Hence, in early 2021, the COCG started work on reforming the code—in particular, expanding its geographical scope and criteria to label a tax regime as harmful, in particular after the criticism that it was not doing enough to halt tax avoidance and evasion.[114]

The Council published a draft Resolution on a revised code of conduct for business taxation amending or confirming the condition under which measures (including measures providing for a significantly lower effective level of taxation, including zero taxation) would be considered harmful:[115]

- ring-fenced from the domestic market (de jure *or* de facto);
- absence of real economic activity and substantial economic presence;
- profit determination departs from internationally (OECD) recognized principles;
- no transparency in the tax measure.[116]

In the analysis of the measures, the COCG will also review:[117]

- whether the measure is accompanied by appropriate anti-abuse provisions to counter non-taxation or double or multiple use of tax benefits;
- whether the measure significantly affects the decision on the location of the business activity in the EU.

According to the draft revised code of conduct, MS will also apply the principles regarding harmful tax practices as broad as possible at global level, including when analyzing jurisdictions in the framework of the EU list of noncooperative jurisdictions, next to the implementation of the BEPS measures.[118]

12 STATE AID

State aid and TP may feel like mixing oil with water from a pure TP technical perspective. Indeed, an independent market operator is a "weird" concept when grappling with TP. Such a party is ordinarily by definition deprived of transacting with enterprises under some form of economic and/or legal solidarity whatsoever. As the

113. *See* Overview of EU Member States' preferential regimes examined since the creation of the COCG in March 1998, available at https://data.consilium.europa.eu/doc/document/ST-8602-2020-REV-2/en/pdf, accessed January 6, 2022.
114. *See*, for example, S. Paez, "EU Code of Conduct Reform Would Expand Harmful Tax Criteria," *Tax Notes International*, December 6, 2021.
115. Text available at https://data.consilium.europa.eu/doc/document/ST-14354-2021-INIT/en/pdf, accessed January 6, 2022.
116. *Ibid*, pp. 6-7.
117. *Ibid*.
118. *Ibid*., p. 12.

(political) stakes remain high, it seems as if the EC State aid specialists have a duty to keep focused on the rear mirror rather than to put their lens fully on the challenge for MS to satisfy surging (imminent) public funding needs. Looking back is helpful if there are lessons learned for the future. What we see, however, is a myriad of complex State aid rules that may—in the best of cases—eventually lead to a one-off recovery of funds from a handful of companies. Although several commentators have already argued that State aid proceedings are not the most efficient way to tackle TP[119] and despite several unfortunate outcomes in court for the EC, it seems as if the EC is still persevering in using State aid proceedings in TP cases. This section gives an overview of the most recent developments in old and new TP related State aid cases. Indeed, 2021 was again a pretty busy year on the TP State aid front.

Further to this, Executive Vice-President Ms. Margrethe Vestager indicated that the EC will continue to use all tools at its disposal to fight "unfair tax practices," including State aid enforcement. She also mentioned that this needs to go hand in hand with legislative action in order to be effective. She continued by indicating that the EC actively supports the work at international level on a solution to reform the international corporate tax framework, including the work toward a minimum effective taxation of multinationals' profits (GloBE),[120] which should set a floor to excessive tax competition.[121] In the light of her discourse, commentators opined that the OECD project on Pillar One and Two will not enhance Ms. Vestager's State aid mission "but instead replace what she is doing."[122]

12.1 The Belgian Excess Profit Regime (EPR)

The Belgian EPR saga is perhaps one of the more torturous ones on TP. In summary, the case relates to a provision under Belgian tax law that exempted certain income, which was considered as excess profits, i.e., profits that were—on an arm's-length basis—not considered to relate to the Belgian activities. The Belgian ruling office examined the application on a case-by-case basis and rendered a ruling in which the application of this provision for a company was confirmed, where appropriate. In its decision of January 11, 2016, the Commission took the view that these rulings constitute unlawful State aid as the excess profit provision provided advantages that are selective (i.e., not available to all comparable companies). The EC furthermore considered that the rulings should not be assessed on a case-by-case basis as individual aid but must be assessed as an aid "scheme."

In its ruling of February 14, 2019, the General Court of the EU (General Court) annulled the EC's decision, finding that it made methodological errors by considering that the EPRs are an aid scheme. According to the General Court, the EC should have

119. *See*, for example, R. Mason, "Tax Rulings as State Aid—Part 4: Whose Arm's-Length Standard?," *Tax Notes International*, May 15, 2017, p. 947; R. Goulder, "Amazon and the State Aid Doctrine: Unchecked Mission Creep," *Tax Notes International*, June 14, 2021, p. 1571.
120. *See* Chapter 1 and section 3.
121. Answer given by Executive Vice-President Vestager on behalf of the European Commission to EP Member Hélène Laporte, August 6, 2021.
122. R. Goulder, "Stand Down Margrethe," *Tax Notes International*, August 23, 2021, p. 1102.

reviewed the specifics of each ruling individually. The EC only examined a sample of twenty-two selected rulings out of a total of sixty-six.

The EC appealed the General Court ruling before the European Court of Justice (ECJ) and at the same time opened thirty-nine individual State aid cases against the enterprises concerned.

On September 16, 2021, the ECJ annulled the judgment of the General Court and, by doing so, upheld the final decision of the EC regarding the qualification of the Belgian EPRs as an aid scheme. The ECJ concluded that the three conditions for an aid scheme to exist are met. Consequently, the EC did not have to investigate each ruling individually.[123]

The ECJ has referred the case back to the General Court which will have to decide on the open questions such as the existence of a selective advantage and the identification of the beneficiaries of the alleged aid. The final decision of whether the Belgian EPRs constitute unlawful State aid may still take a number of years. For the time being, the EC has put the individual State aid cases on hold. Certainly to be continued.

12.2 Amazon[124]

On May 12, 2021, the General Court rendered its judgment regarding the appeal brought by Amazon Group companies and Luxembourg against the State aid decision of October 4, 2017.[125]

The case at hand concerns a ruling issued by the Luxembourg tax authorities to a Luxembourg tax resident company of the Amazon Group in 2003, and prolonged in 2011. During the period under scrutiny (until 2014), Amazon EU Sarl (AEU) functioned as the European headquarters of the group and principal operator of Amazon's European online retail and service business, in charge of strategic decisions related to the retail and services business carried on through the EU websites. In order to carry out its operations, AEU used (IP) rights from Amazon Europe Holding Technologies (AEHT—a Luxembourg partnership) under a license agreement. AEHT functions were to hold the IP and participate in the development of that IP under a cost-sharing arrangement with Amazon US.

Under the TP analysis carried out at the time when the ruling was obtained, the royalty that AEU paid to AEHT was determined based on the residual profit split method. The TP report explained why this method was preferable over the comparable uncontrolled price method (CUP) which was also analyzed. In its decision of October 4, 2017, the EC concluded that Amazon received an individual selective advantage in the form of the tax ruling because it set a TP result and methodology that was found by the EC to be not in line with the ALP.

The General Court stated first that, when examining a fiscal measure granted to an integrated company, the EC may compare the tax burden of that undertaking with the

123. *See* Case C-337/19 https://curia.europa.eu/juris/document/document.jsf?text=&docid=246081&pageIndex=0&doclang=en&mode=lst&dir=&occ=first&part=1&cid=1000991.
124. Cases T-816/17 and T-318/18.
125. SA 38944.

tax burden resulting from the application of the normal rules of taxation under national law of an enterprise, placed in a comparable factual situation, carrying on its activities under market conditions.

The General Court stated further that the EC can demonstrate the existence of an advantage in examining the TP methodology used by an integrated company's taxable income only if the remuneration applied leads to a reduction in the taxable profit of the company compared with the tax burden of a stand-alone undertaking transacting on the open market subject to the application of the normal taxation rules. The General Court concluded that the EC did not sufficiently demonstrate the existence of an advantage. As a basis for this conclusion, the General Court stated that the EC:

- relied only on its own functional analysis of AEHT and did not demonstrate that the Luxembourg tax authorities had incorrectly chosen AEU as the tested party in order to determine the amount of the royalty.
- did not establish the existence of an advantage because the "arm's length" remuneration proposed by the EC could not be solely calculated on the basis of the mere passing on of intangible asset development costs to AEHT without taking into account the increase in its intangible assets value.
- was wrong to ascertain the AEHT remuneration on the basis of the supply of "low value adding" services.
- did not prove the undervaluation of the AEU remuneration and did not justify to the requisite legal standard the methodological choice in light of the AEU functions.

On July 22, 2021, the EC brought on an appeal against the judgment of the General Court.[126]

12.3 Engie[127]

Also on May 12, 2021, the General Court rendered its judgment regarding the appeal brought by Engie Group companies and Luxembourg against the State aid decision of June 20, 2018.[128]

The EC investigation was also related to rulings issued by the Luxembourg tax authorities, but now between 2008 and 2014. The rulings confirmed the tax treatment of certain mandatorily convertible instruments issued by two Luxembourg group subsidiaries ("borrowers") to two other Luxembourg companies of the Group ("lenders"). The rulings confirmed that:

- the borrowers treated the instruments as debt and recorded in their accounts accretions which were deductible at their level;
- the lenders entered into a forward sale agreement with a third entity with the receipt being subject to a participation exemption.

126. Case C-457/21 P.
127. Cases T-516/18 and T-525/18.
128. SA 44888.

The EC considered that the rulings granted State aid by incorrectly lowering the tax basis of the Luxembourg companies. The EC also argued that the rulings endorsed an inconsistent treatment of the same amounts as representing deductible expenses on the instruments at the level of the borrowers and income exempt under the domestic participation exemption at the level of the creditors (double non-taxation).

The General Court sided with the EC when it analyzed this intragroup financing structure by looking at its final economic result. It disregarded the specific tax treatment applicable under Luxembourg law at the time for each individual transaction. The transactions were designed to be implemented in three successive but interdependent stages achieving one single economic result.

For the General Court, the EC was allowed to determine that the combined effect of the transactions derogated from the reference framework and represented a selective advantage because the lenders were allowed to benefit from the provisions of the Luxembourg domestic participation exemption on amounts which corresponded from an economic perspective to deductible expenses incurred by the borrowers in relation to the instruments.

In a secondary line of argument, the EC ascertained that the criteria for determining the existence of an abuse of law under Luxembourg law were met, and hence preferential tax treatment was given owing to the nonapplication of the abuse of law provision.

In the light of the objective pursued by the abuse of law provision (i.e., combating abusive practices in tax matters), the General Court considered that the holding companies were in the same factual and legal situation as Luxembourg taxpayers that cannot reasonably expect to benefit from the nonapplication of the abuse of law provision in cases where the conditions for its application have been satisfied and hence the holding companies benefited from a selective advantage.

As a result, the General Court concluded on the existence of State aid under Article 107 TFEU.

On July 22, 2021, the enterprises concerned introduced an appeal against the judgment of the General Court.[129]

12.4 Nike[130]

Another TP case earmarked by some level of evolution concerns the case against the Netherlands and the tax rulings issued to Nike European Operations Netherlands (Nike) (2006, 2010 and 2015 rulings) and to Converse Netherlands (Converse) (2010 and 2015 rulings). The EC started a formal investigation procedure in 2019.[131] The case concerns the payment of royalties from Nike and Converse to other group companies not situated in the Netherlands. According to the EC, the royalties paid were excessive, leading to a non-arm's-length result for Nike and Converse. The Dutch tax was

129. Case C-454/21 P.
130. Case T-648/19.
131. SA 51284.

calculated on an understated amount of profit, and the EC considered this as a selective advantage.

Nike and Converse requested the General Court to annul the opening decision by reason of: breach of the obligation to state reasons, manifest errors of assessment and noncompliance with procedural rights. In its judgment of July 14, 2021, the General Court did not accept the arguments of Nike and Converse and dismissed the request entirely.

12.5 Fiat

On September 24, 2019, the General Court rendered its judgment regarding the action brought by Fiat Chrysler Finance Europe and Luxembourg for the annulment of the final State aid decision of the EC of October 21, 2015, on Fiat.[132] The General Court dismissed the actions and confirmed the validity of the EC's decision.[133]

On December 4, 2019, Ireland and Fiat Chrysler Finance Europe appealed the EC's decision before the ECJ.[134] On December 16, 2021, Advocate General Mr. Priit Pikamäe rendered his (nonbinding) opinion on the appeal brought by Ireland. The Advocate General proposes to set aside the judgment of the General Court of September 24, 2019, to uphold the actions brought by Luxembourg and Fiat Chrysler before the General Court, and to annul the State aid decision of October 21, 2015.[135]

According to the Advocate General, the General Court infringed the provisions governing the division of competences between the EU and the MS.

The Advocate General indicated that the General Court implicitly accepted the premise that normal taxation must include only rules of national law.[136] The concrete nature of "normal" taxation means that it derives from rules of positive law. In order to avoid any encroachment on the exclusive competence of the MS in the area of direct taxation, the existence of an advantage within the meaning of Article 107 TFEU can be verified only by reference to the normative framework outlined by the national legislature in the actual exercise of that competence. The latter alone can ensure that the ALP forms part of the set of rules and principles applicable to the tax affairs of an integrated undertaking, in the absence of the tax ruling at issue.[137]

The Advocate General shares Ireland's view that the approach adopted by the Commission in the State aid decision and endorsed by the General Court ultimately amounts to introducing a new rule (the ALP) into the national tax system which is extraneous to that system. This extended legal framework is then considered the "normal" tax system. The reference to the purported objective pursued by the national

132. SA 38375.
133. Cases T-755/15 and T-759/15.
134. Cases C-885/19 P (*Fiat Chrysler Finance Europe*) and C-898/19 P (*Ireland*).
135. Press Release No 223/21 of December 16, 2021 of the CJEU and Opinion of Advocate General Pikamäe delivered on December 16, 2021, Case C-885/19 P, *Fiat Chrysler Finance Europe v. European Commission*.
136. *Supra* n. 135, §104 of the opinion.
137. *Supra* n. 135, §106 of the opinion.

legislature is not capable of justifying the ALP belonging to the said system.[138] The legal reasoning that the EC followed and was endorsed by the General Court defines the reference framework constituting "normal" taxation by relying on a version of the ALP based on an uncodified element. According to the Advocate General, the undue interference in the MS' tax autonomy has always been carefully condemned until now.[139]

12.6 Conclusion on State Aid

To conclude this section on State aid, the EC has already incurred quite some criticisms on the application of TP or the (EU) ALP for State aid cases. Indeed, the question is whether State aid investigations centered around TP are the appropriate avenue to reach some kind of upward harmonization on corporate tax. At least, according to one commentator it is not: "If we're honest, Ms Vestager's campaign was always a backhanded way to circumvent the lack of qualified majority voting on matters involving direct taxation. A clever attempt, but it's time to recognize the limits of what State aid doctrine can achieve."[140] Another commentator indicated that "the use of the ALP and the assertion of the existence of an EU ALP to assess whether the tax rulings granted an advantage for State aid purposes, and the allegedly intrinsic selectivity of advance tax rulings, seem to unveil an approach to the interpretation and implementation of article 107(1) of the TFEU that could not have reasonably been expected by Member States and taxpayers before at least 2016."[141]

On the other hand, however, the General Court accepted the EC's authority to use Article 107 TFEU in the examinations. The General Court also recognized that the ALP can be used to assess selectivity, even when the domestic tax law did not yet adopt it (*see*, however, the opinion of the Advocate General in Fiat). The EC did not prevail in the General Court because there were issues and errors with regard to the functional analysis and comparability analysis performed in the investigations. In any way, the EC has made remarkable progress in the State aid examinations. Irrespective of their respect for the work of the EC's specialists, the authors tend to agree with the commentator mentioned earlier. Are State aid examinations and the ALP truly the best way to impose the EC's view on TP and corporate income tax and to ultimately help to make the rules "better" for everyone?

13 ENVIRONMENTAL, SOCIAL AND GOVERNANCE (ESG)

Taxes "say something" about a company's role in society. "Responsible growth" is pivotal from a corporate citizenship perspective. Brands serve as a vehicle for a

138. *Supra* n. 135, §107 of the opinion.
139. *Supra* n. 135, §111 of the opinion.
140. *Supra* n. 122, pp. 1101-1102.
141. G. Allevato, "Judicial Review of the State Aid Decisions on Advance Tax Rulings: A Last Resort to Safeguard the Rule of Law," *European Taxation*, 2021 (Volume 62) No. 2, Journal Articles & Opinion Pieces IBFD.

company's values. Consumers "test" how a company delivers on those values. Taxes are not isolated from that.[142]

13.1 The ESG Agenda as an Overlay for Sustainable Tax Management

Today's ESG imperatives serve as an overlay for sustainable tax planning. The role of the tax function within MNEs is changing. Taxes have evolved from a mere cost of doing business to payments for a company's license to operate. There is pressure on MNEs to be clear about their purpose and for that purpose to include a positive social and environmental contribution. Taxes are an important metric where this contribution can be tested empirically.

The ESG mantra glimmers through in companies' tax teams' agendas these days. That probably does not come as a surprise when one sees how it triggers the attention of multiple stakeholders. Polman and Winston,[143] boldly state that "longer-term challenges don't have the short-term dopamine shot to earnings that paying no taxes does."

The concept of ESG is however far from new. The ESG genesis seems to be situated around 2004 with the Conference Report: Investing for Long-Term Value—Integrating Environmental, Social and Governance Value Drivers in Asset Management and Financial Research.[144]

13.2 The Link to TP

ESG strongly relates to transparency, and this touches on the very essence of both the "G" and the "S" angle. CbCR, PCbCR and the Global Reporting Initiative are just a few connotations popping-up. Certain sectors already have known some form of public reporting for quite some time, for example, the banking industry.[145] Extractives are another example.

As ESG also relates to how the MNE is organized, how it takes decisions, how to attract investors, where it operates, where it pays taxes, where it creates value, etc., there are quite a number of TP touchpoints. It relates to the very fundamentals of driving a business and hence high on the C-suite radar.

Examples of the impact of ESG on TP are:

- questions of centralization or decentralization of the business model—where to (re)locate production;
- sustainability of the products/consumer acceptance of products;
- transport footprint: bringing production facilities closer to markets;

142. Excerpt from the author's statement for the European Parliament's FISC Committee of June 22, 2021.
143. Polman and Winston, *supra* n. 2, 193.
144. *See* https://www.scribd.com/fullscreen/16876744?access_key = key-mfg3d0usaiuaob4taki.
145. Banking prudential requirements (CRD IV), Directive 2013/36/EU and Regulation (EU) No. 575/2013.

- supply chain issues: for example, decarbonization of the development/production/distribution processes;
- first mover advantage or disadvantage (e.g., incurring higher costs at first);
- business restructuring issues upon relocation of production/R&D sites;
- effect of "green" grants;[146]
- sustainable financing (e.g., in low carbon technologies, eco- and social-friendly resources);[147]
- etc.

When drilling down to what hard-and-fast TP rules are to be looked into, one needs to start from the delineation of transactions as it is central to the sustainability of the system profit allocation across the value chain. TP practitioners might consider the following considerations:

- accurate delineation of the transaction: is the transaction in line with the ESG metrics (Key Performance Indicators or KPIs) or goals;
- control over risk: does the party concerned has control over the ESG related risk, for example, can it reach its environmental targets;
- comparability: what is the impact of the ESG KPI or goals on the selection of potential comparables (e.g., ESG or non-ESG comparables, are comparability adjustments possible; setting of the same or similar goals; measurement of the goals; etc.).

13.3 The "E" Angle

With its "Fit for 55 package,"[148] the EU takes a prominent position. A carbon border adjustment mechanism, revision and expansion of the emission trading system, revision of the energy taxation directive, etc., will all create new or expand existing levies. As already indicated under section 5, some of these will be used as their own resources. Environmental taxation will become essential in the company's future tax strategy and management.

13.4 ESG as a Catalyst Toward "Meaningful" Transparency[149]

Meaningful transparency would be a catalyst for restoring trust in the international tax system and between its main actors. ESG could serve as a stepping-stone for a stronger focus on real-time cooperation between taxpayers and tax administrations.

146. But be mindful of the minimum ETR of 15% under the GloBE rules.
147. D. Ledure et al., "International Sustainable Financing and Transfer Pricing—How Environmental, Social and Governance Considerations Seep Through into the Arm's Length Principle," *International Transfer Pricing Journal*, 2022 (Volume 29), No. 1.
148. *See* I. Verlinden and J.P. Van West, forthcoming.
149. Recommendations inspired by the author's appearance before the EU Parliament FISC Committee on June 22, 2021.

13.4.1 Time to Rethink DAC6?

The introduction and consecutive updates of the DAC fueled the international exchange of information. Rulings or APAs and CbCR reports are one example, but more can be observed:

- The pace at which new transparency rules are launched puts pressure on both taxpayers and tax officials. Particularly, the lack of alignment across MSs is troublesome. DAC6, for example, provides for a number of options upon transposition in domestic legislation by each MS. In the absence of EU wide guidance, there are significant interpretation differences. This requires businesses active in the internal EU market to understand the legislation in each MS. This brings a number of challenges, especially for smaller companies.
- One may question the actual usefulness. As mentioned above, "business restructurings" are a good example. Events such as the COVID-19 pandemic and the ocean freight crisis (where a vessel blocked the Suez Canal in late March 2021) force companies to implement contingency emergency plans to ensure actual product supply. Fragmentation of the global or regional distribution footprint may imply that net earnings in a particular country drop significantly as a result of sound business decisions. It would be unfortunate if an MNE would "discover" after three years that it subliminally engaged in deemed tax planning under DAC6. Both taxpayers and tax administrations would benefit from clear definitions.

13.4.2 Exploiting the Potential of DAC7?

While the rationale of DAC6 is clear, its implementation risks morphing it into a mere administrative compliance task. Its merit lies in its potential to serve as a critical stage in a journey toward proactive and open communication with the tax administration.

DAC7 offers a tremendous opportunity to the EU to design an ecosystem where taxpayers and authorities can interact in a transparent way. Issues to be addressed are actual tax risk mapping, the design of a tax control framework, timing of interaction and confidentiality issues, just to name a few.

Contemporaneous interaction is important.

A well-functioning internal market commands a solid multilateral foundation. Shortening the time lapsing between taxable event, securing the tax implications and levying the actual tax bill is an investment in economic fundamentals of a best practice international tax architecture. This is where the OECD's work can serve as a source of inspiration, more precisely the Forum on Tax Administration's proceedings on "Tax Administration 3.0."[150]

150. OECD (2020), Tax Administration 3.0: The Digital Transformation of Tax Administration, OECD, Paris. http://www.oecd.org/tax/forum-on-tax-administration/publications-and-products/Tax-administration-3-0-the-digital-transformation-of-tax-administration.htm.

Real-time cooperation between taxpayers and tax administrations will be the governing principle within a few years. It has the potential to leapfrog a number of ongoing initiatives to enable taxpayers to deal with tax compliance in a cost-effective way and tax authorities to focus on "where true tax risk lies."

Maybe good to illustrate: innovation is key for companies to realize economic growth, and it is by definition *proprietary*. This applies equally to small as well as large companies. The pandemic has simultaneously created and lowered *barriers-to-entry* for companies. Think, for instance, about how young European innovators successfully unlocked their ingenuity via start-ups to reach customers while some larger groups were struggling to move from offline to online sales. There is pressure on all companies to be innovative. Government incentives will undoubtedly remain an important pillar of sustainable government tax policy as a lever to attract foreign direct investment (FDI).

These developments accelerate the need for cooperative engagement combined with investments in tax administrations to achieve the end goal of real-time compliance checks built into business administration systems. "Value creation" is the proxy for the actual determination of taxable income and that requires a level of judgment. It is therefore useful to build in a timely process to discuss and agree between taxpayers and tax administrations.

Critical success factors for a successful implementation of DAC7 are:

- *Trust*: Clearing in advance the tax impact of major transactions through dialog with the tax authorities is crucial. Taxpayers could, e.g., be granted a "tax risk label" depending on the outcome.
- *Reduce the time* between the taxable event and the inspection or the assessment.

14 THE FATE OF THE ALP

A valid question is whether all the recent developments will *increase* or *decrease* the relevance of TP rules as we currently know them (i.e., fundamentally based on the use of the ALP as the relevant standard).

14.1 A Hybrid System of Income Allocation: Tricky?

The ongoing global tax reform (the Pillars) with the EU Directive as European embodiment introduces a hybrid income allocation system with two different tax bases and two different allocation methods. The ALP continues to apply unchanged for companies in the financial services sector and natural resources industry and for all MNEs with consolidated revenues of less than 20 billion euros and accounting profits margins (Profit Before Tax (PBT)) of less than 10% of revenue. It will in other words only be supplemented with a formulary override for a relatively small number of highly profitable companies. Dispute resolution and—more importantly—avoidance will be a key success factor, as "surrendering" profits that are at face value arm's length to market jurisdictions under a new set of rules may be torturous for tax authorities and also for companies should double or multiple taxation persist. It will be a daunting task to design rules ensuring that pools of residual profits are recognized so that the relevant primary taxing rights over such profit can be granted to market jurisdictions and taken away from those countries to which these profits would accrue under the ALP.

14.2 A Post-BEPS "Messy Interregnum"?

Two former OECD officials, Joe Andrus and Richard Collier,[151] expect that the integration of Pillar One with the ALP will take priority for the next few years and will eventually lead to a disregard of key ALP technical and policy issues. That probably does not come as a surprise. Speaking on October 28, 2020, before the European Parliament's permanent subcommittee on tax matters (FISC), OECD's Pascal Saint-Amans said members need to work toward an agreement to reform "durably" transfer pricing rules, even if it takes years. "The deadline cannot be postponed eternally," and if the process fails, it will be "adjourned until political conditions are met to restart global discussions."[152]

This would then be preceded by a rather "messy interregnum"[153] with higher reliance on profit split approaches that are even further detached from transactions between independent parties, an expansion of diverted profits and similar taxes and a greater attempt by tax authorities to rely on safe harbors and formulas. Even if Pillar One will never see the light, they argue that a Pillar Two-only approach will not remediate the operational problems of the ALP. Examples given are the difficulties in finding (sufficiently) comparable open-market references, the pervasive complexity, the treatment of capital and what "control over risk" and value creation actually mean in practice. Indeed, business functions associated with controlling risk have become central to the determination of where within the MNE group various business risks should be deemed to reside. The crux of the matter is whether the OECD BEPS Actions 8-10 exacerbate the risk that contractual arrangements as main allocation criterion have been exchanged for value creation as the prevalent paradigm in international tax law and what this means when grappling with TP. An acronym not even known a decade ago, "DEMPEs," is often called the culprit. What is meant by "development, enhancement, maintenance, protection and exploitation" may raise eyebrows as it is anything but easy to be interpreted unambiguously, definitely when one scares away

151. J.L. Andrus and R.S. Collier, "Transfer Pricing and the Arm's Length Principle after the Pillars," *Taxes Notes International*, January 31, 2022, 543-555.
152. E. Lamer, "Status Quo on Digital Taxation Isn't an Option, Saint-Amans Says," *Tax Notes Today International*, October 29, 2020.
153. Andrus and Collier, *supra* n. 151, at 555.

from deploying a healthy level of facts-specific judgment. For the more cynically enhanced, this raises the question of whether the OECD relies on an unspecified notion of economic substance for which the concept of value creation is used as a proxy. Such negative tone does not come entirely as a surprise when, e.g., flipping through recent literature. The OECD BEPS project in general and Actions 8-10 in particular probably served a noble cause to improve or modernize the application of the ALP through alignment of profit allocation with value creation. The final BEPS reports may hence not have reached their goal to provide guardrails under the ALP when dealing with intangibles and control over risk.

14.3 The ALP as Scapegoat?

14.3.1 The Fundamentals of the ALP

One may question whether we have not become overly critical with the ALP. It may be worth exploring the merits of allocating it (even) more relevance post-implementation of the Pillars. Let us first refresh memories on what it actually does (or what it is meant for). The history of the ALP is captured through several (outside the scope of this chapter's) interesting reads,[154] particularly when analyzing how it evolved since initially being sparked by the intent of anti-avoidance.[155] In the absence of unitary taxation, abuse was the inspiring source of its conception under Mitchell B. Carroll.[156]

Today's debate around the ALP predominantly stems from the incidence that TP is not an exact science.[157] TP practitioners factor in the flaws caused by industrial organization economics when funneling open-market references into the holy grail aka *the arm's-length range*. The taxpayer is left with a margin of appreciation and some like that more than others. It is tempting for the practitioner to become creative or complacent (or both), especially when reading about transfer pricing being rather an art than a science. On the other hand, there is academic work claiming that the margin of appreciation left to the taxpayer leads to unhealthy results, particularly as the ALP sets the door open to countries to use that same flexibility to improve their competitiveness or the global competitiveness of their businesses.[158] TP may be seen as an (alleged) tool for luring inbound intragroup cross-border investment, an instrument of TP (unfair) tax competition or even illegal State aid. Needless to say, when capital

154. R. Collier and J. Andrus, "Transfer Pricing and the Arm's Length Principle after BEPS," 2017, Oxford University Press; L.E. Schoueri, "Arm's Length- Beyond the Guidelines of the OECD," *Bulletin for International Taxation*, 2015 (Volume 69), No 12.
155. G. Kofler and I. Verlinden, "Unlimited Adjustments: Some Reflections on Transfer Pricing, General Anti-Avoidance and Controlled Foreign Company Rules, and the 'Saving Clause'," *Bulletin for International Taxation*, 2020 (Volume 74, Nos 4/5).
156. M.B. Carroll, "Taxation of Foreign and National Enterprises," Volume 4: Methods of Allocating Taxable Income, League of Nations, 60.
157. I. Verlinden, "The Value of a Principle ... The Arm's Length Principle," *Intertax*, Editorial, March 2021 (Volume 49).
158. P.J. Wattel, "Stateless Income, State Aid and the (Which?) Arm's Length Principle," *Intertax*, 2016 (Volume 44, No. 11), 791.

import/export neutrality becomes under pressure, surging political attention does not come by surprise.[159]

Prof Lorraine Eden[160] makes a plea for honoring the ALP, particularly for those using what she calls the "arrows of logic, economics and pragmatism." She sets aside allegations about TP as ordinarily *abusive*, being unworkable to accommodate the digital economy and unable to actually work in the absence of comparables and due to the presence of synergies.

Prof Mihir Desai[161] uses even more colorful language by referring to what he calls pre-US 2017 tax reform "pathologies and problematic behavior" rather than to deficiencies in the ALP in itself. In his view, these stemmed from the 35% US corporate income tax rate, the US worldwide regime and the fact that US companies had an abundance of low-tax jurisdictions to choose from to shift profits to. He is of the opinion that TP is not an existential threat to the corporate income tax. It is his strong belief that TP and avoidance should not preoccupy the public imagination the way it does today as one risks fighting last year's battle in that process simply due to (legacy) distortive incentives for companies. Moreover, he feels that the figures that float around on so-called artificial profit shifting of up to USD 200 billion yearly are overstated and lacking sound foundation.

This is probably a slippery slope for the authors to comment on other than to refer to particularly interesting academic work. According to Prof Jennifer Blouin and Prof Leslie Robinson, actual profit shifting by MNEs risks to be overstated by researchers' misunderstandings of the accounting treatment of indirectly owned foreign affiliates in the US international economic accounting data.[162] The result is double income counting and its misattribution to incorrect jurisdictions.

As a complementary remark, and not immune to the charge of lacking modesty, the authors feel that the ALP requires a certain level of expertise and experience. Detrimental to the well functioning of the ALP are lack of investment in capacity building and resources for governments, as well as in cooperation programs between taxpayers and tax administrations. This is something those setting the rules of the games need to be cognizant of. Whatever standard will be chosen, at the end of the day, one cannot compromise on (investing in) quality when dealing with avoidance and remediation of situations leading to more or less than single taxation.

159. Andrus and Collier, *supra* n. 151, 547.
160. L. Eden, "Insight—David and the Three Goliaths—Defending the Arm's Length Principle," Bloomberg Tax Transfer Pricing Report, https://news.bloombergtax.com/transfer-pricing/insight-david-and-the-three-goliaths-defending-the-arms-length-principle, September 14, 2020 (accessed November 25, 2020).
161. A.M. Desai, "The Myths and Mysteries of the Corporate Income Tax," Musgrave Lecture, March 24, 2021, International Institute of Public Finance accessed at https://www.youtube.com/watch?v=lqjcMAGBORk
162. J. Blouin and L. Robinson, "Double Counting Accounting: How Much Profit of Multinational Enterprises Is Really in Tax Havens?," September 2020, https://ssrn.com/abstract=3491451.

14.3.2 *Satisfying a Legitimate Need*

The current era of multi-stakeholder capitalism creates an interesting dynamic. The PwC submission to the OECD Pillar One blueprint[163] stresses the need to design a set of agreed international tax rules anchored by a grounding force that has some tolerance for swift changes in tax policy, business models, and economic/trade evolution in the years to come.

The current international profit allocation regime has remained in place so long is its anchoring in a rationally articulated principle: the ALP. Since many years, it is helping governments to identify the circumstances in which corporate profits are recognized in one jurisdiction versus another. While criticized for various perceived deficiencies, it has been an animating principle that has helped preserve some measure of certainty in the international tax arena for a substantial period of time. The legal and economic rationales behind the ALP are known and shaped by multilateral consensus, providing reasonable certainty and administrative grounding.

14.3.3 *Be Careful when Looking for Greener Pastures*

Leveling the global playing field amidst the societal, environmental and economic pressures, the world economy appears to provoke a strong political appeal to criticize the ALP.

There are few objective, subjective, economically sound, purely political, crazy, or even emotions-driven angles from which the ALP has not (yet) been assessed, screened, criticized, challenged, ditched, applauded or commented on. Formulary Apportionment fans dream of OECD Pillar One becoming the ultimate door-opener toward BEFIT. The ALP is "wounded." It will need to be seen how resilient it will be in preserving its status as a prevailing standard. Nothing is perfect and that applies to the ALP as well. As eighteenth-century author Carveth Read said, however, "it is better to be approximately right than precisely wrong."[164] It is almost ironic, but a valid expectation could be that exactly the tax authorities will strengthen the reliance on the ALP. Both Pillars may serve as catalysts, each based on their particular merits. Indeed, for Pillar One, "everything" that can be safeguarded as within the 10% PBT threshold does not need to be "surrendered" to other countries. For Pillar Two, the requirement to (re)construe consolidated results according to the ALP incentivizes tax administrations to secure tax base that otherwise may fade away under the IIR, UTPR or Subject-to-Tax Rule (STTR). This latter point strengthens the need for making sure the tolerance of the OECD, the EU and other institutions setting the rules of the game for unfounded TP adjustments is wearing thin and embedded in corresponding rules that leave no room for unfounded opportunistic adjustments.

---

163. PricewaterhouseCoopers International; December 14, 2020, published December 16, 2020, on the OECD website.
164. A quote often (mis)appropriated to John Maynard Keynes as well.

15 CONCLUSION

The European institutions are unstoppable in their efforts to issue hard-and-fast rules. Whether this leads to catching two birds with one stone is premature to say. Stepping up its efforts to satisfy increased funding of public needs is probably the more plausible bird it will catch. The other one is to make the tax system "better" as societal progress does not appear to have kept pace with economic growth.

No stakeholder can hardly disagree with both of them as a matter of principle. This being said, taxpayers deserve *certainty*. Knowing how the tax bill will look like is a key foundation of tax morale, i.e., the willingness to pay taxes.

In this context, there is probably little room for taxpayers to doubt the importance of financial transparency for tax purposes. The rationale of the DAC is clear, and the direction of travel understood. Its implementation proves to be a torturous journey, and lessons can be learned by the "architects," such as related to DAC6. DAC7 has the potential to become the standard for "meaningful transparency." Targeted and harmonized implementation can make it a true game changer toward effective and proactive mutual exchange among MSs and taxpayers and a parameter of trust in the tax system.[165]

Besides being a *first* mover in many areas, the EU is also a *fast* mover. This is quite understandable as there is currently political momentum to change the international tax system. *And one must strike when the iron is hot*!

A fundamental question is whether (political) haste is a guarantee for "good" legislation. A standstill is no option, but more reflection would probably do no harm, to the contrary. No one is helped with unclear legislation or legislation that may need to be changed even before it becomes applicable, let alone legislation that is fundamentally ambiguous and hence open for different interpretations. This is even more true given the "power" of union law to override other taxation rules. The more cynically enhanced feel the risk of the EU becoming a sort of "nicest pupil in the classroom," while legislators outside the EU might interpret things in a more "relaxed" way. Pillar 2 implementation is expected to serve as "proof of the pudding."

Nobody will deny that revisiting the international tax framework is needed. But in a way, one could say that there was always a constant change in the international framework. References can be made to the regular updates of the OECD Model Tax Convention, OECD TPG, the updates of the EU directives, and the work of the (unfortunately abolished but not yet replaced) EU Joint TP Forum. There has always been a political dimension in the development of tax policies, and building "political capital" along the lines of introducing new rules is a plausible "cherry on the cake." Whether this means that the public opinion is served well when complex international rules and court cases are "justified" in 140 characters or so via (social) media feeds is food for thought.

As the reader has discovered throughout this contribution, the focus on TP within the EU lies on audit, tax transparency of all sorts and the crusade against tax avoidance,

165. *Supra* n. 144, Statement author before EP FISC Committee.

tax evasion and (aggressive) tax planning (all on one pile). To the authors, it is not yet clear what the EC considers as tipping point(s) as from which tax planning shifts from "normal" to "aggressive" or from "unfair" to "fair" taxation, not to mention from which moment on tax competition becomes "harmful." The EC is undeniably taking an "assertive" stance toward MNEs. There seems to be a somewhat dogmatic (political) sense that MNEs at all times *salute the tax minimization mantra.*

The authors aim to refrain from making unfounded allegations. This being said, what can be illustrative is that only one initiative discussed in this contribution can be considered beneficial to both MNEs and tax administrations: the ETACA project. This project marries transparency (beneficial to the tax authority) and tax comfort (beneficial to the taxpayer and the tax administration alike). The authors welcome this approach of course for the reasons explained in the relevant section, but one initiative beneficial to MNEs out of a dozen well seems pretty meager. Indeed, the other initiatives are rather skewed toward the tax administrations' interests only.

Administrative complexity is becoming a critical impediment to doing business smoothly. In its special report on Business and the State, *The Economist* draws attention to the red tape that continues to spread inexorably.[166] That section describes excellently the avalanche of laws and regulations—and soft law being interpreted more and more as hard law—that is coming onto us.

Prof. Wolfgang Schön probably rightfully points out that an international tax framework is still not there.[167] That may be a prerequisite for a fruitful dialog with all stakeholders, and particularly civil society on what is needed to ensure trust in the international tax architecture.

ESG can play an important role. Complex relationships between biodiversity loss, climate change, inequality, economic growth and social cohesion have become increasingly clear to many. Companies' sustainability initiatives increasingly include a fiscal dimension. The goal of companies evolves to reaping financial gains *because* of sustainability, rather than *despite* those efforts which can boost mutual stakeholders' empathy.

To end on two very positive notes:

(1) almost every new initiative allows for the public—including MNEs—to let their voice be heard through a public consultation. It might be good to seize the opportunity in a constructive yet firm way. It is important for the EC to take these consultations at heart. Engagement with stakeholders is enriching. The process of establishing public consultation may be lengthy and burdensome at times, but then, Rome was not built in one day!
(2) the ALP may be under pressure for many reasons, but drilling down in its merits may lead to the conclusion that there will always be one reason more to keep it as a pole star for trust in the international tax architecture than to give it up.

166. The Economist, Special Report Business and the State, p. 9, January 15, 2022.
167. Prof. Dr. W. Schön, "Is There Finally an International Tax System?," *World Tax Journal*, 2021 (Volume 13), No. 3.

CHAPTER 3

Transfer Pricing Developments in the United States

Marc M. Levey[*]

* Thank you is extended to Yuyao Leng for her kind research assistance.

1 INTRODUCTION

This chapter seeks to cover the significant transfer pricing cases of 2021 and will address the Coca-Cola Tax Court decision, the implications of the *Altera* Tax Court and 9th Circuit decisions, four pending cases of potential significance, the OECD's Guidance on the Transfer Pricing concerns involving COVID-19, the Multistate Tax Commission Enforcement and Collaborations in Transfer Pricing cases and the impact on tax enforcement given the Biden Administration's lack of funding for the IRS. And the question to be considered is what, if anything, does this means to the future of transfer pricing?

2 THE COCA-COLA TAX COURT CASE

On November 18, 2020, the Tax Court ruled that respondent IRS had not abused its discretion under section 482 of the Code when it reallocated more than USD 9 billion in income for tax years 2007 to 2009 to petitioner Coca-Cola from its foreign manufacturing affiliates.[1]

This significant transfer pricing case is factually straightforward and evaluates the relationships among the US parent company (Coca-Cola), its foreign manufacturing affiliates (known as "Supply Points"), its local foreign service companies ("ServCos"), its independent foreign bottlers, and its "extremely valuable" intangible assets, including trademarks, logos, patents, secret formulas, and "the best known brand in the world." The taxpayer had relied on the terms of an IRS Closing Settlement Agreement in applying the transfer pricing method on which its return position was based, and would have sought competent authority relief, but had been turned away by the IRS, which anticipated litigating the case. The structure is depicted in the figure below:

1. *Coca-Cola v. Commissioner*, 155 T.C. No. 10 (November 18, 2020).

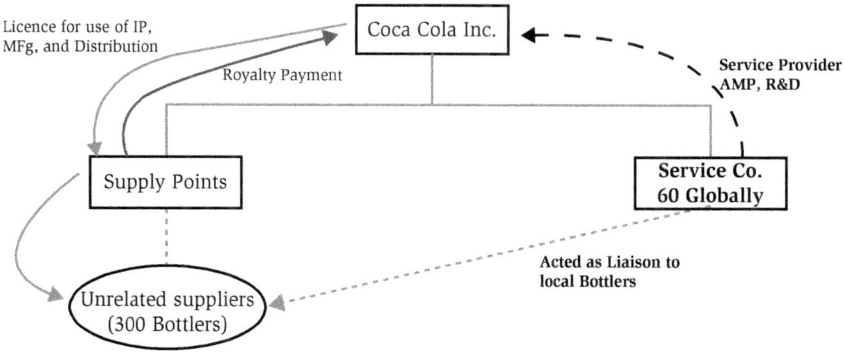

Specifically at issue was whether the court would follow the 10-50-50 apportionment formula for allocating income from the sale of beverage concentrate to its Supply Points pursuant to an old IRS Closing Agreement for the year 1987 through 1995. This formula was followed by Coca-Cola for years after the expiration of that Agreement. Coca-Cola argued that the IRS's use of a new method, namely, the Comparable Profits Method (CPM), was both inappropriate and its use misplaced. The Tax Court also concluded in the earlier decision that the taxes were creditable because the taxpayer met both prongs of the compulsory test. The decision tackles so many distinct transfer pricing topics. Below is a summary of key decision points.

2.1 CPM Judged Most Appropriate

The Tax Court considered in detail the IRS's use of a CPM analysis to be an appropriate, reliable, and conservative transfer pricing method for determining the amounts that the Supply Points should have paid Coca-Cola for using its intellectual property. The Tax Court found that Coca-Cola's Supply Points were essentially "wholly-owned contract manufacturers" executing steps in the beverage-production process, and that Coca-Cola, rather than its Supply Points, owned "virtually all the intangible assets needed to produce and sell" the company's beverages. In light of these findings, the Tax Court concluded that the CPM was "ideally suited" to determine Coca-Cola's compensation for the use of its intellectual property because the CPM was capable of determining an arm's-length profit for the Supply Points without reverting to the value of Coca-Cola's particular valuable intangible assets. The Trial Judge went into extraordinary detail in analyzing the Supply Points' Profit and Loss Statement, noting that its return on assets dramatically exceeded both the comparable firms reviewed and their returns on assets at times by 5 to 7 times their returns. The Tax Court agreed with the IRS that Coca-Cola's appropriate comparable parties for the CPM analysis were the unrelated bottlers because they operated in the same industry, with similar relationships to Coca-Cola, using its items of intangible property to perform similar functions. Further, because the Tax Court found that these bottlers generally were entitled to a higher rate of return than the Supply Points, had less restricted rights, and could be terminated at will, the Tax Court considered the IRS' CPM conservative.

The Tax Court evaluated the theories proposed by Coca-Cola to establish that the Supply Points owned valuable marketing intangibles, namely, legal ownership and economic, beneficial ownership. The court also considered the secondary argument that the Supply Points owned intangible assets in the form of "long term licenses." Citing Treasury Regulations section 1.482—4T(f)(a)(i)(A), which provided in part that the "legal owner of an intangible pursuant to intellectual property law of the relevant jurisdiction ... or contract terms ... will be considered the sole owner of the respective intangible unless such ownership is inconsistent with the economic substance of the underlying transactions." Hence, the court found after reviewing the trademark registrations, the Supply Points were not the legal owners of the trademarks or marketing intangibles. Key considerations were the lack of adequate contractual terms to support this action. Specifically, the court reviewed the legal agreements to determine if the marketing intangibles were conveyed by contract, that the contracts granted no specific rights of ownership interest to the Supply Points, and the contracts made clear that any marketing intangibles were the property of Coca-Cola. Further, the contracts provided that the long-term licenses were terminable at will and did not grant territorial exclusivity, nor guarantee a supply of production.

Key points to be gleaned here are: (1) marketing intangibles to be asserted by a taxpayer must be established by contract, (2) the nonexclusivity and termination at will of the licenses would not constitute a "sale" or conveyance under intellectual property law; (3) taxpayers cannot affirmatively use the economic substance doctrine to assert marketing intangibles; (4) pure advertising is an annual expense and likely would not constitute brand building or "non routines" expenses; and (5) the agreements were not economically sustainable as noted above.

Applying the CPM during audit, the IRS determined that the ratio of operating profit to operating assets ("ROA") for six of Coca-Cola's seven Supply Points during the years 2007 to 2009 was between 21.5% and 94%. The interquartile range of ROAs of Coca-Cola's independent bottlers was 7.4% and 3.8%. After the IRS reallocation of income from the Supply Points to Coca-Cola, the ROAs of the six Supply Points were between 34.3% and 20.9%. The Tax Court noted that these ROAs remained higher than almost 80% of the manufacturers analyzed by the IRS, which included Pepsi, Nestle, and other prominent beverage firms.

2.2 Three Proposed Alternatives Rejected

Coca-Cola proposed three alternative transfer pricing methods to support its contention that, in arm's-length transactions, Coca-Cola's foreign Supply Points would receive most of the income that Coca-Cola derives from foreign markets. The Tax Court rejected all three.

2.2.1 Proposed Alternative 1: CUT Method

The Tax Court first analyzed Coca-Cola's proposed Comparable Uncontrolled Transaction (CUT) method. This method generally compared Coca-Cola's Supply Points to fast food master franchisers such as McDonalds. The Tax Court identified several flaws in this comparison, including that beverages and fast food products are not similar products nor in the same general industry or market. Further, the Tax Court observed that Coca-Cola's Supply Points did not have similar long-term contracts, territorial exclusivity, nor management responsibilities of fast food master franchisers. Also, because Coca-Cola's analysis did not include data from unrelated party transactions involving the transfers of trademarks, secret formulas, and other intangible property used in producing branded beverage products, the Tax Court concluded that the CUT method's reliability was questionable. The Tax Court described the application of the CUT method as "aggressive" and "mathematically and economically" unsound.

2.2.2 *Proposed Alternative 2: RPSM*

Next, the Tax Court analyzed Coca-Cola's proposed Residual Profit Split Method (RPSM), again finding it "wholly unreliable." The proposed RPSM involved estimating a value for nonroutine intangibles that Coca-Cola asserted were the property of the Supply Points. This estimate was based on capitalized advertising costs less amortization, rather than on external market benchmarks nor brand building expenditures. The Tax Court found this estimation method unreliable for two basic reasons: (1) the lack of consensus about whether the costs of advertising can be capitalized into intangible assets, particularly as these expenditures were annual expenses and not typically susceptible to capitalization; and (2) these assets would have no value to an unrelated party because an unrelated party could not use the asset without infringing Coca-Cola's trademarks.

The Tax Court also identified several other flaws in the proposed RPSM. As in analyzing Coca-Cola's proposed CUT method, the Tax Court found that the Supply Points were the relevant controlled taxpayers under the section 482 regulations, and that it was not appropriate to consider a combination of Coca-Cola's Supply Points and local foreign service companies to be the relevant controlled taxpayer instead. The Tax Court also found that Coca-Cola, not its Supply Points, was the owner of the intangible assets involved in the transactions at issue and was not persuaded by the evidence (or lack thereof) presented to the contrary by the Petitioner. Even if the Supply Points themselves owned any intangible property, the Tax Court found that it would not be appropriate to exclude the value of Coca-Cola's own intangible property determinations of the relative value of non-routing intangible property in the RPSM.

2.2.3 *Proposed Alternative 3: Unspecified Method*

The Tax Court then analyzed Coca-Cola's proposed unspecified method, which was based on the fee structure typically used to compensate hedge fund managers. The Tax Court noted that this method "does not remotely resemble any of the 'specified methods' for valuing intangibles under the section 482 regulations" because this method proposed to compensate Coca-Cola only for asset management services, and not for the use of Coca-Cola's intangible assets.

2.3 Blocked Income Ruling Reserved

The Tax Court reserved ruling on Coca-Cola's argument that Brazilian law would have prevented Coca-Cola's Brazilian Supply Points from paying more than a small fraction of the hundreds of millions of dollars of additional income that the IRS determined should be reallocated from the Brazilian Supply Points to Coca-Cola. The IRS asserted that under Treasury Regulations § 1.482(h)(2), the "blocked income" regulations, the provisions in Brazilian law should not be considered when determining an arm's-length transfer price. Coca-Cola argued, alternatively, that the regulation is inapplicable, that the regulation's conditions for taking Brazilian law into account were met, or that the regulations are invalid.

Because the validity of the blocked income regulation is currently before the Tax Court in *3M Co. & and Subs. v. Commissioner*, the court in the *Coca-Cola* case decided not to rule on these arguments until an opinion is issued in the *3M* Case.[2] The *3M* Case was fully briefed in 2016 and is awaiting decision. Interestingly, these cases will challenge the validity of the IRS Treasury regulations issued in 1994 which made standards for challenging blocked income rigorous, if not practically unachievable. The two pending cases each involve licensing of intangibles by a US corporation to its Brazilian affiliates. IRS concedes that Brazilian law limited the royalties that could be paid, but argues that these affiliates could pay dividends, which they could have reported at royalty increase. Notwithstanding the withholding tax implications, the IRS argues that the Revenue Procedure provided a route to pay and collect funds for the US licenses. Hence, the IRS asserts that these taxpayers cannot rely on foreign restrictions to avoid including these amounts income. Of course, the taxpayers argue that they are under no obligation to pay dividends in satisfaction of the royalties the IRS assert that are due.

2.4 Collateral Adjustments Allowed

The Tax Court also allowed two types of collateral adjustments for the years 2007 to 2009: (i) the IRS's adjustment of Coca-Cola's losses under section 987 for its Mexico Supply Points after the IRS reallocated income from the Mexico Supply Points to Coca-Cola, and (ii) reductions or offsets of the royalty amounts owed by Supply Points to Coca-Cola as a result of the adjustments, equal to the amount of dividends these Supply Points had previously remitted to Coca-Cola to satisfy their royalty obligations.

For the section 987 adjustment, the Tax Court rejected Coca-Cola's arguments and found that the court had jurisdiction to review the adjustment, that the computation of the adjustment was neither premature nor dependent on Mexican law, and that the recomputation was a necessary part of "produc[ing] the same result that would have occurred if [Coca-Cola] and its Mexican branch had reported income consistently with the arm's-length standard from the outset."

2. *3M Company v. Commissioner*, T.C. Dkt. No. 5816-13.

For the dividend offsets, the Tax Court rejected the IRS's argument that any offset was barred by Coca-Cola's failure to file the explanatory statements required for taxpayers electing dividend offset treatment for taxpayer-initiated section 482 adjustments. This was only taxpayer win in the case. The Tax Court instead found that Coca-Cola substantially complied with this requirement in the "peculiar circumstances of this case," where the explanatory statements "would have added nothing to the IRS' sum of knowledge" about Coca-Cola's adjustments and offsets.

2.5 The Appeal

On the day after the Tax Court's opinion was published, Coca-Cola stated that it was "disappointed with the outcome," is considering "potential grounds for its appeal," and "intend[s] to continue to vigorously defend our position."

Based on press clippings from the documents filed for an en banc review by the full court, Coca-Cola specifically asked the court to consider that the Trial Judge ignored in holding that the accounting for those licenses by Coca-Cola to its Supply Points resulted in a spend of billions of dollars in marketing the brand.[3] The Supply Points purportedly paid for and bore the risks of marketing expenses in their regions, and Coca-Cola believed that they should be compensated for their contribution. Coca-Cola argues that the Tax Court's erroneous conclusion was simply premised on the fact that Coca-Cola is the legal owner of the trademarks which ignores the Treasury Regulations that takes into account Supply Point's valuable licenses and its concomitant significant spend. As a backdrop to this argument, Coca-Cola argues that as a matter of administrative and constitutional law, this new IRS approach disregards the IRS' approval of this issue for over a decade of time, in addition to the apparent approval from a past Advance Pricing Agreement. Here a renowned constitutional lawyer was retained for this argument. However, the request for review was denied by the Tax Court on December 2, 2021.

Hence, the next step is to the Sixth Circuit Court of Appeals. Considering that Appellate courts typically address errors in the application of the law or a misrepresentation of the factual record, it will be interesting to see the approach by the Appellant Coca-Cola. One issue in the findings of fact appears to be the statement that the Supply Points did not have similar nonroutine intangibles. One would think this may be different than what was represented to the IRS in the "old" APA, and, further, was the Trial Judge Finding Facts accurately depicting the trial record.

3 THE IMPACT OF THE ALTERA DECISION

3.1 Background to the *Altera* Decision

On July 27, 2015, the Tax Court ruled in a landmark decision in favor of the taxpayer in *Altera Corporation & Subsidiaries v. Commissioner* and invalidated a Treasury

3. *See* Bloomberg Daily Tax Report, dated June 4, 2021, "Coca-Cola Disputes IRS Logic Behind $3 Billion Tax Bill."

Regulation that had been promulgated under Code section 482. Treasury Regulation § 1.482-7(d)(2) (2003) (the "Final Rule") required controlled participants in a qualified cost-sharing arrangement (QCSA) to include amounts attributable to stock-based compensation in their cost pool. The Tax Court, sitting in conference, held that the Final Rule failed to satisfy the reasoned decision-making standard in *Motor Vehicle Manufacturers Association of the United States, Inc. v. State Farm Mutual Auto Insurance Co.*, and was therefore invalid. All fifteen voting judges supported the opinion. There were no concurring or dissenting opinions.

The case arose because the Commissioner exercised his discretion under section 482 to allocate income from Altera International to Altera US by increasing Altera International's cost-sharing payments by an amount relating to stock-based compensation. The sole purpose of the Commissioner's adjustments was to bring Altera into compliance with the Final Rule, and the Final Rule was the sole basis for such adjustments.

During the rulemaking process, interested parties submitted written comments to Treasury in which they opposed the requirement that controlled participants in a cost-sharing arrangement (CSAs) include amounts attributable to stock-based compensation in the cost pool. Commentators informed Treasury that they knew of no transaction between unrelated parties, including any CSA, service agreement, or other contracts, in which one party paid or reimbursed the other party for amounts attributable to stock-based compensation. Commentators also provided evidence in the form of member surveys, searches of the SEC's EDGAR system, arm's-length agreements, accounting procedures pertinent to government contracts, and detailed economic analysis all of which suggested that unrelated parties would not agree to share amounts attributable to stock-based compensation.[4]

Because Treasury and the IRS intended the Final Rule to have the force of law, the Tax Court held that the Final Rule was a legislative rule subject to the notice-and-comment rulemaking requirements in 5 USC § 553(b) of the Administrative Procedure Act (APA Act). The court also concluded that the reasonableness of agency decision-making is analyzed under State Farm and 5 USC § 706(2)(A) of the APA Act. For purposes of determining whether Treasury satisfied its obligations under the APA, the Commissioner argued that *Chevron, U.S.A., Inc. v. Natural Resources Defense Council, Inc.*, provided the appropriate standard of review, and that the court should not review the Final Rule under State Farm because, among other reasons, "the Supreme Court has

4. In the preamble to the Final Rule, Treasury did not respond directly to any of the evidence provided by commentators. Instead, Treasury asserted that the "uncontrolled transactions cited by commentators do not share enough characteristics of QCSAs involving the development of high-profit intangibles to establish that parties at arm's length would not take stock options into account in the context of an arrangement similar to a QCSA." The Tax Court responded that "[t]his was a mere assertion; Treasury offered no analysis addressing the extent of the supposed differences or explaining why any differences make the cited transactions irrelevant or unpersuasive." The files maintained by Treasury at the time that it issued the Final Rule did not contain any unrelated party cost-sharing or other agreement, expert opinion, empirical data, published or unpublished article, paper, survey, or report that supported its belief that unrelated parties engaged in a cost-sharing arrangement would agree to share amounts attributable to stock-based compensation. Treasury's position was that it was not required to engage in fact-finding or evidence-gathering procedures in promulgating the Final Rule, and that section 482 allocations are not required to be made by reference to uncontrolled party conduct.

never, and [the Tax Court] has rarely, reviewed Treasury regulations under *State Farm*." The court, however, concluded that "whether *State Farm or Chevron* supplies the standard of review is immaterial because *Chevron* step 2 incorporates the reasoned decision making standard of *State Farm*." Accordingly, the court reviewed the Final Rule under *State Farm* and 5 USC § 706(2)(A), which requires courts to "hold unlawful and set aside agency action, findings, and conclusions" that are "arbitrary, capricious, an abuse of discretion, or otherwise not in accordance with law."

To engage in reasoned decision-making, "the agency must examine the relevant data and articulate a satisfactory explanation for its action including a 'rational connection between the facts found and the choice made.' Generally, an agency considered the data to be arbitrary and capricious if the agency has relied on factors which Congress has not intended it to consider, entirely failed to consider an important aspect of the problem, offered an explanation for its decision that runs counter to the evidence before the agency, or is so implausible that it could not be ascribed to a difference in view or the product of agency expertise."

Although an agency's violation of any of the *State Farm* standards renders a regulation invalid, the Tax Court invalidated the Final Rule on multiple grounds under *State Farm*. First, the court concluded that the Final Rule lacked a basis in fact because "by failing to engage in any fact finding, Treasury failed to 'examine the relevant data'." Further, Treasury's belief that unrelated parties would share amounts attributable to stock-based compensation in a QCSA was not supported by any of the evidence in the administrative record and "every indication in the record point[ed] the other way." Second, the court concluded that Treasury failed to articulate a rational connection between the facts found and the choice made. The court was unpersuaded by the Commissioner's argument that the Final Rule was reasonable because it eased administrative burdens because "Treasury failed to give this or any other explanation for treating all QCSAs identically in the preamble to the final rule," and the court could not "reasonably discern that this was Treasury's rationale for adopting a uniform final rule because the administrative benefits of a uniform final rule are entirely speculative." Finally, the court stated that Treasury's failure to respond to significant comments "frustrate[d] [its] review of the final rule and was prejudicial to affected entities." The court also concluded that the Final Rule was contrary to all of the evidence before Treasury.

In arriving at its holding, the Tax Court focused primarily on Treasury's disregard of the facts and evidence in the administrative record, and the lack of evidence or information to support its belief that unrelated parties to an ACSA would share amounts attributable to stock-based compensation in every case. "Indeed, Treasury's *ipse dix* it conclusion, coupled with its failure to respond to contrary arguments resting on solid data, epitomizes arbitrary and capricious decision making." The Tax Court's application of the reasoned decision-making standard demonstrates that fundamental administrative law principles affect the analysis of the validity of Treasury Regulations.

On June 7, 2019, the U.S. Court of Appeals for the 9th Circuit, in a split decision 2-1 opinion, overturned the Tax Court's decision in *Altera Corp v. Commissioner*, 145 T.C. No. 3 (July 27, 2015). Generally, the 9th Circuit held that companies in CSAs should share the cost of employee stock-based compensation in the cost pool of their CSAs.

The 9th Circuit focused on the development of the tax Code, the perceived intent by Congress and the Tax Reform Act of 1986 that led to the addition of the "commensurate with income standard." In short, the 9th Circuit decision held that Treasury's requirement for stock-based expenses to be shared under a CSA was reasonable despite any empirical evidence that showed that unrelated parties dealing under a similar arrangement would not share such an expense.

The Tax Court also found the Treasury's adherence to the APA Act met the Act's intent and further that the public comments were not particularly helpful.

On February 10, 2020, Altera filed a petition for a writ of certiorari asking the U.S. Supreme Court to review the 9th Circuit's decision. The Supreme Court denied Altera's petition for certiorari, so the 9th Circuit stands, at least if and until another Circuit hears the case and there is split among the Circuits.

3.2 The Non-SBC CSAs and Reverse Claw Bank Provision

In July 2021, the IRS Office of Chief Counsel released AM 2021-004, a memorandum regarding "Non-SBC CSAs" and "reverse claw-back" provisions triggered by, e.g., *Altera v. Commissioner*, 926 F.3d 1061 (9th Cir. 2019), rev'g 145 T.C. 91 (2015), cert. denied, 141 S. Ct. 131 (2020).[5] Specifically, AM 2021-004 provides guidance on the timing of IRS adjustments related to the non-stock-based compensation (SBC) CSAs and on double-counting issues related to such adjustments. AM 2021-004 also signals the IRS' confidence that it can hold taxpayers to their reverse clawback provisions, despite the statute of limitations being closed for years in which the taxpayers incurred the SBCs at issue.

In AM 2021-004, the IRS first addressed the appropriate year for a section 482 adjustment to include SBCs for Non-SBC CSAs that contained a reverse clawback provision. Some taxpayers drafted their CSAs to allow for the possibility that any adjustment for SBCs would be taken into account in the year of the triggering event. AM 2021-004 states that the IRS should make adjustments to any open year in which the SBCs were incurred. Because Taxpayers in Non-SBC CSAs have "IDC shares that are not equal to their RAB shares... the IRS has the authority to correct this imbalance by, for instance, adjusting the results of a CST [cost sharing transaction] in the year in which the IDCs or intangible development costs, were incurred" (AM 2021-004 at 5 (citing Treas. Reg. § 1.482-7(i)(2))). The IRS authority to make allocations clearly "exists regardless of the existence or lack of a reverse claw-back provision ..." (AM 2021-004 at 5). Accordingly, the IRS concluded that an adjustment to an open year (as described above) would reduce the amount of the true-up due in the year in which the triggering event occurred (again, regardless of what the reverse clawback stated (or did not state)). This prevented double-counting of SBCs. *See* AM 2021-004 at 5-6.

AM 2021-004 also addressed where the IRS could make adjustments, even if the year in which IDCs incurred was closed, clarifying that it could make allocations "in an

5. This section was derived from a Baker McKenzie Client Alert dated November 21, 2021, and authored by Angela Chang (SF).

appropriate year" under Treas. Reg. § 1.482-7(i)(5) (allocations when cost-sharing transactions are consistently and materially disproportionate to RAB shares)—i.e., in closed years as well (AM 2021-004 at 6). For example, if taxpayers disregarded their reverse clawbacks and failed to include the true-up payments due in their income, despite the triggering event, the IRS could use the tax benefit rule to make adjustments for the unshared SBCs in the year of the triggering event. Also, if taxpayers tried to remove or modify the reverse clawbacks, the IRS could make "appropriate adjustments" to reflect the unmodified contract or otherwise to ensure the results are consistent with arm's-length principles (AM 2021-004 at 7).

3.3 Thoughts on the Conclusion

AM 2021-004 makes clear that the IRS should make adjustments to include SBCs to open years in which the IDCs were incurred. The IRS further emphasizes that the IRS can hold taxpayers to their reverse clawbacks to pursue adjustments, where the SBCs were incurred in closed years.

4 PENDING CASES OF IMPORTANCE

4.1 *Medtronic, Inc. et al. v. Commissioner*, U.S. Tax Court Docket # 6944-11

In a 2016 Tax Court case, Medtronic provided in a matter that centered around which transfer pricing list reflected the contributions from the company's Puerto Rican subsidiary when calculating the arm's-length royalty rates for an intercompany licensing transaction. In refuting the IRS USD 1.36 billion tax deficiency, the Trial Judge rejected the IRS' use of the CPM which considered the level of profit made by a company in a controlled transaction. Instead, the Trial Judge used an uncontrolled transaction method (CUT) that relied upon transactions by and between unrelated parties to benchmark the related party intercompany transaction. The Trial Judge also disagreed with aspects of the taxpayer's CUT analysis, noting that it failed to make adjustments to account for significant differences between the license of devices and led to Medtronic Puerto Rico and the third-party (Pacesetter) agreement, which arose from a litigation settlement. Thus, the court favored an outcome that it believed was arm's length with certain adjustments to arrive at an arm's-length royalty rate.

In 2018, a three-judge panel disregarded the Trial Judges' opinion requiring a more extensive determination that Medtronic could use a settlement with another supplier. Of note was that the Eighth Circuit found that the Trial Judge's decision was devoid of "making a specific finding as to what amount of risk and product liability expense was properly attributable the Medtronic Puerto Rico." Accordingly, the Eighth Circuit vacated and remanded the Tax Court's decision finding that the lack of certain factual findings prevented it from evaluating whether the CUT method was the best method, and whether proper adjustments were made.

The decision led to a second Tax Court decision which addressed those issues. The second trial began in June 2021 and has been concluded. This second trial focused on the selection of the most reliable transfer pricing method, as well as the determination of any necessary adjustments to the results of applying the CUT method. In the second trial, Medtronic and its experts continued to assert that the CUT method was the most reliable method to price the instant licensing agreement, while the IRS and its experts continued to assert that the CPM was the best method. More particularly, the IRS asserted that the differences between the third-party agreement and the instant royalty transaction were too significant to be resolved through adjustment and that the CPM determined profit that more accurately reflected an arm's-length result.

At the conclusion of this second trial, the Trial Judge suggested the use of the CUT method as the best method. The Trial Judge did however observe that it may be possible to use the third-party agreement as an unspecified method. This may imply that the Trial Judge still does not believe the CPM is a reliable method in this case.

This case highlights the most important transfer pricing concepts, namely, concepts that involve what functions were performed, what risks were assumed, and what assets were employed more specifically; the Trial Judge did not identify the risk in the comparable transaction. One can posit that the IRS is moving away from basic arm's-length principles in a manner that simply justifies its position and gets the best answer for it.

The most reiteration of Medtronic hopefully will answer those questions and particularly the breath of use for the CPM. Post-Trial Answers are due on February 4, 2022.

We observe that the *Amgen, Inc.* case, which is similar to *Medtronic*, has been recently filed with the US Tax Court. Here, gleaning from the petition filed in this case, the IRS asserted a USD 3.6 billion plus interest tax deficiency for taxable years 2010 to 2012. Proposed tax adjustments for taxable years 2013 to 2015 have also been issued. It appears the issues center around the Company's Puerto Rican manufacturing facility and how profits are allocated between the US company and this Puerto Rican manufacturing operations. The Answer to the Petition filed on August 2021 was filed in November 2021; thus, the case has been joined. While this case is just getting underway, it will prove interesting to follow in the wave of transfer pricing cases presently pursued by the IRS.

4.2 *Facebook Inc. and Subsidiaries v. Commissioner*, U.S. Tax Court Docket # 21959-16, Trial 10/18/2021

The key issue in Facebook is how it should value its intangible property, e.g., trademarks and copyrights, regarding its licensing transaction with its Irish affiliate. The IRS assessed the value here as USD 13.6 billion rather than the USD 6.5 billion by the taxpayer. The case appears to be a battle of experts and what is the appropriate valuation to acquire this intellectual property at the time of the transfer. The key issue for the court is whether the company paid its taxes on what an unrelated company to Facebook would have paid for Facebook's September 2010 platform technology.

The trial started in early 2020 where dozens of current and former Facebook employees testified. Following a 16-month delay due to the COVID-19 pandemic, the trial resumed in person in October 11, 2021, and is expected to pick up again in January 2022. The court as it continued heard vast amounts of testimony from researchers, consultants on matters of accountancy, and digital marketing and monetization efforts Market growth and whether intangible assets could be hidden from financial statements were pursued by the IRS Counsel.

Stay tuned—this will be an interesting analysis of Facebook's technology notwithstanding the significant money involved. It may also shed some light on the OECD's Approach to Highly Valuable Intangibles.

4.3. Amazon's Tax Fight with the EU

While not a US case per se, it involves one of a number of cases in which the European Union (EU) has challenged the transfer pricing practices of US multinational enterprises (MNEs).

More particularly, the European Commission challenged a transfer pricing ruling granted by Luxembourg to Amazon that applied to the years 2006 to 2014, when the Commission opened an investigation into that ruling. Here, the Commission said that Luxembourg offered Amazon illegal State Aid by allowing Amazon to underpay EUR 250 million through royalty payments attributable to European profits to an entity that was not taxable in Luxembourg. EU law generally prohibits Member States from granting certain selective advantages to one company that are not otherwise granted to others, hence, the State Aid issue. Those advantages may include applying a different tax treatment to one company over another by means of agreements made by the tax authority.

Generally, the European Commission argued that Amazon's holding company, which held the intellectual property that was licensed to its operating companies impermissibly shifting profit to the holding company, took advantage of a mismatch in the tax laws thus avoiding taxation under Luxembourg tax law. Accordingly, the holding companies' royalties were not taxed in Luxembourg because it was a tax transparent entity, nor were they taxed in the United States because they were not distributions to Amazon US. We note that since this transaction, anti-hybrid legislation in the EU and the United States have made such "mismatches" moot.

Amazon rejected the Commission's assessment because the Commission failed to establish that the rulings conveyed an advantage for the company, ignoring that the Operating Company paid an arm's-length pricing for the royalties and was a Luxembourg taxpayer. Amazon argued also that the Commission argued from the OECD Guidelines in place from 2017 which were not applicable to the tax years in issue.

The court held in favor of Luxembourg and Amazon, stating that the Commission failed to prove that the Luxembourg ruling granted an advantage to Amazon under the EU State Aid law. Specifically, the court noted that the Commission failed to understand the functions of the holding company in exploiting its intangible assets, which is critical in determining how much profit should be attributable to a company. Nor did the Commission prove an advantage in the use of the transfer pricing method.

There have been a number of similar cases brought by the Commission against US MNEs such as Nike and Apple involving State Aid claims. It will be interesting to see the impact of this case on those pending cases. Of course, given the changes in the OECD Transfer Pricing Guidelines and BEPS Actions as well as the US tax law, one may expect not to see many of these cases in the future.

4.4 *Eaton Corp. et. al v. Commissioners*

Eaton Corporation (Eaton) entered into two APAs with the IRS. The first was for Eaton's tax years 2001 to 2005. The second for its 2006 to 2010 tax years. The scope of the APAs was their related manufacturing plants in the Dominican Republic and Puerto Rico and Eaton Electrical, Inc. (Eaton Electrical).

In December 2016, the IRS notified Eaton that it was cancelling both APAs effective January 1, 2005, and January 1, 2006, respectively. The IRS asserted that Eaton had material deficiencies in APA compliance, to wit, noncompliance with the terms of the APA, errors in supporting data and computations of its transfer pricing methodologies. The cancelations resulted in tax deficiencies for 2005 and 2006 of USD 19.7 million and USD 55.3 million, respectively, plus accuracy-related penalties aggregating USD 51.6 million. Eaton contended that this cancelation was an abuse of discretion by the IRS.

On July 26, 2017, the US Tax Court held in favor of the IRS and particularly that Eaton did not transfer intangibles under section 367 and that Eaton's bonus payments represented employee compensation allowing Eaton a deduction under section 162. Specifically, the court acknowledged that there can be ground for a cancelation such as mistakes as to a material fact or failure to state a material fact. They noted that APA cancelations should be a rare occurrence and should only be done for valid reasons consistent with the Revenue Procedures.

The court evaluated nine cases of detail related to the APA negotiations and believed that the IRS had access to all relevant information. Interestingly, the court stated that a "different viewpoint is (not) the same as a misrepresentation." Significantly, Eaton reported the errors to the IRS where they became known. Accordingly, the court held in favor of the Eaton.[6] In October 2018, there was a hearing that Eaton and the IRS reached an agreement on certain cancelations of the APAs; however, the court needed to rule in the application, if any, of the penalties that were asserted. In a supplemental opinion released in October 2019, the IRS reasoned that Eaton was not liable for any penalties.[7] However, the court denied Eaton relief from double taxation under Revenue Procedure 99-32.

Cross Appeals were filed to the Sixth Circuit Court of Appeals. Eaton filed its brief on December 23, 2021. The IRS' brief is due January 24, 2022. Eaton is requesting,

6. *Eaton Corp. v. Commissioners*, T.C. Memo 2017, 147.
7. *Eaton Corp. v. Commissioners*, T.C. Memo No. 6.

generally, that the Tax Court's opinion be upheld, but challenging the court's denial of relief from double taxation. The IRS is seeking a reversal of the Tax Court's decisions.

In short, the issues before the Appellate Court per the Appellee's brief are:

(1) Whether the IRS must show valid grounds for cancelation of an APA.
(2) Whether the IRS unlawfully canceled its binding APAs because of mathematical errors in implementing the APAs, which were brought to the IRS' attention and corrected.
(3) Whether the IRS year late arguments to the Tax Court and lack of supervisory approval ban the application of penalties.
(4) Whether Eaton is entitled to relief of double taxation under Revenue Procedure 99-23 for overpayments to its foreign affiliates.

5 OECD GUIDANCE ON THE TRANSFER PRICING IMPLICATIONS OF COVID-19

5.1 Background

On December 18, 2020, the OECD published Guidance on the Transfer Pricing Implications of the COVID-19 Pandemic ("OECD Guidance"), providing guidance to taxpayers when applying the arm's-length principle and applying the OECD Transfer Pricing Guidelines for Multinational Enterprises and Tax Administrations 2017 ("OECD TPG") for periods impacted by the COVID-19 pandemic.[8]

This guidance emphasizes the use of the existing OECD TPG and the arm's-length principle to tackle difficulties caused or aggravated by the COVID-19 pandemic. It focuses upon transfer pricing and operating transactions but notably does not deal with transfer pricing of financial transactions such as interest on intragroup debt; other important intracompany transactions, such as management fees, are also not dealt with in the OECD Guidance.

The OECD Guidance should not be viewed as an extension nor as a modification of the OECD TPG.

5.2 The Analysis

5.2.1 Comparability Analysis

COVID-19 has created challenges in the execution of comparability analyses, particularly because sole reliance on historical data to determine transfer pricing in the very unique economic situation encountered in 2020 ("FY20") has in many cases become

8. The section was derived from a Baker McKenzie Client Alert dated January 31, 2021, authorized by Marc M Levey (NY), Donna McComber (DC and Chris Raybould (Toronto)). *See also* Wrappe and Felgran, "Insight: Its Different This Time Pandemic Induced Recession Drives Transfer Pricing Changes Tax Management Transfer Pricing Report," June 26, 2020.

unreliable as well as that years data may not be publically available until 2021. Taxpayers and tax administrations therefore need to adopt a practical approach to address these timing issues and other related information deficiencies. The first section of the OECD Guidance outlines several possible approaches and considerations that may support the preparation of comparability analyses for FY20:

- Use publicly available information documenting the effect of the pandemic on the economically relevant characteristics of the controlled transaction, and analyze financial information of the MNE group and/or parties to the transaction (e.g., sales volume, capacity utilization, costs, government assistance or intervention, interim financial statements, macroeconomic and industry-specific indicators, statistical analysis). It is important to recognize that where interim (e.g., quarterly) financial information for independent firms is evaluated, there may be significant variability among companies regarding the impacts of COVID-19.
- The use of taxpayer financial forecasts and/or budgets to support the manner in which arm's-length prices were set and subsequently to compute adjustments to actual results may be an appropriate way to address the impacts of COVID-19, where P&L variances attributed to COVID-19 can be demonstrated. Companies with a record of establishing periodic budgets for their operations should be prepared to demonstrate the historic reliability of those budgets in order to enhance the basis for attributing changes in financial outcomes to COVID-19.
- In line with the OECD Transfer Pricing Guidelines (OECD Guidance), contemporaneous uncontrolled transactions are considered the most reliable information for comparability and may be publicly or internally available reflecting the unusual economic outcomes of the pandemic. When contemporaneous information is not available (e.g., when using the TNMM), the OECD Guidance prescribes to use "whatever current year information is available" to support the transfer prices.
- Tax authorities should be flexible, and taxpayers should use reasonable commercial judgement supplemented by contemporaneous information. The OECD Guidance also discusses the advantages of using the outcome-testing approach (as opposed to the price-setting approach used by some tax authorities), such as providing for flexibility to taxpayers, as well as the option of using more than one transfer pricing method for corroborative purposes. The timing of available information can impact the usefulness of this approach if, for example, transfer pricing adjustments after the close of the financial period are barred or limited by local legislation (e.g., post-closing changes that reduce taxable income are not allowed). It may be possible to include price adjustment mechanisms in controlled transactions combined with the outcome-testing approach. These adjustments should be formalized in intercompany agreements, if possible.
- Comparability analyses should include the actual economic circumstances of the controlled transaction. Hence, sole reliance on precedents such as financial

outcomes contemporaneous to the global financial crisis 2008/2009 would be viewed as inadequate because the impacts of the COVID-19 crisis may differ significantly from those of the 2008/2009 global financial crisis.
- The use of loss-making comparable companies may be appropriate where reliability can be demonstrated (i.e., the comparable companies should assume similar levels of risk and be similarly impacted by the pandemic). In these cases, outcomes such as similar revenue declines as well as characteristics, such as similar industries and similar supply chains, are critical components of the analysis. Modeling may help illustrate these outcomes.

5.2.2 Losses and the Allocation of COVID-19 Specific Costs

During the COVID-19 pandemic, many MNE groups have incurred losses due to challenges including reduced demand, difficulty in obtaining supply of goods or services, or exceptional and nonrecurring operating costs (e.g., expenditure on personal protective equipment, reconfiguration of workspaces to enable physical distancing, specific IT infrastructure). The allocation of these losses or COVID-19 specific costs between related entities increases the complexity of applying the arm's-length principle and the risk of disputes with tax authorities. The OECD Guidance outlines three main issues for consideration to mitigate this risk:

(i) The allocation of profits or losses between related parties to an arrangement should follow the allocation of risks as described in Chapter I of the OECD TPG to be consistent with an arm's-length arrangement. The OECD Guidance specifically addresses the case of entities operating under limited-risk arrangements and emphasizes the following points:
   - Though the term "limited-risk" is commonly used in transfer pricing, it is not defined in the OECD TPG, and the functions performed, assets used and risks assumed by "limited-risk" entities may vary. It is impossible to establish as a general rule that these entities should or should not incur losses; rather, the facts, circumstances and contractual provisions need to be analyzed on a case-by-case basis. This statement may provide some relief to taxpayers with limited-risk entities bearing losses as a result of COVID-19, provided these losses can be further supported at arm's length.
   - According to the OECD TPG, limited or low-risk enterprises are typically not expected to generate losses for a long period of time. It is thus possible for the limited-risk enterprises to generate losses, albeit for a limited time, provided these losses are supported by a robust comparability analysis and contractual provisions.
   - Whether a limited-risk enterprise can incur a loss will be largely informed by the risks (albeit limited) that the enterprise generally assumes. For example, a limited-risk distributor that assumes some marketplace risks may, at arm's length, earn a loss due to the decline in demand as a result of COVID-19. Conversely, it will not be appropriate

to allocate losses associated with the decline in demand if the limited-risk entity does not bear these risks. Ultimately, the determination of the extent of an arm's-length loss should be based upon a comparability analysis, following the most appropriate transfer pricing method to the circumstances.

- The OECD Guidance advises that any changes to the risks assumed by a party before and after COVID-19, and to the allocation of losses, are likely to come under the scrutiny of tax administrations. Consideration should be given to reexamining whether, prior to the outbreak of COVID-19, the accurate delineation of the transaction and resulting allocation of risks was supportable. If a prior risk allocation is recognized under an accurate delineation for a reallocation of that risk to be accepted, it must be supported by an updated facts-and-circumstances analysis, along with evidence of similar commercial arrangements between independent parties under comparable circumstances. In this respect, the guidance in Chapter IX of the OECD TPG in relation to business restructurings may be relevant.
- Based on this OECD Guidance, MNEs looking to allocate or share the burden of losses with limited-risk entities should ensure that its approach: (i) reflects an accurate allocation of risks between entities prior to COVID-19, or can be substantiated by an updated facts-and-circumstances analysis reflecting any new risks borne or activities performed by the entity, and (ii) be supported by an appropriate comparability analysis.

(ii) The allocation of exceptional, nonrecurring operating costs, as a result of COVID-19 should be based on an assessment of how they would have been allocated between independent parties under comparable circumstances:

- The arm's-length allocation of these costs should align with the delineation of the controlled transaction; i.e., the party responsible for performing the activities and assuming the risks associated with such costs would typically bear such costs. If, however, these exceptional costs are centrally borne by one entity of the MNE group, it may be appropriate to charge out those costs to the other parties benefiting from them.
- The OECD Guidance clarifies that certain operating costs resulting from COVID-19 (e.g., teleworking costs) may not be exceptional or nonrecurring if they become permanent or long term.
- Reference should also be made to market conditions, such as the competitiveness of the industry, for the allocation of exceptional costs.
- When performing a comparability analysis, exceptional costs need to be considered carefully in three main instances; (i) they should generally be excluded from the net profit indicator of the tested party and comparables, unless they are associated with the accurately delineated controlled transaction; (ii) it is important to consider whether these costs should be included in the cost basis of the controlled transaction

and, when included, whether to be passed through at cost or with a profit element; and (iii) adjustments for accounting inconsistency between the controlled and uncontrolled transactions may be required to improve comparability (e.g., when exceptional costs are accounted for as operating items in one jurisdiction and as nonoperating items in another).

(iii) Intercompany agreements may be appropriately revised, modified, or revoked as a result of the COVID-19 pandemic, including through the invocation of force majeure clauses, though caution should be taken with any such approach:
  - Renegotiating the terms of intercompany agreements, including pricing terms, as a result of COVID-19 should be well documented and substantiated by evidence of similar unrelated party behavior operating under comparable circumstances.
  - In renegotiating the terms of an intercompany agreement, the OECD Guidance advises that consideration about the options realistically available to the parties and the long-term effects on the profit potential of the parties should be made to assess whether the new terms of the agreement (including the revised pricing and any potential compensation for the renegotiation itself) represent the best interest of the parties. The parties should likewise consider whether indemnification to the "harmed" party is required as a result of a renegotiation.

Where one party to a controlled transaction seeks to invoke force majeure, the agreement and underlying legal framework should form the starting point of the transfer pricing analysis. The OECD Guidance does not define force majeure in the context of the pandemic and instead defers to the contractual definition of force majeure and the conduct of the parties to determine whether the invocation of the force majeure clause is permissible under applicable law. The OECD Guidance further notes that the companies should consider the long-term nature of the relationships and short-term nature of any related disruption before invoking the force majeure clause. Where the agreement does not contain such a clause, companies may seek to assert that a renegotiation would have occurred at arm's length based on a similar basis; however, tax administrations are advised to carefully review these assertions, given the transaction and economically relevant circumstances.

A review of existing contractual arrangements and past year transfer pricing documentation will most often be the starting point for determining and supporting the allocation of risks and losses among related parties. That being said, the COVID-19 situation has created circumstances that often exceed what was reasonably anticipated in intragroup arrangements, and these circumstances need to be identified and quantified. Further, many groups have adapted their governance and decision-making processes to cope with this unique environment.

5.2.3 *Government Assistance Programs*

Due to COVID-19, many governments have provided grants, subsidies, and/or loans; they have also initiated job retention programs or introduced additional tax incentives to eligible taxpayers to mitigate the decline in business activity due to COVID-19. The OECD Guidance provides that these programs potentially have transfer pricing implications, as they may be provided to a member of an MNE group (i.e., the tested party) directly or made available to independent parties within the market so that the behavior and financial results of enterprises engaged in comparable transactions are altered. Due consideration must be given to the terms and conditions of these government assistance programs (such as the availability, substance, duration and take-up).

The extent to which the receipt of government assistance is an economically relevant characteristic may vary. The OECD refers to the provision of a wage subsidy, a government debt guarantee or short-term liquidity support as examples that may be more economically relevant as they may directly affect the controlled transaction and comparable transactions between independent parties. If the government assistance can be considered an economically relevant characteristic, the OECD Guidance directs taxpayers to evaluate and note the impact thereof on accurately delineating the controlled transaction and performing the comparability analysis (as outlined in paragraph 1.33 of the OECD Guidance) and to include this assessment as a part of the documentation to support the transfer pricing analysis.

Taxpayers can rely on existing guidance under the OECD Guidance on other local market features by analogy, which provides that government interventions should generally be treated as conditions of the market and be considered in evaluating the taxpayer's transfer price in that market. The analysis of receiving government assistance as a local market feature (including the nature of assistance) may help determine not only whether its receipt affects the price of a controlled transaction but also how it affects the comparables and the arm's-length prices of uncontrolled transactions.

The potential effect of the receipt of government assistance on the pricing of a controlled transaction will depend on economically relevant characteristics thereof, such as the availability, purpose, duration or other conditions imposed by the government, and the allocation of the economically significant risks. In addition, the OECD Guidance indicates that the economic circumstances of the market in which the party receiving government assistance operates could influence the pricing. For example, factors such as the level of competition, the elasticity of the demand, or the availability of the benefits to competitors in the market could be relevant factors in determining whether receiving government assistance would be translated into an entity's pricing strategy. Furthermore, the impact of price change on taxpayers' sales to third-party customers would also be relevant to determine the impact of the government subsidy on the controlled transaction.

The OECD Guidance recognizes that the impact of different government assistance available in a market may impose additional challenges to the comparability analysis, as government assistance and the specific circumstances of the COVID-19 pandemic may vary across different markets, and hence may impact the arm's-length prices of uncontrolled transactions in different ways. Here, the OECD indicates that, when using one-sided methods, adopting a mechanical approach without further analysis (e.g., recognizing the government assistance as an extraordinary income, offsetting the government assistance against the party's cost base) should be avoided. Moreover, when identifying comparables, taxpayers are urged to consider not only the availability, the duration, and the purpose of the government programs but also the divergence in accounting treatment of the subsidies under different accounting standards, which may impact different levels of profitability. For example, the accounting treatment of a conditional loan differs from that of an outright grant.

Absent reliable local market comparables, adjustments may be required to account for the impact of government assistance on the arm's-length prices of goods transferred or services provided between uncontrolled taxpayers. However, one challenge that the OECD Guidance does not address is the lack of detail in, and the availability of, publicly available data on comparables to conduct this level of analysis. This is particularly so when using European or Asian databases. This level of information is also not available in the United States as there is no explicit GAAP accounting standard for the accounting for government assistance. FASB is developing rules that will require public companies to disclose the amount of their government subsidies.

The OECD Guidance also discusses the impact of receipt of government assistance on the allocation of risk in a controlled transaction. Chapter I of the OECD Guidance provides that the provision of government assistance to an associated party will not change the allocation of risk in a controlled transaction for transfer pricing purposes as the contractual arrangements, the entity's capability and actual performance of decision-making functions remain unchanged.

The OECD Guidance does not address the allocation of risk where a limited-risk entity that has contractually transferred all its risks to a related counterparty in exchange for a guaranteed return receives a government subsidy. Would this subsidy offset the transfer pricing adjustment due from the counterparty? One argument could be that an independent enterprise in a similar circumstance would have insisted on payment from the counterparty despite receiving the government subsidy. In analyzing this type of situation, consideration should be given to local legislation that might prohibit the direct or indirect transfer of government grants or subsidies to other parties.

The OECD Guidance also does not address unilateral directions from individual jurisdictions as to how any government assistance should factor into determining transfer prices, which may create challenges for taxpayers where such local direction may run counter to the OECD Guidance or be contrary to the views of other jurisdictions and complicate any potential resolution of disputes through the Mutual Agreement Procedure.

The transfer pricing treatment of government assistance can have a very significant impact on entities that are remunerated using a targeted return approach (e.g., a cost-based method or a targeted operating margin). Of course, the application of this assistance may vary from jurisdiction to jurisdiction.

The OECD maintains that even in times of a pandemic, APAs remain a compelling instrument to achieve tax certainty and prevent tax disputes. However, taxpayers and tax administrations can only rely on the agreements in APAs if the critical assumptions on which the APA is agreed remain valid. It is likely that the COVID-19 pandemic and the response of governments have dramatically affected the economic and market conditions, which may lead to a breach of the critical assumptions, or cause the need for a revision to the critical assumptions.

For existing APAs, tax administrations should consider case by case whether a breach in critical assumptions should lead to a revision, cancelation or revocation of the APA. The OECD Guidance states that a mere change in business results during the pandemic would likely not result in a breach of a critical assumption. Instead, for both existing and new APAs, the OECD calls on tax administrations to apply a flexible and collaborative approach in dealing with the unusual circumstances caused by the pandemic. Many tax administrations have set up COVID-19 teams to address these issues, e.g., the US APMA team. The OECD Guidance correctly suggests that tax administrations can consider several approaches to mitigate a breach of critical assumptions or failure to adhere to the agreed transfer pricing system, such as the following:

- Separating an APA into distinct phases to address: (1) the period affected by the pandemic; and (2) the post-COVID-19 period. This has the attractiveness of simply focusing on the COVID-19 year(s) as an aberration.
- Incorporating provisions in the APA that the impact of COVID-19 will be analyzed separately, including an agreement on a mechanism for potential adjustments. In this instance, adjustments will be deferred until data relevant to COVID-19 is available for some comparison. A review of the specific impact upon the taxpayer's industry would be most helpful.
- Extending the period of the APA to mitigate the short-term impact of the APA, in particular when the extension is combined with testing the transfer pricing on a multi-period basis.
- Applying a multi-period term-test to assess whether the transfer pricing complies with the APA provisions, rather than evaluating the transfer pricing for each separate financial year. Here multiyear averaging may smooth over the results of COVID-19. In addition, evaluating the arm's-length nature of the transfer pricing based on a targeted range rather than a fixed target may give taxpayers some flexibility to address the impact of COVID-19.

The OECD emphasizes that taxpayers need to provide tax administrations with transparency regarding the impact of COVID-19 on their operations. Taxpayers are expected to inform tax authorities proactively when they foresee that the critical assumptions of an APA may be impacted by the pandemic. The OECD lists various examples of sources of information that taxpayers can use to document the impact of the pandemic, such as segmented P&L data, updated budgetary/revenue projections and modifications to legal agreements or information about third-party behavior. An interesting approach would be attempt to normalize or model the taxpayer's P&L statement for the specific impact of COVID-19 on its results. This can be done by estimating lost revenues and fluctuations to variable costs to show to which extent

COVID-19 has created a gap between a taxpayer's expectations and the actual operating results. This modeling can be most helpful as it would depict the situation that is unique to the taxpayer, which may not be the same as some of the comparable firms used in the APA Request. It is stressed that all parts of the respective documentation should contain a clear assessment that the perceived impact is attributable to the pandemic.

When considering the implications of COVID-19 for a transfer pricing analysis, taxpayers should document their specific information relating to how and the extent to which they have been impacted, and the measures they took to minimize the impact. This, with the financial modeling noted above, should be quite helpful in any future discussions and negotiations with the respective tax administration(s).

Taxpayers who have entered into APAs that contain guaranteed profit margins for low-risk entities may be willing to rediscuss the application of the APA conditions to 2020. This can prove a difficult exercise in practice. APAs in the US where COVID-19 has an impact will be reviewed and considered by a special COVID-19 committee. Each jurisdiction may take different approaches to this issue, so it is important to consult with the local team to understand that local criteria.

On March 23, 2021, the IRS issued its announcement and Report Concerning Advance Pricing Agreements, Announcement 2021, by which provided general information on the operation of the office. Despite unprecedented challenges of the COVID-19 pandemic, new APA filing remained constant. APA Renewals, however, not significant high levels, and new bilateral APAs slightly declined. However, the pandemic and remote working efforts did slow down the time to process APAs. APA Terms increase on average from typical five year terms to six year terms. The CPM/Transactional Net Margin Method continued to be the most commonly applied method. Most interesting is that many taxpayers are reevaluating their business models due to COVID-19.

On November 22, 2021, the OECD released statistics covering 118 jurisdictions regarding the increased caseload of MAPs and APAs. For example, in the United States, the APA closed a total of 295 transfer pricing cases, Canada had 74 cases and Mexico 19 cases. Presumably, many of this increase was the need for certainty in the COVID-19 environment. Interestingly, in Germany, the number of cases increased to 747 with similar percentage increases in France, Belgium and Spain. As for MAP cases, almost 2,500 were started in recent years within 25 jurisdictions leading about 95% of these cases. Approximately 75% of those cases are resolved successfully with only 3% closed without mutual relief. The average time to close MAP and APA cases increased by 4.5 months, most likely due to remote working conditions from COVID-19. The Unites States was one example of this.

6 THE MULTISTATE TAX COMMISSION STEPS UP ITS COLLABORATION AND ENFORCEMENT INITIATIVES

The Multistate Tax Commission is set to revamp its transfer pricing collaboration and enforcement initiatives following the first public meeting of its State Intercompany

Transactions Advisory Service ("SITAS") Committee in over four years. On March 23, the SITAS Committee hosted representatives from state revenue agencies, practitioners, taxpayers, and other members of the public in a virtual conference to present the results of a multistate survey regarding intercompany transactions and transfer pricing. Notably, 70% of the states surveyed indicated that confidential information-sharing agreements with other states for audits would be "extremely valuable." To this end, the SITAS Committee Chair encouraged interested states to execute the State Intercompany Transactions Advisory Service Committee Commitment and Exchange of Information Agreement. Furthermore, 18% of the participating states responded that they currently utilize an advance pricing agreement process, whereby taxpayers currently under audit can agree with the state on a specific transfer pricing methodology to be used over a specific timeframe. Indiana as an example is stepping up its APA process. The vast majority of participating states also reported being very interested in developing their transfer pricing mechanics and abilities through formal training sessions to identify intercompany transactions prone to improper income shifting.

Looking further ahead into 2021 and beyond, we expect the SITAS Committee to continue to build on the momentum set by its most recent meeting with the goal of securing the interest and required financial backing of Member States to move the program forward after years of inactivity.

7 BIDEN AGENDA FACES REVENUE DOUBT WITH BOOST LIKELY LEFT OUT

A major IRS enforcement boost will likely be omitted from any forthcoming top-line revenue estimate of the Democratic's tax-and-spend package. The complicating question is whether the legislation will be fully paid for as Biden promised.

The Biden administration estimates a better-funded IRS with USD 400 billion over a decade through more aggressive audits of corporations and wealthy taxpayers. However, under budget rules set by Congress and the Executive Branch, the government's nonpartisan analysts cannot officially count money that will be spent as increasing revenue when estimating the cost of legislation. Accordingly, the Congressional Budget Office will likely limit its analysis of the IRS plan to a footnote in its official report because the increased funding will not be "score-able." This means that the revenue will be likely much less than that which the Biden administration projected.

What this all means is that IRS examinations of cross-border transactions, including but not limited to transfer pricing, may be significantly affected. With the IRS very limited with its resources, there is limited ability to train revenue agents or any changes regarding current tax matters. Further, IRS will be required to focus on those cases where the recouping of tax dollars is significant, or the deterrent factor is essential. Excepted from this criteria will likely be advance compliance programs such as APAs.

Having said all this, the IRS announced on January 21, 2022, that it plans to hire up to two hundred attorneys nationwide to take on perceived abusive tax schemes. These attorneys are supposed to provide advice during audits, handle cases in Tax Court, and serve on trial teams. The IRS' victory in Coca-Cola, Altera and its performance in

Medtronics indicate that the IRS will not be intimidated from taking on big cases and has learned well how to handle these cases.

8 CONCLUSION

So how do these developments bode for the future of transfer pricing? Of course, the Tax Court decisions and pending cases are fact specific in this highly factual area, but there is always a message to be learned. Coca-Cola makes me wonder about the propriety of Coca-Cola's legal agreements. They argued that the Supply Points possessed nonroutine marketing intangibles, but this argument was not supported by their own legal agreements. In fact, the Trial Judge focused on the fact that Supply Points merely and passively held Service Co's marketing expenses without any headcount to monitor nor manage the function. This later point was indeed fatal to Coca-Cola's argument. Also, how was the marketing intangible, or simply put the justification for the profit allocation to Supply Points, represented in the prior Closing Settlement Agreement where the formulary split of 10-50-50 with Coca-Cola and Supply Points each at 50% of the residual profit.

The starting point to assert that Coca-Cola's affiliates possess economically beneficial marketing intangibles starts with the legal relationship by and between the respective parties. Hence, one would typically look to the Distribution and/or License Agreements for those positions as was done by the court. This was done in a painstaking manner by the Trail Judge. So the clear message here is pay close attention to your legal agreements and whether your transfer pricing policy is closely aligned with it. OECD Action Items 8 to 10 make this point abundantly clear. Further, there did not appear to be a delineation of what branding costs or "non-routine" costs were incurred by the Supply Points and whether those costs, as opposed to basic advertising costs, give rise to a marketing intangible. The Trail Judge here makes a clear distinction between advertising costs which are an annual expense versus those susceptible to capitalization, i.e., branding costs.

Another significant lesson from the Tax Court's opinion is that the Trial Judge thoroughly reviewed Supply Point's Profit and Loss Statement. This is typically done by seasoned transfer pricing practitioners because the easiest way to understate a party's functional and risk profile is to understand how they spend their money.

Further, this decision as well as that pending *in 3M Co. v. Commissioner* may give some much-needed guidance to the blocked income concept under the 1994 regulations.

As for *Medtronics*, the CUT method, a primary method, must assure that adjustments for functions and risks are couched in the factual profile of the tested party. This is true whether one is using a pure CUT or a modified CUT, sometimes known as an "unspecified method." Absent this analysis, the IRS will always default to a CPM method because not only it is easy but also it can be more fashioned to the IRS desires. Knowing this, prudence would suggest using the CPM as a corroborative measure to support the CUT or unspecified method.

Facebook presents the unique and difficult issue of benchmarking a highly valuable item of intangible property. Contemporary databases are not always helpful here because those types of companies are virtually integrated; thus, using them as a CUT is difficult at best. This is why the OECD issued its "Hand-to-Value Intangible Guide" to give some level of assistance to this difficult issue besides defaulting to a profit split or residual approach. Facebook may be the first case to give us some judicial thinking on the significant issue. Amazon's (and Nike's) battle with the EU and its State Aid cases may by the nature of recent global tax reforms be minimized in the future—hopefully. But two of the cases are on appeal to the European Court of Justice, so stay tuned as again they are grappling with hard-to-value intangibles.

Eaton presents the simple case of whether and under what standard the IRS may cancel a binding APA. Among the key questions to be answered are what is the precise criteria for an APA to be canceled. This case however seems to be an outlier as in the twenty-five plus years of the APA program, this issue has never arisen, and the vast majority of taxpayers in the APA program are highly compliant.

But the real message comes out of the Biden administration to not adequately fund the enforcement efforts of the IRS. This may force the IRS to simply put its efforts where it can achieve either significant revenues or a strong deterrent value. This may be contradicted by the IRS' recent announcement to hire two hundred attorneys to assist in tax controversies, but it is not clear if these attorneys are new additions or replacing its depleted staff. Otherwise, prudent taxpayers may go through the APA routes for pure certainty and MAPs to avoid double taxation despite the time commitment of a MAP. And herein lies the future for dispute resolution in the transfer pricing area unless taxpayers can pay the toll of large litigation.

The OECD's Guidance on issues involving COVID-19 is particularly useful, and APMA has paid great heed to it. The issue however regarding comparable date is difficult because of the time lag in receiving relevant date that has companies which may or may not have been so impacted. Using ranges of operating profit does give flexibility to taxpayers during the COVID-19 years more so than simply targeting a specific number. Using contemporaneous forecasts as a measure to show arm's-length returns as if the forecast were met can be a useful tool in arguing that the transfer pricing policy sought to achieve arm's length as well as using multiyear averages to smooth out the results. Of course, in COVID-19, there were "winners and losers," so this approach is most useful for those companies which were adversely impacted.

There is a lot to look forward to as these cases and applications of the OECD Guidance unfold!

CHAPTER 4

Transfer Pricing Developments in Developing Countries and Emerging Economies

Mukesh Butani & Seema Kejriwal

This chapter focuses on transfer pricing developments in emerging markets and developing countries in the calendar year 2021. It discusses changes in transfer pricing legislation and practices, together with landmark court decisions in select jurisdictions. The chapter also addresses developments in transfer pricing guidance for developing countries and emerging economies by the Organisation for Economic Co-operation and Development (OECD) and the United Nations (UN). It also seeks to provide insights into the interplay of key global developments with transfer pricing policies of developing countries and emerging economies. Finally, the chapter attempts to provide an outlook for transfer pricing in developing countries and emerging economies, in light of the combined developments in 2021.

The IMF World Economic Outlook[1] classifies 40 economies[2] as "advanced," based on such factors as high per capita income, exports of diversified goods and services, and greater integration into the global financial system. The remaining countries (156) are classified as "emerging market and developing" economies. Of the 156 countries, 59 are classified as low income developing countries (LIDC).[3] Countries which are not LIDCs are classified as emerging market and middle income economies. Thus, for the purposes of this chapter, countries other than those classified as advanced economies have been considered. Of the 40 advanced countries, 37[4] are members of the BEPS Inclusive Framework. Of the 156 identified emerging market and developing economies, 88 are members of the BEPS Inclusive Framework.[5]

Emerging market and developing countries are spread across geographies – of the 156 countries, Asia comprises 40% (62 countries), Sub-Saharan Africa comprises 29% (45 countries), Latin America and the Caribbean comprises 21% (33 countries) and

1. Statistical Appendix, Page 5 to IMF World Economic Outlook, October 2021.
2. The forty advanced economies are Andorra, Australia, Austria, Belgium, Canada, Cyprus, the Czech Republic, Denmark, Estonia, Finland, France, Germany, Greece, Hong Kong SAR, Iceland, Ireland, Israel, Italy, Japan, Korea, Latvia, Lithuania, Luxembourg, Macao SAR2, Malta, the Netherlands, New Zealand, Norway, Portugal, Puerto Rico, the Slovak Republic, Slovenia, Spain, San Marino, Singapore, Sweden, Switzerland, Taiwan Province of China, United Kingdom, and United States.
3. Syria has been excluded due to lack of a fully developed database. Thus, out of 156 countries, 59 are low income developing countries, 96 are emerging and middle income economies and 1 (Syria) does not have adequate information. Refer Statistical Appendix mentioned in *supra* n. 1.
4. Cyprus, Puerto Rico and Taiwan are not part of the BEPS Inclusive Framework.
5. The balance 14 out of 141 countries in the BEPS Inclusive Framework are not covered by the IMF World Economic Outlook. These are Anguilla, Bermuda, the Cayman Islands, Curacao, the Faroe Islands, Gibraltar, Greenland, Guernsey, the Isle of Man, Jersey, Liechtenstein, Monaco, Montserrat, and the Turks and Caicos Islands.

Europe comprises 10% (16 countries). Tax and transfer pricing developments are probably impacted more by regional influences than by virtue of grouping as emerging markets or developing countries. For example, all emerging and developing countries in the European region, barring two, are part of the BEPS Inclusive Framework; however, in Sub-Saharan Africa, only twenty-two out of the forty-five emerging and developing countries are part of the BEPS Inclusive Framework.

1 KEY TRANSFER PRICING LEGISLATION DEVELOPMENTS

1.1 India

The budget of 2021 introduced certain transfer pricing measures with respect to the transfer pricing audit time limit and computation of minimum alternate tax for additional income from advance pricing agreements (APAs) or secondary adjustments.[6] Further, the application of transfer pricing safe harbor rules was extended to the financial year 2020-2021.[7] While it was widely anticipated, no relief was given on the margins, which continue to remain the same for a fifth consecutive year, without giving any cognizance to COVID conditions. India's tax administration, during tax audits, continues to recognize captive entities as risk-bearing entities bearing single customer and other risks, while taxpayers generally consider captive entities as largely de-risked entities. No reduction in safe harbors even during COVID presents a dichotomy in the approach of the administration toward risk issues for captive entities.

1.2 Mexico

The Mexican Government introduced its Economic Package for 2022 on September 8, 2021, proposing a slew of tax changes to the country's transfer pricing rules.[8] The domestic intercompany transactions have been proposed to be treated the same way as foreign intercompany transactions; that is, the obligation to keep transfer pricing documentation will be applicable in operations with domestic related parties.[9] Further, comparability elements would be required to be documented for each transaction for each related party including the comparability adjustments.[10] Information of the

6. Finance Act, 2021 dated March 28, 2021, available at https://egazette.nic.in/WriteReadData/2021/226208.pdf introduced section 115JB(2D) that provides where there is an increase in book profits of the previous year due to income of past year or years on the account of APA (section 92CC of the Income Tax Act, 1961) or secondary adjustments (section 92CE of the Income Tax Act, 1961), the taxpayer can file for recomputation, and further the Indian government by notification has prescribed Rule 10RB in the Income Tax Rules, 1962 for computation of tax relief in this regard. The ramification of such a provision is that it ensures that the Minimum Alternative Tax payable on past income, for the previous year does not surpass the same after including transfer pricing adjustment.
7. CBDT, Notification No. 117/2021/F. No. 370142/44/2021-TPL dated September 24, 2021.
8. https://home.kpmg/us/en/home/insights/2021/09/tnf-mexico-transfer-pricing-proposals-in-economic-package-for-2022.html.
9. Article 76, Mexican Income Tax Law (MITL).
10. Article 179, MITL.

comparable companies would need to be for the year under analysis, and the use of information from two or more years would only be acceptable if it is shown that the business cycle or commercial acceptance of a product covers several years.[11]

It has been proposed that companies will be required to prepare Statutory Tax Report, and their related parties performing intercompany transactions will be required to file returns.[12] The determination of accrued income and authorized deductions would need to consider not only the prices but also the profit margins that independent companies would have used, being consistent with the transfer pricing rules. Lastly, the deadline for filing the local file and informative transfer pricing return was also extended.

Special proposals have been made regarding *Maquiladoras*[13] that will only be able to comply with their transfer pricing obligations through safe harbor rules established in the Mexican Income Tax Law.[14] Further, under the Economic Package 2022, such companies have now been restricted from obtaining an APA.[15]

1.3 Malaysia

The Malaysian government enacted its proposed legislation on transfer pricing on January 1, 2021, which included provisions for imposition of penalty for the failure to furnish transfer pricing documentation within a stipulated time, granting power to tax authorities to disregard a structure in controlled transaction or a transaction between related parties and to re-characterize any structure adopted by a person and imposition of surcharge of 5% for transfer pricing adjustments even when such adjustments do not result in additional tax liability.[16] Such new measures evidences a punitive approach with more powers being granted to the Malaysian Tax Administration.

The Malaysian Inland Revenue Board (MIRB) also released a report on common transfer pricing issues identified in relation to intragroup services and MIRB's expectations from taxpayers in banking, insurance, oil and gas sectors, after conducting discussions with stakeholders.[17]

1.4 Kenya

The budget for 2021-2022 brought about notable developments to the Transfer Pricing mechanism of Kenya, including amendment to the definition of Permanent Establishment which reduced the duration required by service providers (on behalf of nonresidents) and aggregated the time of connected activities in calculation of duration;

11. Article 179, MITL.
12. Article 76-A, MITL.
13. A Maquiladora is a foreign-run manufacturing operation in Mexico that exports goods to other countries.
14. Article 182, MITL.
15. https://research.ibfd.org/#/doc?url=/data/tns/docs/html/tns_2021-03-08_mx_1.html.
16. The Finance Act 2020, December 31, 2020, Government of Malaysia.
17. https://home.kpmg/us/en/home/insights/2021/06/tnf-malaysia-common-transfer-pricing-issues-arising-intra-group-services.html.

included any dependent agent acting on behalf of the principal playing a material role in conclusion of contracts as well as introduced activities like warehousing and farming under the scope of the definition.[18] It also proposed the introduction of requirement for the Ultimate Parent Entity (UPE) of an MNE to submit a return to the Commissioner containing information related to revenue, employees, tangible assets, among others. Such a provision has been introduced to align with the OECD BEPS Action Plan 13 on CbC reporting and will result in additional transfer pricing documentation.[19] This provision has come into effect from January 2022.

1.5 Morocco

Morocco introduced changes with respect to transfer pricing, introduced by its parliament as part of the Finance Law. Some of the significant changes were:

- introduction of a sanction for failure to produce transfer pricing documentation of 0.5% of the amount of the transactions concerned with a minimum amount of MAD 200,000 per concerned fiscal year;
- limitation of the scope related to the obligation to submit transfer pricing documentation to large enterprises with reported turnover or gross assets (reported on balance sheet) equal to or greater than MAD 50,000,000;
- clarification of the scope of the preliminary tax consultation request from the tax administration regarding the application of the tax legislation to specific situations.

1.6 Jordan

The Hashemite Kingdom of Jordan issued Executive Instructions No. 3 for 2021 dated September 16, 2021, detailing the transfer pricing Regulation covering multinational entity groups headquartered and/or operating in Jordan. The main provisions clarified by the instructions are set out below.

The instructions state that taxpayers are required to submit a disclosure form (TP disclosure form) if the total value of controlled transactions exceeds the threshold of JOD 500,000 within a period of twelve consecutive months. Article 4 of the instructions provides that the TP disclosure form must include details on specified information. The TP disclosure form has to be completed and filed by qualifying taxpayers together with the tax return within four months from the end of the financial year concerned.

The instructions clarify that taxpayers must specify and justify the reasons for choosing the applied TP method. Article 10 of the instructions adds the obligation to submit an affidavit from a certified accountant confirming the consistent application of

18. Budget Statement for Financial Year 2021/2022, "Building Back Better: Strategy for Resilient and Sustainable Economic Recovery and Inclusive Growth" available at, https://www.treasury.go.ke/wp-content/uploads/2021/06/FY-2021-22-Budget-Statement.pdf.
19. https://home.kpmg/content/dam/kpmg/ke/pdf/tax/2021/Budget-brief-2021-22-Kenya-final.pdf.

the TP policy of the group and its impact on the financial statements. However, the deadline and the format of the affidavit are to be clarified.

Articles 6, 7 and 8 of the instructions provide details regarding the format of the Country-by-Country Report (CbCR), Local File and Master File, respectively, and on the requirements for submitting these documents to the Jordan tax authority within twelve months from the end of the financial year concerned.

The instructions provide specific requirements on the expected content of the industry analysis in the Local File (i.e., major competitors, power of suppliers and buyers, availability of substitutes, size, demand and supply trends, etc.). The instructions also provide table 1, table 2 and table 3 templates for the CbCR, which are in line with the OECD format.

Article 10 of the instructions provides that if the taxpayer has adopted any of the TP methods for a related party transaction, the Jordanian tax authority expects the same TP method to be used consistently for subsequent tax years.[20]

1.7 South Africa

The South African Revenue Service (SARS) has published a proposed model for establishing an APA program in South Africa as well as the draft legislation.

The draft legislation deals, among other things, with the following:

- definitions of APA, APA application, advance pricing arrangement, affect transaction, arm's-length allocation, arm's-length transfer price, associated enterprise, compensating adjustment, transfer price, transfer pricing method;
- the purpose, scope and persons eligible to apply;
- fees for APAs; pre-application consultation;
- application for an APA;
- amendments to an application, withdrawing an application and rejection of an application;
- processing an application and finalization of an APA;
- compliance report, extension of an APA; and
- termination of an APA and record retention.[21]

1.8 Vietnam

Further to introduction of transfer pricing guidelines in late 2020, vide an official letter dated August 25, 2021, Vietnam has introduced guidelines for tax departments of the

20. Jordan—Jordan Issues Transfer Pricing Executive Instructions (September 27, 2021), News IBFD.
21. South Africa—South Africa Revenue Service Proposes Model for Establishing Advance Pricing Agreement Programme (December 17, 2021), News IBFD.

provinces and municipalities with respect to amendments made to its APA mechanism.[22] An APA would no longer include in its scope any contemplated or future transactions and can include only those transactions which have already occurred and have the basis for determining tax liabilities. Further, newly established enterprises are restricted from applying for an APA. Besides these changes, stricter documentation requirements have been introduced, and the maximum applicability period has been shortened from five years to three years. Further, commercial databases have officially been made the reference point for tax administration for conducting transfer pricing studies and APA application process.

While some of the abovementioned changes to the APA framework are stringent and may bring lesser legal certainty to taxpayers, the overall APA mechanism has been made holistic and clear for applicants.

1.9 Poland

The Polish government has announced the inauguration of a project entitled "Strengthening the Transfer Pricing Legal System Against Tax Evasive Behaviour." The project envisages the analysis and evaluation of current Polish transfer pricing regulations, including electronic reporting obligations (TPR). The aim of the project is to increase the competitiveness of Polish regulations and effectiveness of TPR.

The Minister of Finance emphasized that an important element of the project is the exchange of good practices with partner countries in the field of documentation obligations, electronic reporting and analysis. As part of this initiative, Poland established cooperation with five countries that are recognized as leaders in the field of competitive transfer pricing regulations, i.e., the United Kingdom, Germany, the Netherlands, Sweden and the United States. Experts from these countries will share their experiences and technological solutions with the Ministry of Finance officials.

The work of the project working group was formally launched on November 19, 2021. The project will run for two years and will be entirely financed by EU funds.[23]

1.10 Ghana

Ghana introduced new Transfer Pricing Regulations in late 2020 which repealed its old regulations. The 2020 Regulations not only maintain many of the provisions of the previous regulations but also provide requirements for more extensive information to be included in the annual TP return and in the TP documentation as detailed below.

Whereas TP documentation was required in the previous regulations, the 2020 Regulations now require that the TP documentation includes both a master file and a local file. The TP documentation is not required if the related party arrangement does

22. Official Letter No. 3194/TCT-DNL, August 25, 2021; Circular 45/2021/TT-BTC (Circular 45) dated June 18, 2021; Tax Administration and Decree 126/2020/ND-CP (Decree 126) dated December 5, 2020.
23. Poland: Poland Launches "Strengthening Transfer Pricing Legal System Against Tax Evasive Behaviour" Project (November 29, 2021), News IBFD.

not exceed the Ghana Cedi equivalent of USD 200,000. The 2020 Regulations, however, empower the GRA to aggregate two or more arrangements between related persons if they view the arrangements as tax avoidance schemes.

The 2020 Regulations also require the submission of a CbC report by the UPE of an MNE Group that is resident for tax purposes in Ghana and has annual consolidated group revenue of GHS 2.9 billion. A constituent entity, which is not the UPE, may file a CbC report if certain conditions are met. The CbC report is due twelve months after the last day of the relevant fiscal year of the MNE Group.

The 2020 Regulations now clearly distinguish between the TP return and the income tax return, and mark it as a stand-alone return to be filed annually. Therefore, penalties will be triggered for not meeting the filing requirements of the TP return and documentation.

1.11 Brazil

Brazil, currently not a member country of the OECD, has been aligning itself in the area of transfer pricing to eventually accede to OECD as a member country. An interministerial working group has been set up by the Brazilian Government for this purpose. Historically, Brazil has had its own isolated set of transfer pricing methods, which have deviated from arm's-length principle, thereby resulting in failure to prevent BEPS. In 2019, an extensive report entitled "Transfer Pricing in Brazil: Towards Convergence with the OECD Standard" was officially released. A survey was also launched seeking public collaboration in the development of safe harbors and other simplification measures on Brazilian transfer pricing matters.

The Brazilian Tax Department will need to train multiple tax inspectors to start reviewing transactions under the arm's-length principle. The identified issue with Brazil's transfer pricing regime, especially in practice, is that the margins are not adjusted according to the economic reality of a taxpayer. It is also important to understand the nontax and political environment of the country to track the progress of its accession to OECD. Besides continuing economic impact of COVID-19, 2022 is also the year of presidential election. Overall, the country's future accession wholly depends upon its capacity to successfully implement much-needed tax reforms.

1.12 Conclusion

It is evident that emerging markets and developing economies across regions have increased focus toward transfer pricing. Developments such as those in Poland indicate that governments in emerging economies recognize the need of aligning with best practices when it comes to transfer pricing administration. Even a country such as Ghana which is classified as an LIDC, and which is not a part of the BEPS Inclusive Framework, has recognized the importance of transfer pricing compliance and understanding transfer pricing impact in the context of global operations of an MNE by mandating submission of CbC reports. This increasing focus by governments indicates a recognition of need to plug tax leakages owing to transfer pricing, irrespective of the size of economy or administrative burden associated.

2 DISPUTE RESOLUTION: KEY RULINGS, APAs AND MAPs

2.1 Kenya

In October 2021, the Kenya Tax Appeal Tribunal delivered a judgment wherein the matter related to convergence of transfer pricing and customs methodologies. The taxpayer had adopted the transaction value method under customs for valuation and placed heavy reliance on its transfer pricing study, wherein the transactional net margin method (TNMM) was used to determine the transfer price and demonstrated that the transaction was at arm's length. On the other side, the KRA rejected the transaction value of the taxpayer and advocated that the deductive value method under customs should have been used. The KRA had doubts that the prices applied were not influenced by the group relationship of the seller and the buyer. The Tribunal ultimately ruled in favor of the taxpayer since the KRA was not able to demonstrate its case and that its decision rejecting the transaction value was wholly arbitrary. However, it is noteworthy that the KRA had a very strong case, and it should have merely relied on the transfer pricing documentation to point out that the TNMM method is equivalent to the deductive value method for customs purposes. This also points to an important facet on strengthening technical skills on transfer pricing and customs of the revenue officers.[24]

2.2 India

The Karnataka High Court of India ruled[25] that in the absence of management or control, no AE relationship can be established, even if the enterprises were deemed AEs under India's transfer pricing laws. Accordingly, transfer pricing provisions would not be applicable in such scenarios.

The Madras High Court ruled[26] that foreign-associated enterprises can be treated as tested party under Indian transfer pricing regulations. The Court also permitted the change of tested party during the course of audit proceedings.

In December 2020, the Madras High Court ruled[27] that a transfer of shares by parent to subsidiary contributed as a gift (without consideration) was not a gift in the circumstances of the taxpayer, and ruled that the income would be chargeable to tax as

24. https://mnetax.com/kenya-trial-to-bridge-transfer-pricing-and-customs-in-landmark-customs-audit-case-46336.
25. *Principal Commissioner of Income-tax v. Page Industries Ltd.* [2021] 431 ITR 409 (Karnataka).
26. *Virtusa Consulting Services (P.) Ltd. v. Deputy Commissioner of Income Tax*, Company Circle 5(2), Chennai (T.C.A. No. 997 of 2018) [2021] 124 taxmann.com 309 (Madras).
27. *Principal Commissioner of Income-tax-5, Chennai v. Redington (India) Ltd.* (T.C.A. NOS. 590 & 591 OF 2019) [2020] 122 taxmann.com 122 (Madras).

capital gains, and hence transfer pricing provisions would be applicable to such transfers.

Several High Courts[28] issued rulings in favor of taxpayers where final assessment orders were erroneously raised under India's newly introduced faceless audit system. When there is a transfer pricing audit adjustment in India, the tax officer has to issue a draft order setting out the proposed adjustment. If the taxpayer objects to the adjustment, a panel of three Commissioners look into the objections and give their orders. The Officer has to pass a final order only after this process. In many cases, the final orders were raised without going through the process, owing to system glitches; however, since a tax officer does not have the power to recall his own order, the orders had to be set aside using a court process. Additionally, the Bombay High Court also set aside[29] an assessment order, and directed the tax office to grant a personal hearing as was requested by the taxpayer, even though the assessment took place under the faceless regime.

2.3 Mongolia

On March 18, 2021, Mongolia announced that it had made its first transfer pricing assessment of a multinational enterprise for approximately USD 228 million and a denial of USD 1.5 billion in carried-forward losses; however, it has been reported by the OECD that the TP assessment is currently disputed.[30] This assessment is perceived as an important milestone in transfer pricing and combatting BEPS in the mining sector. The said ruling pertains to a joint venture between a Mongolian company and a Canadian Company which was involved in the exploration of copper, gold and other metals. The concern of the Mongolian tax administration revolved around the high development costs and projections of lower corporate taxes to be paid over the next thirty years. Two specific issues were raised related to the following two charges/expenses exceeding arm's-length pricing: (i) management service charges paid to the Canadian Company by one of its holding companies; (ii) high-interest expenses.[31] Hence, taxes of USD 228 million and penalties based on reductions in the amount of these two expenses on the claim that they exceeded arm's-length pricing were imposed.

28. *Anand Nvh Products (P.) Ltd. v. National e-Assessment Centre Delhi* [W.P.(C) NO. 7936 OF 2021] [2021] 130 taxmann.com 257 (Delhi), *Marvell India Pvt Ltd v. National Faceless Assessment Centre, DCIT & Another* (Writ Petition No. 19932 OF 2021) (Kar HC).
29. *Piramal Enterprises Ltd. v. Additional/Joint/Deputy/Assistant Commissioner of Income-tax/Income-tax Officer* (Writ Petition (L) No. 11040 OF 2021) [2021] 129 taxmann.com 18 (Bombay).
30. https://www.oecd.org/tax/mongolian-tax-administration-partners-with-international-organisations-and-issues-first-transfer-pricing-tax-assessment-for-usd-228-million.htm.
31. https://mnetax.com/mongolias-first-transfer-pricing-assessment-what-could-be-the-issues-43088.

2.4 China

On October 29, 2021, the State Administration of Taxation issued its annual report regarding China's advance pricing arrangement (APA) program for 2020. According to the APA annual report for 2020, China's tax authorities signed a total of twenty-nine APAs in 2020, consisting of fifteen unilateral APAs and fourteen bilateral APAs—a new all-time high. Of the fifteen unilateral APAs signed in 2020, most (thirteen cases) were completed within one year.

2.5 OECD's MAP Report for 2020: Trends from Emerging Markets and Developing Economies

OECD's MAP statistics also shows regional similarity between emerging markets and developing countries. Of the top twenty countries with the highest number of MAP cases pending closure, only three (India, China and Poland) are from emerging markets and developing economies.

Among the twelve emerging markets and developing countries in the Sub-Saharan region which reported their MAP details, only five had open MAP cases. Barring South Africa, which had eighteen TP and nineteen other cases pending, all the others had less than five TP or other cases pending under MAP.

Eleven emerging markets in the European region reported their MAP details. Of these two reported zero, North Macedonia had one case, and all the other had five or more TP or other cases pending. Poland had the highest with seventy-five TP and eighty-two other cases pending closure.

Twenty-one emerging markets and developing countries in Latin America and the Caribbean reported their MAP details. Of these ten reported zero MAP cases, and eight had five or less MAP or TP cases. Mexico reported forty-five TP and ten other cases, Brazil reported twenty-three TP and six other cases and Argentina reported nine TP and ten other cases pending.

Asia exhibited a mixed trend. Of the 22 countries which reported their MAP statistics, India reported the highest at 709 TP and 164 other cases pending closure. China had 65 TP and 87 other cases pending. Ten countries reported 0 MAP cases, and 4 had 10 or lesser cases. The others had between 10 and 50 cases pending closure.

According to the WTO report of 2019, exports and imports from developing countries grew at a faster pace than the developed countries. Once COVID is behind us, or as the world learns to adapt to living with COVID and its many variants, and as cross-border trade from emerging markets and developing countries stabilizes and grows, it is possible that trends in MAP outcomes pending closure may further change—capacity building for MAP negotiations should thus be on the radar of tax policy priorities for emerging markets and developing economies.

3 IMPACT OF COVID-19 ON TRANSFER PRICING IN DEVELOPING COUNTRIES AND EMERGING ECONOMIES[32]

In its second year, COVID continues to remain a global pandemic. As of January 2022, more than 330 million people were infected, and over 5.5 million people lost their lives to COVID-19. The global health emergency continues as the infection rate is yet to be contained although nearly 50 percent of the global population has been fully vaccinated as of September 12, 2021.[33]

The global economy contracted by approximately 3.3% in 2020. Advanced economies shrunk by 4.7% and emerging and developing economies by 2.2%. The People's Republic of China was one of the few countries in the world whose economy grew in 2020. Latin America and the Caribbean was the most affected region; its economy contracted by an estimated 7.0%.

Advanced economies were able to muster an unprecedented response to the crisis, accounting for the vast majority of the USD 16 trillion on fiscal policy actions announced globally. Output in advanced economies is expected to rebound to precrisis levels faster than some developing economies—advanced economies have received the vast majority of vaccines produced to date and fiscal policies implemented during the pandemic protected against long-term scarring.

In general, developing countries were restricted to a much more limited fiscal response; most were constrained by high debt levels coming into the crisis, capital flight at the start of the crisis, and a sustained, significant fall in public revenues during the crisis.

Concerns are growing about a divergent and asynchronous recovery between advanced and developing economies that would significantly increase global inequalities. Over three decades from 1990 to 2019, developed and developing countries alike grew almost uninterruptedly. Per capita gross domestic product (GDP) and wealth rose, extreme poverty declined sharply, middle classes emerged in a large number of developing countries and living standards improved across multiple dimensions. However, this was also characterized by widening inequality within countries; the fact that not all well-being indicators followed the same upward trend as income and did not reach all parts of the population; the strains imposed on the global labor force; and the worsening environmental catastrophe.

The COVID-19 pandemic has compounded a number of these fault lines, with the most vulnerable members of societies the world overbearing the brunt of the harm caused to health and livelihoods. Technology is exacerbating a number of these phenomena: digital divides are worsening inequalities and leaving some people feeling more alone or less satisfied with their lives, while the increasing use of online networks to share information risks exacerbating polarization. Global poverty, unemployment and inequality have risen as a result of the pandemic, which has undone many of the gains in living standards achieved over the past three decades.

---

32. https://www.oecd-ilibrary.org/sites/405e4c32-en/index.html?itemId=/content/publication/405e4c32-en.
33. https://covid19.who.int/table.

While it is impossible to predict the long-term consequences of the pandemic, most developing economies are expected to take much longer to recover than advanced economies.

On December 18, 2020, the OECD released "Guidance on the Transfer Pricing Implications of the COVID-19 Pandemic" (OECD TP-COVID Guidance). This Guidance represents the consensus view of the then 137 member countries of the Inclusive Framework on transfer pricing considerations in COVID-19.[34]

Emerging markets or developing countries did not come up with separate transfer pricing guidelines for COVID-related situations. The Dominican Republic came up with guidance that would cease to apply the corresponding rate of APAs to the hospitality industry.[35] A number of developing countries introduced extensions of timelines for tax payment as well as transfer pricing documentation and filing before tax authorities,[36] while some have reduced fine for late submission of transfer pricing documentation.[37] In fact, Argentina's Federal tax Authority suspended its inspection, assessment, appeal procedures in light of the pandemic.[38]

The OECD TP-COVID Guidance released states that it represents the consensus view of 137 countries in transfer pricing considerations of COVID-19. It would be helpful if national governments of developing countries take a cue from some advanced economies and introduce transfer pricing guidance that is tailored to individual crisis situations and transfer pricing practices. Some key issues to consider while introducing such specific guidance, *inter alia*, are balanced approach to the problem of enhanced transfer pricing audits owing to increasing pressure on tax collection, revision and extension of APAs, measures to ease compliance and reduce penalties to discourage litigation and lastly, need for closer cooperation between jurisdictions and treaty partners pertaining to documentation. This will not only boost resilience but also capacitate the developing countries to fight the pandemic. More so, it shall play an important role in tax certainty for the taxpayers.

Conclusion

Advanced economies have adopted a proactive approach in providing certainty on transfer pricing matters to taxpayers. However, a clear emphasis on the need to document the economic impact on the business is something that very much applies to taxpayers in developing countries. Affected taxpayers must demonstrate and justify allocation of losses to particular jurisdictions. Further, supply chain disruption through contract frustration and remote working of employees form important aspects in FAR

34. https://research.ibfd.org/#/doc?url=/data/tns/docs/html/tns_2020-05-07_o2_1.html.
35. https://assets.kpmg/content/dam/kpmg/us/pdf/2020/03/covid-19-tax-developments-summary.pdf.
36. Argentina: https://research.ibfd.org/#/doc?url=/linkresolver/static/tns_2020-07-15_ar_2#tns_2020-07-15_ar_2; Sri Lanka: https://research.ibfd.org/#/doc?url=/data/tns/docs/html/tns_2020-04-23_lk_1.html; India: Notification S.O. 3906(E) [NO. 88/2020/ F. NO. 370142/35/2020-TPL], dated 29.10.2020.
37. Thailand: https://research.ibfd.org/#/doc?url=/data/tns/docs/html/tns_2020-09-11_th_1.html.
38. Argentina: https://research.ibfd.org/#/doc?url=/data/tns/docs/html/tns_2020-11-12_ar_1.html.

analysis of any business that much be reflected in reported documents. For developing and emerging economies, the opportunities in transfer pricing policy-making are:

- increasing reliance on taxpayer's internal data by the tax administration;
- simplification measures/safe harbors, perhaps on a temporary basis;
- amplifying mutual trust, flexibility and reasonable efforts;
- targeted capacity development and/or enhancement.

4 DEVELOPMENTS PERTAINING TO ENGAGEMENT OF MULTILATERAL BODIES WITH DEVELOPING COUNTRIES AND EMERGING ECONOMIES

4.1 OECD Developments with Respect to Emerging Markets and Developing Economies

The OECD engages with developing countries on several fronts, and notable developments in 2021 are as under.

(1) BEPS Inclusive Framework

The OECD/G20 Inclusive Framework, established in 2016, currently has 141 members, including 88 emerging markets and developing countries. Developing countries are also well represented on the Steering Group of the OECD/G20 Inclusive Framework, which includes deputy chairs from the People's Republic of China and Nigeria and other members from Argentina, Brazil, India, Mongolia, Saudi Arabia, Senegal, South Africa and Zambia.[39]

Action Plan 5 of the BEPS Inclusive Framework deals with Countering Harmful Tax Practices and is a minimum standard. Under this minimum standard, the compulsory spontaneous exchange of information on tax rulings (the "transparency framework") provides tax administrations with timely information on rulings that have been granted to a foreign-related party of their resident taxpayer or a permanent establishment, which can be used in conducting risk assessments and which, in the absence of exchange, could give rise to BEPS concerns. The transparency framework requires spontaneous exchange of information on five categories of taxpayer-specific rulings: (i) rulings related to certain preferential regimes; (ii) unilateral advance pricing arrangements (APAs) or other cross-border unilateral rulings in respect of transfer pricing; (iii) rulings providing for a downward adjustment of taxable profits; (iv) permanent establishment (PE) rulings; and (v) related party conduit rulings. The requirement to exchange information on the rulings in the above categories includes certain past rulings as well as future rulings, pursuant to predefined periods which are outlined in each jurisdiction's report and that varies according to the time when a certain jurisdiction has joined the Inclusive Framework or has been identified as a jurisdiction of relevance. The OECD, in December 2021, released its fifth annual report which

39. https://www.oecd.org/tax/beps/steering-group-of-the-inclusive-framework-on-beps.pdf.

covers the steps jurisdictions have taken to implement the transparency framework during the calendar year 2020. Forty-six jurisdictions out of the 131 reviewed received recommendations for improvement. Of these 46, 7[40] were advanced economies and 39 were emerging markets or developing economies. The recommendations for emerging markets and developing economies were to largely strengthen information gathering processes and developing processes to complete the templates on rulings for exchange of information. The recommendations for advanced economies were largely on delays experienced in exchange of information. The Philippines, an emerging market, though not a part of the BEPS Inclusive Framework, is one of the jurisdictions reviewed as a jurisdiction of relevance.[41]

(2) Forum for Tax Administration

At its plenary meeting on December 16 and 17, 2021, OECD's Forum for Tax Administration (FTA), *inter alia*, agreed to prioritize tax capacity building initiatives to assist developing countries with the implementation of the Pillars and the further digitalization of tax administration. The FTA, together with the African Tax Administration Forum, also released a report titled "Supporting the Digitalisation of Developing Countries by Tax Administrators." The primary purpose of the report is to share information that will assist developing country tax administrations as they consider digitalization, facilitate dialog among tax officials on tax administration issues, and identify opportunities to improve tax administrations' ICT systems.[42]

(3) Tax Inspectors Without Borders

The Tax Inspectors Without Borders (TIWB), an initiative for emerging markets and developing countries, released its annual report for 2021. Tax Inspectors Without Borders, a joint initiative of the OECD and UNDP, is a unique approach to capacity building that embeds expert tax auditors in emerging markets and developing country tax administrations, to provide practical, hands-on assistance on actual tax audits of MNEs and related international tax issues. More than hundred experts have been deployed to work directly with tax administrations having requested assistance on real-life cases covering international taxation matters. Six years on, TIWB assistance has helped collect USD 1.4 billion additional tax revenue for developing countries, and USD 3.9 billion in tax assessed through June 2021. In December 2020, Mongolia completed its first transfer pricing audit and issued its first transfer pricing tax assessment for approximately USD 228 million and a denial of USD 1.5 billion in carried-forward losses. In Egypt, TIWB helped in finalizing transfer pricing adjustments amounting to EGP 685 million (USD 98 million) leading to an additional tax of EGP 154 million (USD 22 million) collected, as well as USD 10 million in related penalties and in reaching equitable settlements with taxpayers subject to deemed

40. Andorra, the Czech Republic, France, Israel, the Netherlands, Spain and Switzerland were the seven advanced economies which received recommendations.
41. https://www.oecd-ilibrary.org/sites/f376127b-en/index.html?itemId=/content/publication/f376127b-en.
42. https://www.oecd.org/tax/forum-on-tax-administration/publications-and-products/supporting-the-digitalisation-of-developing-country-tax-administrations.pdf.

assessments. TIWB also assisted in developing end-to-end processes to ensure actual payment of additional transfer pricing-related tax revenues in Egypt.[43]

(4) International Compliance Assurance Program

The OECD in a joint initiative with ATAF released a report on Revenue Statistics in Africa 2021. The report shows that the average tax-to-GDP ratio in Africa was 16.6% in 2019, an increase of 0.3 percentage points (p.p.) from 2018. The report covered thirty African countries representing 75% of Africa's GDP. Tax-to-GDP ratios in the region ranged from 6.0% in Nigeria to 34.3% in the Seychelles and Tunisia, and increased in sixteen countries between 2018 and 2019 while declining in fourteen. The rise in the Africa (30) average tax-to-GDP ratio between 2018 and 2019 was driven by increases of over 2.5 p.p. in three countries (Equatorial Guinea, Mali and Tunisia) that were partly attributable to tax policy and administration reforms. In spite of this increase, the average tax-to-GDP ratio for Africa in 2019 remained below those of the Asia-Pacific, Latin America and the Caribbean (LAC), and the OECD at 21.0%, 22.9% and 33.8%, respectively.[44] The OECD's Global Forum launched its Train the Trainer pilot program under the umbrella of the Africa Initiative in April 2021. The project is designed to assist participating jurisdictions in providing local training to tax auditors and investigators. It aims at raising awareness on cross-border administrative assistance in tax matters, in particular the exchange of information on request, and building administrations' capacity to use these instruments effectively in their day-to-day work.[45]

(5) Other engagements

The Tunisian Ministry of Finance, the OECD and the European Union (EU) have decided to extend their program "Improving Domestic Resource Mobilisation Through the Establishment of an Efficient Tax System and Enhanced Tax Transparency" and to expand it to new key areas of assistance including the implementation of the landmark agreement on international taxation (Pillar One and Pillar Two). This program, initiated in 2019 and financed by the EU over a total period of five years, aims to assist Tunisia, an emerging market, in the implementation of international tax standards, to improve its analytical capacity in tax policy, and to strengthen tax morale.[46]

The OECD released a report on Building Tax Culture, Compliance and Citizenship. According to the OECD, developing countries face a combination of challenges: narrow tax bases (resulting in fewer taxpayers), low revenues and low reported levels of tax morale. Therefore, while taxpayer education initiatives are important in all countries, they are especially important to developing countries. They serve as a tool to help reach, and encourage, new taxpayers; explain the role of tax in society; build tax

43. http://www.tiwb.org/resources/reports-case-studies/tax-inspectors-without-borders-annual-report-2021.pdf.
44. https://www.oecd.org/tax/tax-policy/africa-the-rising-debt-burden-highlights-the-need-for-further-progress-in-domestic-revenue-mobilisation.htm.
45. https://www.oecd.org/tax/exchange-of-tax-information/gobal-forum-secretariat-launches-train-the-trainer-pilot-programme.htm.
46. https://www.oecd.org/tax/tunisia-oecd-and-eu-strengthen-tax-cooperation-to-improve-domestic-resource-mobilisation-in-tunisia.htm.

morale; and ultimately increase revenues. It is therefore primarily with developing countries in mind that this report has been prepared.[47]

4.2 Platform for Collaboration on Tax Partners

The Platform for Collaboration on Tax Partners (PCT) is a collaboration between the International Monetary Fund (IMF), the Organisation for Economic Co-operation and Development (OECD), the United Nations (UN) and the World Bank Group (WBG). The PCT continued to deliver toolkits on key areas of significance for developing countries. Two new toolkits on Transfer Pricing Documentation and Tax Treaty Negotiations were released between the period July 2021 and 2021.

The PCT also conducted three regional workshops in partnership with the African Tax Administration Forum (one workshop for Africa) and the Asian Development Bank (ADB) (two workshops: one each for small and large states in Asia) to facilitate better exchange of information on the Medium Term Revenue Strategy Initiative (MTRS) and how it can benefit countries' tax system reform priorities, particularly, in the light of the COVID-19 pandemic. Overall, nearly 550 participants including ministers of finance and/or senior government officials from 53 countries, staff from PCT Partners, regional partners (ATAF and ADB) and development partners attended the workshops. Several emerging markets and developed countries have engaged with the PCT on their MTRS initiative—these include Egypt, Liberia, Papua New Guinea, Uganda, Senegal, Bangladesh, Benin, Ethiopia, Indonesia, Thailand, Pakistan, Rwanda and Vietnam.[48]

4.3 United Nations

4.3.1 UN Practice Manual on TP for Developing Countries Updated

Almost all emerging economies and developing countries are members of the United Nations. In April 2021, the UN released its updated Transfer Pricing Manual, the third edition of the Manual after 2013 and 2017. The United Nations Practical Manual on Transfer Pricing for Developing Countries ("UN TP Manual") forms an important guiding toolkit for developing as well as least developed countries. The Manual was prepared in response to the need, often expressed by developing countries, for clearer guidance on the policy and administrative aspects of applying transfer pricing analysis to some of the transactions of multinational enterprises (MNEs) in particular.[49] The Guidance has become even more relevant due to complexity in business operations and increase in disputes that demand relevant examples and simplifications for developing countries to embrace compliance with transfer pricing in a global environment. The

47. https://www.oecd-ilibrary.org/sites/18585eb1-en/index.html?itemId=/content/publication/18585eb1-en.
48. https://www.tax-platform.org/sites/pct/files/publications/PCT%20Progress%20Report%202021.pdf.
49. https://www.un.org/development/desa/financing/sites/www.un.org.development.desa.financing/files/2020-03/UN_Manual_TransferPricing.pdf. Refer note at para. 3.

inputs are practical and are gathered from useful capacity building exercises with tax administrations from developing and emerging economies.

4.3.2 Update on UN International Tax Committee

A new group of twenty-five tax experts from around the world was appointed by the United Nations Secretary-General António Guterres to serve as members of the Committee for the 2021 to 2025 term. The group contains representatives from emerging markets and developing countries such as India, China, Nigeria, Chile, South Korea, Malawi, Mexico, Ireland, Indonesia, Myanmar, Angola, Russia, apart from advanced economies such as Canada, Norway, Germany, Italy, Sweden, and China. The new committee met in October 2021. The Committee established various subcommittees, including on updating the treaty manual and transfer pricing. On updating the treaty manual, there was general agreement that the Committee should focus on issues with the most impact for developing countries as well as technical issues arising from specific UN Model provisions. Low or no priority should be given to changes to align with the OECD Model unless they represent an issue of practical importance for developing countries. The transfer pricing subcommittee's mandate is that it considers, reviews and proposes guidance on Article 9 of the United Nations Model Convention, and the Arm's-Length Principle embodied in it, and its consistency with relevant Commentaries of the UN Model, that the subcommittee identifies and considers the transfer pricing topics where guidance from the Committees is the most useful, that it reflects the realities for, and the needs of, developing countries, at their relevant stages of capacity development, that it gives due consideration to relevant work in other fora, including the BEPS Inclusive Framework.[50]

It will be interesting to see the new areas of work that will be handled by the new subcommittee on transfer pricing in the near future. The prospective work areas should certainly include practical guidance on Pillar One and Pillar Two for developing countries, with the consensus on theoretical frameworks agreed by the OECD/ Inclusive Framework member countries. The practical guidance and country examples on complex financial transactions, which form a part of the updated transfer pricing manual have been helpful for developing countries to a large extent. Further, the sector-specific guidance like on extractives and mining sectors have been especially prioritized for underdeveloped countries in transfer pricing. Practical toolkits on risk assessment (adaptable to developing countries) could be another prospective work area, which could be distinguished from the OECD's reports on risk assessment. Other prospective work areas could include adding practical examples on DEMPE analysis, bilateral APAs, environmental taxes, etc. Lastly, since most of the developing countries have not released specific COVID-19 related guidance on transfer pricing, this could be another work area to be undertaken by the UN subcommittee.

50. https://www.un.org/development/desa/financing/sites/www.un.org.development.desa.financing/files/2022-01/Report%20of%20the%2023nd%20Session%20Final%20Advance%20unedited%20version_1.pdf.

5 DEVELOPMENTS IN TAXATION OF DIGITAL ECONOMIES

The current treaty rules of allocating taxing rights favor capital exporting or developed countries based on residence principle rather than capital importing or developing countries based on source principle. Hence, they are not well equipped to tax digital economy and enable MNEs to pay a fair share of taxes.

Emerging economies and developing countries, especially populated nations with a high number of digital users, foresee increasing number of economic justifications to broaden the scope to tax digital economy. There have been several developing countries that either proposed or adopted new tax measures seeking larger allocation of taxing rights, in the absence of a global consensus-based solution. Countries like India, Israel, Nigeria and Indonesia have introduced their own versions of "significant economic presence" (SEP), whereby the foreign entity's taxable presence in a market jurisdiction is evidenced by a purposeful and sustained interaction with the users in that jurisdiction through the means of technology and other prescribed thresholds. SEP follows the principle of allocating taxing rights where value is created and is based on the assumption that demand creates considerable value, especially in the context of digitalized business models. Resultantly, part of the income should be allocated to the marketplace or where the customers are based.[51] It is obvious that income can only be created if there is a market or demand for the supply. The aim is to prevent profit diversion by ensuring that the significant global MNEs reflect the economic substance of its activities in market jurisdictions. The biggest issue in implementing SEP is its unilateral nature resulting in juridical double taxation, where residence countries may deny granting tax relief. Moreover, if strictly implemented, countries may foresee other retaliatory international trade measures.

Of the twenty-seven countries that have currently enacted legislation for digital taxes, nine are developed countries. Sixteen other countries have either announced intention to implement or have draft legislation in place, of which six are developed counties.[52] Thus taxing digital companies has equally been an area of concern for both developed and developing countries. During October and November 2021, the US reached an agreement with several countries under which the US will terminate the trade tariff actions it had announced in June 2021 against India and several other countries such as the UK, Austria, France, Italy, Spain and Turkey, in response to the levy, and will not take any further actions. In turn, the countries have agreed to grant a credit on specified digital taxes and/or not impose digital levies after a specified time frame [coming into effect of Pillar 1 or up to December 31, 2023 (March 31, 2024, for India) whichever is later].

51. Eric C.C.M. Kemmeren, *If We Need a Destination-Based Corporate Income Tax, Do We Also Need a Production-Based Consumption Tax?*, in *International Taxation in a Changing Landscape – Liber Amicorum in Honour of Bertil Wiman*, edited by Jérôme Monsenego & Jan Bjuvberg. Alphen aan den Rijn: Kluwer Law International, 2019, p. 148.
52. https://tax.kpmg.us/content/dam/tax/en/pdfs/2021/digitalized-economy-taxation-developm ents-summary.pdf.

6 OUTLOOK FOR DEVELOPING COUNTRIES AND EMERGING ECONOMIES

As can be seen from the 2021 legislative developments, transfer pricing continues to be an area of increased attention and scrutiny by tax authorities. It is widely believed that pursuant to COVID, tax authorities have intensified transfer pricing scrutinies in an attempt to protect/expand their tax base. Emerging economies and developing countries are characterized by increasing quantum of intragroup trades, capacity constraints in tax administration and lack of good quality publicly available databases. The BRICS nations, all of which are emerging market economies, Brazil, Russia, India, China and South Africa, play a key role in the global economy. The five countries collectively represent approximately 42% of the world's population, 23% of global GDP and 18% of international trade. BRICS countries generally play an important part in the value chain for global organizations, and, hence, transfer pricing is key to tax risk management and compliance in these countries.

With the growing participation of emerging markets and developing countries in multilateral frameworks, and increasing support being provided by the OECD, emerging markets and developing countries will continue to align themselves with global best practices. Tax administrators will seek to balance sovereignty concerns with operating harmoniously in a multilateral framework.

Developing countries and emerging economies will continue to align themselves to global best practices and with support from various initiatives from the OECD and UN (such as the UN Manual on transfer pricing, the transfer pricing documentation toolkit developed by the PCT, the Tax Inspectors Without Borders initiative of the OECD, and the developments in the OECD/G20 BEPS Inclusive Framework) will significantly augment their audit and dispute resolution capabilities. Regional organizations like ATAF have been actively engaging with tax administrations of African countries by introducing various demand-driven initiatives on transfer pricing. Such initiatives target capacity building, training and conducting workshops on areas like MAPs, APAs and implementation of safe harbors for reducing transfer pricing disputes and enhancing certainty.

Lastly, reasonable tax and transfer pricing certainty continues to dominate the mindset of multinational taxpayers when it comes to their operations in emerging markets and developing countries. While there is extensive engagement in capacity building for tax administrators between developed and developing counties, preventing and resolving disputes in a speedier fashion still has some miles to go. Countries such as India which were able to provide fabulous certainty to taxpayers on concluded APAs would do well to augment their APA resources and provide quicker closure to taxpayers. Administrations will be well advised if they introduce reasonable safe harbors as a first step in providing certainty to taxpayers. This coupled with a more engaged approach with taxpayers would go a long way in giving multinationals confidence in transfer pricing and tax regimes of emerging economies and developing countries.

CHAPTER 5

Recent Developments on Transfer Pricing in the Post-Covid-19 Era

*Gianni De Robertis, Anh Nguyen & Prita Subramanian**

* The authors wish to thank Federico Faccioli and Denis Kondi for their research assistance; likewise, all those other colleagues and clients with whom we have had many interesting discussions on the topic covered in this chapter.

1 INTRODUCTION

Coronavirus disease of 2019 (COVID-19) was first identified in China in December 2019 and shortly after that spread to other countries in the region, and then expanded to Europe and the United States as a global outbreak. In March 2020, the World Health Organization declared COVID-19 a pandemic. Although the COVID-19 vaccine introduced in April 2021 has been a tremendous help in controlling the spread and the death rate, it has not put an end to the pandemic. At the time of writing, over 278 million cases and just under 5.4 million deaths have been reported worldwide.[1] Given the continuing introduction of new coronavirus variants, how the pandemic will evolve is still ambiguous.

At first, in efforts to limit the transmission rate of the virus, countries across the globe implemented stringent measures such as social distancing, intermittent mandatory national lockdowns and border closures. Businesses were closed, factories were shut down, and nonessential workers were required to work from home. All these attempts to control the spread consequently triggered panicked stocking up on necessities, shortages in supply, and in turn, a severe disruption in the global supply chain, which contributed substantially to a global economic contraction. The repercussions also prompted changes at different levels to adapt, survive and recover. Over the past two years of the pandemic, individual behaviors have changed to adjust to the new normal, companies have reshaped to be more resilient, and governments have started to remedy the consequences of the pandemic.

Some of the effects of COVID-19 on the economy are expected to be temporary and are expected to dissipate once the pandemic is brought under control. However, it is also becoming clear that COVID-19 has irreversibly changed certain aspects of the economy. This chapter discusses the ways in which COVID-19 has disrupted the economy—both temporarily while the public health concerns of COVID-19 persist and over the longer term by changing certain fundamental characteristics of the economy. It then goes on to discuss implications of the temporary and longer-term disruptions caused by COVID-19 for transfer pricing. In the short term, COVID-19 has raised challenges in applying transfer pricing approaches developed for normal times to the

1. WHO, *COVID-19 Weekly Epidemiological Update*, Edition 72, December 28, 2021.

unusual economic circumstances caused by COVID-19. In the longer term, while we do not yet have direct experience with transfer pricing in a post-COVID-19 world, we expect the enduring changes to the economy to lead to changing value chains and relationships within MNEs, with corresponding transfer pricing implications. Additionally, we see COVID-19 magnifying some tensions that have been developing in the global transfer pricing system around digitalization and the application of existing guidance around risk and intangibles.

This chapter is structured as follows. Section 2 analyzes how COVID-19 has impacted the economy in the short term and provides observations on changes that are expected to persist in the long term. Section 3 examines the transfer pricing implications of COVID-19 in the short term. Section 4 discusses how certain aspects of the transfer pricing landscape may change in the long term, followed by concluding remarks in section 5.

2 COVID-19 IMPACT ON ECONOMY

2.1 Short-Term Economic Impact of COVID-19

COVID-19 delivered a sudden and significant shock to the global economy. Two years after the first outbreak of disease, the pandemic and its associated economic effects still linger. We refer to as the short term the period during which economic effects of COVID-19 arising directly from its public health concerns exist. The short term, therefore, includes the period during which the pandemic is active and the period directly following the end of the pandemic during which economic repercussions of the measures taken by governments (through their policies) and individuals (through temporary changes in behavior) to combat the negative effects of the pandemic will linger. The following sections discuss the short-term impact of COVID-19 on the global economy.

2.1.1 Recession and Recovery

The COVID-19 lockdowns and other precautions taken in early 2020 swiftly drove the global economy into a recession. The world Gross Domestic Product (GDP) growth rate in 2020 was minus 3.4%, which is lower than the GDP growth rate of minus 1.3% post the 2008 financial crisis.[2] The recession saw unusually high and rapid increases in unemployment in many countries. In April 2020, the US unemployment rate reached 14.8%—the highest rate observed since data collection began in 1948.[3] In Australia, the effective rate of unemployment jumped from 5.4% in March 2020 to 11.7% in April

2. The World Bank, *GDP growth (annual %)*, https://data.worldbank.org/indicator/NY.GDP.MKTP.KD.ZG (accessed January 4, 2022).
3. Falk G., Romero P., Nicchitta I., Nyhof E., *Unemployment Rates During the COVID-19 Pandemic*, Congressional Research Service, August 20, 2021.

2020.[4] The global unemployment rate in 2020 was 6.5%, the highest recorded within the 2010-2020 period.[5]

Although the pandemic is a global phenomenon, its effects are not evenly spread across territories, industries, and companies. Among the world's seven largest economies, as of the 3rd quarter of 2020, China experienced a positive GDP growth rate of 4.9%, while most other countries such as the United States, France, Germany, Japan, India, and the United Kingdom were negatively affected by the pandemic, during that same period.[6] Various analyses of industrial sectors provide further insights into the uneven effects of the pandemic. The tourism sector has been particularly hard hit as it was directly affected by the travel restrictions. The European Union's tourism industry is estimated to be losing around Euro 1 billion in revenue per month as a result of the outbreak.[7] At the same time, the oil and gas drilling, auto parts and equipment, and restaurants were severely impacted by COVID-19.[8] Sectors revolving around software and the Internet, and online services, however, have risen drastically because social distancing measures have driven up the demand for at-home entertainment, learning through online courses, and telemedicine.

The recovery in global economic activity has been more vigorous than what was expected in June 2020. Toward the end of 2021, the world GDP was close to or above pre-pandemic levels. This reflects the effective supporting policies by governments, the prompt adaptation by businesses and workforce, and perhaps most importantly, the rapid rollout of effective vaccines.[9]

---

4. Suomi A., Schofield T., Butterworth P., *Unemployment, Employability and COVID19: How the Global Socioeconomic Shock Challenged Negative Perceptions Toward the Less Fortunate in the Australian Context,* Front. Psychol., October 15, 2020.
5. Statista, *Global unemployment rate from 2010 to 2020,* https://www.statista.com/statistics/279777/global-unemployment-rate/ (accessed January 4, 2022).
6. Statista, GDP growth rate of the world's seven largest economies as of 3rd quarter of 2020, by country, https://www.statista.com/statistics/1207780/gdp-growth-rate-of-the-world-s-seven-largest-economies-by-country/ (accessed January 4 2022).
7. Niestadt M., *COVID-19 and the tourism sector,* European Parliamentary Research Service, PE 649.368, April 2020.
8. Haydon D., Kumar N., *Industries Most and Least Impacted by COVID-19 from a Probability of Default Perspective,* S&P Global Market Intelligence, https://www.spglobal.com/marketintelligence/en/news-insights/blog/industries-most-and-least-impacted-by-covid19-from-a-probability-of-default-perspective-september-2020-update (accessed January 4, 2022).
9. OECD, *OECD Economic Outlook,* Volume 2021 Issue 2, Ch 1. General assessment of the macroeconomic situation.

Figure 5.1 The Global Recovery Has Outstripped Predictions but Is Not Complete

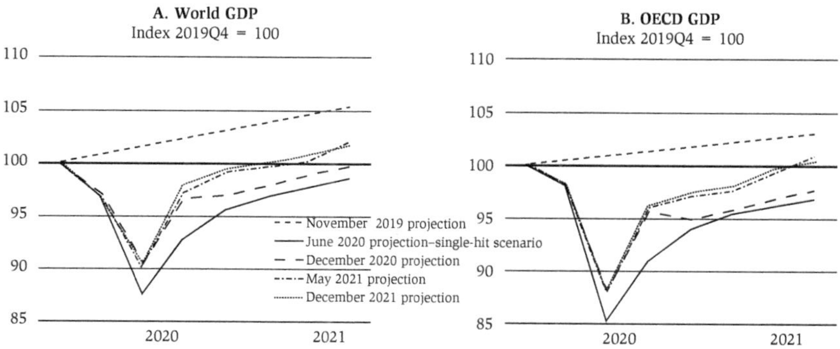

Source: OECD Economic Outlook 110 database; OECD Economic Outlook 106 database; OECD Economic Outlook 107 database; OECD Outlook 108 database; OECD Economic Outlook 109 database; and OECD calculations. StatLink: htps://stat.link/9vr0w2.

Although the economic outlook seems optimistic, it is worth noting that the world had foregone the growth that would have occurred in 2020 and the first half of 2021: global GDP in mid-2021 was still 3.5 per cent lower than projected before the pandemic. Moreover, this foregone growth has not been distributed equally: the loss has been proportionately greater for middle-income emerging-market economies than for advanced economies, and greatest for low-income developing countries.[10] Organisation for Economic Co-operation and Development (OECD) Economic Outlook projects the recovery is continuing with a global economic growth of 4.5% in 2022 (Figure 5.1).[11] However, the emergence of the Omicron variant recently may jeopardize the recovery.

2.1.2 *Supply Chain Disruptions*

Since the emergence of the coronavirus in early 2020, supply chains across the world drastically slowed down for a variety of reasons, including but not limited to disrupted supply (both labor and material shortages) and fluctuating demand. Based on an analysis by the U.S. Institute for Supply Management, 75% of companies have reported disruptions in their supply chain.[12] At the beginning of the national lockdowns and required quarantine, people stocked up on foods, hygiene products and other necessities. Other goods that were in unusually high demand included surgery masks and certain medical equipment, which were required for both household use and hospital

10. *Ibid.*
11. OECD, *OECD Economic Outlook sees recovery continuing but warns of growing imbalances and risks*, https://www.oecd.org/newsroom/oecd-economic-outlook-sees-recovery-continuing-but-warns-of-growing-imbalances-and-risks.htm (accessed January 4, 2022).
12. Fernandes N., *Economic Effects of Coronavirus Outbreak (COVID-19) on the World Economy*, IESE Business School Working Paper No. WP-1240-E, Revised April 2020.

use. There was an extremely high demand in tech and office products as people started working remotely as part of the social distancing mandate. At the business level, companies began ordering extra parts and materials, anticipating a shortage of supply in the future. Following the national lockdowns, closed borders, and extended shutdown of parts of the world's economy was the shortage of supply in raw materials and finished goods. Transportation was canceled, and manufacturing capacity was cut, resulting in a delay and temporary interruption of supply. Consequently, global trade witnessed a huge downturn followed by a fall in global economic activity. The value of international trade in goods started declining in Q1 2020 and plunged in Q2 2020 (see Figure 5.2).[13]

Figure 5.2 Quarterly World Trade Statistics from 2016 to 2021

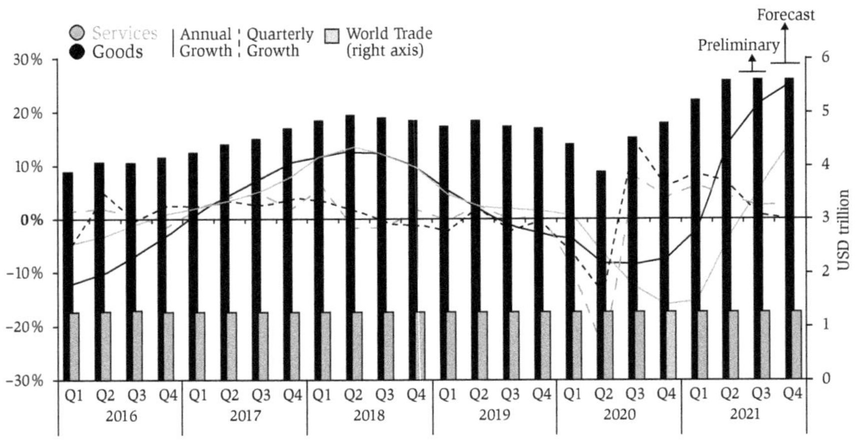

Source: UNCTAD calculations based on national statistics.
Note: Quarterly growth is the quarter over quarter growth rate of seasonally adjusted values. Annual growth refers to the last four quarters.

Manufacturing restarted, and international trade resumed in the second half of 2020 after governments in several countries started loosening up social distancing measures. However, turning back on the global manufacturing machine after the initial shock was difficult. The complex and interconnected supply chain that moves raw materials and finished products around the globe requires predictability and precision.[14] The unexpected shift in demand on different types of goods had disturbed both factors. The panicked stocking by both consumers and companies early in the pandemic made the historical demand data unreliable. It is nearly impossible to predict how long the high demand would last or whether a new demand is permanently created and suppliers should invest in new capacity.

13. UNCTAD, *Global Trade Update*, November 2021.
14. Friesen G., *No End in Sight for the COVID-Led Global Supply Chain Disruption*, https://www.forbes.com/sites/garthfriesen/2021/09/03/no-end-in-sight-for-the-covid-led-global-supply-chain-disruption/?sh=20e895033491.

A prime example of the pandemic disruptive supply-demand is the shortage of microchips. As the pandemic gripped the world in early 2020, demand surged for technology products such as computers, televisions, and monitors; and cloud computing grew substantially to facilitate remote working. Technology companies absorbed all the capacity the chipmakers had. When the economy roared back, carmakers and their parts suppliers found that chipmakers had little capacity available for them.[15] As a result, automobile manufacturers have been forced to cut back on production, leading to significant unmet demand for automobiles in the market. For example, chip shortages forced Ford to reduce production significantly in the second quarter of 2021, which resulted in a quarterly decrease of 28% in its wholesale units.[16]

2.1.3 Remote Working

Remote working is defined as "a flexible work arrangement whereby workers work in locations, remote from their central offices or production facilities, the worker has no personal contact with co-workers there, but is able to communicate with them using technology."[17] Although many of the technologies for enabling remote working have existed for at least a decade, most firms did not adopt them or only adopted them for certain focus groups. COVID-19 has, however, elevated the importance of the virtual dimension of work. In responding to social distancing requirements and quarantine measures, nonessential businesses around the globe were closed, and large numbers of firms were forced to shift to remote working. The transition to remote working was one of the most immediate and pronounced effects of the pandemic on mobility and access to workplaces. For instance, during the pandemic, around 90% of Morgan Stanley's 60,000 employees worked remotely from home.[18] The rapid development of technology, including virtual private networks, voice over Internet protocols, virtual meetings, cloud technology, work collaboration tools and even facial recognition technologies over the pre-pandemic years, has enabled a smooth transition to remote working. Before then, it was expected to take more than a year to implement the level of remote working that took place during the crisis. In actuality, it took an average of eleven days

15. Sheffi Y., *What Everyone Gets Wrong about the Never-Ending COVID-19 Supply Chain Crisis*, https://sloanreview.mit.edu/article/what-everyone-gets-wrong-about-the-never-ending-covid-19-supply-chain-crisis/.
16. Ford, *Q2 2021 Earnings Review*, https://www.cnbc.com/2021/06/30/chip-shortage-causes-ford-to-cut-vehicle-production-at-several-plants.html https://s23.q4cdn.com/799033206/files/doc_financials/2021/q2/Ford-2Q2021-Earnings-Presentation.pdf (accessed January 12, 2022).
17. Wang B., Liu Y., Qian J., Parker S., *Achieving Effective Remote Working During the COVID-19 Pandemic: A Work Design Perspective*, Applied Psychology: An International Review, 2020, 0 (0), 1-44 doi: 10.1111/apps.12290.
18. Stanley M., *Dear Fellow Shareholders: Retrieved 2-9-20*, https://www.morganstanley.com/about-us-2020ams/pdf/2020_Letter_to_Shareholders.pdf.

to implement a workable solution, and nearly all the companies have stood up workable solutions within a few months.[19]

2.1.4 Decrease in Tax Revenue

COVID-19 has not only disrupted businesses and changed the way of working but also deteriorated government fiscal positions in the short term. During COVID-19, governments around the globe faced the dilemma of balancing public health and the economy. Mandate lockdowns and social distancing on the one hand limited the virus transmission and on the other hand hindered the economy. Governments, therefore, introduced a range of tax reforms, among other public policies, to support the economy and social welfare. Tax filing deferral, introduction of new tax allowance and credits, and targeted tax rate cut were most common measures applied to support households. For businesses, multiple support measures focusing on business liquidity and cash flow, such as deferrals of tax payments, tax refund acceleration, accelerated deduction and depreciation, were implemented, etc. While these measures provided tremendous help to households and businesses during COVID-19, they created pressure on tax revenues. Overall, COVID-19 has reduced tax revenues in two-thirds of OECD countries (see Figure 5.3).[20]

19. McKinsey, *How COVID-19 Has Pushed Companies over the Technology Tipping Point—And Transformed Business Forever*, https://www.mckinsey.com/business-functions/strategy-and-corporate-finance/our-insights/how-covid-19-has-pushed-companies-over-the-technology-tipping-point-and-transformed-business-forever (accessed January 4, 2022).
20. OECD, *Revenue Statistics 2021: The Initial Impact of COVID-19 on OECD Tax Revenues*, https://www.oecd-ilibrary.org/sites/6e87f932-en/1/3/2/index.html?itemId=/content/publication/6e87f932-en&_csp_=989e3029323a6936ab9fa6df32f709e4&itemIGO=oecd&itemContentType=book#section-d1e13372 accessed January 6, 2022.

Figure 5.3 Changes in Nominal Tax and Nominal GDP, 2019-2020[21]

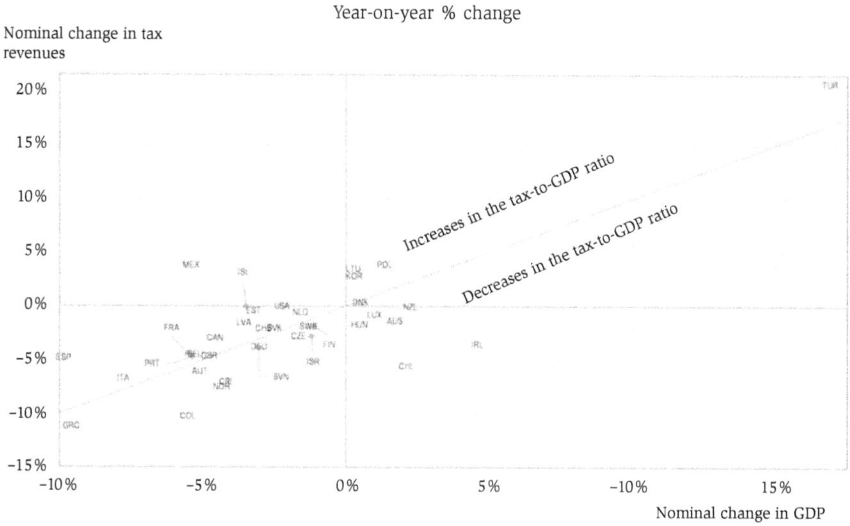

Source: OECD Revenue Statistics 2021: The initial impact of COVID-19 on OECD tax revenues

2.2 Medium- and Long-Term Changes to the Economy Resulting from COVID-19

As discussed above, COVID-19 has caused an immediate and significant disruption to the global economy. Once the public health concerns of COVID-19 subside and the measures put in place to address them are removed, changes to the economy that are the direct result of the extraordinary circumstances of the pandemic are expected to fade. However, in addition to the changes imposed by COVID-19 as a matter of necessity in the short term, COVID-19 has fundamentally altered aspects of the global economy that are expected to outlast the pandemic. At the macroeconomic level, the recession and the measures taken by governments to combat the negative effects of COVID-19 have reduced tax revenues, as discussed above, and added to the public debt. They have also led to above normal inflation. While it is uncertain as to how long this inflation will last, the increase in public debt and inflation are sufficiently meaningful to drive economic policy post-COVID-19, at least in the medium term. At the microeconomic level, companies and individuals have made changes or are planning to make changes to how they work or do business that are expected to persist into the longer-term post-COVID-19. The following sections focus on the long-term

21. *Ibid.*

economic impact of COVID-19 for businesses since that will be most relevant to our discussion of the transfer pricing implications of COVID-19 later in this chapter.

2.2.1 *Supply Chain Restructuring*[22]

Pre-pandemic, global supply chains already had certain inherent issues which were exposed during COVID-19. Pressure to compete on prices and to be more efficient motivated companies to offshore parts of their production to certain countries that have low labor costs or cheaper materials and consequently become overly reliant on a single geography to source particular goods. Companies started adopting lean production and just-in-time inventories to minimize inventory levels and to improve the efficiency of manufacturing processes. With regard to products that require sophisticated manufacturing processes and have high intellectual value, companies tend to rely on a limited number of suppliers to control product quality and intellectual property risk. Subcontracting became more prevalent. The increased use of subcontracting resulted in a deep web of multiple tiers of suppliers in which one supplier relies on the other and so on. The multiple tiers system created a lack of visibility into one's own supply chain. In fact, only under half of the companies understand the location of their tier-one suppliers and only 2 % has visibility into their supply base beyond second tier.

While the above strategies existed for a reason, businesses bore great loss when the pandemic broke the weakest links and disrupted the whole supply chain. The impact of COVID-19 on global supply chains was far-reaching, and its long-lasting effects call for a reimagination of supply chain operating models. Companies have started reassessing their supply chain risks to mitigate future disruption. In a survey performed by McKinsey, 93 % of supply chain leaders said they plan to increase resilience across their supply chain. As of May 2020, planned actions to build resilience and actions implemented within the prior twelve-month period are represented in Figure 5.4.

22. McKinsey, *How COVID-19 Is Reshaping Supply Chains*, https://www.mckinsey.com/business-functions/operations/our-insights/how-covid-19-is-reshaping-supply-chains (accessed January 4, 2022).

Figure 5.4 Planned and Implemented Actions to Build Resilience

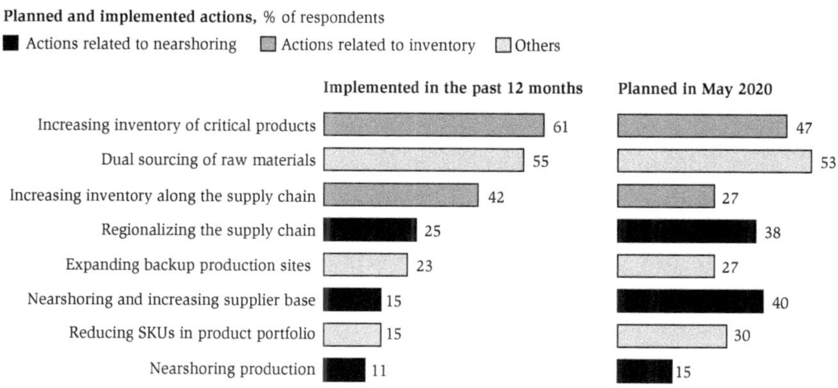

Source: McKinsey survey of global supply-chain leaders (May 4–June 16, 2021, n = 71).

While companies in different industries may strategize their supply chains differently depending on the circumstances, major restructurings of global supply chains are summarized as follows.

Increasing inventories: Just-in-time production has helped companies reduce their need for working capital, but a supply chain designed for maximum efficiency is more fragile to shock. The key is to balance the benefit of lean production and minimal inventories with the ability to meet consumer demand on time and in the right locations. While reserving a safety stock does not entirely mitigate the risk of disruption, it builds in a critical buffer that can minimize the financial impact of disrupted supplies.

Diversifying suppliers: Diversifying supply base reduces the overly dependence on suppliers and offers more protection against shocks. While diversification of supply base for parts and components also means sacrificing economies of scale and therefore is challenging to implement, dual sourcing of raw materials is another lever to build a more resilient supply chain. Together with increasing stock, expanding the source of supply for raw materials has been implemented by many companies (*see* Figure 5.4).

Reshoring, nearshoring, or regionalizing supply chain: Perhaps the most immediate reaction to the supply chain disruption is relocating sourcing and production closer to the market by reshoring, nearshoring, or regionalizing supply chain. Regional production near major consumer markets allows companies to promptly respond to market demand. Almost 90% of companies surveyed by McKinsey expect to pursue some degree of regionalization during the next three years. While companies may implement certain targeted adjustments to fix the weakest points in their supply chain, the decision to reshape the global production networks also depends on geopolitics, the tax and investment landscape, and industry characteristics, among other factors. Therefore, the overall global production footprint may not change drastically.

For example, very few of the surveyed companies in the semiconductor and advanced electronics industry plan on nearshoring. This industry is well established with strong economies of scale which makes it illogical to replicate the production in another location. In contrast, two-thirds of surveyed automotive companies plan to nearshore suppliers.[23]

Digital transformation for supply chain: Digitalization of supply chain helps companies strategize and achieve supply chain resilience. Big data analytics assist firms in streamlining their supplier selection process, predicting market demand more accurately, and providing more visibility into logistics processes. Cloud computing facilitates supplier relationships as it enables buyers to share demand data in a timely manner.[24] Automation and the use of robotics can reduce the dependence on physical workforce.

2.2.2 Dispersion of Workforce

The pandemic pushed companies and consumers to rapidly adopt new behaviors that are likely to persist. Perhaps the most obvious impact of COVID-19 on the labor force is the dramatic increase in employees working remotely.

Before the pandemic, there was a stigma that remote working would be less productive. However, research performed by McKinsey shows that about 20% to 25% of the workforces in advanced economies could work from home between three and five days a week without a loss of productivity. This represents four to five times more remote work than before the pandemic and could prompt a large change in the geography of work.[25] While there is no change in productivity, remote working offers flexibility to workers, reduces time commuting to work, and cuts down CO_2 emissions, among other benefits. Some companies are already planning to shift to flexible workspaces after positive experiences with remote work during the pandemic, a move that will reduce the overall space they need as fewer workers go into offices each day. A survey of 278 executives by McKinsey in August 2020 found that on average, companies planned to reduce office space by 30%.[26]

In an effort to dissect the potential of remote working, McKinsey performed research to quantify the physical proximity required in more than eight hundred occupations by grouping them into ten work arenas. The greater the required physical proximity score, the lower the expected potential for remote work, all else being equal. Factoring in other characteristics of the occupation in addition to the proximity score, McKinsey drew conclusions on the potential for remote work in the ten work arenas. The research

23. McKinsey, *Risk, Resilience, and Rebalancing in Global Value Chains*, https://www.mckinsey.com/business-functions/operations/our-insights/risk-resilience-and-rebalancing-in-global-value-chains (accessed January 4, 2022).
24. Baker McKenzie, *Beyond COVID-19: Supply Chain Resilience Holds Key to Recovery*, https://www.bakermckenzie.com/-/media/files/insight/publications/2020/04/covid19-global-economy.pdf?la=en (accessed January 4, 2022).
25. McKinsey, *The Future of Work after COVID-19*, https://www.mckinsey.com/featured-insights/future-of-work/the-future-of-work-after-covid-19 (accessed January 4, 2022).
26. *Ibid.*

finds that the computer-based office work arena, which accounts for roughly one-third of employment in advanced economies and has a relatively low proximity score, has the greatest potential for remote work. Other work arenas with higher levels of physical proximity such as retail and banking will likely migrate to e-commerce and other digital transactions to a certain extent.[27] Outdoor production and maintenance arena, which although has the lowest score, has lower potential for remote work and was less impacted by COVID-19 as the work requires few interactions and is performed outdoor (Figure 5.5).

Figure 5.5 Overall Physical Proximity Score by Work Arena[28]

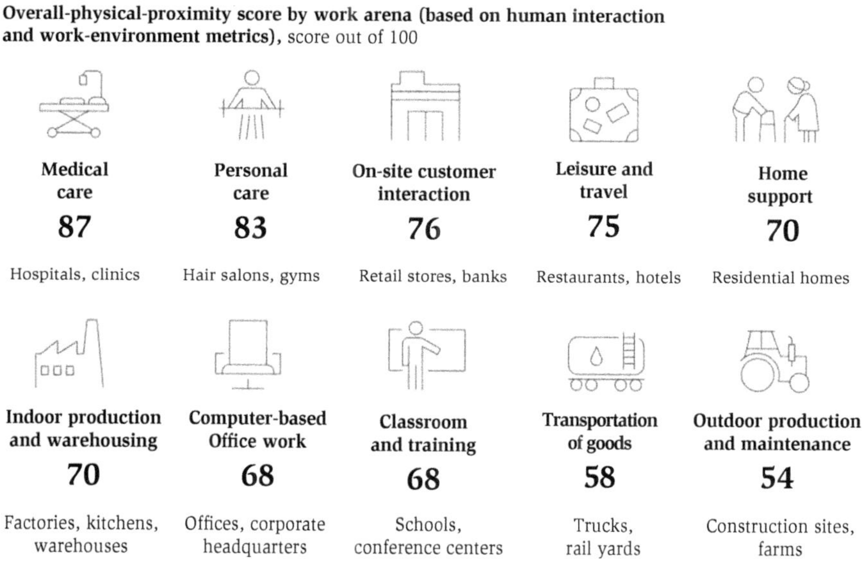

Source: McKinsey, The future of work after COVID-19

Studies have shown that a majority of US companies intend to offer hybrid models going forward as they see flexible work options help increase retention, recruit talent, improve work-life balance and employee wellness, among other motivations. According to a survey performed by KPMG, 81% of surveyed companies planned to allow hybrid work arrangements, and 59% agreed that workforce flexibility is part of their talent acquisition/retention agenda.[29] Surveys conducted by the Centre for Economic Performance show that in February 2020, at the onset of the pandemic, more than 60%

27. *Ibid.*
28. Physical proximity score represents the proximity between workers and their coworkers/customers, the number of interpersonal interactions involved, and their on-site and indoor nature.
29. KPMG, *Employer Trends in the Remote Work World, 2021 Remote and Multistate Payroll Reporting Survey Report,* visit.kpmg.us/Employment Tax.

of surveyed companies rarely or never allowed remote work, whereas that percentage is expected to be dramatically lower from January 2022 onwards to a little over 20% (Figure 5.6).[30]

Figure 5.6 Patterns of Remote Working (Days per Week)

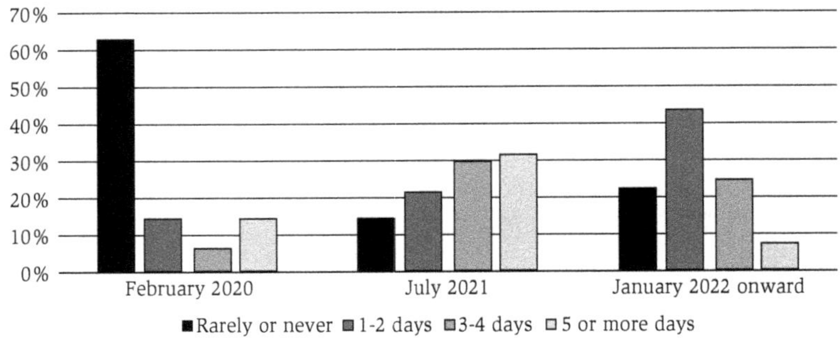

Source: Velero A., Riom C., Oliveira-Cunha J., The business response to COVID-19 one year on: findings from the second wave of the CEP-CBI survey on technology adoption, COVID-19 Analysis Series, Centre for Economic Performance, November 2021, No. 24.

With businesses going remote, technology created numerous potential job opportunities for individuals around the globe. With working from home becoming the new normal, it enabled companies to tap into a vast and diverse talent pool, which can be an effective way to bring people with different perspectives and ideas to organizations.[31]

In a survey performed by KPMG, 40% of the surveyed companies responded that they have not restricted the locations where their employees can work remotely. According to the same survey, only 54% currently use or are considering using a technology solution to identify employee taxing jurisdiction (Figure 5.7).[32]

30. Velero A., Riom C., Oliveira-Cunha J., *The Business Response to COVID-19 One Year On: Findings from the Second Wave of the CEP-CBI Survey on Technology Adoption*, COVID-19 Analysis Series, Centre for Economic Performance, November 2021, No.24.
31. XpertHR, *Most Employers Plan to Offer Hybrid Work After the COVID-19 Pandemic*, https://www.prnewswire.com/news-releases/most-employers-plan-to-offer-hybrid-work-after-the-covid-19-pandemic-according-to-xperthrs-latest-survey-301395043.html (accessed January 4, 2022).
32. KPMG, *Employer trends in the remote work world.*

Figure 5.7 Survey Results on Remote Working Restriction and Tracking

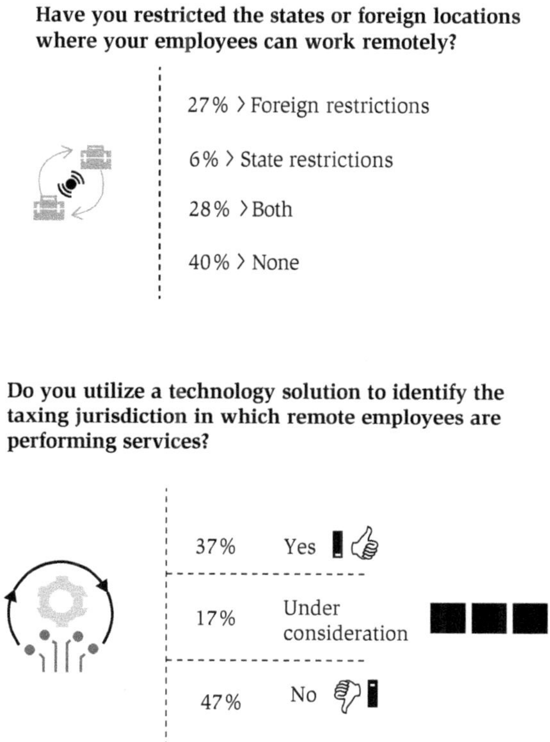

Source: KPMG, Employer trends in the remote work world

2.2.3 Digitalization

Before the pandemic, digitalization had been driven by the need to improve business processes, cooperation and customer engagement, and a faster pace of innovation. COVID-19 is a great accelerant to the existing global trend toward embracing new technologies and digital platforms to adapt to new business needs. More than half of businesses refocused operations or moved operations online due to COVID-19, and the majority say these changes are permanent.[33] The adoption of digital technology was applied to a wide range of business functions, most markedly to sales and marketing, people management and remote working (Figure 5.8).

33. Velero A., Riom C., Oliveira-Cunha J., *The Business Response to COVID-19 One Year On: Findings from the Second Wave of the CEP-CBI Survey on Technology Adoption*, COVID-19 Analysis Series, Centre for Economic Performance, November 2021, No.24.

Figure 5.8 Business Functions That Digital Technologies Related To[34]

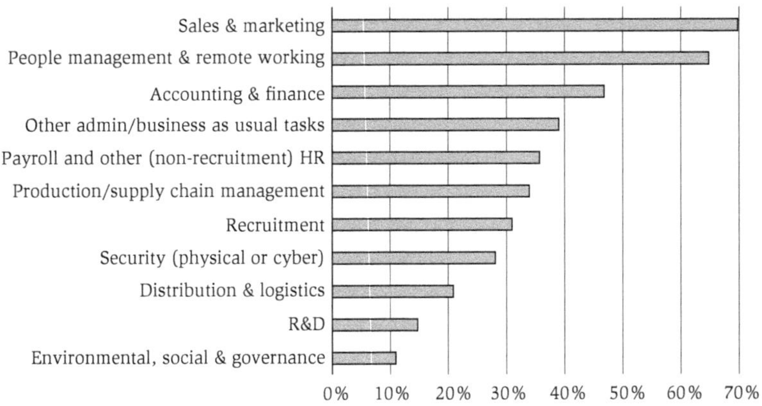

Source: Velero A., Riom C, Oliveira-Cunha J., The business response to COVID-19 one year on: findings from the second wave of the CEP-CBI survey on technology adoption, COVID-19 Analysis Series, Centre for Economic Performance, November 2021, No. 24.
Notes: N = 307 (Adopters that answered this questions).

The pandemic has changed consumer behavior and product demand and called for a digital transformation in sales and marketing, and products portfolio. During the pandemic, many consumers increasingly utilized the convenience of e-commerce and other online activities. Roughly three-quarters of people using digital channels for the first time around the world during the pandemic say they will continue using them when things return to "normal."[35] Other kinds of virtual transactions such as telemedicine, online banking, and streaming entertainment have also taken off given the need for social distancing. As consumer preferences drastically shifted to virtual online channels, companies and industries have responded in turn by funneling their investment into technology and accelerating digitalization to swiftly meet the market demand. This effort sped up the creation of digital products and services or digitally enhanced offerings, especially in healthcare and pharma, financial, and professional services. According to a new McKinsey Global Survey of executives, companies have accelerated the digitization of their customer and supply chain interactions and of their internal operations by three to four years, and the share of digital or digitally enabled products in their portfolios has accelerated by seven years.[36]

34. *Ibid.*
35. McKinsey, *The Future of Work after COVID-19*, https://www.mckinsey.com/featured-insights/future-of-work/the-future-of-work-after-covid-19 (accessed January 4, 2022).
36. McKinsey, *How COVID-19 Has Pushed Companies over the Technology Tipping Point—And Transformed Business Forever*, https://www.mckinsey.com/business-functions/strategy-and-corporate-finance/our-insights/how-covid-19-has-pushed-companies-over-the-technology-tipping-point-and-transformed-business-forever (accessed January 4, 2022).

Advanced data analytics has become more crucial to analyze economic and business circumstances, make intelligent predictions, and streamline management and operations during the pandemic, which is expected to continue post-pandemic. The disruption in markets and operations during COVID-19 requires companies to have more accurate insights and timely assessment of the situation in order to steer their organizations in the right direction. Descriptive and diagnostic analytics play a role in drawing insights from big data to help management make well-informed decisions about the future of work (human resources and organizational behavior changes), market demand (consumer behavior changes), product/service development and innovation (new product mix), and global value chains (more visibility into the supply chain and its pressing points). Predictive and prescriptive analytics concern what will happen in the future; determine actions and evaluate their impact on business objectives, requirements and constraints; and help mitigate severe impacts should similar events happen in the future.[37] Deploying advanced data analytics therefore generates great intelligence and value for businesses in both the short term and long term.

Acceleration in technology adoption to promote remote working happened early in the pandemic, as noted in section 2.1. The cloud migration allowed for a streamlined movement toward the new way of working. As the future of work will likely be a hybrid model, the digital need required to facilitate virtual collaboration continues to persist. The use of messaging, videoconferencing platforms, shared sites and collaboration tools has increasingly become the norm. In tandem with the virtual operation setting is the cybersecurity concern and the need to invest in data security. Investment in data security is one of the changes that is identified as helping to position organizations better than they were before the crisis.[38]

3 TRANSFER PRICING IMPLICATIONS OF COVID-19 IN THE SHORT TERM

As discussed above, COVID-19 has caused an immediate and significant disruption to the global economy, which continues today. Some of the effects of COVID-19 on the economy are expected to be temporary and are expected to dissipate once the pandemic is brought under control, whereas other changes to the economy are expected to endure into the future. The previous section discussed the ways in which COVID-19 has disrupted the economy—both temporarily while the public health concerns of COVID-19 persist and over the longer term by changing certain fundamental characteristics of the economy. This article correspondingly discusses the implications of the temporary and longer-term disruptions caused by COVID-19 for transfer

37. Sheng J., Amankwah-Amoah J., Khan Z., Wang X., *COVID-19 Pandemic in the New Era of Big Data Analytics: Methodological Innovations and Future Research Directions*, British Journal of Management, Vol. 32, 1164-1183 (2021).
38. McKinsey, *How COVID-19 Has Pushed Companies over the Technology Tipping Point—And Transformed Business Forever*, https://www.mckinsey.com/business-functions/strategy-and-corporate-finance/our-insights/how-covid-19-has-pushed-companies-over-the-technology-tipping-point-and-transformed-business-forever (accessed January 4, 2022).

pricing. This section discusses the transfer pricing implications of COVID-19 that are expected to linger in a post-COVID-19 world in the short term.

The disruption created by COVID-19 has impacted the way companies manage their transfer pricing. Since the short-term economic effects of the pandemic are not expected to stop immediately with the end of the pandemic and there is often a lag in the availability of economic data used for transfer pricing analyses, the post-COVID-19 transfer pricing landscape in the short term will continue seeing similar issues as during the pandemic.

On the compliance side, the economic downturn has challenged well-established policies and processes, which have had to be reassessed in light of the exceptional market conditions caused by the pandemic. Various aspects of day-to-day compliance with transfer pricing rules have had to be reassessed and, in many cases, adjusted to reflect the new reality. These aspects include, for example:

- the treatment of exceptional costs arising in connection with the pandemic;
- the renegotiation or suspension of existing contracts;
- the treatment of government subsidies;
- the selection of the most appropriate transfer pricing method;
- the sources and types of information used for transfer pricing analyses;
- the use of comparable companies/comparable data;
- the need for comparability adjustments;
- year-end price or margin adjustments/true-ups;
- how to deal with existing APAs and with nearly completed APA procedures;
- possible modification of the structure of transfer pricing documentation; and
- the treatment of widespread losses.

During 2020, tax authorities published guidance and clarifications, and introduced special measures to tackle the general tax implications of COVID-19 for specific matters such as custom duties or Value Added Tax. A few countries (e.g., Australia, New Zealand, Singapore and the United States) and, toward the end of 2020, the OECD published guidance on the various practical transfer pricing challenges that companies were encountering in determining the correct arm's-length pricing under such unusual market conditions.

In particular, the 'Guidance on the Transfer Pricing Implications of the COVID-19 Pandemic' (OECD Guidance),[39] published by the OECD in December 2020, represented the consensus view of the members of the OECD Inclusive Framework on BEPS (Inclusive Framework) and provided companies with clarification on how to manage the complexities of intra-firm pricing.[40]

The objective of the OECD Guidance was to provide clarifying comments on and examples of the application of the arm's-length principle and the 2017 OECD Transfer

39. OECD, *Guidance on the transfer pricing implications of the COVID-19 pandemic*, OECD Policy Responses to Coronavirus (COVID-19), OECD Publishing, Paris (December 18, 2020) ("OECD Guidance").
40. For a more detailed discussion, *see also KPMG Report: OECD Guidance on the Transfer Pricing Implications of the COVID-19 Pandemic.* KPMG (December 23, 2020).

Pricing Guidelines (OECD TPG)[41] to the technical issues arising from the pandemic, and it does indeed provide new guidance beyond that already included in the OECD TPG.

Overall, the OECD Guidance establishes some general principles and gives a few examples of how to apply the arm's-length principle to some of the pricing issues that have arisen during the pandemic. However, it does not necessarily offer specific solutions or answers to the many challenges faced by companies and tax administrations. It starts from the assumption that the *arm's-length principle* and the OECD TPG apply to intragroup transactions in both good and adverse economic conditions and that the intragroup transaction should be evaluated in comparison with the *behavior of unrelated parties* engaged in comparable transactions. *Consistency pre- and post-pandemic* and a *constructive, flexible, collaborative, and transparent* approach to the technical issues—by tax administrations as well as taxpayers—are indicated as extremely important.

The short-term impact of COVID-19 on the management of intragroup transactions (including the topics illustrated above) was covered in detail in "Transfer Pricing Developments Around the World 2021."[42]

Two years after the start of the pandemic, this section will focus on one of the most debated issues that companies have had to face in the aftermath of the pandemic: the application of the Transactional Net Margin Method (TNMM) in an economic environment of widespread losses, with a focus on the selection of comparable transactions/companies and comparability adjustments.

3.1 The Application of the TNMM During the Pandemic

The TNMM is arguably the pricing method most used by multinational enterprises (MNEs) and is the method most affected by the economic disruption generated by the pandemic. In a time of high volatility and unusual economic circumstances, various challenges are posed by the application of a transfer pricing method that is based on the determination of a stable profit margin for affiliated entities performing routine functions and bearing limited risks. In several sectors, the financial results of MNEs reflected the full impact of the pandemic, with unusual financial results (mainly losses). This has created significant difficulties in the identification of the right profit level indicator (PLI) and the correct comparable transactions to be used for the transfer pricing analysis.

In this context, MNEs have had to decide whether to allow routine and limited-risk companies to incur losses or to make significant year-end price or margin adjustments. For many MNEs, in many sectors, the extent of losses does not allow the possibility of stable, positive, profit margins for group affiliates performing routine activities.

41. OECD, *OECD Transfer Pricing Guidelines for Multinational Enterprises and Tax Administrations 2017*, OECD Publishing, Paris (2017) ("OECD TPG").
42. De Robertis G., *Recent Developments in Transfer Pricing and COVID-19* in *Transfer Pricing Developments Around the World 2021* edited by Lang M., Petruzzi R., 2021, Chapter 6.

The decision is complicated by the fact that any transfer pricing analysis must rely on third-party behavior and third-party comparable data, which are not available in real time.[43]

In the short term, therefore, MNEs have had to consider how to tailor the application of the TNMM to the unusual market conditions. The main aspects considered by MNEs include the following.

1. Revising comparable screening procedures

Revision of the application of a TNMM may start with the revision of the procedure used to select and screen potential comparable transactions and comparable companies. For example, in normal circumstances, it is not unusual to exclude loss-making companies from comparable sets, on the basis that routine companies would not expect to make losses. This assumption may not hold good in extraordinary economic circumstances; hence the exclusion of loss-making companies may need to be reconsidered.[44]

2. Using the best comparable data

While in normal market conditions companies may often rely on comparable data of previous years, during COVID-19 the market conditions are so unusual that this approach would be incorrect in many industry sectors. This is also pointed out by the OECD Guidance,[45] which indicates the reduced possibility of relying on historical data, as they do not reflect current economic conditions. Companies, therefore, have aimed to use either real-time data (e.g., from interim financial reports) or, alternatively, to adjust historical comparable data to reflect current market conditions.

3. Making comparability adjustments

Comparability adjustments can take many shapes and forms, from very simple to very complicated ones.[46] For example, adjustments can be made using one of the approaches set out below:

(i) Modification of target margins: for example, by using the lower quartile rather than the median or the interquartile range of the comparable set.

(ii) Adjustments to company data: tax managers may adjust the financial data of their own company to a precrisis level, to cancel out the effect of the crisis. For example, they may modify the level of turnover, variable costs, capacity

43. OECD, *OECD Guidance on the transfer pricing implications of the COVID-19 pandemic, OECD Policy Responses to Coronavirus (COVID-19)*, OECD Publishing, Paris, Chapter I (December 18, 2020).
44. *See also* OECD Guidance, paragraph 33.
45. OECD, *OECD Guidance on the transfer pricing implications of the COVID-19 pandemic, OECD Policy Responses to Coronavirus (COVID-19)*, OECD Publishing, Paris, paragraph 9 (December 18, 2020).
46. Chroustovsky S., Petutschnig M., *Comparability Adjustments—A Literature Review*, WU International Taxation Research Paper Series, No. 2018-08, pp. 19 (2018).

utilization, share of fixed costs, bad debts, and one-off costs,[47] or consider budget figures.

(iii) Adjustments to comparable companies: based on the facts and circumstances, historical data from comparable companies may be adjusted in various ways according to the type of data and type of statistical technique that are used. Broadly speaking, comparable sets for which no current data are available can be adjusted by using:
   - current/real-time macroeconomic data: e.g., change in GDP, level of unemployment, stock markets; or
   - current/real-time microeconomic data: e.g., change in sales, selling, general and administrative expenses (SG&A), capacity utilization, fixed costs, extraordinary costs, bad debts.

The data needed to make adjustments could have been obtained from the market, i.e., not only from interim financial statements or economic statistics available in real time but also from the comparables themselves, by looking at their performance in past recessions or their historical performance overall.[48]

4. Considering how to address the "survival bias"

This fundamental issue is often underestimated and may greatly affect the reliability of any transfer pricing analysis. Comparable sets tend to understate the impact of economic downturns on company margins. In particular: "good comparable sets are composed of independent companies and, very often, these companies are small and medium-sized. These independent companies will be affected to different degrees by a recession: a limited number of them may not be affected or may even benefit from the economic turmoil while the majority are likely [to] be affected severely and some of them very severely. While the companies that are less affected by the recession will survive and will appear in the comparable sets, some of the severely affected companies will not survive and will not appear. Therefore, comparable sets identified in years of deep recession have an intrinsic bias, often referred to as a survival bias, where only the relatively less affected companies will appear in the final set. As a result, such sets do not show the full impact of the recession on company margins. Arm's length margin ranges will decrease—but not as much as might be expected in such conditions."[49] Companies that are part of MNEs are generally more likely to survive during deep recessions and to absorb losses for one or more years, as they can benefit from the support of the group overall. Conversely, stand-alone companies are less resilient when facing heavy losses.

47. For an example, *see* De Robertis G., *Recent Developments in Transfer Pricing and COVID-19* in *Transfer Pricing Developments Around the World 2021* edited by Lang M., Petruzzi R., 2021.
48. Subramanian R., Krustev V., Eisenberg H., Hughes M., *Transfer Pricing Adjustments to the COVID-19 Economic Downturn,* Tax Management Transfer Pricing Report, TPR, 07/06/2020.
49. De Robertis G., *Recent Developments in Transfer Pricing and COVID-19* in *Transfer Pricing Developments Around the World 2021* edited by Lang M., Petruzzi R., 2021, section 6.3.3.

Not all MNEs have pursued the same strategy when dealing with the implications of the pandemic for intragroup transactions and the application of the TNMM. Many companies operating in sectors which have not been severely affected by the economic fallout of the pandemic have decided to apply the TNMM in the same way as in the past, while companies which have been significantly affected by the economic downturn have decided to adjust their TNMM analyses to account for one or more of the four aspects listed above.

As foreseen in "Recent Developments in Transfer Pricing and COVID-19," in deciding whether to make adjustments and, if so, which ones to make and what technique to use, companies have considered both their own specific facts and circumstances (e.g., industry sector, functional profile, value chain and impact of the downturn) and the characteristics of identified comparable companies. Taxpayers have also considered the trade-off between simplicity and accuracy, generally preferring simpler adjustments – which may be less subjective and easier to audit – to more accurate but more complex ones that rely on many assumptions.

3.2 Some Evidence from the Market

In the tables below, we illustrate some examples of comparable analyses which have been performed in relation to various functional profiles and industries. The examples show how the estimated 2020 margin ranges, obtained by using historical data from European comparable sets (2017-2019), compared with the actual 2020 ranges now available. The analysis focuses on five examples of comparable sets, which used different types of comparability adjustments.

In particular, the adjustments applied to the sets can be briefly described as follows:

– Statistical adjustment to the comparables' financials based on macroeconomic indicators

This approach estimates the effects of COVID-19 pandemic on the selected comparables by considering the statistical correlation between revenues and costs of a large sample of entities operating in the industry under analysis and a macroeconomic variable (e.g., GDP, change in GDP, level of unemployment, stock market performance). The correlation coefficients derived through models of statistical regression are used to estimate how (and to what extent) the change observed in 2020 in the macroeconomic variable selected (e.g., a 10% decrease in the GDP) is applied to the financial data of the selected comparables.

– Statistical adjustment to the comparables' financials based on microeconomic indicators

This approach estimates the effects of the pandemic on the selected comparables by analyzing the effects that COVID-19 had on the tested party's (or to the group's) financials: microeconomic variables generally considered are change in sales, SG&A, capacity utilization, fixed costs, extraordinary costs, bad debts. In particular, through statistical regression models, it is determined how (and to what extent) the change in the microeconomic variable selected (e.g., change in sales experienced by the tested party in 2020) transmits to the financial data of the selected comparables.

– Use of information from the 2008-09 crisis rollback

This approach estimates the effects of COVID-19 pandemic by analyzing the performance of a set of comparable companies during previous crisis periods (e.g., 2008-2009 crisis). The analysis of the differences in their performances between normal times and crisis times provides useful insight for estimating the potential change in the comparables' PLI to be expected in 2020 due to COVID-19 pandemic.

The analysis can be performed using the most recent comparable set available (recent comparables) or a comparable set selected for fiscal years immediately before the past crisis, e.g., 2006 or 2007 (old comparables).

The content of the tables is briefly explained below:

- The first column shows 2020 data for the comparable set. These data became available only toward the end of 2021 (when companies published their figures and databases were updated); hence, they were not available when MNEs had to apply their TNMM and make their final decision on prices and margins for 2020.
- The second column shows historical data for the same comparables - data which were available at the end of 2020.
- The other columns show estimates of 2020 data obtained using some of the statistical methods listed above.

Looking at the actual 2020 data, a few interesting facts emerge from these examples:

- In all cases, the median margin decreases, compared to the average of the previous three years. This confirms the significant impact of the economic downturn across a range of industries.
- In all cases, the range of margins dips into negative profit, and in one case, the first quartile is also negative. This compares to a pre-pandemic period in which only two sets displayed a negative minimum margin and, in all cases, the first quartile was positive. This confirms that in difficult economic conditions, a share of routine independent companies does make losses.
- Not all companies can be found (or, in some cases, no data can be found) for 2020. This may be due to incomplete updating of the database or to some companies being no longer in existence.

Looking at the estimated 2020 data, the estimated median PLI for 2020 is always lower than (or in one case equal to) the actual PLI for 2020. The difference varies significantly on a case-by-case basis. Similar considerations apply to the profit ranges and quartiles:

Example 1: Retail European Union (EU) (apparel sector)

	Actual comparable data	Historical data	Estimated 2020 OM data starting from historical data
	Operating Margin (OM) 2020	Average OM 2017-2019	Based on microeconomic data
Maximum	22.4%	15.1%	19.7%
75th percentile	6.8%	6.6%	5.6%
Median	1.4%	2.8%	0.2%
25th percentile	–3.3%	1.5%	–5.3%
Minimum	–26.5%	–3.6%	–56.3%
No. of companies	30	36	
No. of companies not present or lacking 2020 data	6		

Example 2: Wholesale EU (specific industrial sector)

	Actual comparable data	Historical data	Estimated 2020 OM data starting from historical data
	OM 2020	Average OM 2017-2019	Based on macroeconomic data
Maximum	14.5%	30.5%	29.1%
75th percentile	4.3%	6.4%	4.5%
Median	1.7%	3.6%	1.6%
25th percentile	0.2%	1.4%	–0.6%
Minimum	–2.3%	0.8%	–1.3%
No. of companies	12	12	
No. of companies not present or lacking 2020 data	0		

Example 3: Manufacturing EU (specific industrial sector)			
	Actual comparable data	Historical data	Statistical adjustment to historical data (NCPM)
	Net Cost Plus Mark-Up (NCPM) 2020	Average NCPM 2017-2019	Based on macroeconomic data
Maximum	19.2%	12.9%	8.1%
75th percentile	8.6%	7.6%	3.0%
Median	2.9%	5.0%	0.5%
25th percentile	2.2%	3.7%	–0.7%
Minimum	–7.7%	2.4%	–2.0%
No. of companies	10	12	
No. of companies not present or lacking 2020 data	2		

Example 4: Wholesale EU (electrical/electronic sector)				
	Actual comparable data	Historical data	Estimated 2020 OM data starting from historical data	
	OM 2020	OM 2017-2019	Based on macroeconomic data	Based on microeconomic data
Maximum	4.8%	10.5%	7.8%	11.1%
75th percentile	2.8%	4.8%	1.7%	4.2%
Median	1.8%	3.3%	0.5%	1.8%
25th percentile	0.4%	1.4%	–1.5%	0.6%
Minimum	–1.0%	–0.5%	–3.5%	–2.0%
No. of companies	11	14		
No. of companies not present or lacking 2020 data	3			

Example 5: Wholesale EU (consumer sector)

	Actual comparable data	Historical data	Estimated 2020 OM data using data from the 2009 financial crisis		
	OM 2020	Average OM 2017-2019	Method 1 (using old comp sets)	Method 2 (using recent comp sets)	Average
Maximum	87.2%	15.8%	13.9%	3.7%	8.8%
75th percentile	4.6%	5.6%	4.6%	4.0%	4.3%
Median	2.4%	4.2%	2.9%	1.7%	2.3%
25th percentile	0.5%	2.8%	1.8%	1.4%	1.6%
Minimum	–5.8%	0.6%	–2.6%	–5.5%	–4.1%
No. of companies	13	20			
No. of companies not present or lacking 2020 data	7				

There are at least two key points which we can infer from these examples:

(1) The use of historical data to set arm's-length pricing for 2020 would have generally and significantly overstated the margins earned by routine European entities in the industries/sectors in the examples above.[50] Therefore, the application of comparability adjustments is justified and is likely to improve the compliance of the TNMM with the arm's-length principle for 2020 for such routine entities.

(2) The decrease in profitability revealed by the actual data seems lower than might be expected, given the severity of the economic downturn and the pandemic and the economic data and industry-sector figures which have been published for 2020. This may be due to several reasons, including the fact that the comparable companies are routine entities, and thus less exposed to certain economic risks or the various public programs which have been implemented to support businesses during the pandemic. But it could also reflect a "survival bias," which has been explained earlier in this section, since the companies most affected by the pandemic may no longer appear in the database and in the final set, following their liquidation or closure due to the economic downturn.

50. Other industries, sectors, and regions might not be equally affected.

3.3 Post-COVID-19 Short-Term Transfer Pricing Implications

Once the public health concerns of COVID-19 subside and the measures put in place to address them are removed, changes to the economy that are the direct result of the extraordinary circumstances of the pandemic are expected to fade. Economic activity has already picked up since the steep decline in 2020, businesses are expected to find solutions for the temporary supply chain disruptions and the necessity of working from remote locations will recede (although the longer-term trend toward remote work is expected to remain). However, while the immediate public health disruptions of COVID-19 are expected to end with the pandemic, the economic repercussions of the extraordinary circumstances of COVID-19 may persist for a short period after the end of the pandemic.

More importantly for transfer pricing purposes, given the typical reliance on historical data and multiple years of data, the transfer pricing implications discussed above that companies are grappling with during COVID-19 are expected to continue for a short period post-COVID-19. COVID-19 has exposed shortcomings of transfer pricing approaches for dealing with extraordinary circumstances and risks. As a result of COVID-19, some companies have taken a fresh look at their transfer pricing policies and contracts. Further, as noted above, one of the most notable questions arising in the context of COVID-19 is whether any adjustments should be made to profit margins of routine entities under the TNMM. In this context, companies have had to evaluate whether they could still support the "routine" or "low-risk" characterization of their routine entities or whether the transfer pricing adjustment may be construed as a more fundamental change in the characterization of the entity. Such evaluations are expected to continue in the post-COVID-19 short term where companies make or have made adjustments to the profit margins of their routine entities. Additionally, the unusual financial results, adjustments to tested party or comparable data and renegotiation of contracts, among other issues, will be audited some years post-COVID-19. Therefore, we can expect to see greater scrutiny from tax authorities and increased controversy in the post-COVID-19 short term, particularly since tax authorities will have the benefit of hindsight to evaluate adjustments and atypical transfer pricing approaches.

The variability of profit margins of routine businesses by industry, sector, and year over year because of the pandemic also holds lessons for the Inclusive Framework's work on Amount B under Pillar One, which seeks to come up with standardized profitability margins for routine marketing and distribution activities.[51] One of the key stated goals of the Amount B work is to simplify application of the arm's-length principle to certain routine transactions. As the experience from the pandemic has shown, there can be significant variability in profit margins of businesses that are typically considered routine. The Inclusive Framework will, therefore, need to balance the need for simplicity with the risk of significantly misstating profit margins under certain circumstances.

51. Pillar One is the OECD BEPS pillar that addresses the broader challenges of the digitalized economy and focuses on the allocation of taxing rights.

4 TRANSFER PRICING IMPLICATIONS OF COVID-19 IN THE LONG TERM

As discussed above, COVID-19 has fundamentally altered aspects of the global economy, such as altering supply chain relationships, geographically dispersing employees of businesses and accelerating digitalization. Further, in doing so, COVID-19 has exacerbated conditions that have in recent years either led to a rethinking of international tax systems, such as increasing digitalization of businesses, or deepened tensions in application of existing rules, such as interpretation of the transfer pricing guidance related to risk and intangibles. The following sections discuss transfer pricing trends in the long term that have been created or accelerated by COVID-19.

4.1 Business Restructurings

As discussed earlier, COVID-19 has laid bare risks in the global supply chain structures of the last few decades. In response to the disruptions to supply chains brought about by COVID-19 and the associated declines in revenues and profits, MNEs are undertaking supply chain restructurings—they are increasing inventories, diversifying suppliers, increasing domestic production, and digitally managing supply chains.

These supply chain restructurings are expected to lead to new transfer pricing issues. There will be new transactions to price, for instance, where an MNE moves the location of its controlled manufacturing activities to be closer to its markets, or where an MNE sets up new procurement companies to tap into sources of supply not previously considered. As MNEs reorganize supply chains, they will also need to reconsider transfer pricing policies for existing types of transactions. For example, the MNE might have transfer pricing policies for the sale of product by controlled manufacturers based on profit margin benchmarks derived from comparable companies. As the MNE moves manufacturing locations, the existing comparable company benchmarks may no longer be appropriate. More importantly, if the new manufacturer has been established to manage an economically significant supply risk, then the MNE may need to rethink its value chain and how the new manufacturer fits within it as it works through the new transfer pricing policies.

The restructuring of supply chains will also lead to exit tax considerations. Countries have different rules on exit taxes, and MNEs will need to evaluate the different rules to determine if they will be subject to exit taxes in any jurisdictions as they restructure their supply chains.

More generally, Chapter IX of the OECD TPG provides guidance on business restructurings. It defines a business restructuring as the cross-border reorganization of the commercial or financial relations between associated enterprises, including the termination or substantial renegotiation of existing arrangements.[52]

Some business restructurings may involve cross-border transfers of something of value, e.g., of valuable intangibles. More generally, business restructurings are often

52. OECD TPG, para. 9.1.

accompanied by a reallocation of profit potential among the members of the MNE group. A reallocation of profit potential per se does not require compensation at arm's length, but companies will need to consider the extent to which such a reallocation of profit potential is consistent with the arm's-length principle in evaluating potential exit charges for their business restructurings.

In order to determine whether at arm's length the restructuring itself would give rise to a form of compensation, it will be essential to understand the restructuring, including the changes that have taken place, how they have affected the functional analysis of the parties, what the business reasons for and the anticipated benefits from the restructuring were, and what options would have been realistically available to the parties.[53] MNEs will need to work through these questions as they restructure their supply chains. Given the differing rules of jurisdictions and differing viewpoints of tax authorities, MNEs can also expect challenges to any transfer pricing positions related to supply chain restructurings from tax authorities.

4.2 Dispersed Workforce

As discussed in section 2.2.2, COVID-19 has had the effect of dispersing an MNE's workforce. The proximate cause of much of this dispersion has been travel restrictions and quarantine requirements imposed by various governments. As a result of these restrictions, many cross-border workers have been unable to physically work in their countries of employment. Such dislocation of an MNE's workforce is expected to be temporary—as the COVID-19 health crisis wanes and governments relax travel restrictions, some of the more significant impediments to workers working in their countries of employment will be lifted.

However, as discussed earlier, there is a broader and more permanent shift in employment practices underway. As remote work becomes easier and companies vie to attract talent, allowing employees to work from home or their location of choice is becoming increasingly common.

Remote work is raising a plethora of tax issues since taxing rights under the current international tax system have been built around physical presence in a jurisdiction. In our discussion here, we focus on transfer pricing issues related to the taxing rights of countries in connection with remote work. In particular, we focus on the following two key issues relevant to transfer pricing that are increasingly arising as a result of the longer-term trend toward remote work:

- Do the remote workers create permanent establishments (PEs) in their remote work location? If so, how should profit be attributed to the PE created by the remote worker?

53. OECD TPG, para. 9.42.

- Should existing transfer pricing policies be modified to account for the dispersion of an MNE's workforce, particularly of employees with decision-making and control functions related to risks and the development, enhancement, maintenance, protection and exploitation (DEMPE) of intangibles?

These two questions are not unrelated. The attribution of profit to a PE is broadly comparable to the transfer pricing question. We start below with a discussion of PEs arising from remote work and then move on to the pricing question.

4.2.1 Remote Workers Creating PEs

The OECD Model Tax Convention on Income and Capital that forms the basis of most tax treaties defines "permanent establishment" as a fixed place of business through which the business of an enterprise is wholly or partly carried on.

At the start of COVID-19, several governments[54] and the OECD Secretariat[55] released guidance based on tax treaty rules around whether dislocated employees created PEs in their locations of remote work. This guidance generally clarified that the exceptional and temporary change of location of work because of COVID-19 should not create new PEs for the employer. Similarly, the temporary conclusion of contracts in the remote location because of COVID-19 should not create a PE in the remote location.

Not all countries have provided such guidance and among the countries that have provided guidance, the guidance is not uniform. However, one aspect of the guidance is clear—the guidance only applies to the exceptional and temporary change in location resulting from COVID-19.

Therefore, any longer-term shift in employment practices toward remote work that is a result of company policy as opposed to COVID-19 public health measures is not expected to be covered by the temporary relaxing of PE rules.

As remote work becomes increasingly common as a standard employment practice, we can expect to see greater incidence of PEs going forward.

In fact, companies are grappling with issues around the determination of new PEs resulting from dispersed employees. This determination comes with all the considerations that have traditionally accompanied PE determinations, e.g., whether to change employment location of the remote worker, whether to establish an entity in the jurisdiction of the employee's activities or whether to allow the employee to create a PE. Over time, as a dispersed workforce becomes more widespread, companies are likely to develop internal policies around remote work to manage the number and locations of PEs within the MNE group. As discussed in section 2.2.2, approximately 60% of surveyed businesses in a 2021 KPMG study had restricted the states or foreign locations where their employees could work, and 54% were utilizing or considering

54. These include Australia, Canada, Ireland, India, UK, and US. *See*, for instance, Rev. Proc. 2020-20 released by the US Internal Revenue Service.
55. OECD Policy Responses to Coronavirus (COVID-19): *OECD Secretariat analysis of tax treaties and the impact of the COVID-19 crisis*, April 3, 2020. The OECD Secretariat subsequently updated this guidance in January 2021. *See* OECD Policy Responses to Coronavirus (COVID-19): *Updated guidance on tax treaties and the impact of the COVID-19 pandemic*, January 21 2021.

utilizing technology to track the taxing jurisdictions of their employees. These percentages are likely to increase over time. Therefore, there may be some stabilization in the incidence of PEs over time. Nevertheless, companies will likely need to deal with greater PE issues as more employees start working remotely as a matter of company policy rather than an exigency imposed by COVID-19.

New PEs create various tax issues to work through. Most relevant from a transfer pricing perspective is how much profit to attribute to the PE. Here we note that tax treaties are not uniform in their treatment of profit attribution and neither are domestic rules. Therefore, companies will need to carefully evaluate domestic rules and treaties to determine appropriate approaches for profit attribution. Having said that, under any rules that follow transfer pricing principles for profit attribution, there is significant overlap in the principles for attribution of profit to a PE and the pricing of controlled transactions, and therefore we discuss both together below.

4.2.2 *Transfer Pricing Challenges of a Dispersed Workforce*

Before we discuss pricing and profit attribution issues related to a dispersed workforce, we first take a short detour to provide an overview of key elements of the OECD Guidance on the attribution of profits to a PE and the pricing of controlled transactions.

4.2.2.1 *Overview of Key Transfer Pricing Principles*

Under the OECD TPG, the fundamental principle underlying the determination of profits of associated enterprises of an MNE group is the arm's-length principle. The arm's-length principle treats the members of the MNE group as separate entities rather than as inseparable parts of a single unified business, and seeks to price the controlled transactions between such members by reference to prices independent enterprises would have agreed to in comparable transactions under comparable circumstances.

4.2.2.1.1 Attribution of Profit to a PE

With regards to attribution of profit to a PE, while there is variation in the practices of countries and tax treaties, the Authorized OECD Approach (AOA) attributes profit to a PE by treating the PE as a separate and independent enterprise and applying the guidance in the OECD TPG to its dealings with other parts of the enterprise.[56]

However, since a PE is not in fact legally separate from the rest of the enterprise of which it is a part in the way that an associated enterprise is legally separate from other enterprises within the same MNE group, it is first necessary to hypothesize appropriately the PE and the remainder of the enterprise as if they were associated enterprises. The AOA accomplishes this in the first step of its analysis using a functional and factual analysis to attribute risks, economic ownership of assets and capital to hypothesize a

56. OECD: *2010 Report on the Attribution of Profits to Permanent Establishments*, July 22, 2010 ("OECD PE Report").

separate and independent PE. The AOA attributes to the PE those risks for which the significant functions relevant to the assumption and/or management of risks are performed by people in the PE and attributes to the PE economic ownership of assets for which the significant functions relevant to the economic ownership of assets are performed by people in the PE. Additionally, the AOA allocates capital to the PE needed for assuming the risks attributed to the PE.[57]

Once the PE has been hypothesized as a separate and independent enterprise, the second step of the AOA applies the OECD TPG to the dealings of the PE with other parts of the enterprise as it would to any controlled transactions between associated enterprises.[58]

Thus, attribution of profit to a PE under the AOA differs from regular transfer pricing for associated enterprises primarily in the additional first step required to hypothesize the PE as a separate and independent enterprise. Unlike in the context of associated enterprises where contracts or legal arrangements reflecting the conduct of the parties provide a basis for the determination of which enterprise owns assets, which bears risk and which possesses capital, the AOA assigns risks, assets and capital to the PE based on its significant people functions.

We next discuss some recent changes in transfer pricing rules that are important for the transfer pricing discussion around a dispersed workforce.

4.2.2.1.2 Control over Risk and DEMPE

The OECD, and subsequently the Inclusive Framework, embarked on an ambitious project in 2013 to address perceived shortcomings of the international tax system to prevent base erosion and profit shifting (BEPS) through double non-taxation. The OECD came up with fifteen actions to address BEPS and issued final reports on its findings and recommendations in 2015. Three of the actions, Actions 8-10, addressed transfer pricing issues.[59]

Leading up to BEPS Actions 8-10, tax authorities had expressed concern that MNEs were artificially shifting income to low tax jurisdictions by transferring their valuable intangibles and/or economically significant risks to group companies in those jurisdictions. The MNE often did not have much operational activity in the low tax jurisdiction but earned significant profits there by virtue of its contractual assumption of risk or intangible property (IP) ownership. One approach the OECD took to addressing this particular concern was to include specific functional requirements for an entity to reap the economic benefits of intangible ownership or assumption of risk. According to the OECD, these requirements are consistent with arm's-length behavior.

The starting premise of the OECD's approach to assumption of risk and intangible ownership is that at arm's length, all members of an MNE need to receive appropriate compensation for the functions they perform, assets they use and risks they assume. The approach presumes that important functions related to the control of risk and the

57. OECD PE Report, section B-3.
58. OECD PE Report, section B-4.
59. OECD *Action Plan on Base Erosion and Profit Shifting*, 2013.

DEMPE of an intangible contribute to the returns for the assumption of risk and the creation of the intangible's value, respectively. The OECD's approach, therefore, concludes that contractual assumption of risk alone or legal ownership of an intangible alone does not generate a right to the returns from risk assumption or the intangible. The legal owner of an intangible must provide a share of the returns from the intangible to the provider of DEMPE functions commensurate with the importance of those functions. A legal entity that assumes an economically significant risk must also control the risk.

In this way, the OECD's guidance on control over risk and DEMPE is intended to prevent companies with no significant employees or minimal operational activity from earning significant risk-related or intangible-related returns.[60]

4.2.2.2 *Pricing Dispersed DEMPE and Risk Control Services*

As noted above, dislocated employees may create PEs in their new jurisdiction of work. Alternatively, their employment may shift to other group entities. Whether the MNE needs to attribute profit to a PE or price new transactions arising from a shift in employment location of a worker, similar considerations arise—identifying how the activities of the employee fit within the MNE's value chain, determining the dealings or intercompany transactions involving the employee, and transfer pricing the dealings or intercompany transactions involving the employee. As noted above, in the case of a PE (assuming profit attribution under the AOA), there is an additional interim step of hypothesizing the PE as a separate entity.

We will focus on the transfer pricing question in the context of associated enterprises below and briefly get back to the question of PEs later in the section.

While the basic questions that need to be answered are the same irrespective of the level of the employee, the most interesting and challenging issues arise in the context of senior employees who control economically significant risks or perform important DEMPE functions. As companies vie for talent, the dispersion of senior employees within the MNE group is only expected to get more common in the future. This dispersion of senior employees is further exacerbating tensions in the interpretation and application of the revised guidelines on control over risk and DEMPE that have already arisen in recent years.

While the OECD TPG make it clear that legal ownership or contractual terms alone do not entitle an entity to returns from the assumption of risk or the ownership of intangibles, the guidance is less clear on degree; i.e., how much "substance" in the form of risk control and important DEMPE functions is required for an entity to earn the returns from risk assumption and intangible ownership. In practice, different tax authorities have interpreted this guidance differently, leaving taxpayers with the challenge of determining the appropriate level of substance to satisfy the functional requirements for earning the rewards of risk assumption and intangible

60. *See* Subramanian P., *Ten Questions on the OECD's DEMPE Concept and Its Role in Valuing Intangibles*, Tax Management Transfer Pricing Report, Vol. 26, 06/01/2017 for the discussion above and a summary of the DEMPE guidance.

ownership—e.g., how closely involved the decision-makers need to be in the making of decisions, how senior the decision-makers need to be, how many decision-makers, how often they need to meet, etc.[61]

The role of contracts in determining returns is a related issue that has also been interpreted differently by different tax authorities. While per the OECD Guidance, contracts alone cannot determine who is entitled to returns from risks and intangibles, contracts are the starting point for accurately delineating a transaction, including determining which entities assume risk or own intangibles. Where multiple entities perform decision-making functions, contractual assignments of rights to one or more of those decision-making entities will be respected under the OECD TPG. However, the language of the OECD Guidance has been interpreted in different ways by tax authorities to support differing opinions on the role of contracts. For example, the OECD TPG note that where the associated enterprise contractually assuming risk controls that risk and has the financial capacity to assume it, "the fact that other associated enterprises also exercise control over the same risk does not affect the assumption of that risk by the first-mentioned enterprise ... ."[62] Thus, the OECD TPG allow for multiple parties to exercise control over a risk but for that risk to be assumed by just one of the parties controlling it. However, the OECD TPG also note that "[i]n circumstances where a party contributes to the control of risk, but does not assume the risk, compensation which takes the form of a sharing in the potential upside and downside, commensurate with that contribution to control, may be appropriate."[63] Some tax authorities have read this latter language as implying that control over risk functions should be entitled to sharing in the returns from risk irrespective of contractual compensation terms in contradiction of the guidance cited previously.[64]

Based on this reading of the OECD TPG, some tax authorities are using a functional analysis that identifies DEMPE and risk control functions as the basis for an application of a profit split, to the exclusion of contractual terms and other comparability analyses. In this regard, these tax authorities are in effect pricing controlled transactions as if they had hypothesized the entities that are parties to the controlled transaction by attributing risks, intangible assets and capital to those entities based solely and pro rata on their risk control and DEMPE functions, without regard to the legal and contractual arrangements that do in fact make these attributions. These tax authorities are doing so, effectively overriding contractual arrangements, even where the conduct of the parties is in fact consistent with the contractual arrangements. Further, they are ignoring, or at least giving short shrift to, comparability analyses for selecting the most appropriate transfer pricing method in favor of an application of profit splits based on DEMPE and risk control functions.[65]

61. Blough S., Subramanian P., Uceda A., Gorgas T., BEPS Actions 8-*10: Current State of Play*, June 13, 2019, KPMG LLP.
62. OECD TPG, paragraph 1.94.
63. OECD TPG, paragraph 1.105.
64. Blough S., Subramanian P., Uceda A., Gorgas T., BEPS Actions 8-*10: Current State of Play*, June 13, 2019, KPMG LLP.
65. *See* Hickman A., *Arm's Length Principle Mutations: Control of Risk in the OECD Guidelines and Variations in Practice*, MNE Tax, January 13, 2021.

An underlying issue is that the language in the OECD TPG is consensus language; i.e., no participant to the BEPS project objected to the revised guidelines. Therefore, tax authorities with potentially different points of view needed to agree on the language in the revised guidelines. The result is that at least some of the language in the OECD TPG is amenable to differing interpretations, which has been a source of increased controversy.[66]

The dispersion of important DEMPE and risk control functions within MNEs is bringing the differing interpretations of the OECD Guidance around control and DEMPE functions and the challenges with implementing the guidance into increasingly stark contrast. Some tax authorities are treating every individual with important DEMPE or risk control functions as a basis for a pro rata allocation of profits to their jurisdiction, overlooking contractual arrangements in delineating the controlled transaction and paying scant attention to a comparability analysis under the arm's-length principle. Accurate delineation of the transaction that would start with an examination of contracts and continue with a review of the conduct of the parties may confirm that the entity with the senior employee is not allocated risk, especially where the MNE may have no activities in the location other than the activities of the single senior employee. A further comparability analysis may show that the most appropriate method for pricing the dealings of the newly acquired senior employee is not the profit split method but some other transfer pricing method. By ignoring these steps in the application of the arm's-length principle and moving directly to a pro rata allocation of risks and (effectively) intangible ownership and subsequently to a profit split, tax authorities risk misapplying the arm's-length principle. Further, there are inevitable conflicts with tax authorities who do not subscribe to this reading of the OECD Guidance.

A dispersed workforce is increasingly laying bare the challenges with the OECD Guidance around DEMPE and risk control in application of the arm's-length standard and in providing tax certainty. Under the pro rata profit split approach, the dispersion of an MNE's senior workforce could mean potentially significant profits moving with individuals and being dispersed in locations where the MNE does not have much activity at all. It could introduce significant volatility in the distribution of MNE profits to jurisdictions as individual senior employees move locations. Additionally, it will likely continue leading to greater controversy for MNEs and tax authorities and compliance costs for MNEs in the future.

We note that the long-term trend in dispersion of an MNE's workforce as a matter of policy could also complicate the treatment of temporary dislocations of workforce that were forced upon the MNE due to COVID-19. As discussed above, some governments and the OECD released guidance on whether temporarily dislocated employees create PEs in their remote jurisdictions. However, to our knowledge, countries have not released guidance on how the activities of dislocated employees will be considered for transfer pricing purposes, e.g., when applying DEMPE and control of risk concepts. While it would make sense for a country that ignores the presence of a temporarily

66. Subramanian P., *Ten Questions on the OECD's DEMPE Concept and Its Role in Valuing Intangibles,* Tax Management Transfer Pricing Report, Vol. 26, 06/01/2017.

dislocated employee for purposes of determination of a PE to do the same with respect to the allocation of income, some countries may determine that substance issues present different policy concerns from residency and PE issues.[67] Therefore, MNEs face risk of controversy related to the pandemic years during which local management teams may have been forced to perform certain decision-making functions or the key decision-makers might have been unable to perform such functions from their jurisdictions of employment. Additionally, where employees permanently change jurisdictions after their temporary dislocation due to COVID-19, tax authorities may be disinclined to give the MNE the benefit of any relaxation of rules related to temporary dislocations, even where the initial dislocation was forced upon the employee due to COVID-19. Thus, the longer-term trend in employee dispersion may compound PE and transfer pricing controversy risks associated with initial dislocations too that arose out of necessity rather than a matter of company policy.

Finally, to circle back to the issue of attribution of profit to a PE, we note that similar challenges arise in the attribution of profit to a PE. The AOA requires hypothesizing the PE as a separate and independent enterprise by attributing risks, assets and capital to the PE based on its significant people functions. Similar challenges arise in identifying significant people functions and key decision-making functions in the context of PEs and associated enterprises, respectively, although differences in the definitions of significant people functions and important DEMPE/risk control functions could lead to different conclusions as to which functions are significant people functions and which are DEMPE/risk control functions. While there are no legal contracts to help determine risk allocations in the case of a PE, once the PE has been hypothesized as a separate and independent enterprise, and its dealings defined, there are similar challenges with selection of the most appropriate transfer pricing method, which need not simply be a profit split based on significant people functions but some other transfer pricing method. The similarities and differences in attributing profit to a PE in comparison to pricing a controlled transaction will further add to the challenges of MNEs and tax authorities in evaluating the transfer pricing implications of dispersed employees.[68]

We understand that the OECD is considering providing guidance on tax issues related to a dispersed workforce, including the transfer pricing issues around DEMPE and risk control activities.

4.2.2.3 Challenges with Sustaining IP Structures

In recent years, the guidance related to control over risk and DEMPE functions has been a significant catalyst for taxpayers to take a closer look at their international tax

67. Horowitz M., Martin M., Bettge T., *INSIGHT: Transfer Pricing Substance in Flux—DEMPE, BEPS 2.0, and COVID-19*, Bloomberg Tax, July 31, 2020.
68. For a more detailed discussion of the AOA in comparison to transfer pricing of controlled transactions of associated enterprises, *see* Andrus J.L., Collier R.S., *OECD Discussion Draft: Additional Guidance on the Attribution of Profits to Permanent Establishments*, Brit. Tax Rev. 5, p. 509 (2017) and Collier R.S., Dykes I.F., *The Virus in the ALP: Critique of the Transfer Pricing Guidance on Risk and Capital in the Light of the COVID-19 Pandemic* in Bulletin for International Taxation December 2020.

structures. Since the release of the revised transfer pricing guidance, taxpayers have taken stock of their end-to-end value chains, identifying significant intangibles and economically significant risks, identifying key DEMPE and risk control functions and determining where those functions are performed. Based on a detailed understanding of their value chains and international tax structures, taxpayers have identified tax risks given the BEPS Actions 8-10 guidance and determined appropriate changes to their tax structures.[69]

Several of the MNEs which did hold significant intangibles in "cash boxes" have moved or are moving them to other entities with greater DEMPE and risk control functions. MNEs have also evaluated the appropriate level of substance in their principal companies or intangible-holding companies. Some MNEs have worked to bolster the DEMPE and risk control functions in these entities, while some others have migrated their intangibles to other entities that do have sufficient decision-making functions.[70]

The question of what level of decision-making functions is "sufficient" under the BEPS Actions 8-10 for risk assumption or intangible ownership has been a challenging one for many companies. Where not all DEMPE and risk control functions are in the principal or IP-holding company, companies have worked on clarifying contractual arrangements and ensuring that the principal companies do have sufficient decision-making authority related to important DEMPE and risk-related activities. In this context, MNEs have considered committees that make important decisions related to the key intangibles and risks (based on the facts of the industry and business of the MNE) in which employees of the principal company participate and appropriate levels of decision-making authority in the Board of Directors of the principal company.[71]

The dispersion of an MNE's senior workforce post-COVID-19 will raise important questions for MNEs regarding the sustainability of the IP and principal structures that so many of them have worked to ensure meet "substance" requirements of the revised OECD TPG. Notwithstanding the amount of thought and effort companies have put into designing their structures to be compliant with the revised OECD TPG, companies already faced challenges given the different interpretations of the DEMPE and risk control concepts by tax authorities. The dispersion of DEMPE and risk control functions within the MNE will exacerbate such challenges. As a response, companies will likely need to redouble efforts toward developing processes to manage and continually monitor the viability of their IP and principal company structures, given the risks arising from the dispersion of senior professionals. More generally, MNEs and tax authorities will likely need to prepare for increased controversy going forward—MNEs through proactive engagement with tax authorities such as through advanced pricing agreements (APAs) centralized and improved documentation, etc., and tax authorities through resources devoted to dispute resolution and prevention programs.

69. Blough S., Subramanian P., Uceda A., Gorgas T., *BEPS Actions 8-10: Current State of Play*, June 13, 2019, KPMG LLP.
70. *Ibid.*
71. *Ibid.*

4.3 Digitalization of Businesses

Digitalization is not a new phenomenon, but, as noted above, COVID-19 has accelerated the trend toward digitalization. With COVID-19 restrictions making in-person work more difficult, companies have increasingly turned to digital means for conducting their business. As discussed above, this has included a digital transformation in sales and marketing, increasing utilization of e-commerce, acceleration of the digitization of customer and supply chain interactions, increasing use of remote work technologies, and acceleration of virtual transactions such as telemedicine, online banking, and streaming entertainment.

Accompanying the greater digitalization of businesses is the increased need for transfer pricing new types of transactions or rethinking the pricing for existing transactions. For example, digitalization has enabled the collection and analysis of data on a much larger scale than was feasible historically. It has also opened new avenues for the monetization of data. With the increased collection and use of data, companies need to evaluate whether new transactions related to the transfer of data need to be priced. Companies also need to evaluate whether transfer pricing approaches developed for intercompany transactions in a less digital world need to be revisited as they become increasingly digitalized. For example, as digital sales and marketing becomes increasingly important in relation to physical sales and marketing efforts, companies need to evaluate whether transfer pricing approaches developed for physical sales and marketing services need to be revised to adapt to increased digitalization of such services. Comparable company benchmarks may need to be rethought. For instance, companies may need to consider whether distributors of products through physical sales force that they have historically used as benchmarks for their routine distributor returns provide appropriate benchmarks for e-commerce distribution.

The increased digitalization is also leading to an evolution of the value chains of businesses. Historically, in many industries, digital assets were not considered key value drivers. For example, these might have been back-office systems that were required for operating a business, but which did not distinguish the business from its competition. That is changing, with new digital assets emerging in a broad spectrum of industries that are increasing in importance. This transformation of value chains is not a result of COVID-19, but COVID-19 has significantly accelerated the process as noted in section 2.2.3. Through the COVID-19 pandemic, companies in the industry have accelerated their integration of digitalization across functions, creating efficiencies and even reducing costs.

To the extent that digital approaches can drive efficiencies, we may expect to see a corresponding change in the value chain and value drivers of businesses, in turn leading to changes in transfer prices and profit allocations within MNEs. With the increased digitalization of businesses and evolving value chains, the following will be important ingredients of a transfer pricing analysis and, more generally, a determination of the international tax structure of an MNE: (1) where development is occurring for the proprietary software, algorithms, and solutions; (2) how revenue is generated from the digital assets developed by the company; and (3) what defines the routine and nonroutine activities occurring in the digitalization efforts for a company's value chain.

Given how rapidly digital solutions are being developed and used during the COVID-19 pandemic, companies need to be particularly vigilant in monitoring where costs are incurred for digital development activities, as well as identifying how and where key activities are occurring to manage their international tax structures and appropriately price any new or modified controlled transactions.[72]

4.3.1 *Increasing Tension Between Actions 8-10 and Ongoing International Tax Reform*

As discussed above, the OECD released its final recommendations on the 15 actions to combat BEPS in 2015. Under the transfer pricing actions—Actions 8-10—the OECD provided revised guidance on risk and intangibles, which it positioned as a reinforcement and clarification of the arm's-length principle. Through its work on Actions 8-10, the OECD concluded that special measures "beyond the arm's length principle" were not required to meet the objectives of Actions 8-10 but that clarifying and strengthening the guidance on the arm's-length principle were sufficient.[73]

Under the BEPS Action Plan, Action 1 covered challenges with taxing the digital economy. The final report identified broader tax challenges raised by digitalization and considered options for addressing them. None of these options were ultimately recommended in the Action 1 Report, but it was agreed to continue to monitor developments in respect of the digital economy, with a further report to be delivered by 2020.[74]

Subsequent to the release of the final reports under the BEPS Action Plan, the OECD and Inclusive Framework have increased their focus on the digital economy. The Inclusive Framework's work on taxing the digital economy has travelled a long way, with many twists and turns along the way. What started out as an effort to tax the digital economy has now morphed into a broader effort covering all parts of the global economy. Not an insignificant part of the equation is the general view that it would be difficult, if not impossible, to "ring-fence" the digital economy from the rest of the economy for tax purposes because of the increasingly pervasive nature of digitalization. The current proposal is to introduce international tax reform in two pillars. One pillar addresses the broader challenges of the digitalized economy and focuses on the allocation of taxing rights (Pillar One), and a second pillar addresses remaining BEPS issues (Pillar Two). Per the OECD, the two-pillar approach recognizes that the digitalization of the economy is pervasive, raises broader issues, and is most evident in, but not limited to, highly digitalized businesses.[75]

72. Minnear M., Subramanian P., Che R., Farooqui I., *COVID-19's Impact on Transfer Pricing in the Life Sciences Industry*, Tax Notes Federal, June 29, 2020.
73. OECD/G20 Base Erosion and Profit Shifting Project: *Aligning Transfer Pricing Outcomes with Value Creation* ACTIONS 8-10: 2015 Final Reports.
74. OECD/G20 Base Erosion and Profit Shifting Project: *Addressing the Tax Challenges of the Digital Economy*, Action 1: 2015 Final Reports Cite Action 1 Report.
75. OECD/G20 Base Erosion and Profit Shifting Project: *Addressing the Tax Challenges of the Digitalisation of the Economy*—Policy Note. January 23, 2019.

While the BEPS Actions 8-10 work reaffirmed the arm's-length standard and described the functional substance (in terms of people) required for earning a share of the MNE's profits, paradoxically, the new debate on the digital economy is trying to attribute residual profits to jurisdictions without any, or only limited functions (DEMPE or otherwise). With this new debate on the taxation of the digital economy, countries are in effect backtracking on their commitment to the OECD's earlier conclusion in BEPS Actions 8-10 that the arm's-length principle would continue as the unchallenged standard for transfer pricing in all cases.[76]

Underlying this backtracking are increasing doubts among some tax authorities that the arm's-length principle can be relied on to give an appropriate result in all cases in the face of the increasing digitalization of the economy and its enablement of significant economic presence of an MNE in a market without corresponding physical presence there. Against that background, the proposed Pillar One would supplement arm's-length pricing with a formulaic allocation of profit to market jurisdictions for the largest and most profitable MNEs.

As the global economy becomes more digitalized, a process accelerated by COVID-19, pressures on the arm's-length principle are likely to increase. The scope of Pillar One under the current proposal is limited to the approximately hundred largest and most profitable companies. The current proposal is to lower the threshold in seven years so that Pillar One will then apply to a larger group of companies. With the increasing pace of digitalization in part due to COVID-19, an interesting question is whether governments will stop there or whether this is just a first step in the departure from the arm's-length principle, whether the formulaic approach of Pillar One will become more pervasive in the future, and, if so, at what pace this move toward formulary and away from the arm's-length principle will proceed in the future.

We note that there is uncertainty as to whether Pillar One rules will in fact become law. Passage of the new rules in the United States Congress is far from certain. However, even if the rules are not globally adopted, the discussions of the past three years have presented countries with a blueprint for possible departures from the arm's-length principle. Further, even for companies not falling within the scope of Pillar One, tax authorities now have a formula for computing a share of global income to attribute to their jurisdictions. Therefore, even if the global effort for adopting and implementing Pillar One fails, the discussions and proposals may have irreversibly changed the future of international taxation and the fate of the arm's-length principle. COVID-19 has likely hastened and confirmed that change by accelerating the conditions driving the push for new rules, in particular the digitalization of the global economy.

76. Blough S., Subramanian P., Uceda A., Gorgas T., *BEPS Actions 8-10: Current State of Play*, June 13, 2019, KPMG LLP.

4.4 Increased Controversy

As noted earlier, COVID-19 has negatively impacted GDP and tax collections in many countries. As a result, there is pressure on governments to find additional sources of revenue or increase tax compliance. This pressure to make up for lost revenues, along with all the other structural changes underway in the international tax arena, is likely to further increase transfer pricing controversy.

Per the OECD's Mutual Agreement Procedure (MAP) Statistics 2020, Inventory Trends, the inventory of transfer pricing MAP cases has continued to grow since 2016 (Figure 5.9).[77] COVID-19 is likely to continue the trend toward increased controversy as governments look to maintain tax revenues.

Figure 5.9 MAP Inventory Evolution (Transfer Pricing Cases)[*]

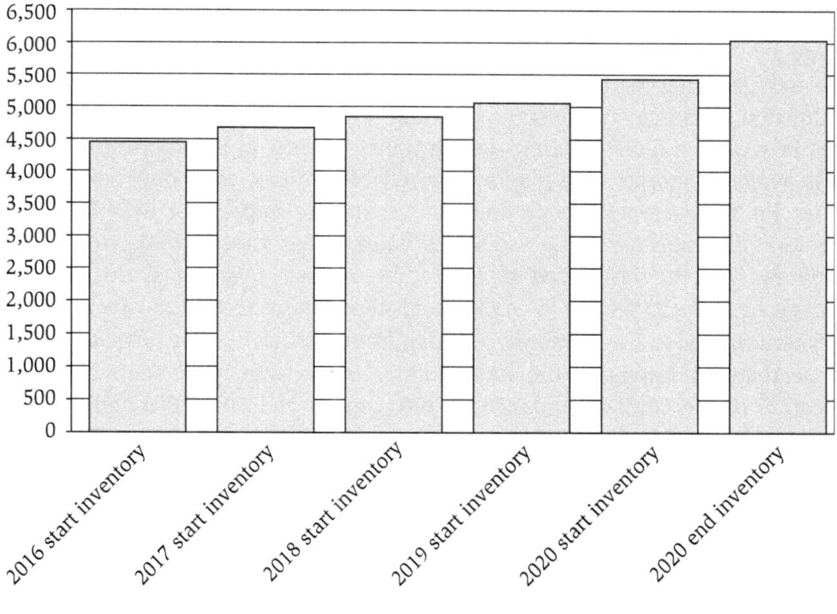

Source: OECD, Mutual Agreement Procedure Statistics 2020-Inventory trends

* The evolutions depicted are based on cumulative numbers reported by individual jurisdictions (i.e., on the sum of all cases reported by each reporting jurisdiction) and therefore do not eliminate double counting. These numbers should only be used for comparative trends. More information on the differences as compared to the numbers used on the MAP Statistics page is provided in the FAQs.

77. OECD, *Mutual Agreement Procedure Statistics 2020—Inventory trends—OECD*, https://www.oecd.org/tax/dispute/mutual-agreement-procedure-statistics-2020-inventory-trends.htm accessed January 6, 2022.

Dispute prevention and resolution are likely to be a greater focus of MNEs and tax authorities alike post-COVID-19. The BEPS project recognized the importance of measures to improve tax certainty, devoting Action 14 to improving the effectiveness and timeliness of tax-related dispute resolution mechanisms. Pillar One similarly acknowledges the need to promote tax certainty and proposes various dispute prevention and resolution mechanisms. Additionally, new innovations will likely be needed in the tax certainty area to deal with the evolution of international tax systems, including any departure from the arm's-length standard. Pillar One takes a step toward such innovation in its proposals, such as in the proposal for a new early certainty process. COVID-19 has reaffirmed the need for effective dispute prevention and resolution, which is expected to be a policy focus in a post-COVID-19 world.

5 CONCLUSION

COVID-19 has caused an unprecedented short-term impact on the economy and paved the way for long-term changes in fundamental characteristics of the global economy. These have affected MNEs' operations and raised numerous transfer pricing issues. The unusual economic circumstances during the pandemic years have created challenges in setting and testing arm's-length transfer prices in the short term, since the readily available market data may not be reliable without additional adjustments to account for the macroeconomic and microeconomic impacts of COVID-19. In the longer term, the expected changes in MNEs' value chains, the dislocation of their senior employees, and the fast-paced digitalization of their operations are expected to introduce further challenges in pricing and allocating profit within the group. The longer-term trends in the economy resulting from COVID-19 have further highlighted or exacerbated tensions in the international tax system, particularly around the application of the OECD's guidance on risk control and DEMPE functions and the current work of the Inclusive Framework on redistribution of taxing rights to market jurisdictions under Pillar One. These changes, along with the pressures on governments to raise revenues, are likely to create greater tax uncertainty and controversy in the future and greater need for new and improved approaches for dispute prevention and resolution.

CHAPTER 6

Recent Developments on Transfer Pricing and Substance

Scott Wilkie

1 WHAT "HAPPENED"? WHAT IS "HAPPENING"?

This chapter addresses what appears to be the creeping normalization of economics-based perceptions, even reconstructions of transactions as taxpayers undertook them, not merely as analytical heuristics to enable the orderly testing of taxpayers' reported incomes according to the "arm's length standard (or principle)" (ALS) but seemingly as the primary determination in a transfer pricing analysis. The heuristics, modalities, and objects of transfer pricing analysis, shared by more expansive reactions to "tax avoidance" generally, increasingly are dominated by the question, "What is the substance," the "economic reality" as the precursor to ensuing analysis of any kind. The significance of this requires thoughtful reflection.

Analytical insights derived from industrial economics have long played an important role in understanding the nature and effects of transactions occurring between the legally distinct elements of an economic unity that is a multinational enterprise (MNE). But the modalities of analysis in any area touched by the law are not "the law." Rather, they serve its effective interpretation, application, and administration. Recent developments, however, suggest something else in the lore and mythology of transfer pricing, even absent excesses typically ascribed to MNE planning that the ALS was devised to discipline.

Has there been a change in the role of transfer pricing analysis? If so, is it necessary? Is there an alternative to more and more refined, pseudoscientific "analysis," the deluge of which this chapter does not canvass, that would be faithful to the ALS and transfer pricing's analytical competencies and aspirations?

This chapter considers these questions, by asking questions about what legal analysis properly entails, and what the evolution of important features of past and present transfer pricing guidance communicate about the role of law and the primary significance of how taxpayers organize themselves and conduct business. The objective is not to justify or facilitate perceived excesses of transfer pricing in the ongoing assault on income shifting, but instead to reconsider the compatibility of informed legal analysis as part of transfer pricing analysis, not something to be regarded as merely precious and even archaic in the present environment.

2 WHAT (IS) "SUBSTANCE"?

Transfer pricing analysis now hosts a trio of self-reinforcing notions, "accurate delineation," "commercial rationality," and, served by them, "value creation." Together, they frame and orient the thinking about the "substance" of arrangements tested by the ALS and transfer pricing's catalog of analytical methodology. Accompanied by ongoing related "refinements" of supporting transfer pricing "analysis" that the transfer pricing industry propagates on an industrial scale, they beg two questions.[1] To what end? According to what standards? This chapter is a spiral of narrowing questions asked and explored to prod these primary questions.

The overarching objective of transfer pricing is conceptually clear enough, under the banner of the ALS guided in its application by the Organisation for Economic Co-operation Development's (OECD's) Transfer Pricing Guidelines (TPG) and similar guidance published by the United Nations Tax Committee. It is to ensure an international allocation of income of an MNE according to its constituent members' demonstrable contributions to earning it, where they earn it, undistorted and not diverted by opportunities afforded by common control of all organizational and transactional elements. Implicitly, this also entails an income (tax base) allocation among taxing jurisdictions—countries—just as much as if they were private economic actors contracting with each other vicariously through their taxpayers, their entitlements, too, consequently needing to be reconciled. Theirs also are contributors to the production processes that MNEs "front" to earn income. They are public inputs of production that are just as important, valuable, and compensable, as those obtained privately. Tax is their price; the conditions and relations of private taxpayers' transactions are effectively the "market" for their "trade."

Answers to any questions, in particular to the two questions asked at the outset, assume the existence of standards, reliable reference points apart from philosophical abstractions and aspirational judgments for answering them. Yet, in transfer pricing, as analytical granularity multiplies, the largely methodological guidance offered by supranational organizations increasingly seems to be perceived as being or having equivalent status as statutory law, as or perhaps a substitute for the law.

It is inevitable, however, that the bespoke tax and general laws of countries are just as important. Within what framework, otherwise, can orderly and enforceable conduct take place? In what other way can the contours of effective commercial life be orchestrated and understood? The law is needed to activate parameters of transfer

1. These notions are addressed specifically in section D.2 of the OECD Transfer Pricing Guidelines for Multinational Enterprises and Tax Administrations (recently updated in 2022 but still including changes made in the 2017 edition to embrace these notions as an outgrowth of the OECD's base erosion project). This chapter is critical of these notions as normative standards and indeed substitutes for legal analysis and reliance on legal constructions that necessarily, in a "rule of law environment," ground every manner of human and commercial interaction. Lying at the core of these notions is the OECD's overarching focus on "value creation" as the most contemporary mantra and label for detecting and measuring the "source" of income. Yet, the notion of "value creation" prompts many questions. *See* for useful commentary: A.J. Martín Jiménez, *Value Creation: A Guiding Light for the Interpretation of Tax Treaties?*, (2020) 74(4/5) Bull. Intl. Taxn. 1; M. Lennard, *Act of Creation: The OECD/G20 Test of "Value Creation" as a Basis for Taxing Rights and Its Relevance to Developing Countries*, (2018) 25(3) Transnational Corporations 55; R.S. Collier and I.F. Dykes, *On the Apparent Widespread Misapplication of the OECD Transfer Pricing Guidelines, Risk and Post-BEPS Problems for the Arm's Length Principle*, (2022) 76(1) Bulletin for International Taxation; and J.L. Andrus and R.S. Collier, *Transfer Pricing and the Arm's Length Principle after the Pillars*, taxnotes, January 28, 2022 at https://www.taxnotes.com/special-reports/base-erosion-and-profit-shifting-beps/transfer-pricing-and-arms-length-principle-after-pillars/2022/01/28/7d40m.

pricing in a properly enforceable way.[2] But, there is a detectable turning away from, possibly even a lack of awareness or willingness to consider the significance of legal analysis. This is unhelpful, unrealistic, and unnecessary nevertheless to serve the objective of transfer pricing in a reliable and predictable way. The law is relevant; it is necessary. It is more than a mere formality. It is not the same as "formalism"; it is not form for its own sake, as if a mere "picture" did tell a conclusive transfer pricing story of a thousand words. Recognizing this does not, however, require discarding the force of contemporary transfer pricing analysis. But it does contribute to understanding the

2. For example, Canadian and Australian courts have made it quite clear that at most the transfer pricing guidance may have probative analytical value but falls short of being or being the equivalent of law, unless possibly that guidance is actually incorporated directly or by reference in countries' tax laws as Australia, recently, and the United Kingdom before it purports to have done. These cases, also, in line with the thesis of this chapter adopt and rely on analysis that is fundamentally and profoundly "legal," oriented to the "legal substance" of parties' arrangements as they have portrayed and implemented them, and then, to those arrangements, the courts do what Article 9 of the OECD Model Tax Convention—the ALS—call upon them (and taxpayers and tax authorities) to do, namely determine whether the terms set for those and those kinds of arrangements comport with the terms on which independent parties would have set for those arrangements. That is, are those terms the terms that independent parties looking out for their own interests would have agreed and as part of that determination would justifiably have expected (analyzed later in this chapter in relation to "justifiable reliance") their counterparties to be able to honor and perform functionally and financially as independent enterprises. *See*, for example, the important Canadian Transfer pricing cases, *GlaxoSmithKline* (*Canada v. GlaxoSmithKline Inc.*, 2012 SCC 52, [2012] 3 SCR 3) and *Cameco Corporation* (*The Queen v. Cameco Corporation*, 2020 FCA 112 (FCA) upholding *Cameco Corporation v. The Queen*, 2018 TCC 195 (TCC)), referred to in post, notes 8 and 15 as the case may be. There are like reactions by Australian courts, including recently. *See*, for example, *Chevron Australia Pty Ltd v. Commissioner of Taxation*, [2017] FCAFC 62, *Commissioner of Taxation v. Glencore Investment Pty Ltd*, [2020] FCAFC 187, and most recently *Singapore Telecom Australia Investments Pty Ltd v. Commissioner of Taxation*, [2021] FCA 1597. In these three important transfer pricing cases, decided in all material ways in line with the decision of the Canadian courts, these courts relied on an evidence based assessment of the "legal substance"—my term, not theirs—to proceed with the transactions sculpted, legally, by the parties even where significant equity-like overtones were present. The courts then did what the ALS contemplates and the analytical capabilities and resources of industrial economic analysis facilitates, that is, to evaluate whether independent enterprises would have undertaken *those* transactions, with the characteristics that the tested taxpayer had including those influenced or grounded in its group membership, with the terms selected by the parties or whether, with reference to hypothetical like transactions, the terms would have been different and therefore, for example, charges should enjoy less tax recognition, not be deductible, despite having the legal character they had. It is to be noted that at least some of these courts and the decisions they rendered speak about "commercial rationality," but interestingly the implicit sense of this notion is informed by questions of "legal substance"—again my words—informed by evidence about whether independent parties would have "justifiably relied"—my words but explained later in this chapter—according to the terms of their agreements or, without changing those terms, the tax effects ought to be moderated in line with the ALS, informed by the TPG, because those terms had dimensions or context that was not consistent, for commercial relations of the sort undertaken, with what independent parties would have done. That said, however, these cases do not seem to address what "commercial rationality" means or might mean as a "principle" rather than an impression and a conclusion drawn for evidence in the circumstances. This way of approaching the ALS and the utility of the TPG as a "toolkit" of analytical devices reflects the approach advocated in this chapter. There are interesting public law questions nevertheless raised by such approach about what appoints to delegation of legislative authority and function in favor of "guidance" that is ambulatory as determined not in a legislative context but by, in the pertinent case, the OECD.

inherent significance of that analysis and how it may be mobilized so as to limit even more protracted and abstract debates about where "value" is "created."

We need to refresh the substantive significance of legal analysis and legal constructions as necessary features of effective transfer pricing analysis. These comments seek to do that. They canvass the desirability of retrenching from the persistent economic determinism of transfer pricing, in the direction of an informed reconsideration of the role of "the law" to ascertain what is "substance" undistracted by organizational and transactional technique, nevertheless assisted by "economics" as by any other evidence of what transactions "really" entail. This marks the essence of proper legal analysis of the "legal substance" of events that derive their features from the law and on which tax law consequently operates.

Otherwise, as experience increasingly reflects, "substance," which essentially is in the transfer pricing context more a *judgment*—may devolve to be a loaded moral judgment—about circumstances and outcomes according to perceptions of what taxpayers ought to have done, without substantive, analytical, or temporal, boundaries. Devoid of objective limitations, "substance" may be too easily seen in the preconceived image of those anticipating certain outcomes and guided accordingly in their "analysis," conflating analysis with judgment. Without a more objective anchor, where transfer pricing begins and ends and indeed "who wins" are difficult to know reliably and predictably.[3] As much as anything, in international tax, it may be more the "process" within which rules operate, and demonstrably are able to operate effectively, which is important less than the "rules" themselves.[4]

3 BEYOND TRANSFER PRICING'S CATECHISM

A healthy dose of skepticism about the ALS as commonly understood offers a helpful but humbling start. Pivoting on measures of wisdom and worldliness that eludes most members of the transfer pricing "club" inspired by Thomas Khun's study of scientific revolutions, Robert Couzin perceptively writes:

3. The open-ended nature of transfer pricing at the best of times but now abetted by the notions associated with "recharacterization," which exacerbate the infirmity of arrangements as undertaken by taxpayers, draws to mind the "Caucus-race" in L. Carroll's *Alice's Adventures in Wonderland*, in *The Complete Works of Lewis Carroll, A Wonderland of Stories, Nonsense and Wit* (London: Penguin Books, 1988), 31: "'What *is* a Caucus-race?' said Alice ... 'Why,' said the Dodo, 'the best way to explain it is to do it.' ... First it marked out a racecourse ... ('the exact shape doesn't matter,' it said,) and then all the party were placed along the course, here and there. There was no 'One, two, three, and away!' but they began running when they liked, and left off when they liked, so that it was not easy to know when the race was over. However, when they had been running half an hour or so, ... the Dodo suddenly called out 'The race is over!' and they all crowded round it, panting, and asking 'But who has won?' This question the Dodo could not answer without a great deal of thought, ... At last the Dodo said '*Everybody* has won, and all must have prizes.'"
4. *See*, for example, R. M. Bird, *Reforming International Taxation: Is the Process the Real Product?*, Georgia State University Andrew Young School of Policy Studies, International Center for Public Policy Working Paper 15-03, June 2015.

> The members of a scientific community have a similar education and similar experiences; they belong to the same organizations; they read the same technical literature in the same way; they employ common theories, metaphysical understandings; they share values and commitments. Personal and professional advancement depends upon adherence to and promotion of the paradigm. ... [Transfer-pricing practitioners who are members of various private and public constituencies and the organizations to which they belong] are engaged in and dependent upon the continued existence of a particular system. ... When a crisis arises, a fact or conception that threatens to undermine the [scientific] paradigm, scientists do not renounce it. To do so would be to abandon science itself as they know it. Similarly, transfer-pricing practitioners approach such practical difficulties as the crisis of intangibles by expanding or adjusting rather than replacing the paradigm. Like the ether in physics or phlogiston in chemistry, transfer pricing is no longer merely a technique or tool but has become a way of understanding reality—in this case fiscal reality. ... By the 16th century, ... [Khun] observed, "astronomy's complexity as increasing far more rapidly than its accuracy." So too with transfer pricing. Paradigms do change, generally after a period of intense insecurity. Revolutions do occur.[5]

"Substance," increasingly loosely, tends to be defined within the transfer pricing paradigm perpetuated by those whose methodological perceptions and inclinations tend are identified with and as the ALS and not merely as heuristics to apply it. This tendency now seems to entail a primary unbounded inquisition about whether to accept events as undertaken by taxpayers as the starting point for a transfer pricing analysis. Increasingly, what is perceived to be the legitimate scope of transfer pricing analysis seems to be wary and even less respectful of the legal foundations of the events that generate the income of an MNE's and its internal income allocation meant to be tested by transfer pricing analysis for distortions attributable to the gratuitous exercise of corporate control.

Has the law become a casualty of a self-generated problem—the problem of "substance." as framed by porous and amorphous transfer pricing notions labeled "accurately delineated," "commercial rationality," and "value creation," along with their derivatives? Is this the "right" or even a necessary focus of transfer pricing? Is it even an accurate interpretation of the ALS even allowing for its attention to the "conditions" of and "commercial or financial relations" among members of a commonly controlled corporate group, an MNE?

What is the role of the law in establishing the circumstances to which transfer pricing regulation applies? What is "legal substance" and should that be, indeed is that, the real underlying focus for which these new or recalibrated labels in fact may be unhelpful distractions no matter how well meaning? In light of transfer pricing's objective, is it time for a more thoughtful, open-minded reconsideration of fractional or formulary apportionment as an achievable manifestation of what Article 9 of the OECD Model Tax Convention presents as the ALS?[6] As noted later, it is remarkable that the present

5. R. Couzin, *Policy Forum: The End of Transfer Pricing?*, (2013) 61:1 Canadian Tax Journal 159-178.
6. This chapter draws on research and ideas considered in a number of earlier commentaries, including: R.S. Wilkie, *Reflecting on the "Arm's Length Principle": What Is the "Principle"? Where Next?*, in W. Schön and K.A. Konrad eds., *Fundamentals of International Transfer Pricing in Law and Economics* (Berlin: Springer, 2012), 137-156; J.S. Wilkie, *The Definition and Ownership of*

workplan of the OECD guardedly advanced as Pillar One adopts a formulary or fractional approach built around various indicators of where income should be considered to have its "source" depending on the nature of an in-scope affected enterprise.

4 THE QUEST AND THE CONTEXT

The members of the transfer pricing community are the "Indiana Jones's" of tax law.[7] They search valiantly, but largely in vain, for the utopian ideal of perfect multinational income allocation explained by a universal understanding of the "substance" of taxpayer's arrangements. "Substance" is perceived mostly from an economic perspective. There is polite acknowledgement of the legal manifestations of transactions according to how they are "written" in contracts. But transfer pricing as generally understood has evolved to treat the law as less and less important even as the beginning point for transfer pricing analysis. Transfer pricing for some time has existed as a discipline unto itself in the context of taxation, even to the point of justifying by its own means and mantra the superimposition of economic reconstructions on transactions for transfer pricing purposes regardless of how they are constructed in fact and according to applicable law. Under the vanguard of "recharacterization" and more polite synonyms, transfer pricing would like to separate events from their legal foundations as the initial step in then allocating "economic income" according to indicators that sound profound but themselves lack "substance."

The mutually reinforcing notions "accurate delineation," "commercial rationality," and "value creation" in the most recently updated TPG are surrogates for "substance."[8] The title, even, of the update's precursor, the Actions 8-10 OECD Base Erosion and Profit Shifting Project (BEPS) Report reflects these notions almost as a

Intangibles: Inside the Box? Outside the Box? What Is the Box? (2012) 4:3 *World Tax Journal* 222-248; J.S. Wilkie, *New Rules of Engagement? Corporate Personality and the Allocation of "International Income" and Taxing Right*, in B.J. Arnold, ed., *Tax Treaties after the BEPS Project: A Tribute to Jacques Sasseville* (Toronto: Canadian Tax Foundation, 2018), 349-371; J.S. Wilkie, *Transfer Pricing Aspects of Intangibles: The License Model*, in M. Lang, A. Storck, and R. Pretruzzi, *Transfer Pricing in a Post BEPS-World* (The Netherlands: Wolters Kluwer, 2016), 62-96; and J.S. Wilkie, *Policy Forum—The Way We Were? The Way We Must Be? The 'Arm's Length Principle' Sees Itself* (for What It Is) in the 'Digital' Mirror, (2019) 47(12) Intertax 1087-1102.

7. Indiana Jones is a well-known fictional movie character who engaged in exploits and adventures in search of the long lost "Holy Grail" of Biblical significance. The adventures involved great drama, exciting special effects, and belief-suspending departures from reality, in unsuccessful searches for the venerated relic. *See*, for less "adventurous" commentary, Couzin, *supra* n. 5, and Wilkie, *Reflecting on the "Arm's Length Principle": What Is the "Principle"? Where Next?*, *supra* n. 6.
8. OECD TPG, in particular Ch. 1, paras. 1.6, 1.33 and 1.34, and 1.139-1.145. The TPG have been recently updated (January 20, 2022) to include commentary previously circulated by the OECD concerning profit splits and various financial transactions, both bearing to some extent on the comments made in this chapter about specific aspects of the TPG.

catechism—*Aligning Transfer Pricing Outcomes with Value Creation.*[9] The open-endedness and orientation of these terms as the OECD has so liberally adopted them, however, seem to marginalize or perhaps misunderstand not only the nature and significance of legal analysis in transfer pricing generally but also the connection between the ALS as a "principle" and "substance" as set out in Article 9 of the OECD Model Tax Convention. Certainly, the pretense of legal arrangements being the starting point of a transfer pricing analysis remains. But the continuing recalibration of transfer pricing analysis suggests that this is an almost precious concession to the "old days" of transfer pricing. "Economics," it seems, is more than an analytical device. It has become the original and primary "delineator" of transactions—of their "substance"—against which the transactions as actually delineated by taxpayers ought to be measured and if found wanting by this standard discarded. This is a step considerably beyond what judicial authorities confronted with "recharacterization" have been willing to embrace as a suitable role for alternative transactions as surrogate comparables where none otherwise exist.[10] It is also a step beyond what the ALS requires, even foreshadows. And, as these comments later chronicle, it is not what the TPG as they have developed have required or, as normative analysis even envisioned.

Does the quest for more "granular" pseudoscientific economic insights into and describing what taxpayers could have done obscure the substance of "substance" in transfer pricing? Indeed, curiously, the essence of the ALS is judging taxpayers and their transactions according to standards that are in fact antithetical to the economic and resulting organizational and transactional imperatives that cause MNEs to exist in the first place to avoid the risks and costs of unrestricted dealings, in that sense according to a fiction that they are what undeniably and by design they are not.[11] The

9. The BEPS project included a significant reconsideration of the adequacy and application of the TPG. It is well beyond the scope of the comments in this chapter to address the various reports prepared under the OECD's auspices. Some of the more notable reports and other developments include "*OECD, Base Erosion and Profit Shifting, Action Reports (2015), "Aligning Transfer Pricing Outcomes with Value Creation,* Actions 8-10—2015 Final Reports," (Paris: OECD, 2015) and subsequent OECD BEPS materials including recent revisions of the OECD *Transfer Pricing Guidelines* published in 2017 and 2022. Also significant is the extension of the BEPS project in the OECE's proposals in its work on Pillar One, Pillar Two and the GloBE: *see*, in particular, *OECD/G20 Base Erosion and Profit Shifting Project Two-Pillar Solution to Address the Tax Challenges Arising from the Digitalisation of the Economy* (Paris: OECD, October 2021) and *Tax Challenges Arising from the Digitalisation of the Economy—Global Anti-Base Erosion Model Rul*es (Pillar Two) (Paris: OECD, December 2021) and the even more recent commentary announced and linked in OECD, *OECD Releases Detailed Technical Guidance on the Pillar Two Model Rules for 15% Global Minimum Tax,* https://www.oecd.org/tax/beps/oecd-releases-detailed-technical-guidance-on-the-pillar-two-model-rules-for-15-percent-global-minimum-tax.htm referring to three reports published in December 2021 and March 2022.
10. *See*, most recently, also referred to *supra* n. 2, The *Queen v. Cameco Corporation*, 2020 FCA 112 (FCA) upholding *Cameco Corporation v. The Queen*, 2018 TCC 195 (TCC), *Commissioner of Taxation* v. *Glencore Investment Pty Ltd*, [2020] FCAFC 187, and *Singapore Telecom Australia Investments Pty Ltd v. Commissioner of Taxation*, [2021] FCA 1597. *See* commentary on the *Cameco Corporation* case in J.S. Wilkie, *Transfer Pricing Rules Past Cameco and Digital Tax on Tech Giants*, (2021) September/October *IBFD International Transfer Pricing Journal* 307-319 and Scott Wilkie's commentaries referred to in that chapter.
11. *See*, for example, S.I. Langbein, *Transaction Cost, Production Cost, and Tax Transfer Pricing*, (September 18, 1989) 44 Tax Notes 1391; and S.I. Langbein, *The Myth of Arm's Length and the*

law, though, is accustomed to dealing with fictions; legal constructions of many kinds are fictions.[12] But they are nonetheless important fictions on which there is general reliance for good order; a "deep dive" into convergent legal theory is not required to understand this. It cannot be that inevitable reliance on and choices among legal constructions disqualify respect for them where relevant evidence sustains taxpayers' conduct consistent with them.[13] The utility and significance of these fictions with which the ALS contends are tested even more by the increasingly common detachment of enterprises from any—at least, any necessary—business forms locations, for which oddly the law seems to have become the scapegoat.

The fictions that are embedded in the nature of the tested taxpayers, MNEs, and their transactions and for that matter the theory behind the ALS make the "substance" of persons and events primary in transfer pricing. But this is hardly new. More and more, though, tools of transfer pricing—the analytical guidance—are taken for granted as being the ALS rather than a matrix of analytical devices to serve it. To that end, "substance" in transfer pricing's lexicon is treated as if it were a conclusion of economics with legal status and significance. The present lightning rod for this is transfer pricing's predilection for wanting to "recharacterize," or indeed formatively "characterize," taxpayers' circumstances as the first step in a transfer pricing analysis, according to economic connotations.

However, the essential questions animating "substance" in transfer pricing, contrary to popular belief, are "rule of law" and practical tax administration questions.

"Substance" is not, and to serve transfer pricing's essential objective does not need to and this chapter asserts cannot possibly, involve a determination made apart from the law regarding and to detect what taxpayers "actually" did. The law is not some kind of dispensable or discretionary accessory; it is trite but accurate to note the common observation that tax law is accessory to the general law. The general law shapes the contours and gives life to persons and arrangements between them. "Substance" does not have to be an economic judgment that then is slotted or packaged into one of possibly several accommodating legal constructs. Neither is testing the viability of applicable law as the justification for a chosen path of dealing new to the law. Location and nexus questions are familiar to the general law, which of course hosts the events that concern transfer pricing. In a conflict of laws analysis according to well-established legal principles, for example, legal determinations become facts one proved. The proof includes establishing with evidence whether parties are justified to rely on the legal parameters and constructs they have selected according to the law's discipline on what is justifiable reliance. The notion of justifiable reliance, as addressed later with reference to the seminal scholarship of Professor Lon Fuller concerning the nature of contracts and legitimate claims for damages for nonperformance, is a

Arm's Length Method, (February 17, 1986) 30 Tax Notes 625; and Wilkie, *Reflecting on the "Arm's Length Principle": What Is the "Principle"? Where Next?*, *supra* n. 5.

12. *See*, for example, H.D. Rosenbloom, *Banes of an Income Tax: Legal Fictions, Elections, Hypothetical Determinations, Related Party Debt*, (2004) 26:17 Sydney Law Review 17-35 (published in a different form in Tax Notes International Vol. 32, December 15, 2003 at 989).
13. Wilkie, *Transfer Pricing Aspects of Intangibles: The License Model*, *supra* n. 6, and the references to the scholarship of Lon Fuller in that paper.

common feature of the law of contract. The sense of "substance" framed by the trio of "accurate delineation," "commercial rationality," and "value creation," however, is that these somehow are terms of legal art, which is not the case. In the first instance as they frame the parameters of transfer pricing analysis, an impression is to be created of "economically relevant characteristics" of taxpayers' dealings, the repository for which then may or may not be the transactional formulations that taxpayers "actually" implemented to achieve economic outcomes that may well be achievable in a variety of ways though with different legal connotations.

It is reasonable to ask whether there is as much point to the focus on "substance" as a determinant of appropriate transactional characterization as is commonly thought, to justify transfer pricing's attachment to it as having almost primordial significance. A theme of these comments is that pricing analysis would be more faithful to its purpose and origin, and would be more reliable if the focus shifted away from more and more open-ended ostensible refinements of "substance" to objectively observable elements of how products (including "digital products") are "made" and sold. In this connection, in this chapter, where helpful I will draw on particular Canadian experience.

5 LURKING QUESTION(S)

"Substance" in the present transfer pricing context both provokes and masks these critical but within the accepted transfer pricing environment possibly uncomfortable questions:

1. Are tax authorities entitled to superimpose, *ex post*, on a taxpayer's formulation of its circumstances when properly effected under applicable law another legal formulation that yields different tax outcomes possibly inconsistent with attendant corporate, commercial, and property law outcomes? Should the events as "seen" through a tax lens be different than as they occur and are portrayed for other purposes? More grandly, perhaps, other is the invisible hand of contemporary transfer pricing, a free-form inquiry into the fiscal significance of legal institutions and legal constructions, a license of sorts to "raise the corporate veil"?
2. Are taxpayers, too, entitled also to depart from their transactional formulations if it suits them to assert tax consequences inconsistent with those that otherwise would flow from their adopted transactional? There is an old adage of tax practice that taxpayers should be very careful arguing against their own form.
3. If those tax authorities are enabled with a (broader) permission to superimpose on otherwise legally effective organizational and transactional formulations, alternative fictions or hypotheses generated by economics, does it apply as the first step in a transfer pricing analysis even absent evidence of taxpayers' "bad behavior"? Does such authority exist where according to an entirely unremarkable evidence-based legal analysis it can be shown that taxpayers have conducted themselves consistently with to be the intrinsic expectations of the legal constructions they have selected to host their organizational and commercial existence and dealings? In other perhaps more inflammatory words, are tax authorities (and to be evenhanded, taxpayers too) allowed to "recharacterize" the circumstances to which tax law manifest in transfer pricing applies?

4. Finally, is "substance" even the right or necessarily a relevant notion for achieving the ALS' objective? Or is it a distraction that possibly deflects from that objective, considering other available ways to test the defensible allocation of MNEs' income among country hosts for their transactions? Effectively, is illuminating, even helpful to perceive countries as being vicariously engaged with private taxpayers in their enterprises, in the nature of constructive partners in so far as a country's tax base is a subset of a taxpayer's profits?

"Substance" as the trio of new or restated transfer pricing determinants, "accurate delineation," "commercial rationality," and "value creation," would have it determined, perhaps is not expressing the "right" question, at least in the most useful way. The "right" question is how and where income is earned, where it has its "source." "Substance" is not a term of art in law or economics. It is as inherently disputatious as it is uncertain. And, certainly, as a notion held out to serve such an important role in transfer pricing and more generally measures to combat unacceptable tax avoidance, it prompts and engages unique underlying legal questions which cannot be avoided by assigning presumptive significance to the notion.

6 START WITH: "WHAT (ACTUALLY) HAPPENED?"

Transfer pricing analysis of transactions has to start somewhere. It starts with the events as formulated by taxpayers—what actually, including as a matter of law in the fullest sense of what legal analysis entails, happened. Though the TPG "say" this, as these comments later parse, the manner and context of this acknowledgment cast doubt on whether "actual" transactions are first to be redetermined with reference to their "economically relevant characteristics" and then assigned a (possibly among several) "convenient" legal formulation among others that could have been selected nevertheless to achieve a materially equivalent economic outcome. But a taxpayer's organizational and transactional affairs are not merely a diagram. What they are entails, rather, a conclusion of law drawn from applying well-understood legal standards to assess the parties' justifiable reliance on the implications of how they have depicted and documented their relations. Is that not how transactions are customarily "delineated," before the specific regulatory regime determines consequences? Is it not the case, even obvious, that economically equivalent outcomes are possible with quite different regulatory consequences depending on how they are effected according to the precepts of and choices offered by applicable law?

Some orientation offers helpful direction. The core transfer pricing questions, embedded in Article 9 of the OECD Model Tax Convention which frames the mandate of the ALS, are the following. Through typical levers of corporate governance, did the parties exercise the common control of all transaction parties in a chauvinistic way to direct income away from where it was earned? If so, with due regard to relevant contributing factors of production (in the broadest sense which includes manifestations of ingenuity and risk assumption—intangibles), the destination of sales, and the uniqueness of a "firm" according to well-known microeconomic theory, what would be a more reasonable allocation of the group income? Then, with reference to the compensatory elements of the events that took place rather than those that might be (re)imagined, should suitable *income* adjustments be implemented? None of that invokes "substance" in a sense either that a selection among viable legal formulations is necessarily determinative as such of an appropriate transfer pricing outcome or that a particular means selected by a taxpayer to effect an economic outcome is colorable because it impairs achieving transfer pricing's objective. It is a separate kind of question for other parts of tax law whether, for example, statutory determinations of taxable income have been properly applied or adjustments within the contemplation of the applicable tax law are appropriate. For example, this might include whether deductions that otherwise are justifiable in principle should be constrained because they are overstated, unreasonable, or otherwise disconnected from statutory requirements nevertheless examined according to and constrained by those requirements.

In aid of a determination so directed, an alternative transactional formulation may be useful and used as an analytical heuristic in order to enable via an alternative transactional formulation that does have an arm's-length analog a typical transfer pricing analysis to take place. This is what, for example, recent Canadian court decisions in *Cameco Corporation*[14] clearly and forcefully express with respect to the specific anti-tax avoidance aspect of the transfer pricing provision of the Canadian *Income Tax Act* applicable for transactions having no arm's-length analog. The alternative is a kind of "reality check" surrogate or reference point where otherwise a reference point does not exist. As but only as such, that alternative formulation would be examined in relation to the taxpayer's circumstances, as disclosed by relevant evidence. The object of the exercise is not to tax on the basis of substituted transactions but to evaluate the compatibility of the taxpayer's reported income in relation to the expectations of transfer pricing otherwise in the usual way. If warranted, an adjustment to its income—in the Canadian transfer pricing lexicon, the "quantum" or "nature" of an amount—would be made. What would not happen, however, is that the "substance" of the arrangements would be the jumping-off point for "recharacterizing" them, something the courts explicitly denied is permissible according to the ALS as ingested in the Canadian transfer pricing provision.

If this is what is meant to be reflected by "accurate delineation," "commercial rationality," and "value creation," this is far from clear directionally or otherwise. But if this is what is meant, two important observations are irresistible.

First, this envisages nothing different in any material respect from the purpose or objectives of transfer pricing from its modern inception in the work of the International Chamber of Commerce and the League of Nations almost one hundred years ago.[15]

Second, transfer pricing has only ever sought to determine a suitable allocation of multinational group income—compensation commensurate with where "value is created"—that may have been diverted from where it was earned through the common

14. *See Cameco Corporation*, *supra* n. 2.
15. *See* Wilkie, *Policy Forum—The Way We Were? The Way We Must Be? The 'Arm's Length Principle' Sees Itself*, *supra* n. 6.

control of all organizational and transactional elements which MNE group unity necessarily implies, effectively with the acquiescence of all interested parties.[16]

7 "SOURCE" IS STILL THE REAL FOCUS AND THE (HARDEST) QUESTION

Even this understanding of transfer pricing's formative objective obscures the singular question that pervades the entire contemporary regeneration of transfer pricing notions captured by attention to "substance." It is a question that cannot be answered by economics except in the role that any probative evidence has. That question is: What is the "source" of income?

Fundamentally, that presents a legal question, not a question of economics.

Even the most mundane of legal problems entails an evidence-based analysis, to identify and probe all facts and circumstances (as considered later in this chapter with reference to a more critical understanding about what a legal analysis entails and what "legal substance" is) in relation to the pertinent legal framework. That is what a legal analysis, an inquiry into "legal substance," is. Tax and its subset transfer pricing are not unique in this way. Law-based analysis involves verifiably establishing all the relevant circumstances, including what the law considers to be the *justifiable* reliance of parties on their selected legal formulations. This is far from the same thing as being guided by "form" alone. Form is only reliable as a general legal matter if probative facts and circumstances based analysis of the inherent expectations of the legal formulations adopted to accomplish outcomes can be shown to have been satisfied and accordingly justified.

Did the transaction parties do what they say they did, what their selected legal formulations reflect by their nature that parties needed to and according to the intrinsic expectations of those formulations were expected to do and keep on doing for those formulations to be effective according to their terms? An evidence-based analysis invariably will disclose this. It will illuminate whether the parties to the arrangements actually relied on each other, and had objectively justifiable reasons to rely on each other, to be able to execute the obligations and enjoy the rights that the depiction of their arrangements suggests. If, instead, the analysis discloses that for *those* parties in *their* circumstances, their legal formulations on which they ostensibly relied are essentially beside the point or, as a matter of law, reveal a different transactional configuration than written projections of their circumstances, then the legal substance of their arrangements will be so determined to be what it is—and always to have been as a matter of law. This sounds a little like the TPG's justification in the guise of "accurate delineation," "commercial rationality," and "value creation" for subordinating legal analysis to determinations not bounded by recognizable standards. However, if properly understood, this is the essence of a *legal* analysis, not an economics-based reconstruction. Legal analysis has normative standards that withstand the immediacy

16. This is an approach taken, for example, in anti-income diversion provision of the *Income Tax Act* (Canada), subsection 56(2).

of their practical application. Even allowing for countries not necessarily having the same or equivalent legal systems, legal analysis is standards-based and for this reason projects a measure of universality, that is, normative reliability, although the actual legal principles may be different and need some measure of reconciliation—which lies at the heart of "international taxation." As earlier noted, the legal discipline of conflict of laws is used to reconcile divergent legal standards by determining, in relevant contexts, parties' entitlements to have their arrangements determined according to the legal regimes they have selected to animate them, reflecting that the terms of applicable law are effectively adopted by reference in how transaction parties deal with each other and memorialize the expectations of their dealing in contracts.

What is a useful next step in this analysis building on the realization that "recharacterization" in the guise of "accurate delineation," "commercial rationality," and "value creation" is essentially a search for a norms-based determination of the "source" of income?

There cannot be much that is more fundamental to a "facts and circumstances" separate entity transactional analysis than its (legal) substance, that is, whether what seems to have occurred actually did as and with the effect according to applicable law that the adopted means of accomplishing an outcome implies should have been the case.

Can even more seemingly "precise" analytical markers, jargon it might be said, be a reliable substitute for examining thoroughly, as a legal matter, how taxpayers have accomplished their outcomes? Would transfer pricing be better off, more faithful indeed to the nature of economic analysis, to adopt a possibly less "perfect" approach? Is that "second best" foreshadowed albeit tentatively by the prevailing Pillar One proposal? Does fractional or formulary apportionment offer a more hopeful direction, at least, than what seems to be a pursuit of goals and strategies suggesting a quest for universal homogeneous tax and law regimes with a common tax base, common relevant tax legislation, and unique governance institutions?[17]

---

17. It is interesting to note that this grand and perhaps laudable objective has proved elusive in the "hard law" European Union environment in which though there is harmonized VAT, achieving harmonized corporate income tax through the Common Consolidated Corporate Tax Base (CCCTB) and its precursors, now to be replaced by the proposed "Business in Europe: Framework for Income Taxation" (and a concomitant more highly developed notion of "own resources" for the European Union) has not proved to be successful. The European experience is in microcosm what the international experience is for transfer pricing and, for that matter, the Pillars. *See* the excellent pending paper by A.M. Jiménez, *The EU Own Resources and Budget After the COVID Pandemia: Still Far From a Closer 'European Union'* (publication pending at the time of writing as a chapter in an upcoming book). Notably, the OECD has invited comments as part of a public consultation on the extensive use of tailored factors based allocation keys to establish taxable nexus and allocate international income with obvious transfer pricing implications; *see* OECD, *Public Consultation Document, Pillar One—Amount A: Draft Model Rules for Nexus and Revenue Sourcing*, February 4, 2022-February 18, 2022. Amount A, of course, in many ways reflects the hardest aspect of allocating international income of MNEs by determining its "source(s)" because it entails the intangible essence of being an MNE and the implicit sharing of all elements of the economic unity that is an MNE among its legally diffracted elements and legal fragments.

8 THE NEW "NORMS" OF THE MOMENT: "ACCURATE DELINEATION," "COMMERCIAL RATIONALITY," AND "VALUE CREATION": A CLOSER LOOK AT THE (NEW) SUBSTANCE OF "SUBSTANCE"

8.1 Accurate Delineation

According to terms seemingly unrefined by any normative or empirical standards, the beginning point of a transfer pricing analysis is foreseen as an original economic construction (or reconstruction) of events undertaken by taxpayers, to establish their "accurate delineation," according to their "commercial rationality," in aid of establishing where "value was created." What any of these phrases means or ought to mean for transfer pricing or indeed any legal analysis is far from clear, as terms of art or even by necessary implication. Regardless of how a taxpayer has expressed itself organizationally and transactionally, it seems that the first order of business is to determine events to establish according to their "economically relevant characteristics," a "substantial" formulation—their "delineation"—for transfer pricing purposes, which can be the events as it has been decided they "realistically" occurred or ought to have occurred, notwithstanding how in fact and law they did occur.

What does "accurate delineation" mean? By what incontrovertible, predictable, principled, objectively reliable standard is it to be determined? How is it held out as a distinct feature of transfer pricing analysis, relevant for the objective served by the ALS? Is it a legal notion? An economic notion? The TPG except possibly by descriptive but imprecise implication do not respond very well; the standard, if there be one, is not known or, more likely, is unknowable *as a standard* in the nature of a legal prescription.[18] It only needs to be recognized almost as a truism that economically equivalent outcomes can often be achieved via various legal formulations with different organizational, legal, commercial, and tax connotations and consequences, to know that choice among alternatives is not, in itself, and never has been a "bad thing."

So, then, what is being accurately delineated, i.e., characterized or "recharacterized," and indeed why based on a more thorough appreciation of the objectives of transfer pricing analysis? Why is what happened, as it happened according to its legal substance as this chapter contemplates legal substance properly is to be determined, not the accurate delineation, indeed the only enforceable delineation, of the events? Scrutinizing them for their transfer pricing implications, i.e., to determine the "sources" of income as allocations of MNE income according to where the income can

18. *See Canada v. GlaxoSmithKline Inc.*, 2012 SCC 52, [2012] 3 SCR 3, and *Cameco Corporation*, *supra* n. 2 in which the Canadian courts made clear that the TPG are not law, including neither embroidery of the ALS as legislated in the law nor a substitute for it, although they may be useful and have some significance in conducting a transfer pricing analysis. Australia's courts have taken a like view in cases decided before the recent incorporation by reference of the TPG in Australia's statutory tax law. For example, *see* the *Glencore* and *Singapore Telecom* cases, *supra* n. 2 as well as the comments in note 8 about their significance, and the like significance of the *Chevron*, *GlaxoSmithKline*, and *Cameco Corporation* cases in relation to the thesis of this chapter.

be considered to have been earned, is a separate matter, is it not? Economic analysis, subsuming elements of enterprise business valuation and industrial economics, no doubt may supply useful evidence as in any legal proceedings to determine the legal substance of the arrangement. But evidence is not "a law unto itself," as some approaches to transfer pricing seem to project. While it serves legal, including tax, analysis to detect legal quality of parties' arrangements, it is not a substitute or alternative for what in law and fact they are.

8.2 Commercial Rationality

The license to restate taxpayers' arrangements implied by "commercial rationality" is equally puzzling, and troubling for the same reasons. Transfer pricing is all about "judgment"—it is a truism that transfer pricing is an art not a science.[19] That term suffers from the same frailties as "accurate delineation," including the uncertain vantage from which and priority with which such a determination would be made in light of and maybe despite an explanation by taxpayers of why they did what they did in a particular way. According to what principled standard, as if the standard was or could be universally applicable, is a choice to be made and judged to be rational or not among legally sustainable ways to accomplish the same economic objective? Indeed, in the service of the ALS, why does that question even need to arise?

8.3 Accurate Delineation + Commercial Rationality = ?

Separately but also deliberately in combination, these phrases are euphemisms for "substance" as transfer pricing would like it to be understood. A concern, though, is that they may imply a formative entitlement on the part of tax authorities, i.e., without any necessary indication of colorable "tax avoidance," to make a primary determination of taxpayers' circumstances, unconstrained by what a legal analysis would determine those arrangements to be. In transfer pricing's contemporary setting, they seem to be triggers, perhaps even rationalizations and justifications, for "recharacterizing" taxpayers' arrangements according to an economic imperative that does not necessarily recommend only one possible transactional formulation—from the perspective of tax authorities. If they are not that, then as this chapter tries to develop, should events as undertaken by MNEs not be a sufficient foundation for doing what transfer pricing analysis is supposed to do, to determine the alignment of reported income and contributions made to earn it? The significance accorded these new or newly emphasized, or recalibrated, notions *as points of departure* for a transfer pricing analysis and not consequential from determinations of untoward tax avoidance attributable to gratuitous or pointless or contrived conduct by taxpayers as disclosed by evidence to be inconsistent with organizational and transactional formulation, is the notable undercurrent of these phrases. In this neat, understated elision of legal arrangements to imply a code of economic conduct with the imprimatur of law, the law

19. The Supreme Court of Canada referred to it this way in the *GlaxoSmithKline* case, *supra* n. 2.

that establishes the terms of dealing manifest in "real transactions" of the "real parties" is conveniently marginalized and may be displaced in favor of essentially standardless abstract determinations.

The dominance of economic tools in transfer pricing, even if understood only as analytical devices and not principles or "rules," may have obscured this in practice. But this is highly relevant to how the substance of "substance" ought to be perceived.

"Accurate delineation" and "commercial rationality" are mobilized to detect where "value is created." Yet again do we find deference to this equally untethered notion. It may merge with notions or perceptions of the *source* of income, the *origination* of income, the *nature and location* of physical and intellectual contributions in a production function or supply chain, and the like. But, unlike its cousin, the "old fashioned" discipline of business valuation, "value creation" as a euphemism for profit allocation knows no empirical or principled boundaries. In the TPG, it is closely connected to the TPG's indicators of "substance"—what is thought to be the "accurate delineation" as a primary analytical step of taxpayers' arrangements according to what also is thought to be "commercially rational." Yet, those using these terms may be hard pressed to explain indisputably the frame of reference for judging how these determinations associated with "value creation" ought to be made. More "granular" economic analysis based on more and more finely extracted or labeled economic elements of commercial activity subsumed in transactions is an impostor for the delineation of events that have and can in evidence grounded analysis can be shown to have fundamental legal significance. Interestingly, transfer pricing's separate entity transactional orientation has never denied, or needed to deny, the inherent reliability of transactions as taxpayers have undertaken them except, possibly, when there is demonstrable and overt colorable tax avoidance. This has been a mainstay of transfer pricing analysis.

In any event, regardless of the jargon or "bumper sticker" of the moment, has transfer pricing not always been concerned with value creation? How could this not be the case, regardless of the economic models of the moment? Why and how else would questions about compensating value otherwise arise? "Value creation" as a transfer pricing imperative is not new. In fact, in the modern era of transfer pricing, it reaches back almost one hundred years to the work of the International Chamber of Commerce and the United Nations in the 1920s and 1930s.

9 IS "SUBSTANCE" EVEN THE "RIGHT" OR RELEVANT QUESTION?

A key question is: Has "substance"—as the TPG now frame or imply that notion—displaced or marginalized the law? In other words, is an economic inference about "substance" to be treated as the law,[20] as if the economics of "substance" were a "code" like a tax code? Is this so despite that taxation at the best of times is accessory to the relevant private law that enlivens legal personalities and legal

20. *See* the cases referred to *ibid.* and *supra* n. 18.

constructions—organizational forms and personalities and kinds and formulations of transactions?

The starting point of any tax analysis, any interpretative exercise regarding a tax statute, is the private law as if it were spelled out in the statute rather than incorporated by necessary reference or implication. The tax law generally operates on "as found" notions of property, contract, commercial relations, forms of business organization, and the like. If exception is taken to tax effects flowing from personalities or events as the law creates or otherwise conceives them, tax law can be and sometimes is adjusted to preserve the tax consequences appropriate for the affected circumstances as tax policy sees them, though without altering or "recharacterizing" them as such. This, to emphasize, is to accord with the outcomes intended by discernible tax and underlying fiscal policy. The tax response might include mimicking or reflecting outcomes that would be consistent with and could have been effected using a different legal form without it being unnecessary to jettison reliance on legal formulations to achieve a more fiscally sound outcome. Even then, if "recharacterization" is required as statutory embroidery of what the private law otherwise establishes, not infrequently that is made explicit in legislation. It is not commonly left to "chance" or impression, or to the vagaries of administrative fiat, episodic "judgement," and discretion of tax administrators and authorities or for that matter taxpayers and their advisors without reference to suitable criteria on which the fair, in the legal sense of fair, exercise of discretion would be expected to be grounded.[21]

Is the "substance" question as the TPG implicitly poses it, the question itself and how it is framed, the "right question" or a distraction from the right question? The history and seminal guidance on transfer pricing as well as the prevailing Pillars conversation reveal, as already mentioned, an alternative hiding in plain sight, namely tailored fractional (an old euphemism, itself, for formulary) apportionment. Notably, the focus is on where income was earned, without being unduly influenced by the legal mechanics according to which it was earned. Formulary apportionment may not yield the "right" outcome in all cases or even at all. But the limits of its inaccuracy will be evident in its parameters and therefore objectively knowable, capable of objective and empirical calibration in ways that are consistent with what possibly may be the underlying goals of "accurate delineation," "commercial rationality" and "value creation"—and "substance." A corollary is that the legal constructions relied upon by

21. The *Income Tax Act* (Canada) contemplates the restatement or adjustment of the quantum and nature of *amounts* in section 247, but rarely uses the word "recharacterize" with notable exceptions for *amounts* in the remedy for events reassessed according to Canada's "General Anti-Avoidance Rule," in subsection 245(5), and in a unique actual recharacterization of dividends as interest for certain dividends on shares of a foreign affiliate that have debt-like characteristics from a financial point of view. The point, here, is that generally when the Canadian tax law finds tax consequences at odds with the financial connotations of a transaction or financial instrument or, even, the organizational significance of a public partnership or public trust that effectively is partly substitute for a taxable corporation, it does not "recharacterize" the events or instruments or entities but instead alters the manner in which transactions and amounts and entities as they exist and continue to be recognized are taxed or assimilated to taxation. "Recharacterization" is not commonly undertaken for Canadian tax purposes. The analyses of the Canadian Tax Court and Federal Court of Appeal in the *Cameco Corporation* case, *supra* n. 2, are revealing.

taxpayers, as relevant evidence discloses taxpayers have respected them, can be not merely the starting point but the unadulterated framework for transfer pricing analysis consistent with the seminal expression of the arm's-length standard in Article 9 of the OECD Model Tax Convention. Equally, however, the tax outcomes are not dominated by those formulations. The emphasis returns to and is what are the "factors of production" and how were they deployed and ultimately realized. Therefore, the law can readily be embraced and not displaced or marginalized as the restated TPG in their BEPS context seem to invite in the service of "substance" as the further justification of "recharacterization."

In this light, how can the substance of "substance" be further developed?

9.1 The Starting Point: The "Reasonable Expectations" of Transfer Pricing

The ALS is found in Article 9 of the Model. It contemplates nothing more than a realignment of the allocation—the split—of profit among members, associated enterprises, of a commonly controlled multinational corporate group where "conditions are made or imposed between ... two [associated] enterprises in their commercial or financial relations which differ from those which would be made between independent enterprises ...."

What the ALS really seeks to detect is the gratuitous exercise of control within a multinational family—simply because of unlimited possibilities arising from being able to control all organizational and transactional elements of dealings within the corporate family. Despite the frequently disputed comparability of the objective and methods of Article 9, and Articles 5 ("permanent establishment") and 7 (attribution of business income to permanent establishments), the exercise contemplated by Articles 5 and 7 is instructive in so far as they apply to a single legal and economic enterprise that has not undergone fiscal mitosis—cell division—enabled by the simple legal expedient of incorporating its distinct elements and then effectively recombining them using contracts of various kinds to transfer property, provide services, enable the use of "intangibles," and effect financing.[22] Their focus is on parsing production and sales elements to allocate income.[23] The principal difference is that whereas Article 7 imagines a separate taxable presence with a distinct legal personality in the "source" jurisdiction where income-earning activities take place and markets exist, Article 9 relies on the "real thing." Legal personality is a presumptive feature of Article 9 captured by "enterprise" which still, though, in tax treaties is defined in relation to the carrying on of business, is something that attracts muted, if there is any, recognition in

22. In some respects, the Pillar Two minimum tax treats entities and "establishments" in the same way, targeting group profit and positing the direct or effective taxation of group profits on a de facto consolidated basis, and therefore effectively marginalizing the fiscal significance of subdividing MNEs as economic unities into constellations of legal distinct pieces joined together by contracts.

23. The OECD "AOA," recommended to be the standard and means for attributing business profits to a permanent establishment, is built on this premise and despite its controversial history reflects this essence of international taxation generally as well as in the transfer pricing context.

the transfer pricing "club."[24] The point though is both are concerned with where compensable features of business are carried on, not so much who as a distinct of diffracted legal personality ostensibly conducted activities under the veil of legal personality. In the Article 9 case, the economic features and business activities of an *enterprise* have been fragmented from the MNE "unity" in separate legal persons reconnected through contractual and other relations created and defined by the law. These fragments are persons who are persons in the eyes of the law simply because the law says so though the economic and business dynamics conducted through the media of various legal constructions closely parallel the circumstances that would prevail without that legal separation and, indeed, in the closely held commonly controlled world of MNEs have the effect of restoring that functional unity.

The essence of Article 9, of the ALS, is not and never has been to seek the "right" "price" of anything, but to exclude the influence of common control where distortions in the allocation of profit among contributing members of the corporate family are evident. It is to establish where income should be considered to have been earned with reference to the objectively verifiable elements of carrying on business as the business was carried on—referable "inputs" and "outputs" and the processes by which the former become the latter and become sold to consumers—undistorted by excesses of gratuitous corporate governance only possible because of common control. Common control effectively puts MNEs on both sides of the same transactions; it is the absence of adverse self-interests that requires the institutionalized caution and skepticism of transfer pricing. Implicitly the focus is on those elements in their composite result, "income" or "profit." The mechanics of the transformation is not the "rule," not the ALS. The ALS is about sifting "income" for the impurities of gratuitous corporate governance, the influence of legal technique for its own sake, particularly where taxpayers can be shown to have been indifferent to or not justifiably to have relied on the levers of the law that equally engaged and interested countries, that are sources of the law, have made available to private taxpayers.

Despite the lore surrounding the ALS abetted by the transmutation of the TPG as a "rule" or "principle" (or both) rather than a matrix of analytical devices, the ALS is not to be confused with the TPG and, to be even clearer, the TPG are not the ALS. The TPG comprise a suite of analytical tools that may be helpful in detecting the excesses of the exercise of commercially undisciplined control, but the TPG are not the "standard" and more likely than not—notable exceptions are the United Kingdom and Australia—they are not (the) law of tax jurisdictions legislatively attuned to transfer pricing even though the probative influence of the TPG may be significant and even profound—as an analytical expedient or heuristic.

24. Article 9 applies to "enterprises of a contracting state." Article 3 of the Model, as bilateral tax treaties commonly do, defines "enterprise of a Contracting State" and "enterprise of the other Contracting State." They "mean respectively an enterprise carried on by a resident of" the States. And Article 3 defines the fundamental notion of "enterprise" as "appl[ying] to the carrying on of any business." The object of the ALS is the carrying on of business. The proximity of Articles 5 and 7 and of Article 9 is very much closer than commonly acknowledged, and their fiscal focus regarding the allocation of taxing rights in relation to where the law indicates income is "sourced" is exactly the same.

The ALS as defined by Article 9 (for which the TPG are extended OECD Model Tax Convention Commentary for Article 9) says nothing about financial elements—the "stuff"—of contemporary and increasingly more granular transfer pricing: revenue, cash flow, expenses, deductions, legal constructions—comparative or otherwise, "economics," "substance," "characterization" including "recharacterization," or any other methodological rudiment that too often may be taken for granted as or as synonymous with "the ALS." The ALS targets, and the fundamental remedy that it supports is a realignment of *profit* or *income*. In most tax jurisdictions, this is a net notion after taking into account all the intrinsic transactional and financial elements of income measurement.

The ALS and for that matter despite a number of additions and restatements the TPG are fundamentally unchanged in their terms, objectives, and effect from the original conception of the ALS by the International Chamber of Commerce in the early 1920s and the League of Nations, outlined particularly in the highly detailed formative work by Mitchell B. Carroll in his 1930s studies and reports.[25] At least directionally, even before the OECD's first cut at the TPG in 1979, that can fairly be said for the essence of all of the methodological devices and trade-offs found in the TPG and, for that matter, in the BEPS Actions 8-10 Reports and Pillars proposals. The seeds, and more, of all of that can be found in the original attention paid to transfer pricing by the League. Since then, the TPG have been restated following the contours of United States transfer pricing law and regulation. But the changes do not materially alter the objectives or analytical direction of the ALS, albeit in the image of and by the more or less wholesale adoption by the OECD of the United States' modern exposition of transfer pricing.

The goal is not and from the beginning was not to detect the "fair market value" of property or services or their absolutely "right" "price," though each might coincide or overlap as part of a transfer pricing analysis in so far as the sum of the "values" of the elements of an income computation reasonably might be expected to be an undistorted computation and share of income. The guiding objective was and remains to allocate profit free of the chauvinistic, opportunistic, uncommercial exercise of corporate governance manifest in common control for its own sake—doing things that can be done simply because there is no exogenous, disinterested discipline. What the absolute "right" outcome might be was and remains an imponderable. What matters is whether contributing members of a corporate family are sharing in the outcome of their collective, integrated, and indeed "unitary" endeavors in a relatively evenhanded and reasonable way, and consequently that the jurisdictions to which they are primary tax adherents equally are attributed their due shares of the family income.

It is obvious and inevitable in a system of laws that income arises within frameworks comprised of organizational forms and personalities to which the law gives life—corporations, notably—and transactions connecting those personalities together almost, in the closely held setting, as if they had maintained an economic unity transactionally and legally. A core challenge faced by transfer pricing is the fragmentation of such a unity using private law-based legal constructions that have the effect

25. *See* Wilkie, *Policy Forum—The Way We Were? The Way We Must Be? The "Arm's Length Principle" Sees Itself (for What It Is) in the "Digital" Mirror*, *supra* n. 6.

of "sourcing" income as so arranged by taxpayers albeit within the continuing economic unity. It may be that there is a close enough correspondence between tax and economic income despite the intervention of legal constructions and devices, but this is what transfer pricing is concerned to test. In effect, conduct of taxpayers according to typical and enforceable legal arrangements is the platform for transfer pricing. This being so, it would be odd and is awkward to begin a transfer pricing analysis by pretending that the legal premise is inherently frail or marginal and should be disregarded. The formulations of transactions—formulations that have different legal significance even if they might be perceived to frame equivalent economic outcomes—are products of the law and their effectiveness needs to be determined according to the law.

The ALS has nothing to say, either, about how the income *should be* earned organizationally or transactionally—that is, by what legal mechanics or how choices among them ought to be made to nevertheless achieve economically equivalent outcomes. The TPG cannot and do not need to change that to faithfully serve the expectations of the ALS. The TPG are and ought to be, and in fact need to be, only concerned with the outcome of the business and economic *rudiments* of shared enterprise as they have been assigned to MNE group members by the group itself. The ALS is not a surrogate or proxy legal system. Rather, its role is fiscally forensic in relation to the circumstances it finds otherwise to exist, to ensure that effects under competing (including tax) legal systems are reasonable in relation to the application of those legal systems to taxpayers' conduct and, vicariously to the relative entitlements of the countries whose legal systems they are.

In this context, a prime difficulty in determining "substance" is the infinite malleability with which members of MNE may conduct themselves according to business formulations that draw their significance for many reasons from the law. Even if they are "not up to something," they are always on all sides of the transactions. The discipline of independent parties' self-interests, the adversity of interest that contracts take for granted, cannot be expected even if it may be simulated.[26] But, this is not a reason or an excuse to kick the law to the side in the name of correcting unwarranted income diversion, as if the ALS assisted by the TPG constitute an omnibus general anti-avoidance rule (GAAR) that equally applied to the law generally as well as tax law. If, for example, the law permits deductions to be taken in one legal setting but not another, the magic of transfer pricing cannot change that; change, if warranted, is to other aspects of how income is computed and taxable income determined.[27] Transfer

26. *See* H.D. Rosenbloom, *Banes of an Income Tax: Legal Fictions, Elections, Hypothetical Determinations, Related Party Debt*, 26:17 (2004) *Sydney Law Review* 17-35.
27. Canadian tax law, by way of example, offers statutory experience in achieving suitable tax outcomes without "recharacterizing" transactions or disregarding taxpayers' legal formulations. A common and long-standing example of untoward transfer pricing is interest bearing debt being used instead of shares, recognizing that interest is deductible in computing income and dividends are not. In Canada, generally dividends paid between corporations are not taxed in the hands of corporate recipients; in principle, income is taxed only at one corporate level. There are exceptions but that is the principle. Financing transactions were devised, often though not always involving banks, in which loans were effectively made in the guise of fixed value preferred shares, in order to secure the benefit of the intercorporate dividend deduction for what

pricing, built as it is on a curious premise that legally diffracted economic units nevertheless can be examined by disregarding that premise, cannot blithely step away from the premise and, in so doing, pick and choose among the variety of legal formulations that might have been available to taxpayers. Nor does it have to. If there is mischief in how taxpayers respond to the signals they receive from countries' legal and tax regimes,[28] the remedy lies either in modifying those regimes or focusing more plainly and the main and indisputable elements of carrying on business which can be objectively expressed and, if only by the taxpayers themselves, weighted according to their relative significance for the taxpayer.[29]

The transfer pricing conundrum may mask a more fundamental question about why any legal constructions matter fiscally, particularly when both sides of any bargain are essentially the same via the implications of the parties being commonly controlled. But reconstructing the premises of tax systems goes well beyond transfer pricing's remit. To wage that battle guerilla style, as the most recent labels "accurate delineation," "commercial rationality," and "value creation" seem to suggest, is to make a nonsense of the most fundamental assumptions of transfer pricing about the legal framework for transfer pricing analysis. That is, transfer pricing neither dictates nor indeed cares, or for that matter needs to care that much, about how, in terms of legal formulations, taxpayers earn their income. It cares only that allocation of that income among corporate family members who contribute to earn it is not opportunistically distorted by the exercise of control for its own sake. The issue is not whether by some universal standard the resulting allocations among group members are somehow absolutely "right" or possibly different in absolute terms from those that might seem to arise for

otherwise in a transaction effected differently would have been taxable interest. The same technique was used effectively to "sell" tax attributes that a financed party was unable to use. An option familiar in the current transfer pricing landscape would have been to "recharacterize" the shares as debt and the dividends as interest. Instead, the Canadian law denies the intercorporate dividend deduction where objective features of the shares are as or more consistent with debt rather than unrestricted equity. There is not any need to "recharacterize" but simply to adjust the intensity with which the financial return on the transaction is taxed. This is suitable place also to observe that "transfer pricing," that is, income allocations that are tested according to the ALS, is really the convergence of the application of the full range of "other" more typical tax rules yielding income according to tax precepts. It might be that this realization and examples like the Canadian example would be instructive in evaluating why transfer pricing would require transactions and taxpayers' roles in them to be recast rather than the levers of income computation otherwise present in taxing statutes being pulled to ensure that income is suitably measured and allocated.

28. *See* the critique of the current state of the OECD's Pillars proposals, J.S. Wilkie, *Next Steps for the OECD Pillars: Moving from a Political Deal to an Enforceable Law,* (November 22, 2021) 104:2 Tax Notes International 889-903.

29. *See,* for example, the "DEMPE" approach created by the OECD in BEPS Actions 8-10, for allocating income attributable to "intangibles"—not merely intellectual property in the legal sense but all manner of enterprise uniqueness that informs the organizational and commercial essence of an MNE. Recently, a doctoral student at the Vienna University of Business and Economics has closely examined DEMPE in light of the objectives of transfer pricing and the ALS: *see* M.S. Screpante, *Rethinking the Arm's Length Principle in the Era of Value Creation: An Anti-Avoidance Approach to the Allocation of Profits on Intangibles Profit-Shifting Tax Planning Structures* (unpublished), defended in the Defensio on January 20, 2022.

others from business that look a lot like a tested business. That is what Article 9 says, no more and no less.

There is another challenge in this arena, directly bearing on the substance of "substance."

What typically bedevils transfer pricing analysis is how to measure and allocate what economists call "rent"—the idiosyncratic MNE-specific features of economic integration, of the "togetherness" of what could be independent elements, associated with being an MNE and protecting the features if its business and market presence that are considered to be unique and uniquely valuable. Implicitly, the core focus of transfer pricing—continuously from its modern origin in the work of the International Chamber of Commerce and the League of Nations up to the rearticulation of the same issues now through the BEPS and Pillars lenses in the work of the OECD—is what to do about the "intangible" aspect of MNEs. It is that that accounts for their existence as commercially and economically unitary, integrated "entities" facing the commercial world as a unit despite their legally distinct strands reconstituted through contracts as the units they essentially are. The "intangible" element, which is not restricted to legally protected intellectual property, is what constitutes MNEs as such. Despite many pages, and dense and in some respects prolix commentary that comprise the TPG, it is "rent" that is more often than not what the TGP seek to parse. This has been the case, even if understated in earlier versions of the TPG, even before "intangibles" most recently became a focus of the OECD's attention, in revisions of Chapter VI and the introduction of Chapter IX of the TPG, the BEPS project in which transfer pricing in one way or another was dominant, and now in the Pillars and GloBE proposals. It is the intangible element that is the primordial aspect of an MNE. Again, despite possible appearances to the contrary, it is what makes MNEs even as members of the same industrial sector "different" and consequently the implications of transactions among the members of each seemingly similar MNE also "different" than seemingly like transactions conducted by the members of corporate families.[30] Transfer pricing's objective to solve for the allocation of MNEs' international income cannot be solved without reaching a reasonably reliable way to allocate economic rent as allocated income according to the precepts of the ALS. Yet, the TPG seem mostly focused on remediating symptoms of this "problem" without solving the problem itself in a practical and readily and objectively administrable way, i.e., reflecting or significantly influenced by a formulaic or fractional approach, even if less perfectly than the imagined ideal that commonly dominates transfer pricing and justifies even more and more apparently refined expositions of the TPG by the transfer pricing "establishment" as Robert Couzin to whom this chapter referred earlier nominated it.

Both the International Chamber of Commerce and Mitchell B. Carroll in his work for the League of Nations explicitly addressed the question of "intangibles." This too is not a new question. Allowing for the language of the day, their conception of the issue and their offered solutions are fundamentally no different than those that are presented as

30. The Supreme Court of Canada recognized this in the *GlaxoSmithKline* case, *supra* n. 2, observing that genuine comparables can be expected to be quite rare, in relation to analysis that more generally is more art than science.

novel advancements in the BEPS and Pillars context. The International Chamber of Commerce preferred profit splits but understood that they might be hard to actually implement in an international setting. Its solution was a one—sales—factor formula. Carroll took a slightly different tack though to much the same effect. After considering comprehensively the notion of fractional apportionment and its adoption by a number of countries by the 1930s in their tax regimes, he concluded that the sorts of MNE features we call "intangibles"—essentially, the intellectual dimensions of creatively, strategy, and direction—were more likely than not were associated with the head offices or parents of MNEs of which local branches and subsidiaries were functional emanations—what in contemporary transfer pricing terms were more or less "routine" contributors to the mobilization of MNE business.

All of this is to say that experiential transfer pricing analysis has always been known to suffer from serious limitations. And that has not changed. And, again, that is essentially attributable to wanting prescriptive guidance for the substance of "substance" but knowing how elusive that ideal is. Transfer pricing by its nature is a world of "second bests." That this is so does not require disregarding the legal context of events to police the commercial integrity of shared MNE group income, no less, a rubric without the enforceable features of the law to replace it. The substance of "substance" is an enduring undercurrent of transfer pricing, and even the digital modalities of how business is now commonly conducted do not change the essence of the exercise, which is to determine the "source" of income and in particular the shared accountability for and enjoyment of all dimensions of an MNE of what makes an MNE an MNE. The most recent indication of this is the approach contemplated by the OECD's Pillar One.

From the essential thread(s) of transfer pricing, the nuances of the questions these comments ask become even clear as reframed more pointedly:

1. Is the search for "substance" really seeking an ambulatory, universal notion of the "source" of income? Is this what is meant to be expressed by "value creation"? In the absence of a universal legal system (which would entail an even greater cession of fiscal sovereignty than, e.g., implicitly imagined by the Pillars[31]), is it possible to achieve a universal notion of "source" under

31. Sovereignty, more specifically "fiscal sovereignty," is a serious influence, understated though it may be, in any discussions about nations actually or effectively sharing taxing rights, "defining" "income," or taking any action legislatively and in an enduring way, or as may be the case with public law limitations in mind in a way that is difficult to change because of commitments made in a multilateral convention. Yet, the undercurrent of present international developments seems to anticipate or expect increasing degrees of practical and even legal homogeneity or harmonization of the terms and administration of "sovereign" tax regimes. Recalling that tax regimes *enable* countries' distinctive fiscal policies—distinctive because countries are not the same and do not have or project, necessarily, the same cultures, social conditions and values, economic resources or objectives or the like, tinkering or more with "tax"—including in the most mundane transfer pricing settings, raises fiscal issues. An effect of "accurate delineation" and its companions "commercial rationality" and "value creation" is to invoke as a subtext these kinds of fiscal issues, but without normative constraints so as to allow even a determination that countries may have shared and where necessary self-abnegating views on the questions these notions mask. For interesting discussions on the intersection of sovereignty and tax, *see*, for example, L.B. Samuels, *The Sovereign Power to Tax*, in *Treatment of Tax Measures Under International Trade and Investment Agreements: The GATS Compromise*, (April 9-12, 2008) 102 Proceedings of the Annual Meeting (American Society of International Law) 51-55, retrieved

applicable law? Are the BEPS project and its Pillars extension amount to a quest for a universal notion of income's "source" when it comes right down to it, effectively by determining what is *not* the "source" of income, i.e., what amounts to a "negative source" discipline?[32]

2. Has "substance" ever been "the question" in a transfer pricing analysis? Is "substance" as a transfer pricing abstraction more of a distraction that impedes than aids progress to achieve what the ALS as expressed in Article 9 of the Model permits to be done and supposes ought to be done?
3. Is the only difficult, even imponderable, aspect of the analysis of otherwise readily observable conduct of taxpayers the "intangible" element, economic rent which tax commentators have tried to measure in various ways without achieving agreement or a generally agreed empirical model? Not just for "digital" businesses but more generally? Is it an achievable goal to allocate this "royal jelly" of MNE existence incontrovertibly among tax jurisdictions without objective markers? Is it likely that we will translate the economist's theory of the firm into indisputable allocations to the legally diffracted elements of the economic unity that is an MNE without objective parameters as points of reference?
4. How do we reliably, predictably, and more or less incontrovertibly, as part of the ordinary measurement of income and administration of tax regimes, identify and distill the seamless and intrinsic elements of a producer of "goods" and services including their intellectual aspects? Is more and more seemingly "qualitative" analysis the answer?
5. How can tax jurisdictions be accountable to each other for plausible income allocation outcomes on an objective basis? Despite the involvement of private parties, it is the essence of international taxation, including transfer pricing, that the real protagonists are countries identifying and defending their interests in relation to each other, even in a tax world with prevalent multilateral tax pretensions and aspirations?

10 YES, IT IS ALL ABOUT "SOURCE"

In this critique of "substance," a key recurring point is the fundamental underlying quest for establishing the "source" of income, and that this is not an economic notion

from https://www.jstor.org/stable/2566026, and D. Ring, Democracy, *Sovereignty and Tax Competition: The Role of Tax Sovereignty in Shaping Tax Cooperation*, Boston College Law Legal Studies Research Paper Series, Research Paper 171, January 28, 2009. *See also* the comments in this regard in Wilkie, *Next Steps for the OECD Pillars: Moving From a Political Deal to an Enforceable Law, supra* n. 28. *See also* W. Schön, *Taxation and Democracy*, (2019) 72:2 Tax Law Review, New York University School of Law, 235-303. And also *see* D. Rodrik, *The Globalization Paradox Democracy and the Future of the World Economy* (New York, London: W.W Norton & Company, 2011). *See also*, J.S. Wilkie and P.W. Hogg, *Tax Law Within the Larger Legal System* (Winer 2015) 52:2 Osgoode Hall Law Journal 463.

32. *See* Wilkie, *New Rules of Engagement? Corporate Personality and the Allocation of "International Income" and Taxing Right, supra* n. 6. The notion of negative source is a descriptive way of interpreting the effect of the BEPS project's attention notably in its transfer pricing aspects to the functional and financial capacity of MNE group members to conduct business and earn income within the framework of transfer pricing's separate entity and transactional foundations. Effectively, the latent objective is to determine where income cannot reasonably be considered to have been earned, that is, to have its "source," wherever else in an affirmative sense its "source" connections fairly may be established. *See also* A.J. Martín Jiménez, Value Creation: A Guiding Light for the Interpretation of Tax Treaties?, *supra note* 1.

even though economic analysis may inform how the legal notions framing this determination have applied. It is also not floating, not ambulatory, not to be conveniently defined depending on ambient circumstances. It is a legal notion. It denotes and expresses what arises from the legal modalities of relations among parties, depending on and revealing the significance and effect of relations that are not merely addressed but defined by the law. This includes where relations are considered to take place because of how and where they are *enforceable*. What kind of contract it is and how it is to be performed are legal questions. What kind of person it is and the capacity in which and means by which it functions are legal questions. Whether legal personalities conduct themselves in relation to faithful renditions of the intrinsic features and requirements of the legal relations and instruments they adopt to frame their conduct and relationships, which includes whether their intended reliance on selected legal formulations is justified and consistent with their conduct, present determinations of law, albeit informed by evidence of various kinds including insights from financial and economic analysis.

A legal analysis to determine legal consequences necessarily includes an evidentiary inquiry—which is what transfer pricing analysis really is—into how taxpayers conduct themselves. These comments have mentioned law-based and evidence-based inquiry a number of times. What does this mean?

Determining justifiable reliance on legal formulations by the parties to them to achieve commercial objectives includes considering how risk is distributed among and borne by transaction parties as well as their functional and financial capacity to bear the risks ostensibly attributed to them by the legal formulations they adopt. These all are aspects of an informed legal analysis, an inquiry into the "legal substance" of parties' relations.

Transfer pricing analysis is merely a specialized example of the evidentiary inquiry that underpins any legal analysis. It is part of a legal analysis. That evidence is required in a legal analysis does not transform the legal analysis into an economics analysis. Nor does or should it elevate economics any more than any other evidence above its supporting role in a legal analysis. Yet, the contemporary inertia of transfer pricing seems to imply or want otherwise.

Much of what passes for or is passed off as "economic substance" is probably, more accurately, the "legal substance" of events—understood the way these comments explain "legal substance." This is not mechanical form. It entails an evidence-based inquiry into what the legal formulations actually mean in relation to affected taxpayers including, to put "sham" and other like implications in tighter focus, whether the adopted legal constructions "window dressing" or treated by affected taxpayers with detectable indifference, effectively being "beside the point" for them, almost in the nature of a misrepresentation of their circumstances. This engages a legal not an economic analysis. This kind of inquiry might well disclose ulterior or parallel additional legal arrangements that ought to be subject to transfer pricing analysis as the contractual or other relations they are despite their invisibility, as the Supreme Court of Canada in the *GlaxoSmithKline* case analyzed.

This may be what "accurate delineation" could mean, assisted by a law-based evaluation of the "commercially rational" intrinsic expectations of a selected legal formulation taking account of evidence of a taxpayer's circumstances including, importantly, their capacity as independent enterprises to perform the obligations they purport to have undertaken and to enjoy rights that flow from the relationships in which they take on those obligations. But the undercurrent of deference to economic judgments of "substance" as the determinants of the "actual" events to which transfer pricing analysis would then apply suggest the law being relegated to a much inferior role, it being almost presumptively "beside the point" regardless of taxpayer conduct. "Avoided" tax, arising from nothing more exotic than selecting among legally viable ways to achieve equivalent economic outcomes, may be considered undue and potentially impugnable "tax avoidance." This, notwithstanding how the ALS evolved and what it means within the context of legal systems that necessarily animate the circumstances in which it applies.

Two observations are apposite.

Historically and in principle according to the ALS, transfer pricing has always contemplated and relies on legal relations, informed by a typical factual inquiry that in the law is referred to as "evidence." It is unnecessary to look further for the "substance" of taxpayers' affairs than to know what they are, tested to determine their compatibility with how they have been memorialized in contracts and by organizational formulations. That is their "substance" even if there are other formulations of the same economic events that might well have different general legal as well as tax consequences. Whether that accords with suitable rewards for the operational elements of an enterprise is a different question, the question that the ALS addresses.

In many legal traditions, the fact that legal relations among legally distinct fragments of a single economic unit might seem meaningless because of the absence of genuinely independent and adverse interests as would be found in dealings between arm's-length persons does not mean for that reason alone that the legal framework of business relations, even within a non-arm's length setting, ought not to be respected. They are not mere formalities in an environment grounded on observance of the law; the alternative, it must be said, is chaos. It would make the law into a kind of tautology: Legal constructions—what is a contract, what is a corporation, what is property—are artificial constructions of the law; constructions of the law should be disregarded or marginalized because they are constructions of the law.

Testing the significance of organizational and transactional arrangements as matter of law with evidence is to determine, as the legal scholar Lon Fuller[33] analyzed in

33. *See* Wilkie, *Transfer Pricing Aspects of Intangibles: The License Model, supra* n. 6. Professor Lon Fuller's study of the law of contracts and damages, which grounds his examination of the notion of "justifiable reliance" in contracts, has significantly influenced the outlook in this chapter and the paper referred to in this footnote. In short, the question to be asked, in any contractual setting whether parties deal or do not deal at arm's length, is whether a contract party is entitled to rely on its counterparty for the performance of obligations if that contract party knows or ought to know, as may be tested by a typical evidentiary inquiry in the course of a legal analysis, that the counterparty is likely unable to perform its obligations—to use notions found in Actions 8-10 of the BEPS project, that it is financially and functionally incapable of performing its obligations. If so, would it be so strange to conclude, as a legal matter, that reliance on the appearance of the contract for its substantial significance would not be justified, and as a matter of law that the evidence of the parties' circumstances should guide an original determination of

relation to the relationship between the law of contracts and the law of damages arising from breaches of contracts, whether reliance on transactional relations as portrayed by the parties is justified. It involves an understanding of economic context, but it is not an economic question or determination. It does not transmute the law into something else. Evidence serves law as part of a legal analysis. It is not *the law*. For transfer pricing purposes, it does not need to effect such a transmutation.

How is "justifiable reliance" to be evaluated. Again, more probing questions arise.

Are corporations surrogates for natural persons as the corporate law, the law of business associations, contemplates? Do they have the intellectual, functional, and financial capacity to undertake and be responsible for their arrangements, among other things recognizing as the OECD does the legitimacy of "outsourcing" or contracting out functions to be performed under supervision by competent others for suitable compensation? Would an independent party be justified in relying on its counterparty to be what it presents itself to be and to do what it purports to be able to do, based on an objective evidence-based analysis? If the answers to these questions, based on evidence about the circumstances, are no, then the "legal substance" of the tested arrangements is not and never was what it was presented to be. Then what legal relationships are to be inferred from the observed conduct—not recharacterized but, rather, discovered, revealed? As so cast—not *re*cast but *cast* as they intrinsically are, those relationships are no less legal and legally resilient for not, possibly, being transcribed properly or maybe even at all, as such, by the parties. All of that is an inquiry into the legal substance that engages an interpretation of arrangements adopted by economic actors as legal personalities but does not presumptively displace those arrangements in favor of any, let alone an economic reconstruction. It involves interpreting and applying the law, not merely reading it as words in a dictionary or viewing it as pictures on a whiteboard.

It must be said, too, that avoiding the limited implications of "economic substance" which may be inferred from "accurate delineation" and "commercial rationality," as a kind of alt-keystone of contemporary transfer pricing analysis does not impair the TPG's utility. The TPG remain a useful suite of devices for its purpose, to facilitate the kind of evidentiary inquiry that transfer pricing as a subset of the tax law quite naturally entails. But its purpose is not to be "the principle" or a surrogate or substitute for the law. The TPG's role is income measurement, not transactional redetermination, drawing on a variety of analytical heuristics. They offer devices to evaluate the compatibility with reported income of taxpayers' selected transactional "forms" and their outcomes as imagined by the ALS set out in Article 9 of the OECD Model Tax

what their contract, at law, must have been? Would it be that strange, also, to conclude that whatever else may be said about the circumstances, a party demonstrably incapable of performing the contract could not be expected to earn income that would be commensurate with performance? These are the elements of legal analysis; in a manner of speaking the functional analysis grounding transfer pricing reflects a similar inquiry. As evidence that inquiry is useful to detect the "reality" of transactions —the legal reality—without requiring analysts to step entirely outside the normative legal system to be guided determinatively by economics as if economic analysis were the equivalent of legal, indeed statutory, provisions.

Convention. But that is all even though it is a lot. The TPG are not a bespoke legal system for transfer pricing.

In other words, it is unnecessary to disturb or discard the "legal substance" of taxpayers' arrangements to conduct a transfer pricing analysis or reach the determinations that transfer pricing seeks for the international allocation of international business income as Article 9 of the OECD Model Tax Convention projects the essence and parameters of the ALS. And, when an evidence-based analysis of taxpayers' formulations of their arrangements—which is a private law legal analysis—discovers if it does that the legal arrangements are other than what they purport to be, then that discovery is not "recharacterization" but rather the primary determination of the quality—the legal quality—those arrangements according to applicable law. Obviously, legal arrangements, whether as originally formulated or determined in this kind of an analysis, have financial, tax, and yes economic consequences. But that does not require the consequences to be "the rule." That applicable law may not be the same among tax jurisdictions or that the absence of accurate documentation may present analytical complications are familiar situations in any legal analysis in an international setting. Indeed, it is the essence of the discipline of conflict of laws to detect applicable law among a possible range of possibilities based on evidence of the observed conduct of affected persons and their nexus or connection to the legal regimes on which they purport to rely.

It is important to emphasize this because the "source" of income which seems to be at the heart of BEPS and the Pillars and of the quest for "substance" in transfer pricing is a legal notion. There are no normative or indisputably resilient conceptions of economic source because there is no objective referential or normative context for such a determination in the context of countries' relative taxing rights that otherwise exist according to and depend on the law. It is possible to agree or disagree with legal determinations after considering evidence about them in relevant contexts. But any such evaluation is primarily tethered to a normative starting point, against which the compatibility of circumstances disclosed by evidence with the legal notion of concept is measured. "Economic substance" is too easily and malleably in the eye of the beholder.

11 "SUBSTANCE" AND "RECHARACTERIZATION" ARE FICTIONS: AND MISUNDERSTOOD

The next step in this inquiry into the substance of "substance" is to ask whether in the evolution of the TPG as an analytical manifestation of the ALS, there necessarily has been any actual or implied license to "recharacterize" arrangements simply because they yield different regulatory, i.e., tax, outcomes than would have arisen from possible alternative arrangements to achieve the same or equivalent financial and "economic" outcomes. As the TPG have evolved, as the ALS has been evaluated more and more probingly, has a fundamental implication of transfer pricing simply not been noticed? Has it always been or even now in their recalibration is the case that a normative expectation of transfer pricing is first to define events in an image those events might have taken, and then proceed on this basis to measure income test its international allocation within an MNE? Are countries as transaction parties through their taxpayers asked to ignore the significance of their legal systems when it comes time to measure their contributions to the allocation of international fiscal resources?

The short answer to that question is no. "Recharacterization" is not a normative element of the ALS nor have the TPG treated it this way. Indeed, the more evident implication is that any exception to taking taxpayers' transactions "as found" would require demonstrable purposive tax avoidance by taxpayers. Even though an economic inquiry into the financial and economic circumstances of transaction parties may inform the evidence about the legal substance—the substance—of taxpayers' circumstances, the transaction formats have not been dictated by transfer pricing's economic methodology or theory.[34] In other words, what amounts to transactional substitution has not been an inherent transfer pricing tool. As discussed elsewhere in these comments, important judicial determinations in the transfer pricing context are consistent with this observation.

To appreciate this, it is useful to trace key relevant aspects of the modern history of the ALS set out in the evolved TPG from their origin in 1979—to see them on a continuum.

The original 1979 TPG, which essentially brought the United States transfer pricing rule and regulations into the international arena as an adopted "norm," specifically disavowed transactional (substantial) substitution. The TPG said:

> "In general, the approach which is adopted in this report to the adjustment of transfer pricings for tax purposes is to recognize the actual transactions as the starting point for tax assessment and not, other than exceptional cases, to disregard them or substitute other transactions for then ..."[35]

This is an entirely unremarkable statement that fundamentally transfer pricing entails, indeed takes for granted, that the "substance" of transactions is their legal substance, whatever else may be said about splitting an MNE's profit among its legally distinct constituents. This assumes, of course, that evidence about taxpayers' conduct would confirm their arrangements as formulated and memorialized to be, in law, those that they purport to be, an inherently law-based determination and for that very ordinary in the experience of the law. That could only have been said with the awareness, implicit in the ALS as expressed in Article 9 of the Model, that in a setting of commonly controlled entities, the necessary artifice of legal constructions associate with degrees of indifference about which among them may be selected to achieve economically equivalent outcomes must be taken for granted. It is embedded in the notion of transfer pricing.

34. *See* Wilkie, *Transfer Pricing Aspects of Intangibles: The License Model*, and references in that paper, particularly to Lon Fuller, examining the notion of "legal substance," and *New Rules of Engagement? Corporate Personality and the Allocation of "International Income" and Taxing Right*, and *Policy Forum—The Way We Were? The Way We Must Be? The 'Arm's Length Principle' Sees Itself (for What It Is) in the 'Digital' Mirror*, *supra* n. 6.
35. Taken from OECD, TPG 1979.

Refinement of the TPG in the relevant respect between 1995 and 2016 introduced some opacity for those who would want the bedrock of legal substance to be less firm. Still, however, the direction remained consistent. There was an expectation that if taxpayers' legal arrangement were to be ignored or marginalized, the provocation would have to be purposive tax avoidance. Telescoping and to a limited extent paraphrasing several paragraphs of the TPG as they flowed in this period, the TPG said:

> However, there are two particular circumstances in which it may, exceptionally, be both appropriate and legitimate for a tax administration to consider disregarding the structure adopted by a taxpayer in entering into a controlled transaction ... [(1) economic substance varies from form, and (2) though consistent in form and substance the structure is commercially irrational and impairs relevant due tax administration] ... In both sets of circumstances described above the character of the transaction may derive from the relationship between the parties rather than be determined by normal commercial conditions and may have been structured by the taxpayer to avoid or minimize tax. In such cases, ... Article 9 would ... allow an adjustment of conditions to reflect those which the parties which the parties would have attained had the transaction been structured in accordance with economic and commercial reality of parties transacting at arm's length. ... [There is a] difference between restructuring the controlled transaction under review which ... generally is inappropriate, and using alternative structured transactions as comparable uncontrolled transactions ... .[36]

The catalyst for any transactional restatement is a measure of tax avoidance that would need to involve something more than merely avoiding tax that would be payable if the economic outcome had been secured via a different legal formulation. This is clear in the last sentence of the digest of TPG paragraphs quoted above. The analytical force of the two possible judgments expressed in (1) and (2) in that quotation fairly should be understood in relation to the ultimate controlling condition imposed by the last sentence. Also, whatever else may be implied by judging economic substance to be different than the form transactions take, or if consistent with it nevertheless to decide that form impairs tax administration by reflecting a "commercially irrational" arrangement, the remedy does not lie in "recharacterizing." The "substance" of the arrangement is its legal substance, and any disagreement with reliance by a taxpayer on its chosen legal formulation is to be resolved, with the benefit of relevant evidence, by a redetermination of the taxpayer's income and a reallocation of the MNEs' international income accordingly, no doubt using whatever other "technical" lever exist in the affected tax law to accomplish this.

Understood this way, for the same reasons as the original exposition in 1979, there is no (necessary) implication of unlimited "recharacterization" as some sort of normative transfer pricing tool or remedy. Even if understated, however, in common transfer pricing discourse, "recharacterization" is frequently what seems to be meant by or foreshadowed in "substance," largely on economic grounds.[37] Yet, as the

36. Taken as a digest of internally consistent relevant excerpts from OECD TPG 1995—2014.
37. It is also to be noted, in light of this observation, how the Canadian courts in the *Cameco Corporation* case orchestrated their reconciliation of the typical pricing oriented "avoided tax" versus "tax avoidance" aspects of the transfer pricing provision of the Canadian Income Tax Act

concluding phrase of these digested extractions from the TPG suggest it is clearly anticipated that "using alternative structured transactions as comparable uncontrolled transactions" in circumstances where a market comparable does not otherwise exist does not require substituting the alternative for the transactions actually undertaken by taxpayers. Rather, taking account of the general conditions of a taxpayer's arrangements, another formulation posited as a comparable is simply a heuristic device to allow a transfer pricing analysis to proceed as it otherwise would, by drawing on objective reference points, even if once removed from actual market circumstances, to test and infer the adequacy or not of the taxpayer's reported income. In Canadian terms, it is to test whether reported income is defensible (not whether it is correct as an absolute, or otherwise incontrovertible) and if not whether and how the "quantum" or "nature" of *amounts* should be adjusted. This would be the case for any transfer pricing analysis, to yield a commercially defensible income free of distortions attributable to identities of interest among components of a taxpayer's corporate family.

The next step—a giant step, it seems—is to the present. It is not clear whether the present is a (sea) change, is confused, or is an opaque or confused rendition of what has come before.

The notions "accurate delineation," "commercial rationality" and "value creation," notably when used in combination, seem to have the effect of validating as a norm "recharacterization" as a formative step to determine "substance" to which, then, transfer pricing analysis of a typical kind would apply. This effectively would institutionalize a dominant economic influence that is excessive and unnecessary in relation to the seminal statement of the ALS in Article 9 of the OECD Model Tax Convention and its UN analog. As noted earlier, the only permission afforded tax authorities by Article 9 is to adjust profits or income. There is no none to adjust "conditions" and "relations"; at best, these are context and comparators, not alternatives or substitutes for what actually and legally happened.

Has there been a change, to embrace taxation on the basis of "economics" as the primary if not exclusive determinant of transactional "substance"? Or does the substance of "substance" reside in an evidence-based determination of whether the parties actually comported themselves with how they have projected their arrangements according to the legal constructions they adopted and relevant documentation? Has there been a change in emphasis or ordering for the deployment of economic analysis to test transfer pricing?

The way in which "accurate delineation," "commercial rationality," and "value creation" have been mixed as a new transfer pricing concoction is confusing, not only for the reasons discussed in this chapter conceptually. They are internally confusing when commentary about them is parsed together and to some extent telescoped relying on nothing more than of the OECD tries to explain them.

In the section of the TPG entitled "Identifying the commercial or financial relations," the gravity and possibly open-ended scope of "accurately delineating" transactions taking account of judgments about their "commercial rationality" emerges. Before

in paragraphs 247(2)(a) and (c) in relation to paragraphs 247(2)(b) and (d), respectively. *See* the reference to the *Cameco Corporation* case, *supra* n. 2.

delving into the possible implications of "accurate delineation," the TPG somewhat ominously say:

> There are two key aspects in ... [a comparability] analysis: the first aspect is to identify the commercial or financial relations between the associated enterprises and the conditions and economically relevant circumstance attaching to those relations *in order that the controlled transaction is accurately delineated*; the second aspect is to compare the conditions and the economically relevant circumstances of the controlled transactions as accurately delineated with the conditions and the economically relevant circumstances of comparable transactions between independent enterprises. ... [I]n delineating the controlled transaction and determining comparability between controlled and uncontrolled transactions or entities, a functional analysis is necessary[38] [emphasis added].

What is the role of the law? This foundational statement of accurate delineation posits not merely *re*characterization, but *characterization* in the first instance of the taxable event according to economic perceptions. It is to be wondered what principled standards of a kind that legal systems typically would recognize, frame such an alternative determination and the judgments on which it relies, it being undeniable that the transactional context will have a legal complexion. Is legal analysis relegated to a secondary, if any, role? Does the law, which gives "life" to bargains and determines their enforceability as bargains—legally framed and typed bargains—as they have been struck and distinct from other kinds of bargains even to the same or an equivalent financial effect, matter?

The most recent restatement of the TPG continues, somewhat equivocally, to offer this awkward "build out" of "accurate delineation" in relation to "commercially rational" conduct of parties in deciding to engage in transactions in particular ways. The leading indicator of the dominant influence is, perhaps, this primary instruction of the TPG:

> "Following the guidance in the previous section [D.1, the opening of which is quoted above], *the transfer pricing analysis will have identified the substance of the commercial or financial relations* between the parties ***and will have accurately delineated*** *the actual transaction* by analysing the economically relevant characteristics."[39] [emphasis added].

Attention is drawn to the emphasized instruction *cum* conclusion by the TPG, which more than implies that the "actual transactions" are those yielded by economic analysis: "... will have identified the substance ... and will have accurately delineated...." What role is the law expected to play? What is "actual"—the primary (re)imagining of an economic construct consistent with economic outcomes, recalling that economically equivalent outcomes are often achievable in legally different but no less respectable ways? Or is "actual" what taxpayers actually "did" to formulate events that certainly have economic features but are expressed and packaged according to familiar legal constructions that not only are common and capable of being well

38. OECD TPG 2022, section D.1, para. 1.33.
39. OECD TPG 2022, para. 1.139.

understood as such but also are essential for the orderly social and economic affairs generally?

The TPG then, against that backdrop and with that orientation, seem to anticipate what this chapter refers to as an evidence-based legal analysis to assess what may be labeled the "legal substance" of the circumstances. The TPG go on to say:

> "In performing the analysis, *the **actual** transactions will have been **deduced*** from written contracts and the conduct of the parties. Formal conditions recognized in contracts will have been clarified ***and supplemented*** by analysis of the conduct of the parties and other economically relevant characteristics of the transactions. ... *Where the characteristics of the transaction that are economically significant are inconsistent with the written contract, then the actual transaction will have been delineated in accordance with the characteristics of the transaction reflected in the conduct of the parties.*"[40] [emphasis added].

"[T]he actual transactions will have been *deduced* ...", the TPG say. What does that mean? The actual transactions are what actually happened—what the actual transactions are. What needs to be "deduced," particularly in the first instance? Issue may be taken with whether parties were justifiably entitled to rely on those transactions as "written" in relation to their relative "conduct" and interests disclosed by the evidence; i.e., in other words, whether the transactions as presented by the taxpayers are the transactions at law, which is a determination that only an evidence-based legal analysis can make. But that does not necessarily mean that their transactions are not what they purport to be or determine whether they happened as presented. Ascertaining this, what transfer pricing would describe as the functional and financial capacity of parties to undertake transactions entails legal analysis, including an inquiry as part of that legal analysis into the parties' conduct—not whether they ought to have framed their transactions they did but whether according to pertinent evidence about their conduct and an understanding of the intrinsic demands of their selected legal formulations, they did. It considers evidence about how they relied on each other and conceived, and if so were justified in conceiving, their relative rights and obligations according to their adopted legal formulations.

Transfer pricing does not need to reimagine the transaction to which then transfer pricing analysis would apply with reference to economic features and outcomes. There is nothing to "deduce," is there, in such a primary way? That is not to say as commented earlier that a legal analysis would not disclose, for example, embedded other contracts needing to be analyzed for transfer pricing purposes or that correspondingly the transfer pricing, i.e., income allocation, implications of other transactions. But it seems that in the mind of the TPG, it is the "economically relevant characteristics" that are perceived to account for the "delineation" of the contractual relations. Yet, economic relations are only that. Where is the awareness that economically equivalent outcomes may readily be achievable by different legal means with dramatically different legal and tax outcomes?

40. OECD TPG 2022 para. 1.140.

The TPG do not get less opaque in their new incarnation as they try to address and possibly redefine the substance of "substance." The restated TPG caution that "[e]very effort should be made to determine pricing for the actual transaction as accurately delineated under the arm's length principle ...." Yet, as noted earlier, "actual" and "delineated" have been expressed with reference to economic analysis. On this ground, the TPG purport to authorize disregarding transactions as taxpayers have implemented them in favor of other formulations considered to be superior according to the economics of tested arrangements. Seemingly, this is seen as the starting point for transfer pricing analysis, contemplating that transactions as accurately delineated by taxpayers in fact and according to the expectations of relevant law may not be "accurately delineated" as the TPG imagine they should have been, and accordingly still may be disregarded with something else being substituted for the displaced transactional configuration. The TPG say:

> This section sets out circumstances in which *the transaction between the parties as accurately delineated can be disregarded* for transfer pricing purposes. Because non-recognition can be contentious and a source of double taxation, *every effort should be made to determine the actual nature of the transaction*, and to ensure that *non-recognition is not used simply because determining an arm's length price is difficult. ... The transaction as accurately delineated may be disregarded, and if appropriate, replaced by an alternative transaction*, where the arrangements made in relation to the transaction, viewed in their totality, differ from those which would have been adopted by independent enterprises behaving in a commercially rational manner in comparable circumstances, thereby preventing determination of a price that would be acceptable to both of the parties taking into account their respective perspectives and *the options realistically available to each of them at the time of entering the transaction. ...* The key question in the analysis is *whether the actual transaction possesses the commercial rationality of arrangements that would be agreed between unrelated parties under comparable economic circumstances, not whether the same transaction can be observed between independent enterprises. The non-recognition of a transaction that possesses the commercial rationality of an arm's length arrangement is not an appropriate application of the arm's length principle. Restructuring of legitimate business transactions would be a wholly arbitrary exercise the inequity of which could be compounded by double taxation* created where the other tax administration does not share the same views as to how the transaction should be structured. *It should again be noted that the mere fact that the transaction may not be seen between independent parties does not mean that it does not have characteristics of an arm's length arrangement. ... The structure that for transfer pricing purposes, replaces that actually adopted by the taxpayer should comport as closely as possible with the facts of the actual transaction* undertaken whilst achieving a commercially rational expected result that would have enabled the parties to come to a price acceptable to both of them at the time the arrangement was entered into[41] [emphasis added].

The emphasized words in their immediate context and in relation to the proximate statements by the OECD in the TPG are, to say the least, intriguing and even confusing. Possibly among others, these questions arise:

41. OECD TPG 2022 paras. 1.142-1.144.

1. Are the transactions not meant already to have been accurately delineated according to their economically relevant characteristics, to be considered the actual transactions? If so, how can "the transaction between the parties as accurately delineated be disregarded"? Why would this happen? According to what reference standard would this happen, and if "accuracy" is the goal, why would this happen?
2. To avoid "non-recognition," it is admonished that "every effort should be made to determine the actual nature of the transaction." But by this point in the analytical protocol is that not already supposed to have happened, according to this protocol for ascertaining what is to be considered the "actual" transaction?
3. What is an "alternative transaction" to an "accurately delineated" transaction which is to be considered the "actual" transaction according to its economically relevant characteristics?
4. By what standard and for what reasons would "accurately delineated" transactions be considered to be "commercially irrational" and why?
5. Again, if according to economically relevant characteristics an "actual" transaction is considered to have been "accurately delineated"—though *as what* it remains to be seen, why is there any (further) consideration of "options realistically available" to the parties? On what grounds would an alternative formulation of an "accurately delineated" transaction be determined to be a more "realistic" option, and indeed an option that ought to have been selected? What is "actual," factually actual according to relevant evidence, or legally actual in that according to relevant evidence the transactional formulation is enforceable, or both?
6. How is a transaction that would be "commercially rational" between independent enterprises, but which does not have an analog in the conduct of independent enterprises, determined to be "commercially rational" for independent enterprises? And who decides this and on what basis, particularly given that "the mere fact that the transaction may not be seen between independent parties does not mean that it does not have characteristics of an arm's length arrangement"?
7. How can any of the seemingly conflicting instructions to disregard "commercially rational" "accurately delineated" transactions coexist with the also seemingly categorical assertion that not recognizing a transaction "that possesses the commercial rationality of an arm's length arrangement is not an appropriate application of the arm's length principle" and that "[r]estructuring ... legitimate business transactions would be a wholly arbitrary [and inequitable] exercise"?
8. What is a "structure that for transfer pricing purposes" effectively would recast or reinvent the facts in relation to the structure "actually adopted by the taxpayer," that nevertheless "should comport as closely as possible with the facts of the actual transaction"? Why is the original transaction being ignored or embroidered in light of the rest of what these excerpts from the TPG instruct?

Article 9 of the Model says none of this. Nor, for that matter, is any of this needed for a coherent and law-based transfer pricing analysis that informs the effectiveness of taxpayers' relations according to the standards of any worthy, thoughtful legal analysis and confirm the legitimacy of the expected terms of dealing as the platform on which the adequacy of reported income then is examined. These include terms that impinge directly or indirectly pricing with reference to evidence as to the taxpayer's condition in relation to its counterparties and their relative justifiable reliance on each other for what their contracts purport to be, that is, with respect to the outcomes they appear to contemplate in what must be enforceable ways in order to be those contracts.

As the list of questions intends to illustrate no doubt despite good intentions to describe what is understood by the ALS, the internal coherence and sense of what this encapsulation should be is unclear and muddled in the OECD's own expressions, "accurate delineation" and "commercial rationality," and attendant notions of "options realistically available." This compounds the equally imponderable overarching guidance that projects "value creation" seemingly as a self-defining notion.[42] In all of this, there is scant if any recognition of the significance of the law for informing the nature of property interests, the scope and interpretation and application of contracts, or the nature and significance of organizational personalities imbued with their existence only by the law—or why the law's implications are not relatively significant. Or might these conflicting and self-reinforcing statements, made baldly without any apparent authority, simply be a not very elegant articulation of the starting point, and as earlier guidance said more clearly the ending point too as well as the frame of reference, for identifying the legal substance of taxpayers' arrangements? Here, "legal substance" connotes substance as developed in this chapter—the substance of "substance."

What is to be made of this? Does deference to "legal substance" undermine an effective application of the ALS as the test of the undistorted commercial defensibility of a taxpayer's income and an MNE's splitting or allocation of its total enterprise profit? As a way to understand relevant "substance," is attention to "legal substance" instructive in thinking harder and more thoroughly about what transfer pricing really targets? In that vein, is analysis that simply amplifies by kind and degrees more and more qualitative judgments with yet more labels, likely to yield uncontroversial outcomes among tax jurisdictions that cannot be assumed to have the same legal and tax regimes but are able to assert respectable tax claims?

This discussion is meant to illustrate that there is not and has not been, possibly until the most recent statement of the TPG, any expectation that taxable events need or first should be "recharacterized" or redetermined to determine their "substance" in the image of an economic hypothesis about how they might have been undertaken, regardless of how as a legal matter it can be determined they did take place. So-called recharacterization, the assertion of an alternate "substance," was not only exceptional but also extreme in the evolution of the TPG. It would not be advanced except as a reaction to purposive tax avoidance with overtones that might befit why a GAAR ("general anti-avoidance rule") would apply in another tax context. Does the trio of

42. It is possible that in this confused recalibration of how to apply the ALS, the OECD is trying to suggest what the courts in Canada, in the *Cameco Corporation* case, referred to as an alternative transaction to be used as reference point in a case where no comparables otherwise exist, to test the reliability of a taxpayer's reported income. However, the courts did not disregard or otherwise displace the transactions undertaken by the taxpayer. Instead, as an analytical heuristic, the courts sought an interpretation of Canada's transfer pricing rule in subsection 247(2) of the Canadian *Income Tax Act* that reconciled its two aspects as a single coherent rule namely, the typical comparables-based aspect to test for arm's-length terms and conditions and the tax avoidance aspect for transactions that lack an arm's-length analog.

"accurate delineation," "commercial rationality," and "value creation" alter that? Do they elevate transactional *re*construction to the status of a primary regulatory function? Does it present the methodological analysis the OECD has long tried to capture in the TPG as controlling the direction not merely of that analysis possibly but as being determinative of the events to which it applies, though on a false legal premise? What might this suggest about the utility of "substance" as an analytical goal or directive?

12 DISTINGUISHING INCOME MEASUREMENT FROM ACTIONABLE TAX AVOIDANCE

The argument driving this chapter forward so far is that the substance of "substance" ought to be determined with reference to the "legal substance" of taxpayers' organizational and transactional arrangements. But, for that, transfer pricing need not suffer. It is not an endorsement of "schemes" or the primacy of "form" in its most narrow and mechanical sense. As said, "legal substance" is not simply a pictorial or written depiction of what those arrangements could be if implemented faithfully according to applicable law. It is the fact of their implementation that matters, and it is evidence, including transfer pricing analysis, that grounds such a determination, made as the legal determination it is.

The inquiry is one of *justifiable reliance* by the parties on arrangements as they were cast, informed and indeed determined by an evidence-based inquiry that is the essence of legal analysis to interpret and construe both legislation and contracts. Were the parties, by their nature and various manifestations of their capacity to undertake activities of various kinds and assume risk, justified in relying on each other in respect of what appear to be their relative rights and obligations? Or, on the other hand, was such reliance not justified because those parties lacked the capacity and resources, themselves including by reasonable extension through the out-sourcing of activities and the management of inherent risks to contractors, for which they nevertheless remained and had the capacity to be responsible, to orchestrate, and to supervise?

To be blunter, were *those* formulations of *those* arrangements undertaken by *those* parties essentially, as relevant evidence would show, *besides the point*? Were taxpayers either indifferent to their organizational and transactional choices, on purpose or by reason of the natural rhythm of their dealings? The question is not whether they could have achieved their ends in a different way. The question is whether they did. That does not displace the transfer pricing analysis envisioned by the ALS. It simply puts it in its proper place and context, not as a surrogate legal system but a test taking account of all relevant circumstances—"conditions" and "commercial or financial relations" as Article 9 of the OECD Model Tax Convention speaks.

In this regard, it is good to be reminded that whatever else may be said about taxation, tax is a cost, no less so within the compass of transfer pricing. Rational actors treat it that way. Tax regimes react to its fiscal implications as a cost but limiting the recognition of financial costs as tax costs. An implication of the trio of terms the OECD uses seems to suggest an eye to "sham" or the anti-tax avoidance aspects of specific transfer pricing rules even though informed adjudicators have rejected broad assertions so directed and have emphasized the fundamental regard that must be had for an evidence-based legal analysis. Marginalizing the significance of law as the objective framework for the primary step in transfer pricing to ascertain "what happened"—the "substance" of pertinent events as if transfer pricing is primarily animated by an anti-avoidance mindset is problematic. Economic reconstruction is not what the ALS or the TPG require.

13 STRANDS OF TRANSFER PRICING ANALYSIS: DETECTING THE SUBSTANCE OF "SUBSTANCE"

Approaching the substance of "substance" this way reveals two tangled strands of transfer pricing analysis which conflate the income measurement and anti-tax avoidance connotations of transfer pricing.

There is no doubt that the manner in which organizational and transactional arrangements are adopted by taxpayers may entail avoided tax. But "avoided tax" is not the same as "tax avoidance." It is "commercially rational" to regard tax as a business cost as well as a public charge for being able to access the opportunities to conduct business afforded by the sorts of resources taxation, as an enabler of fiscal policy, funds.

What transforms "avoided tax into "tax avoidance"? Tax avoidance as envisaged by transfer pricing and more broadly in the international context involves escaping tax that should and would be paid if the implications—the legal implications—of taxpayer's conduct and evidence about that conduct were properly understood.

The two strands may be untangled this way.

Were the ostensible legal arrangements essentially beside the point for the affected taxpayers because their conduct, willful or not, evidently did not rely on them in the sense those arrangements expect as a matter of law according to the internal implications and expectations of the selected legal formulations? Given the functional and financial capacity of the taxpayers, as a legal matter was justifiable reliance by the parties on each other as held out essentially impossible had the parties been fully informed about each other's condition as transaction counterparties? In that case, the inquiry, based on the evidence, involves an *original* discovery of what the legal arrangements were—as legal arrangements, not as economic reconstructions or hypotheses. It is a legal conclusion, grounded in legal analysis informed as any legal analysis by what transfer pricing describes as "the facts and circumstances," that the legal arrangements were other than they purported to be, that, to use perhaps the most common example, what is presented as debt is really equity. In such a case, a *legal* conclusion to this effect (comporting with the tendency or implications of an evidence-based legal analysis) might be justifiable. But it is not essential nevertheless to attain transfer pricing's objective to accurately measure the allocation of international MNE income.

If, for example, a perceived "mischief" is that debt gives rise to tax deductions for interest so as to unreasonably reduce and redirect income, then address that. That the financial transaction could just as easily, perhaps, have been accomplished by the issuance of equity with nondeductible dividends rather than debt with deductible interest for parties under common control is not enough to warrant reconstructing it or substituting one for the other legal configuration. "Recharacterization" is not an omnibus remedy. More is required than different legal formulations of an economic event yield different tax outcomes. But an original construction of debt might still be possible. The reason, though, would have to be that according to law-based insights from an objective legal analysis based on relevant evidence, the debtor did not have the capacity to be a debtor even if assisted in a "normal" way by other MNE group members through financial supports like guarantees bought and paid for in a typical fashion, and, knowing that, the creditor would not be justified in thinking it had rights as a creditor vis-à-vis the debtor. That is a legal analysis. It involves evaluating the capacity of the parties to be and to do what their organizational and transactional formulations portray—to be "justifiably reliant" on each other. It does not entail a judgment about what otherwise capable but indifferent parties ought to have done based on amorphous standards of "accurate delineation," "commercial rationality," and "value creation." It does entail recognizing the reality of how MNEs function according to overarching corporate guidance and, also, not dismissing events within MNE groups simply because they lack the same adversarial significance as the same events undertaken by independent parties. Despite using the problematic notion of "commercial rationality" descriptively, the recent judicial acknowledgment of "commercial rationality" in the Canadian *Cameco Corporation* case offers little in the way of principled insight about what that phrase "means," contrasted with might be a casual insinuation about what fundamentally is the kind of legal analysis these comments suggest is the essence of these terms used liberally in the TPG.

If taxpayers have demonstrated their justifiable reliance on the legal formulations orchestrating their commercial relations as that would be revealed by evidence-based legal analysis, have they adequately evaluated—"priced"—the terms of their dealing? That is the transfer pricing question. Have their relative competencies in relation to what their transactional counterparties are relying on them to and to be able to do been suitably compensated—including a share of the "rent" attributable to being contributors to the whole economic unit that is an MNE? In other words, is the income of the MNE group members reasonably allocated among them when the excesses of corporate governance, if any, are ignored? This is the mandate of Article 9 of the OECD Model Tax Convention; nowhere in it is the disregard of the law contemplated.

If the strands of "substance" and its companion "recharacterization" are untangled this way in relation to how the ALS is constituted under Article 9 of the Model, two conclusions emerge. These are important not only for giving objective life to the substance of "substance" as the trio of terms in the TPG might seek to try to do, but also in suggesting a way forward, possibly validated by the guarded acceptance in the Pillar One of fractional apportionment.

First, the primary inquiry in a transfer pricing analysis is to understand the legal arrangements on which taxpayers purport to rely for their rights and obligations, based on evidence about how they have conducted themselves, not as a picture but as a legal condition. In the legal sense, is a taxpayer's reliance justifiable after carefully examining the parties' functional and financial features as independent parties engaging in commercial relations of various kinds with each other and expecting to be able to enforce them other than by suasion associated with common control? Again, that is a legal analysis. It may entail what seems like transactional substitution, but only because the legal analysis would disclose that the ostensible arrangements are a mirage as a legal matter. As the Canadian Supreme Court in the *GlaxoSmithKline*[43] case invited to consider, the legal relations and contracts may be other than or additional to what they appear to be, though no less legally enforceable if not written.

This is what gives life, in a legal system, to the admonition in Article 9 of the Model Tax Convention to examine and evaluate "conditions made or imposed" in relation to the justifiable reliance to which independent parties would be entitled with respect to particular formulations of commercial arrangements in their "commercial or financial relation."

This is not inviting judgments about "substance" other than in this sense, and it is *not* authorizing or inviting untethered economic reconstructions of taxpayers' affairs. The law faces in all its guises, including the transfer pricing aspects of tax law, questions about the nature and validity of all manner of circumstances. The substance of "substance" is a legal substance. This involves more than taking for granted organizational and transactional diagrams of flows and reading words in contracts without testing their legal reliability in the circumstances of the parties. The tensile strength of contracts is the parties' justifiable reliance on them in light of their capacities to perform them. This is according to the inherent expectations of the transfer pricing paradigm, based on transaction parties existing and engaging as separate parties despite their membership in an MNE group. An inquiry into the "theory of the firm" is not required to appreciate that in the transfer pricing context, the whole firm is the sum of its parts. The parts are "artificial"—legal constructions, fragments of that whole effectively reassembled through contracts. "Substance" is better and more usefully understood according to the law rather than without it as, for example, the recent US Tax Court decision in the *Coca-Cola*[44] case reflects. There, by engaging in a rigorous legal analysis of the parties' legal rights and obligations as they had configured them legally, the "economics" of the transactions *as outcomes* were revealed and determined by the Court not to be justifiable. Among other things, the Court noted that highly rewarded operational functions ostensibly performed by one party had as a legal matter been assigned contractually to others who according to the evidence had in fact satisfied their obligations to perform those contractually allotted functions. In short, there was nothing to be rewarded as far as the more handsomely (grossly excessively) "compensated" party was concerned. "Functions" and "risks" are not foreign to legal analysis; they are its essence.

43. *See supra* n. 18.
44. *THE COCA-COLA COMPANY & SUBSIDIARIES, Petitioner v. COMMISSIONER OF INTERNAL REVENUE, Respondent,* 155 T.C. No. 10 UNITED STATES TAX COURT. *See* R. Avi-Yonah and G. Mazzoni, *Coca-Cola: A Decisive IRS Transfer Pricing Victory, at Last* (December 14, 2020) *Tax Notes Federal* and (December 30, 2020) *Tax Notes*.

Second, trite and even redundant in these comments though it may be to say, Article 9 concerns the allocation of MNE *profit* or *income*. Methods-based transactional analysis is an assist, not "the rule." The ALS and TPG are means to *that* end, taking account of all relevant features and interactions and sympathetic associations of events and arrangements and contributions with an MNE. The TPG facilitate a particular kind of evidence-based legal analysis of arrangements to identify and test the significance of their terms in the circumstances, not to determine whether the "right" price was paid for anything. The purpose of the ALS is to detect and adjust for the pointless or gratuitous, essentially nontransformative exercise of control within an MNE that results in uncommercial outcomes. The expectation in Article 9's statement of the ALS is that this can be accomplished with some measure of objective reliability without saying what that measure necessarily is. It implies that there should be an international agreement on the outcome, flowing as it does naturally from an "accurate" determination of the organizational and transactional arrangements.

Where might this lead?

14 BACK TO "ACCURATE DELINEATION," "COMMERCIAL RATIONALITY," AND "SUBSTANCE"

The core question addressed by transfer pricing, and also at the heart of all the substantive BEPS Actions and the Pillars, is: What is the "source" of corporate income (leaving aside questions about the incidence of corporate tax), recognizing that the "source" of income is a legal question answered by countries general and tax law. Neither can be presumed to be internationally universal. Something more than what in trade law context might be described as "fair and equitable treatment" unsupported however by any normative commonly accepted prescription or standard must be required.[45] The OECD's BEPS-based restatement of key aspects of the TPG to invent or restate and meld, as the case may be, the notions "accurate delineation" and "commercial rationality" has a detectable implication, though, that FET on a more or less ad hoc basis is what these terms imply and try to justify. "Fair and equitable treatment" may be a sensible enough parameter when only one country's laws are engaged, where the question is whether they were suitably applied in the relevant regulatory context. But the issues of judgment and opacity that pervade transfer pricing arise from the

45. Adolfo Martin Jiménez offers insights into the significance of this term in trade and tax contexts, including the inherent uncertainty and imprecision of this term in an as yet unpublished paper the publication of which is pending, *International Investment Agreements and Anti-Tax Avoidance Measures: Incoherences in International Law System, "Systemic Interpretation" and Taxpayers' Rights*. I refer to this excellent paper for its candid and penetrating examination of how this notion, the sense of which, can be detected as an undercurrent of the kinds of initiatives that offer authorities seemingly limitless opportunities to establish in the first instance how economic and legal events should be seen as a precursor to apply relevant law, such as those examined in this chapter. There is no doubt that equity and fairness are animating norms or principles of public law and taxation, but there is some distance from that to regarding one or another perception of what is or ought to be "just" or "economic" in the eye of the beholder to have the significance of law or to be substituted for what the law would otherwise show in an evidence-based analysis "actually" happened.

application simultaneously of the law and tax law of more than one country, each with its own law and acting in its own fiscal self-interest.[46]

Is "substance" as the TPG seems to imagine it the "wrong" issue, giving rise to unhelpful questions that can only yield unhelpful and disputable answers? And, if so, is there another way that is much more closely attuned to the aspirations and instructions of Article 9 of the Model to establish the relevant substance of "substance" to achieve what the ALS exists to assure?

15 ACHIEVING THE FUNDAMENTAL TRANSFER PRICING OBJECTIVES BY NOT, NOT ACHIEVING THEM: FORMULARY OR FRACTIONAL APPORTIONMENT?

This commentary returns to the place where it started, wondering about the substance of "substance" in the context of what transfer pricing as a subdiscipline of taxation seeks to achieve.

Interpreting the TPG's novel attempt to manifest the substance of "substance" in the opaque notions "accurate delineation," "commercial rationality," and "value creation" as if they could yield a reliable and internationally shared view of the "source" of income, without requiring any country to abandon or limit its own fiscal or tax policies or alter its law that serves both, gives rise to several observations that might guide future inquiries.

1. It is said again that the objective of the ALS assisted by the TPG is to determine the "source" of income in terms of inputs to the production of and of markets for goods and services, including those traded or that by their nature are "digital." The compensable circumstances of incomed generating activity—value creation—has always lain at the core of transfer pricing and, for that matter, its close cousin the "attribution" of profits to "permanent establishments"? Where do the inputs come from? Where are they transformed? Where does the output go, and how? These are not questions that depend on the significance of legal constructions and instrumentalities, though typically the answers to those questions will be attributed to them. In short, the legal constructions and instrumentalities do not determine the outcome. Accordingly, why is there such a preoccupation with them to detect the "source" of income?
2. There is in any event no "natural law" of "source."[47] "Source" is a legal notion that is as much or more determined by the implications of the private the constructions that create and define the features of the legal personalities and the relations among them which transfer pricing addresses and the legal quality of amounts to which those relations give rise and where those amounts should be considered to originate. It is the law that "delineates" transactions, and they are "accurately delineated" if relevant evidence establishes the

46. *See*, for example, D. Rodrik, *The Globalization Paradox Democracy and the Future of the World Economy* (New York and London: W. W. Norton & Company, 2011).
47. I have credited H. Ault and D. Bradford with the notion that there is no natural law of "source," an inherently legal notion: *See* Wilkie, *supra* n. 6, in various publications, notably, *New Rules of Engagement? Corporate Personality and the Allocation of "International Income" and Taxing Right*.

requisite correspondence between the objective intrinsic expectations of relevant legal constructions as legal constructions and evidence about parties' use of and reliance on them to test, again as a legal matter, the justifiability of their reliance on them. Inspired and guided by the scholarship of Professor Lon Fuller to which this chapter refers a number of times, "justifiable reliance" is a legal notion that emanates from the law of contract and the law of damages—damages arising from a loss sustained because a contractor otherwise functionally and financially able to perform obligations meant to create rights of others fails to perform. If the evidence would show that party's original incapacity, functionally or financially or both as a distinct legal person to perform its bargain, then reliance by others aware of that infirmity would not be justifiable and any loss sustained by that party would not and should not to that extent be compensable.

3. The history of transfer pricing offers no authority that "substance" is or otherwise needs to be anything but legal substance, as long as there is clarity about what "legal substance" means. This does not diminish the kind of investigation into "facts and circumstances" that the TPG enshrine. But it does put that inquiry in its proper place as a tool of evidentiary analysis, which is inherently legal in relation to the legal events being texted, and not substantive organizational or transactional discipline on its own. The law is not beside the point. It is the point.

What transfer pricing in the image of Article 9 contemplates is an allocation of income among MNE group members undistorted by excesses of corporate governance that accordingly aligns with relevant commercial circumstances even if those circumstances reflect differences from unrestricted dealing and consequently "rent" to be shared. That is the ALS. To serve that purpose, what is required is an objectively defensible measure of income according to objective measures of how it is earned.

Are countries likely to relegate their fiscal sovereignty to a common or universal tax and legal systems, as implicitly and maybe covertly the Pillars envisage?[48] We will see. But understanding that tax law enables fiscal choices and fiscal choices reflect and activate countries' national psyches and cultures, it is perhaps doubtful that the structural universality that transfer pricing seems to crave—now relying on infinitely malleable notions of "accurate delineation," "commercial rationality" and "value creation" beyond the limits of the law (if necessary)—will replace reliance on the tax and legal systems expressing any country's fiscal character. In any event, even if it were the case that legal and tax regimes would somehow become harmonized or homogenized, that would still not avoid dealing with the alignment of income and relevant factors and markets of production and realization. This is, in a sense, the flaw of the Pillars and particularly Pillar One—it does not solve the "source" issue but simply repackages it.

How to solve the "source" issue is the "the issue." It is what the substance of "substance" engages.

If the status quo is not satisfactory and a universal legal system is not likely,[49] inexorably almost we are driven to consider some form of fractional or formulary apportionment, if not as commonly understood at least directionally according to an

48. *See* Wilkie, *supra* n. 25.
49. *See* Couzin, *supra* n. 5.

objectively satisfying prescription in light of what transfer pricing regulation actually seeks to discipline with as few controversies as possible. There the role of economic analysis is to identify and evaluate the rudiments of what happened—the factors of production—without needing to delineate or judge their character or motivation according to a set of factors agreed to be relevant, whatever the relative weightings of the factors may be. Implicitly, that is what transfer pricing analysis is now, but not in so many words. Guardedly this is what Pillar One seems to concede for in-scope taxpayers, after, it must be said, almost one hundred years of denying the legitimacy of formulary approaches in deference to qualitative functional analysis that has shown itself not to yield universally acceptable outcomes for taxpayers or for the countries that share vicariously through their tax bases in taxpayers' income and therefore are protagonists in the transfer pricing exercise. Indeed, in the Actions 8—10 Report, the OECD has already endorsed the practical utility of fractions and formulae.

This is the essence of "DEMPE" ("Development," "Enhancement," "Maintenance," "Protection," "Exploitation") as the template for testing the reasonable allocation of income from intangibles. Leaving the weightings of the variables—an exclusive list of variables—to taxpayers to explain, DEMPE is a formula: DEMPE = D + E + M + P + E, where each of those variables represents a necessary and indeed inevitable production input, that when combined culminate in market outcomes. While taxpayers are free to assign weights, based on their circumstances as they understand them, to each of the variables, then to be tested by transfer pricing standards, they are not free not to analyze each of the elements. There is no doubt that this is formulaic.

To emphasize, taxpayers must evaluate their circumstances in light of how DEMPE frames relevant commercial activity, and assign weights accordingly, though still these may be tested by tax authorities. Affected taxpayers must account for a discrete set of production factors that frame the transfer pricing exercise for all concerned, taxpayers, tax regulators and adjudicators, and countries acting through their taxpayers in relation to each other—to explain the substance of their "substance" in ways that are possible and well grounded in cognizable reference standards.

Back to the enigmatic title of this section: "Achieving the Fundamental Transfer Pricing Objectives By Not, Not Achieving Them."

There are two ways to achieve what Article 9 of the OECD Model Tax Convention—the ALS—instructs: determine affirmative the (absolute) "right" outcome, or establish an outcome that according to objective responds to transfer pricing's objectives and because of its objective nature allows its imperfections to be readily understood and, if warranted, corrected. In transfer pricing's history, the former has not achieved unqualified success because it calls on kinds and degrees of international legal and tax homogeneity that are difficult if not impossible to achieve in respect of taxpayers whose very nature is the antithesis of the foundational assumptions of the ALS. It is to be wondered whether more and more seemingly refined expositions of the same kinds of analysis found in the TPG with the effect of eroding the significance of the law will or even can achieve the universally acceptable outcomes sought by and with the TPG for the ALS. The fact that the transfer pricing conversation has persisted largely unchanged for as long as it has stokes this curiosity. But, doing something to not, not achieve the objectives of transfer pricing is by negative implication achieving a positive outcome in terms of those objectives and the practical utility of the ALS. Achieving the "not, not" assurance can be more objective but still faithful to the sort of inquiry associated with industrial economics, in a fractional or formulaic approach, even if not all judgment is eliminated.

Is it necessary to settle on what *the* "substance" is to do this? No. Is "recharacterization" required to achieve this objective? No. What matters is some reliable way of apportioning income with reference to indisputable factors of production and related markets, whatever the legal "substance" of the arrangements may be. The substance of "substance" may not even be substance as some sort of exogenous or peripheral determination. And the transfer pricing analysis may be better for it. Is it time to reconsider "formulary" or "fractional" apportionment in a more open-minded and results-driven way?

CHAPTER 7

Recent Developments on Transfer Pricing and Business Restructurings

Monique van Herksen, Clive Jie-A-Joen & Önder Albayrak

1 CURRENT REGIME FOR BUSINESS RESTRUCTURING AND HARD-TO-VALUE INTANGIBLES (HTVI)

1.1 Introduction

Multinational enterprises (MNEs) are continuously restructuring their business operations for legitimate business reasons (e.g., anticipated synergies, changing economies and obtaining economies of scale, competitive pressure, lowering costs and adhering to regulatory developments). Such business restructurings are likely to involve the transfer of functions, risks and/or assets (e.g., intangibles) within an MNE group. In case something of value (e.g., intangibles and ongoing concern) is transferred, unlike unrelated enterprises, associated enterprises are by law required to deal with each other "at arm's length" in such situations with the transfer pricing consequence that an arm's-length compensation payment may be due to the transferor. Transfer pricing valuation principles are used to estimate the transfer price for the transfer of something of value between MNE group entities taking into account the arm's-length principle as the valuation standard. Considering the urgent need for domestic revenue mobilization by governments, scrutiny and transparency requirements related to such transfers have increased dramatically.

1.2 Background to Chapter IX (Transfer Pricing Aspects of Business Restructurings)

The arm's-length principle introduced the requirement of comparability, in essence a purely economic effort that triggers the requirement to perform a benchmark analysis that establishes that the pricing between associated enterprises is comparable to that of unrelated parties, and can therefore be considered to be at arm's length.

Soon after the 1995 OECD Transfer Pricing Guidelines for Multinational Enterprises and Tax Administrations ("OECD Guidelines") were issued, tax practitioners adopted the new rules. They did so by considering their application up front before planning tax structures. The OECD Guidelines present five transfer pricing methods, each of them with a more or less designated application for certain types of functions. They are the Comparable Uncontrolled Price Method (CUPM), Cost Plus Method (CPM), Resale Price Method (RPM), Transactional Net Margin Method (TNMM) and Profit Split Method (PSM). The idea behind these methods was that an associated enterprise will assess functions performed, assets used and risks assumed, and after acknowledging what its functional profile is, choose the most appropriate transfer pricing method for that functionality to determine the arm's-length price or profit margin it would be expected to make in order to operate at arm's length.

What happened, however, was that business structuring and restructurings were planned proactively to fit into the transfer pricing rules by determining up front that centralization with low risk, i.e., "cost-plus" profiled operating and manufacturing functions, could be located in high tax jurisdictions, and the associated enterprises there could then be engaged in business transactions with a centralized high-risk related enterprise in a low-tax jurisdiction. Structuring the transactions as such would lead to an optimal tax result. As a result, local distribution entities were restructured into limited risk distribution entities / commission agents led by centralized "full-fledged or super distributors" responsible for distribution strategies and marketing. Companies owning all relevant valuable intangibles used by the entire group were incorporated into business structures, usually in low-tax jurisdictions or jurisdictions with preferential tax regimes, licensing out the IP to create deductible royalty payments at the level of the other operating companies that were using the IP and tax optimization. Manufacturing entities were restructured into toll or contract manufacturers. Often, the relevant intangibles could be contributed as capital in kind to the newly incorporated IP companies, leading to no direct tax consequences at the level of the transferor entity, and again to tax optimization.

While these tax optimization structures were designed on paper and often did not accurately reflect the business realities, it turned out to be challenging for tax authorities to successfully tackle them. The 1995 OECD Guidelines only contained general guidance on evaluating whether one of the comparability factors, the purported allocation of risk, is consistent with the economic substance of the transaction. However, the allocation of risks assumed between the parties plays a key role in reviewing business restructurings since the assumption of increased risks is expected to be compensated with a higher return.

For several years, the abovementioned tax optimization technique fared well. Eventually, the weak spot in these tax optimization structures ended up being the fact that the designated centralized and high-risk companies, which could be IP or centralized procurement companies, for example, ended up being very lightly staffed. So lightly, it could be questioned whether these centralized entities had de facto control over the risks they were supposedly managing and the transactions that they purported to be engaged in. But as de facto control over risk was not necessarily an explicit requirement in the transfer pricing rules at the time, there was a need to tackle this form of tax avoidance.

1.3 Initial Anti-abuse Steps

Chapter IX of the OECD Guidelines introduced guidance on the transfer pricing aspects of business restructurings to tackle the above described tax avoidance. Although there is no legal definition of business restructurings, this OECD chapter defines it as the "*cross-border reorganisation of the commercial or financial relations between associated enterprises*," including the termination or substantial renegotiation of existing arrangements (e.g., distribution arrangements and manufacturing arrangements) and the cross-border transfers of "something of value," that is typically accompanied by reallocation of profit potential between MNE group entities. As noted, business restructurings often entail the centralization of functions, risks and/or assets (including intangibles) with the accompanying profit potential being reallocated to a central entity acting as the risk-taking entrepreneur. Examples include: (i) full-fledged distributors that are restructured into limited risk distributors or sales agents, (ii) full-fledged manufacturers that are converted into contract or toll manufacturers, (iii) transfers of intangibles to a central IP entity, and (iv) cost contribution arrangements in which preexisting intangibles are transferred to an offshore entity by another entity owning the preexisting intangibles and the joint development of new intangibles by the entities involved.

The discussion draft on business restructurings (dated September 19, 2008)[1] and Chapter IX of the 2010 OECD Guidelines were comprised of four parts that analyzed issues in relation to business restructurings. Among others, the appropriateness of the risk allocation/risk transfer between the related parties and the commercial rationality of transactions in the context of business restructurings were questioned. The four parts were:

- Part I: Special considerations for risks;
- Part II: Arm's length compensation for the restructuring itself;
- Part III: Remuneration of post-restructuring controlled transactions;
- Part IV: Recognition of the actual transactions undertaken.

Tax administrations considered that business restructurings were employed as a tool to minimize tax since business restructurings often involved local entities being restructured into limited risk entities who post-restructuring, received a routine return that is generally lower as compared to the return received during the pre-restructuring situation. This resulted from the lower risks assumed, while the principal risk-taking entity (often located in a low-tax jurisdiction) was allocated the residual return.

The discussion draft on business restructurings and Chapter IX of the 2010 OECD Guidelines, relevantly, started out with providing a framework for analyzing risk allocation in Part I:

- The starting point for assessing which related party assumes the risk regards the contractual arrangements.
- To evaluate whether the contractual allocation of risk between the parties is consistent with the economic substance, it should be evaluated:
  - whether the contractual allocation of risk is consistent with the conduct of parties; and
  - whether the contractual allocation of risk is at arm's length.
    - in case there is reliable evidence of a similar allocation of risks in comparable uncontrolled transactions, the risk allocation in the controlled transaction is regarded as arm's length.
    - in case there is no reliable evidence, the OECD introduced the concept of which party has greater control over risk and whether the risk bearer has the financial capacity to assume the risk in the OECD Guidelines. Control over risk was defined as "the capacity to make decisions on whether and how to manage the risk, internally or using an external provider." This means that the risk-bearing entity should have people (employees or directors) who have the authority to, and effectively do, perform the control functions.

1. OECD, "Transfer Pricing Aspects of Business Restructurings: Discussion Draft for Public Comment", September 19, 2008, to February 19, 2009, www.oecd.org/dataoecd/59/40/41346644.pdf.

The above de facto substance test was interpreted as requiring financial substance and material substance in order to support risk allocation.

1.4 The Next Anti-abuse Steps

In 2013, the OECD launched a major project on Base Erosion and Profit Shifting (BEPS) that served to tackle tax and transfer pricing abuse and resulted in a report with several Action items in 2015. The reports on Actions 8-10 ("Aligning Transfer Pricing Outcomes with Value Creation") were directly relevant for addressing transfer pricing abuse. The guidance on risk allocation in Chapter IX of the 2010 OECD Guidelines was further developed as part of OECD BEPS Actions 8-10 and in particular resulted in more detailed guidance on analysis of risks in paragraphs 1.56-1.106 (i.e., section D.1.2.1 "Analysis of risks in commercial or financial relations") of Chapter I of the 2017 OECD Guidelines, including the following six steps risk allocation framework:

> **Step 1**: Identifying the economically significant risks with specificity. Whether a risk is economically significant depends on the likelihood of the risk arising and the magnitude of possible profits or losses materializing from the risk.
> **Step 2**: Determining which associated enterprises contractually assume which specific economically significant risks based on the contractual terms.
> **Step 3**: Functional analysis in relation to the assumption of risk; determining how the parties operate with respect to the assumption of the economically significant risks, especially which party to the controlled transaction:
> - conducts control functions and risk mitigation;
> - encounters upside or downside consequences of risk outcomes; and
> - has the financial capacity to assume the risk.
>
> **Step 4:** Determining whether the contractual assumption of risk is consistent with the conduct of the associated enterprises and other facts of the case through examining:
> - whether the parties to the transactions follow the contractual terms; and
> - whether the party assuming risk, as analyzed under 4a, exercises control over the risk and has the financial capacity to assume the risk.
>
> **Step 5**: Determining whether reallocation of the risks is necessary which depends on the above analysis.
> **Step 6**: Pricing the actual transaction as accurately delineated by considering the evidence of all the comparability factors of the transaction.

Based on Step 5, if the related party that contractually assumes the risk in accordance with Step 4a does not exercise control over the risk nor has the financial capacity to assume the risk, then the risk (and related returns) should be allocated to the associated enterprise exercising control and having the financial capacity to assume the risk. In practice, it is possible that several parties exercise control over the risks and have the financial capacity to bear those risks, while only one of those parties contractually assumes the risks. In such cases, the contractual risk allocation is respected. However, any other parties that control the risk (or financially support such risk) should receive arm's-length remuneration for exercising that function. To successfully tackle the tax optimalization that was being exploited through restructurings, it became important for tax administrations to evaluate the allocation of risks both before and after the restructuring, to assess whether economically significant risks had been transferred and the consequences of such reallocation for the application of the arm's-length principle to both the post-restructuring intercompany transactions and for the restructuring itself.

Part IV of Chapter IX expanded the guidance on the following two exceptional circumstances when tax administrations would be allowed to disregard or not recognize the actual transactions undertaken by taxpayers (paragraphs 1.64-169 of Chapter I of the 2010 OECD Guidelines) in the context of business restructurings:

(1) the economic substance of a transaction differs from its form; and
(2) the "arrangements made in relation to the transaction, viewed in their totality, differ from those which would have been adopted by independent enterprises behaving in a commercially rational manner and the actual structure practically impedes the tax administration from determining an appropriate transfer price."[2]

However, the act of "disregarding" a transaction was not to be invoked lightly. Part IV makes explicitly clear that the interpretation of the guidance on nonrecognition under exceptional circumstances is restricted to nonrecognition for the purposes of conducting transfer pricing adjustments covered by Article 9 of the OECD Model Tax Convention (only). The arm's-length principle together with the guidance on nonrecognition of the actual transactions under the exceptional circumstances was intended to function as a general anti-abuse measure. Because of that, it was provided that "exceptional" has a similar meaning as "rare" or "unusual." This was supposed to make clear that tax administrations should attempt to make adjustments based on transfer pricing arguments rather than resorting to nonrecognition of controlled transactions. Nonrecognition was not to be the norm, but an exception to the principle that a tax administration's evaluation of a controlled transaction should normally be based on the actual transaction undertaken by the taxpayer.

The inclusion of Options Realistically Available (ORAs) in Chapter IX[3] was considered relevant in determining whether the arrangements adopted differ from those of independent enterprises behaving in a commercial rational manner. As such, the theory holds that an independent enterprise will not enter into a restructuring transaction if it has a realistic option available that is clearly more attractive, including the option to reject the restructuring. It is in general appropriate to evaluate the commercial rationality of a restructuring as a whole in case of economically interrelated transactions (e.g., as opposed to analyzing the transfer of an intangible that is part of a broader business restructuring on a stand-alone basis). The restructuring arrangement should make commercial sense not only at group level but also at the level of each

2. Paragraph 1.65 of the 2010 OECD Guidelines.
3. Paragraphs 9.27-9.31 of the 2010 OECD Guidelines.

group entity that is affected by the restructuring, considering its rights and obligations, ORAs and expected benefits from the arrangement, such as the compensation of the post-restructuring controlled transactions plus compensation payments for the restructuring itself, if any.

However, it was maintained that a business restructuring arrangement that has as an ultimate or additional goal to achieve tax savings does not as such result in disregarding the structure of the business restructuring arrangement. Tax administrations should substitute a nonrecognized transaction with an alternative structure that is consistent with the facts of the case, the functional changes to the taxpayer's business and the commercial rationality of independent parties.

BEPS Action 9 ("Risks and capital") continued the development of guidance on the recognition of accurately delineated transaction resulting in paragraphs 1.119-1.128 of the OECD Guidelines. While the exceptional circumstance of the economic substance of a transaction differing from its form disappeared, the exceptional circumstance that allows for disregarding the transaction of commercial irrationality of a transaction was revised as follows in paragraph 1.122 of the 2017 OECD Guidelines:

> The transaction as accurately delineated may be disregarded, and if appropriate, replaced by an alternative transaction, where the arrangements made in relation to the transaction, viewed in their totality, differ from those which would have been adopted by independent enterprises behaving in a commercially rational manner in comparable circumstances, thereby preventing determination of a price that would be acceptable to both of the parties taking into account their respective perspectives and the options realistically available to each of them at the time of entering into the transaction.

Paragraph 1.122 and paragraph 9.38 of the 2017 OECD Guidelines point out that a relevant indicator of assessing the commercial rationality of a restructuring arrangement regards whether or not an MNE group as a whole is left worse off on a pretax basis.

Despite the expanded guidance on the (exceptional) circumstances under which tax administrations may disregard controlled transactions / business restructurings, the guidance remains in general vague and overly broad and therefore results in substantial uncertainty.[4]

In the updated 2017 OECD Guidelines, the amended Chapter IX on business restructuring is organized into two parts rather than into four parts:

- Part I: Arm's length compensation for the restructuring itself;[5]
- Part II: Remuneration of post-restructuring controlled transactions.

4. For example, it is difficult to interpret the term "commercially rational," since the same circumstances that exist between associated enterprises may not exist between independent enterprises. In addition, the requirement to consider ORAs is an open ended analysis, subject to what options would be taken into account when dealing with third parties, and difficult to apply.
5. The guidance on analysis of risk allocation and recognition of actual transactions, which were described in separate parts in Chapter IX of the 2010 OECD Guidelines, has now been included in Part I.

Part I looks at the arm's-length compensation for the restructuring itself, and serves to analyze whether the business restructuring includes a reallocation of profit potential among MNE group entities. If so, the transfer pricing rules serve to assess whether such a reallocation of profit potential takes place consistently with the arm's-length principle. If there has been a transfer, a buyout or compensation may be due. In this respect, the key transfer pricing issues generally are:

- whether the restructured entity is entitled to an arm's-length compensation for the restructuring itself, and if so, what would constitute an arm's-length amount of compensation;
- determining the arm's-length remuneration for the post-restructuring controlled (intercompany) transactions, if any.

This means that based on the revised Chapter IX, relevant aspects in assessing the arm's-length compensation, if any, for the restructuring itself are:

- understanding the restructuring itself;
- determining under what exceptional circumstances tax administrations can disregard the business restructuring arrangement;
- a restructured entity does not automatically receive compensation in case the business restructuring leads to a decrease in its expected future profits. This depends on whether the business restructuring has led to a transfer of "something of value" (an asset or an ongoing concern) or termination or renegotiation of existing arrangements that would have been compensated between independent enterprises in comparable circumstances. Thus, for each business restructuring, it should be analyzed whether "something of value" (e.g., an asset or an ongoing concern) will be transferred and how that "something of value" should be valued.[6]

It should furthermore be analyzed whether the restructured entity is entitled to any indemnification because of the termination or substantial renegotiation of existing arrangements (e.g., distribution arrangement and manufacturing arrangement), and if so what that arm's-length indemnification would be. The second key issue in relation to a business restructuring is dealt with in Part II of amended Chapter IX that focuses on the remuneration of post-restructuring controlled transactions. It is remarked that

6. Chapter IX recognizes three categories which may constitute something of value: (i) tangible assets (e.g., equipment and inventory); (ii) intangibles or rights in intangibles (e.g., trademarks, patents, designs or models, copyrights of literacy, artistic or scientific work (including software) and contractual rights); and (iii) activity (ongoing concern). Chapter IX makes reference to the guidance provided in Chapter VI of the OECD Guidelines on the use of valuation techniques for transfers of intangibles or rights in intangibles. However, the transfer of something of value may include not only intangibles but also other items. The valuation of the transfer of "something of value" at the moment of transfer can be highly uncertain and has led to disputes with tax administrations witnessing the number of transfer pricing court cases. Tax administrations and taxpayers can benefit from more detailed guidance on the pricing of something of value specifically in the context of business restructurings based on experience gained since the publication of the first Chapter IX in the 2010 OECD Guidelines.

the arm's-length principle should be applied similarly to such transactions as to the transactions that were structured from the start.

Also important as regards business restructurings related to transfers of intangibles and to tackle restructurings that lacked substance, Chapter IX was expanded in 2017 with the introduction of so-called DEMPE functions: Development, Enhancement, Maintenance, Protection or Exploitation of the intangible.[7] Compensation related to intangibles from then on was required to reflect the DEMPE functions performed by the respective associated enterprises with respect to the intangibles, and did not just follow legal title and contractual risk allocation.

1.5 Background to HTVI Approach

A challenge observed with intangibles includes that they may be transferred at a time when their value is highly uncertain, and after the transfer, end up being highly profitable for the transferee. To avoid having to apply a high transfer price, for tax optimization purposes, restructurings between associated enterprises would often regard the transfer of still unpatented research or of patented research which had not yet received the requisite regulatory approvals. At that stage, or without such approvals, the intangibles de facto were relatively worthless. These transfers would often involve transfers to entities located in low-tax jurisdictions or with favorable tax regimes. If post-transfer the necessary regulatory approvals were granted allowing for commercial exploitation, there would be an immediate jump in value for the transferred intangibles. This was characterized as undesirable tax optimization. Based on an update following the 2015 BEPS Report on Actions 8-10, Chapter VI of the 2017 OECD Guidelines addresses this practice in relevant part by providing guidance on how to determine the arm's-length pricing of transactions involving intangibles or rights in intangibles when valuation is highly uncertain at the time of the transaction. They are referenced as Hard-To-Value Intangibles (HTVI).

Paragraph 6.185 of the OECD Guidelines provides that tax administrations should allow the pricing of a transaction involving an intangible or rights in an intangible ("Intangible Transaction") based on a mechanism to deal with high uncertainty if independent enterprises in comparable circumstances would have agreed to such a mechanism. Similarly, if independent enterprises in comparable circumstances would have agreed on renegotiation of pricing arrangements because of a major event, the occurrence of such an event should result in amending the pricing of the transaction.

In this respect, the OECD Guidelines considered that in similar situations, third parties would use (one of) the following mechanisms to deal with the highly uncertain valuation:

- Use of anticipated benefits taking into account subsequent developments that are foreseeable and predictable to the extent possible.[8]

7. Paragraph 9.57 of the 2017 OECD Guidelines.
8. *See* paragraph 6.182 of the OECD Guidelines.

- Use of shorter-term agreements, including price-adjustment clauses in the contractual terms, and adopt a payment structure involving contingent payments to protect against subsequent developments that are insufficiently predictable (e.g., royalty or periodic milestone payments).[9]
- Third parties may (agree to) renegotiate the pricing arrangements in case of occurrence of major unforeseen events or developments.[10]

According to paragraph 6.185 of the OECD Guidelines, the tax administration was granted the right to apply the above mechanisms and determine the pricing of a transaction involving an intangible or rights in an intangible on the basis of one of the above mechanisms if independent enterprises in comparable circumstances would have agreed to the inclusion of such a mechanism to address the high uncertainty in valuing the intangible.

In addition, pursuant to the OECD BEPS project, a special measure was introduced for transfers of HTVI, the so-called HTVI approach.[11] The reason being that there is an information asymmetry between tax administrations and taxpayers, and that it is hard for tax administrations to evaluate which developments or events are relevant for the pricing of a transaction involving the transfer of (rights in) intangibles. Similarly, it is difficult to determine whether the manifestation of such developments or events might have been foreseen or "reasonably foreseeable" at the time of the Intangible Transaction.

Under the HTVI approach that is included in section D.4 of Chapter VI, tax administrations may consider *ex post* outcomes as presumptive evidence about the arm's-length nature of the *ex ante* pricing arrangements adopted in pricing intercompany transfers or licensing of HTVI and the presence of uncertainty at the time of the transaction, in order to protect them from the disadvantage that results from information asymmetry.[12]

Granting the authority to use *ex post* results to determine a valuation based on *ex ante* projections at the time of the transfer is conceptually worrisome. *Ex post* results will *always* differ from *ex ante* projections since the *ex post* actual results mirror a single realization of all potential risk outcomes, whereas *ex ante* projections reflect the average of all potential risk outcomes. It therefore can be considered an extraordinary measure. The HTVI approach provides tax administrations with a proverbial sledgehammer to challenge and adjust *ex ante* pricing arrangements, which will be hard to dispute, in particular for hard-to-value intangibles plus that corrections like this do not necessarily accurately reflect what happens at arm's length.

9. *See* paragraph 6.183 of the OECD Guidelines.
10. *See* paragraph 6.184 of the OECD Guidelines.
11. *See* paragraphs 6.186-6.194 of the OECD Guidelines.
12. As background it is appropriate to note that the HTVI approach was introduced as one of five potential special measures to achieve that transfer pricing outcomes are in line with value creation in the "Discussion Draft on Revisions to Chapter I of the Transfer Pricing Guidelines (Including Risk, Recharacterisation, and Special Measures)" of December 19, 2014. This discussion draft refers to these special measures as "special measures, either within or beyond the arm's length principle." Other special measures included options to address inappropriate returns for providing capital, which did not make it to the BEPS final reports of October 5, 2015.

Nevertheless, the OECD Guidelines maintain that the HTVI approach is consistent with the arm's-length principle. Furthermore, the HTVI approach should not be regarded as using hindsight through using *ex post* outcomes for tax assessment purposes since it is supposed to take into account whether the developments or events whereupon the *ex post* results are grounded might have been foreseeable or reasonably foreseeable at the moment of the HTVI transfer.

HTVI are defined as intangibles or rights in intangibles for which, at the time of the intercompany transfer: (i) there are no reliable comparables and (ii) the projections of future cash flows or income expected to be derived from the transferred intangible, or the assumptions used in valuing the intangible are highly uncertain; therefore, it is hard to predict the success of the intangible at the moment of the transfer of the intangible.

Indicative features that HTVI may exhibit are as follows:[13]

(1) The intangible is only partially developed at the time of the transfer.
(2) The intangible is not expected to be exploited commercially until several years following the transaction.
(3) The intangible does not fall itself within the definition of HTVI, but is integral to the development or enhancement of other intangibles which fall within that definition of HTVI.
(4) The intangible is expected to be exploited in a manner that is novel at the time of the transfer, and the absence of a track record of development or exploitation of similar intangibles makes projections highly uncertain.
(5) The intangible, meeting the definition of HTVI under paragraph 6.189 of the OECD TPG, has been transferred to an associated enterprise for a lump sum payment.
(6) The intangible is either used in connection with or developed under a Cost Contribution Arrangement (CCA) or similar arrangements.

The above list with six indicative features is not intended to be exhaustive, nor does an intangible that bears one or more of these features necessarily constitute an HTVI. The criteria listed above simply serve to draw out what the true essence of an HTVI is, which is that it is difficult to predict its future success because there is a high degree of uncertainty regarding projections of future cash flows or income, and assumptions used in valuing the intangible.

Importantly, besides thoroughly documenting intercompany transfers with robust *ex ante* valuation analyses, taxpayers can only rebut the presumptive evidence resulting from *ex post* outcomes in case at least one of the following exemptions under paragraphs 6.193-6.194 of the OECD Guidelines apply:

(a) The taxpayer is able to provide details of the *ex ante* projections used at the time of the HTVI transfer to determine the pricing arrangements (including how risks were considered in the valuation model (e.g., probability weighted)

13. Paragraph 6.190 of the OECD Guidelines.

and whether reasonably foreseeable events were properly reflected) and "reliable evidence" that any significant difference between the financial projections and actual outcomes is resulting from developments or events that were not foreseeable at the moment of the HTVI transfer.[14]

(b) The transfer of the HTVI is part of a bilateral or multilateral advance pricing arrangement (APA) that is in effect.

(c) Any significant difference between the financial projections and actual outcomes does not reduce or increase the compensation for the HTVI by more than 20% of the compensation determined at the time of the transaction.

(d) A commercialization period of five years has elapsed subsequent to the year in which the HTVI initially achieved third-party revenues for the related party buyer / licensee and during which commercialization period any significant difference between the financial projections and actual outcomes was less than 20% of the projections for that period.

1.6 Precursor of HTVI: The Commensurate-with-Income Standard

It may be interesting to look at historical developments a bit closer when analyzing HTVI. A precursor to the HTVI analysis is the commensurate-with-income (CWI) analysis that is embedded in the US's Internal Revenue Code section 482. The legislative history of the CWI standard, introduced via the Tax Reform Act of 1986, provides an elaborate explanation on the functioning of that standard.[15] The anti-abuse nature of the CWI standard is clear from its legislative history. As reason for change, it is provided in the legislative history that there was a strong incentive for taxpayers to transfer intangibles to related foreign corporations (or possession corporations) in a low-tax jurisdiction, particularly when the intangible has a high value relative to manufacturing or assembly costs. Such a transfer could result in definitive tax deferral or effective tax exemption on the earnings while retaining the value of the earnings in the related group. The problems were considered particularly acute in the case of transfers of high-profit potential intangibles that were transferred to foreign-related corporations (or possessions corporations) at an early stage, for a relatively low royalty

14. Under exemption (a), it seems that the valuation analysis of the taxpayer at the time of the HTVI transfer needs to consider for projections based on various scenarios to take into account events or developments that are foreseeable at the time of the HTVI transfer. The income-based method, which calculates the present value of the projected income streams or cash flows during the useful life of the object being valued making use of a discount rate, is often applied in valuing the transfer of intangibles. The OECD Guidelines do not provide specific guidance on considering various scenarios. The traditional income-based method on which OECD guidance is provided assumes a one scenario approach based in general on the most likely scenario of stream of cash flows or income streams. Paragraph 6.190 of the OECD Guidelines does provide that it is good practice for taxpayers to conduct "sensitivity analysis" to consider the impact of a change in assumptions and valuation parameters on the estimated intangible value. It would be beneficial to taxpayers in case examples can be provided to illustrate in more detail how taxpayers can consider scenarios and the type of sensitivity analysis to be conducted.

15. H.R. 3838, 99th Congress; Public Law 99-514.

and taken the position that it was not possible at the time of the transfer to predict the subsequent success of the product.

The basic requirement introduced through the Tax Reform Act was that payments with respect to intangibles that a (US) person transfers to a related foreign corporation (or possessions corporation) be commensurate with the income attributable to the intangible. This applied to both outright transfers of the ownership of intangibles (whether by sale, contribution to capital or otherwise) and to licenses or other arrangements for the use of intangibles. Congress intended that the inquiry as to the appropriate compensation for the intangible not be limited to the question of whether it was appropriate considering only the facts in existence at the time of the transfer. Congress intended that consideration is also given to the actual profit experience realized as a consequence of the transfer. Thus, Congress intended to require that the payments made for the intangible be adjusted over time to reflect the changes in the income attributable to the intangible. The Act was not intended to require annual adjustments when there are only minor variations in revenues. However, it will not be sufficient to consider only the evidence of value at the time of the transfer. Adjustments will be required when there are major variations in the annual amounts of revenue attributable to the intangible.

The HTVI approach clearly seems inspired by the periodic adjustment rules introduced by the CWI standard embedded in the US transfer pricing regulations in section 1.482-4(f)(2) as follows:

> If an intangible is transferred under an arrangement that covers more than one year, the consideration charged in each taxable year may be adjusted to ensure that it is commensurate with the income attributable to the intangible.

The CWI standard applies to any intercompany transactions of intangible property, and in particular, the CWI was considered a reflection of what happens at arm's length.[16]

The US regulations contain several exceptions to the applicability of the CWI approach,[17] including:

- a comparable uncontrolled transaction exception (based on the transfer of the same intangible to an uncontrolled taxpayer under substantially the same circumstances);
- a comparable uncontrolled transaction exception (based on the transfer of a comparable intangible under comparable circumstances) together with the condition that the aggregate actual profits earned or the aggregate cost savings realized by the controlled taxpayer from the exploitation of the intangible in the year under examination and all past years are not less than 80% nor more

16. The so-called "White Paper" ("A Study of Intercompany Pricing Under Section 482 of the Code, I.R.S. Notice 88-123, 1988-2 C.B. 458") confirmed that the US Treasury considered that the commensurate-with-income standard is consistent with the arm's-length standard. This indicated a shift in the interpretation of the arm's-length standard by US Treasury in the sense that this standard does not always require a comparability analysis.
17. US Treasury Reg. sections 1.482-4(f)(2)(ii).

than 120% of the projected profits or cost savings foreseeable at the time of entering into the related party agreement;
- an extraordinary events exception (an extraordinary event that was beyond the control of the taxpayers and that could not have been reasonably foreseen at the time of entering into the related party agreement);
- an exception incorporating that a method is used other than the comparable uncontrolled transaction method together with the condition that the total actual profits earned or cost savings realized by the controlled transferee from exploiting the intangible in the year under examination and all past years are not less than 80% nor more than 120% of the projected profits or cost savings foreseeable at the time of entering into the related party agreement; and
- an exception consisting of a five-year commercialization period with deviations from projections of less than 20%. There are also periodic adjustments provisions in section 1.482-7 regulations on cost-sharing arrangements with respect to "platform contributions."

While there are many overlaps, there also are some (material) differences between the OECD HTVI approach and the US commensurate-with-income standard. For one, the HTVI approach applies to HTVI only, while the US CWI approach applies to any and all intangibles. In addition, the exemptions under which the HTVI approach is not applicable are not entirely aligned with the exceptions provided under the U.S. 1.482-4 and 1.482-7 regulations, but they do appear inspired by those exceptions.

1.7 Latest HTVI Developments

The 2015 Final Report on BEPS Actions 8-10 referenced that guidance on the HTVI approach would be provided in 2016, and "the practical application of the exemptions, including the measurement of materiality and time periods contained in the current exemptions, will be reviewed by 2020 in the light of further experience."[18] The guidance referenced has been published, but there has been no indication of actions with respect to the mentioned 2020 review.

The OECD guidance of June 21, 2018,[19] is directed toward tax administrations on applying the HTVI approach with the purpose of improving consistency and reducing double taxation risk ("HTVI Guidance"). The HTVI Guidance discusses: (a) the principles underlying the application of the HTVI approach, (b) examples illustrating the practical application of the HTVI approach, and (c) the interaction between the HTVI approach and access to the mutual agreement procedure.

The principles underlying the application of the HTVI approach include:

- Tax administrations can consider *ex post* outcomes as presumptive evidence on the reasonableness of the assumptions of the *ex ante* pricing arrangements.

18. OECD, "Aligning Transfer Pricing Outcomes with Value Creation, Actions 8-10-2015 Final Reports", OECD/G20 Base Erosion and Profit Shifting Project, OECD Publishing, Paris, 2015. http://dx.doi.org/10.1787/9789264241244-en.
19. This guidance is included as Annex II to Chapter VI of the 2022 OECD Guidelines.

- The *ex post* outcomes should provide information on the determination of the valuation that would have been made at the time of the HTVI transfer. However, it is inappropriate that the valuation is based on the actual income or cash flows without considering whether the associated enterprises could reasonably have known the information in connection with the probability of achieving such *ex post* results at the time of the HTVI transfer.
- In case an amended valuation demonstrates that the HTVI was transferred at a value below or above the arm's-length price, the amended price may be assessed to tax considering price-adjustment clauses and contingent payments notwithstanding the pricing structure alleged by the taxpayer.
- Audit practices should be applied by tax administrations to identify and pursue presumptive evidence based on *ex post* outcomes.

On December 16, 2020, the OECD published information on the implementation of the HTVI approach in forty jurisdictions through a questionnaire, including on whether the jurisdiction has adopted the HTVI approach, and if so, under what legal basis.[20] About 21 of these countries indicated that they have adopted the HTVI approach or that there is no impediment to apply the HTVI approach because the OECD Guidelines are followed in applying the arm's-length principle in domestic law.

2 CURRENT DEVELOPMENTS

2.1 The COVID Pandemic

On January 30, 2020, the World Health Organization declared the SARS-CoV-2 ("COVID") outbreak a Public Health Emergency. Strict social distancing and quarantine measures were mandated to avoid the virus spread and protect public health. This included workplace and border closures and led to supply challenges becoming prominent. To keep economies standing, governments started providing subsidies and there was an unparalleled global effort to develop vaccines, sanitizers and disinfectants, to repurpose medical equipment, facilities and product lines and restructure laboratories into diagnostic testing facilities for SARS-CoV-2. Traditionally competitor companies shared information through open science data sharing and entered into collaboration agreements that were hastily structured, sometimes not even considering sales forecasts but only considering estimated costs in order to commence work and develop a common response that would lead to an effective cure for the COVID virus and improved (medical) products to handle and provide relief for COVID patients. Numerous data sets were made available publicly, and an incredible amount of information was spread around swiftly to accommodate breakthrough developments that could help halt the pandemic and keep people from dying. Of course, the unprecedented speed with which products were and are being developed includes significant risks of failure and of unanticipated side effects, but increasingly these

20. https://www.oecd.org/tax/transfer-pricing/transfer-pricing-country-profiles.htm#htvi-approach.

liabilities are being mitigated in novel ways as well. None of these actions would have been imaginable at the scale they are being undertaken and within the brief period of time within which they are being undertaken. In the interest of finding viable solutions, companies simply took (and are taking) significant risks.[21] That said, the pandemic impacted the global economy in very different ways. While some industries experienced a sharp decline, others experienced growth. The hospitality and aviation industries are examples of sectors that experienced a sharp decline, which in turn impacted other industries such as the agricultural sector (since restaurants were largely closed or had restricted opening hours) and services sectors. Digitally provided business and online entertainment continued to reach people or even dramatically increased. Digital broadcasting and games, for example, experienced a significant increase when the pandemic provided for global lockdowns. All in all, there were major demand shortfalls or increases and supply disruptions with spillovers down the entire supply chain. To survive, extreme creativity was required, and many organizations had to de facto restructure themselves to cope and deal with the dramatically changed market circumstances. Over two years into the pandemic, it is still not likely that the world will return to what was considered "normal" before the pandemic hit since not only is an end to the pandemic not yet in sight (while a tapering off of its strength is expected this may still take several years) but also as a result of quite a dramatic change in values that has occurred. The pandemic triggered a reevaluation of how a workforce should be structured since working from home has been the norm for so long together with a strong environmental awareness. Environmental concerns grew as countries were required to report on their national emissions in 2021 under the 2015 Paris Agreement on climate change, while people clearly witnessed environmental benefits of reduced aviation and transportation activity resulting from lockdowns.

Actions undertaken by companies worldwide to weather the COVID pandemic and adjust to the changed circumstances can easily rise to the level of a business restructuring as described by the OECD Guidelines. Once they do, they are to be subject to the issued guidance for the following reasons:

(i) Chapter IX of the OECD Guidelines that presents guidance on the transfer pricing aspects of business restructurings does not offer any legal definition of business restructurings.
(ii) The OECD Guidelines do not provide that the respective analyses and steps serve particularly or solely to address business restructurings that target tax optimization/aim to reduce tax costs. Quite the opposite, the OECD Guidelines emphasize that a business restructuring arrangement that has as an ultimate or additional goal to achieve tax benefits does *not* as such result in disregarding the structure of the business restructuring arrangement.
(iii) The relevant tests relate to whether the contractual allocation of risk post-restructuring is consistent with the conduct of parties and whether there is sufficient substance to control the risk and financial capacity to assume the

21. The global impact of the coronavirus pandemic, by J. Hiscott, et al. https://www.ncbi.nlm.nih.gov › pmc › articles › PMC7254014.

risk. This means that the risk bearing entity should have people (employees or directors) who have the authority to, and effectively do, perform the relevant oversight and control functions.

(iv) The analysis of whether the company considered the ORAs as required pursuant to Chapter IX does not in any way reference situations caused by developments that qualify as or are close to "Force Majeure," which at times may have caused restructuring actions, such as due to COVID. The ORAs simply apply to help determine whether the arrangements adopted intercompany differ from those made by independent enterprises behaving in a commercially rational manner.

The above conclusion means that the OECD's HTVI Guidance applies to business restructurings triggered by the pandemic exactly the same way it does to any other business restructuring. It can be safely assumed that any transfers of intangibles triggered by reacting to the market conditions caused by the pandemic were made at a time there was extreme uncertainty as regards the commercial viability of those transfers. Commercial viability may very well not have been the main rationale for certain transactions; they may have been undertaken largely with an altruistic intent, such as collaborating and trying to assist with stemming the pandemic. As rapid large-scale production of functional vaccines was considered crucial, there was an unprecedented rush to conduct vaccine development research and clinical trials. Technologies that had led a relatively uneventful life so far or collected dust in file cabinets or computer files all of a sudden were jolted back to further development, testing and trials, to see whether they could generate a worthwhile amount of antibodies to the virus, serve to manufacture functional respirators, function as effective disinfectants, or serve some other purpose. Existing technologies and patents were applied in novel ways and fields to try to achieve the same. If any of those technologies were transferred, say, within a five-year period before their new usage, and end up meeting any of the HTVI characteristics listed in paragraph 6.190 of the 2017 OECD Guidelines (that are not intended to be exhaustive), they expose the taxpayer to potential *ex post* pricing adjustments. Considering the broad scope of HTVI, it should not be a surprise that technologies and intangibles used during the pandemic could be considered as HTVI.

That the pandemic caused entirely unforeseen tax consequences has been acknowledged by the OECD. They issued three consecutive papers on the impact of COVID on tax and transfer pricing, namely on April 3, 2020, December 18, 2020,[22] and on January 21, 2021. However, while the guidance dated December 18, 2020 addresses under what circumstances arrangements may be modified to address consequences of COVID and also references force majeure, none of the issued guidance considered that as a result of the length of time the pandemic is taking, ad hoc adaptions by companies could actually present a more permanent restructuring of their operations. For example, there

22. OECD, "Guidance on the Transfer Pricing Implications of the COVID-19 Pandemic," December 18, 2020, https://www.oecd.org/tax/transfer-pricing/guidance-on-the-transfer-pricing-implications-of-the-covid-19-pandemic.htm.

are early indications that (partial) remote working / working from home may be the new normal. As a result thereof, a question may be what the transfer pricing consequences will be of (cross-border) remote working, including the relocation / recruitment of talents conducting DEMPE functions in non-hub entities (i.e., so-called routine entities). Risk control functions may get dispersed across the MNE group in different locations and countries.

2.2 Digitalization

While the COVID pandemic has emphasized more than ever that doing business digitally is a material requirement to reach consumers, whether they be wholesale and retail customers, digital business has soared and been in the spotlight since the Big tech companies like Apple, Microsoft, Amazon, Alphabet (formerly Facebook) triggered a discussion on taxing digital income and the OECD Pillar 1 proposal. The COVID pandemic has only exacerbated the imperative to digitalize.

Platform and App-based solutions have been in vogue for a while now and have managed to excite private venture capital investors and raise tremendous amounts of investment capital. More established examples would be Airbnb, Uber, eBay, and a fast increasing number of food delivery companies. But there is also a steady number of initial public offerings in the tech and fintech field, for example, like Coinbase, with a nearly endless number of start-ups in the tech and fintech areas as well. People more and more speak of an innovation economy, where raw automation, machine learning, artificial intelligence and chatbots are taking over a myriad of functions along the (global) value chain previously performed by human beings. The relevance of this is that these digital innovations are becoming revenue-generating assets on their own. They are not necessarily auxiliary or merely connected to a service or product; they are becoming the service or product in their own right.

Large investment banks are steadily launching updated versions of product-led (digital) solutions. Mobile banking is becoming the norm, biometrics increasingly serves to protect and access sensitive information, artificial intelligence serves to enhance the customer experience or is being used to detect treatments in the healthcare business and machine learning software will prompt customers to make the right (revenue-generating) decisions. Welcome to what is becoming part and parcel of many applications. Not only are professional service providers such as technology developers, consulting and advertising service providers or hospitals digitalizing but also the far more traditional businesses are undergoing digital transformation, including the more classic professional services firms such as architectural firms, law firms and accounting firms. Digitalization is a development that is not likely to be halted anytime soon.

Digitalization generally has the effect of replacing tangible assets with intangibles. It may lead to major restructuring, as companies may decide to reshore certain activities previously offshored or regionalize functions as a result of replacing (part of their) global tangible footprint with a digital one. It should be clear that the relevant software, know-how and intangibles that are involved in the above digital products and services are being scaled, repurposed and developed further on a relatively continuous basis and are being transferred (intercompany) as part and parcel of the dynamic business environments in which many takeovers and mergers take place. Intangibles are regularly transferred intercompany because their intended use was not scaled properly for one market, leading to investment cost for development that simply cannot be recouped in that particular market. It may then be explored whether their use in another market can serve to recoup some of those costs. In other words (almost) all services, functions or products nowadays involve (some form of) digital intangibles and their form and (the location of) use are anything but static.

Realizing that digital innovation and developments have amplified the use of intangibles also means that there is a corresponding increase in the chance that intercompany transfers of such intangibles trigger HTVI aspects. In particular, a lot of digital applications are still relatively novel right now but may take off large scale once made operational.

Earlier, we noted that the OECD felt the need to introduce a special measure for transfers of hard-to-value intangibles (HTVI), the HTVI approach, in addition to the observations in paragraph 6.185 of the OECD Guidelines. In other words, while the uncertainty of valuing intangibles is a generally recognized challenge under normal circumstances, in special situations, namely there where the intangible in issue rises to the level of an HTVI, tax administrations are granted a significantly more favorable position to preserve their taxing rights. The result is that companies are required to provide evidence that they considered, at the time of the transfer of the intangible, that the transferor be compensated in case the intangible outperforms its initial expectations after the transfer, as that is presented as being arm's-length behavior. What is being observed during the onset of the COVID pandemic is that price-adjustment clauses were not really used as the mechanism of choice to deal with uncertainty between unrelated parties. Risk of failure and the upside of success are rather being addressed through milestones, tiered royalties, options, first-review clauses and success fees, rather than the price-adjustment clauses that the OECD appears to envisage. The key consequence of the OECD approach is that a strong assumption results that the taxpayer did not apply an arm's-length price, that the burden of proof is on the taxpayer as regards the appropriate pricing for the transferred intangible and that this burden becomes disproportionally high:

- Tax administrations can consider *ex post* outcomes as presumptive evidence on the reasonableness of the assumptions of the *ex ante* pricing arrangements.
- The *ex post* outcomes should provide information on the determination of the valuation that would have been made at the time of the HTVI transfer. However, it is inappropriate that the valuation is based on the actual income or cash flows without considering whether the associated enterprises could reasonably have known the information in connection with the probability of achieving such *ex post* results at the time of the HTVI transfer.
- In case an amended valuation demonstrates that the HTVI was transferred at a value below or above the arm's-length price, the amended price may be

assessed to tax considering price-adjustment clauses and contingent payments notwithstanding the pricing structure alleged by the taxpayer.
- Audit practices should be applied by tax administrations to identify and pursue presumptive evidence based on *ex post* outcomes.

Section D4 of the OECD Guidelines on HTVI does provide for exceptions to the HTVI approach.[23] However, the exceptions are limited. They require that at least one of the following situations apply that:

(a) The taxpayer is able to provide details of the *ex ante* projections used at the time of the HTVI transfer to determine the pricing arrangements (including how risks were considered in the valuation model (e.g., probability weighted) and whether reasonably foreseeable events were properly reflected) and "reliable evidence" that any significant difference between the financial projections and actual outcomes is resulting from developments or events that were not foreseeable at the moment of the HTVI transfer.
(b) The transfer of the HTVI is part of a bilateral or multilateral APA that is in effect.
(c) Any significant difference between the financial projections and actual outcomes does not reduce or increase the compensation for the HTVI by more than 20% of the compensation determined at the time of the transaction.
(d) A commercialization period of five years has elapsed subsequent to the year in which the HTVI initially achieved third-party revenues for the related party buyer / licensee and during which commercialization period any significant difference between the financial projections and actual outcomes was less than 20% of the projections for that period.

Of the four available exceptions, two are quantitative, one is factual and one is dependent on providing a level of evidence and substantiation that meets the level of being considered "reliable." The two quantitative factors include criteria that can be subjectively interpreted. In sum, it will not be easy to establish qualification for (any one of) these exceptions.

Considering the massive increase in use by business of valuable (digital) intangibles that in turn due to being used large scale can lead to generating enormous amounts of revenue, it can be expected that what was intended to be a special situation for which tax administrations ought to be granted a significantly more favorable position to preserve their taxing rights, albeit to the detriment of the taxpayer, is becoming a much more frequently encountered situation, and anything from special. It can be posited that while the HTVI chapter was drafted and implemented in 2017, the dramatic market developments and corresponding leap in use of (digital) intangibles simply were not (and probably could not be) foreseen, as a result of which the HTVI approach is likely to become the norm rather than a "special" regime.

23. Paragraph 6.193 of the OECD Guidelines.

2.3 Macroeconomic Developments

While the onset of the COVID pandemic triggered a global depression beginning in March 2020, just less than two years later, in January 2022, it was reported that consumer prices in the US jumped 7% in December of 2021, the hottest year-over-year inflation since June 1982.[24] Inflation concerns also exist for the European and Asian markets.

The massively provided global government aid together with interventions by central banks to cut interest rates to historically low and even negative levels to counter the consequences of COVID led to easy money and ravenous market demand. However, business is not able to meet that demand because COVID quarantining and fallout in the workforce are leading to a severe shortage of staff available to be physically on the job. Supply chains are encountering major bottlenecks, such as containers with produce sitting idle in ports and not being processed (thus not being returned empty to be refilled). The job market is doing well, boosting wages (and indirectly increasing costs in the supply chain), contributing in turn to the inflationary trend for some industries and countries. While it is not clear for how long inflation will continue to rise, the concern with rising inflation is that it means that the value of currency and its purchasing power goes down and the prices of products and services proportionally go up.

Extrapolating the impact of rapidly rising inflation on the use of intangibles,[25] inflation de facto means that more currency will be needed to be paid for the use or acquisition of products and services, including intangibles, than before. It also impacts the valuation of intangibles. In a related party setting, this simple fact can exacerbate the reach and impact of HTVI since the definition of HTVI is relatively easily met, and the future income stream resulting from the use of a transferred intangible post inflation may *ex post* appear quite a bit higher than it actually is, also since the valuation discount rates used may have been lower than the actual inflation.

The higher the inflation rate, the more interest rates are likely to rise as well. These macroeconomic developments will impact the valuation analysis, and it is yet unclear how to account for uncertain macroeconomic developments.

Despite the COVID pandemic, 2021 turned out to be a record year for global merger & acquisition (M&A) volumes due to the availability of low-interest rate financing and strong stock markets.[26] This M&A activity is likely to lead to post-acquisition business restructurings and trigger the associated transfer pricing aspects.

24. P. Wiseman for ABC News of January 12, 2021. EXPLAINER: Why US inflation is so high, and when it may ease—ABC News (go.com).
25. The question is whether the inflation rate will decrease once supply shortages and COVID issues dissipate.
26. https://www.reuters.com/markets/us/global-ma-volumes-hit-record-high-2021-breach-5-trillion-first-time-2021-12-31/.

3 CHALLENGES

3.1 The HTVI Approach Is a Very Broadly Applicable Rule

Considering current developments, the reach and application of the HTVI approach are far more broad than initially intended. It is assumed to be a regime applicable (only) in the (relatively special) circumstances where intangibles or rights in intangibles[27] were transferred yet at the time of the intercompany transfer:

(i) there are no reliable comparables;
(ii) the projections of future cash flows or income expected to be derived from the transferred intangible, or the assumptions used in valuing the intangible are highly uncertain; and therefore
(iii) it is hard to predict the success of the intangible at the moment of the transfer of the intangible.

Given the definition of HTVI, there will be differences in interpretation of what constitutes an HTVI resulting in uncertainty. First of all, there may be differences of interpretation on whether "reliable comparables" exist for the intangible in question.[28] Next, intangibles are often hard to value and as such their valuation will often be considered as "highly uncertain."

Paragraph 6.190 of the OECD Guidelines does provide for a list of indicative features that HTVIs may exhibit, but it does not provide a number of characteristics that, if met, tip the scale for an intangible to qualify as an HTVI. The interpretation of these indicative features based on the specific facts and circumstances of a case leads to uncertainty in practice. Consider, for example, a case in which an intangible was developed on a limited test project in one country. Turns out that the intangible used in the test project is not commercially viable in that country. It is decided to transfer the intangible to the parent company which will seek to develop it further. Is this an HTVI? The intangible was already exploited commercially by the local subsidiary, but not commercially viable. The commercial exploitation was—geographically—limited. Perhaps, it will become commercially viable if further enhanced and exploited internationally, but the subsidiary does not have the infrastructure or means to do that. Further developments to try to make the intangible commercially viable will be undertaken by the parent company. Essentially, the HTVI approach requires MNEs to closely monitor *ex post* outcomes compared to *ex ante* projections in the case of HTVI transactions, but this assumes that it is clear that the intangible transferred qualifies as an HTVI.

---

27. Paragraph 6.26 provides that "Limited rights in intangibles are commonly transferred by means of a licence or other similar contractual arrangement, whether written, oral or implied. Such licensed rights may be limited as to field of use, term of use, geography or in other ways. Such limited rights in intangibles are themselves intangibles within the meaning of Section A.1."
28. Paragraph 6.17 of the OECD Guidelines provides that unique intangibles are those intangibles "that are not comparable to intangibles used by or available to parties to potentially comparable transactions."

The rationale for introducing the HTVI approach is grounded on the theory that independent enterprises in comparable circumstances of high uncertainty would have agreed to "such" a mechanism. But it is unclear why the mechanisms mentioned in paragraphs 6.182-6.184 cannot provide for adequate solutions in these situations, as they also consider the implementation of price corrections related to unforeseen developments. Rather, the information asymmetry between tax administrations and taxpayers and that it is hard for tax administrations to evaluate which developments or events are relevant for the pricing of a transaction involving the transfer of (rights in) intangibles seems to be the governing reason for the implementation of the HTVI approach.

Considering the current market developments, which are impacted by great demand from investors to invest in the "next best thing" and the urge to participate in developments and inventions that lead to major improvements and innovation, it is increasingly common that acquisitions or collaborations take place that involve new use of existing intangibles or regard (only) potentially promising inventions, both between associated enterprises and unrelated enterprises. Often the intangibles in issue are:

(a) only partially (and certainly not fully) developed;
(b) the subject of a transaction but may very well not be exploited (viably or sufficiently) commercially until several years following the transaction;
(c) not falling themselves within the definition of HTVI, but may end up being integral to the development or enhancement of other intangibles which may fall within that definition of HTVI.
(d) expected to be exploited in a manner that is novel at the time of the transfer and the absence of a track record of development or exploitation of similar intangibles makes projections highly uncertain.
(e) transferred to an associated enterprise for a lump sum payment (often consisting of part of the cost of development).

This means that increasingly, such transactions may qualify as HTVI transactions, opening them up to an *ex post* outcome-based review and adjustments by tax administrations. In these transactions, future outcomes can fluctuate tremendously upwards or downwards, there is great uncertainty and price-adjustment clauses are not considered viable to be used. Rather, milestones, tiered royalties, options, first-review clauses and success fees are being used to allow for phased or continued investments. Applying an *ex post* outcome-based adjustment in such situations would operate as an anti-abuse rule, when there may not have been any tax abuse. The HTVI rule appears to function more as an anti-abuse rule and to curb tax avoidance, than as a reflection of what occurs at arm's length. The rule could be greatly improved by allowing for the possibility to substantiate that there is no tax avoidance.

It is assumed that a deliberate choice was made by the OECD to not incorporate the CWI standard in the OECD Guidelines. Rather, it was preferred to include a special mechanism to address situations where it can be assumed that associated enterprises seek a (tax) benefit resulting from the presence of uncertainty at the time of the transfer of intangibles by pricing the relevant intercompany arrangements such that they generate tax savings, i.e., lead to tax avoidance. Below we list several solutions to make the HTVI approach operate more in line with the exceptional regime it is intended to be.

While the HTVI approach provides for exemptions (listed under paragraphs 6.193-6.194 of the OECD Guidelines), those exemptions are difficult to meet and could benefit from being updated as follows:

(a) The first exemption is when the taxpayer is able to provide details of the *ex ante* projections used at the time of the HTVI transfer to determine the pricing arrangements (including how risks were considered in the valuation model (e.g., probability weighted) and whether reasonably foreseeable events were properly reflected). Under this exemption, the valuation analysis of the taxpayer at the time of the HTVI transfer needs to consider for projections based on various scenarios to take into account events or developments that are foreseeable at the time of the HTVI transfer. Yet even then, it will be very difficult to provide reliable evidence substantiating that the difference between *ex post* results and *ex ante* projections relating to an HTVI is due to reasonably unforeseeable events or developments. What objective evidence should taxpayers provide to demonstrate that their original valuation properly considered all developments or events at the time of the HTVI transaction and when developments or events occur that were not considered, that these were unforeseeable developments or events? The term "unforeseeable" is not linked to any particular level of knowledge that a taxpayer is expected to have either. The examples discussed in Annex II to Chapter VI (i.e., Guidance for tax administrations on the application of the approach to HTVI) of the 2022 OECD Guidelines also do not illustrate this exemption. Guidance addressing this issue is required. For example, financial projections prepared for business planning purposes (e.g., to obtain a loan from a bank or used by management to make business and investment decisions) may indicate that the projections used at the time of the HTVI transfer were the most reliable projections available. Furthermore, this threshold could also be considered met if the observed milestones, tiered royalties, options, first-review clauses and success fees are explicitly included in intercompany contracts in relation to the pricing. Adherence to those clauses should serve to provide "reliable evidence" that the taxpayer operated at arm's length. Acknowledgement that foreseeability is dependent on knowledge of the (local) market in which an enterprise operates considering its functional profile and the matching required sophistication would be useful as well.

(b) The next exemption provided is that the transfer of the HTVI is part of a bilateral or multilateral APA that is in effect. While this seems an appropriate reason for exemption, taxpayers may choose not to obtain a bilateral or multilateral APA for transfers of intangibles for various reasons and therefore this exemption may not apply. However, the average amount of time to complete bilateral and multilateral APAs is generally longer than that of unilateral APAs, since bilateral and multilateral APAs involve more than one jurisdiction.[29] In addition, it appears that APAs in the context of HTVI pose particular problems. About 25% of transactions covered by APAs concluded in 2020 in the United States' APMA Program regard the use of intangibles. The Announcement and Report Concerning Advance Pricing Agreements of March 23, 2021, provides that the use of intangibles "can be among the most challenging transactions" in its inventory of the APMA.

(c) The third exemption provided is that any significant difference between the financial projections and actual outcomes does not reduce or increase the compensation for the HTVI by more than 20% of the compensation determined at the time of the transaction. First, if and to the extent that payments are relying on milestones, tiered royalties, options, first-review clauses and success fees, applying this compensation level threshold in addition, would seem overkill. Next, if the HTVI approach is to serve as an exception, the 20% threshold is too low, considering the scale on which intangibles may be implemented and applied internationally within a very short period of time. It is unclear how the 20% threshold was determined. This threshold should be increased, perhaps even to 50% or higher to increase its applicability and reduce the use of HTVI to the exceptional situations that it is intended to cover.

(d) Finally, the fourth exemption regards that a commercialization period of five years has elapsed subsequent to the year in which the HTVI initially achieved third-party revenues for the related party buyer / licensee and during which commercialization period any significant difference between the financial projections and actual outcomes was less than 20% of the projections for that period. In the world of intangibles, five years is an eternity. During that period of time, intangibles (and in particular software) are likely to be adapted and improved dramatically in order to be useful. This opens up the initial transfer and transaction to yet another HTVI analysis, namely that the intangible becomes integral to the development or enhancement of other intangibles which fall within the definition of HTVI. The five-year time period should be reduced to perhaps two or two and a half years, and reduce the use of HTVI for the exceptional situations that it is intended to cover.

Considering the above, it seems that it is easy to get into the HTVI approach, but difficult to get out of it. If the HTVI approach were to be applied consistent with its original intention: as a special regime to curb tax avoidance taxpayers should be granted the option to substantiate that there was no tax avoidance. Therefore, in addition to the above exemptions, it would seem appropriate that if the taxpayer can substantiate that income generated with the use of the transferred intangible is subject

29. The Announcement and Report Concerning Advance Pricing Agreements of the US Advance Pricing and Mutual Agreement Program (APMA Program) of March 23, 2021, presents information on various elements of APAs executed in 2020. The average amount of time taken to complete bilateral APAs and unilateral APAs was 40.1 months and 29 months, respectively, in 2020.

to a statutory corporate tax rate that is the same as that in the jurisdiction of the transferor, or in any case subject to a rate of 15% or higher, there should be a strong inference that the intercompany transfer did not serve to obtain tax avoidance.

3.2 The HTVI Approach Is Not Generally Applied Between Independent Enterprises

Can the HTVI approach be considered as consistent with the arm's-length principle?

- The OECD Guidelines in general caution against the use of hindsight and against the use of *ex post* adjustment.[30] For example, paragraph 3.73 of the OECD Guidelines provides that the "mere existence of uncertainty should not require an ex post adjustment without a consideration of what independent enterprises would have done or agreed between them." In addition, paragraph 3.74 states that "Data from years following the year of the transaction may also be relevant to the analysis of transfer prices, but care must be taken to avoid the use of hindsight." Making use of *ex post* results means that tax administrations make use of information known at the time of assessment, which were not reasonably foreseeable at the time of the HTVI transfer. Using information on *ex post* results is using hindsight.[31] While in the case of HTVI taxpayers are offered the opportunity to rebut the presumptive evidence by providing reliable evidence, this is very difficult to do.
- The arm's-length principle is based on what independent enterprises would agree to do. Current developments undermine that independent enterprises would agree on the OECD HTVI approach. Rather than the difference between *ex post* results and *ex ante* projections, unrelated party agreements tend to include milestones, tiered royalties, options, first-review clauses and success fees, rather than the price-adjustment clauses.[32]
- The OECD Guidelines already provide for various mechanisms to deal with highly uncertain valuation at the time of the transaction, such as a price-adjustment clause, in case independent parties would have agreed on such mechanisms. It is unclear how the HTVI approach fits in with these mechanisms, other than providing tax authorities with an anti-abuse rule.
- The HTVI approach results in a reversal of the burden of proof to taxpayer while the allocation of the burden of proof is generally left to domestic legislation.
- It is hard to envisage how independent enterprises would know the *ex post* results at the time of the transaction pursuant to which intangibles were

30. *See*, for example, paragraphs 2.136, 3.73, 3.74, 8.20, 9.24, 49 and 52 of Annex II to Chapter IV.
31. *See* C. Camilo Rodriguez Pena, "Compatibility Between the OECD's Hard-to-Value Intangibles Methodology and the Arm's Length Standard: What Is the Way Forward?," International Tax Studies, 8-2020, IBFD.
32. *See* also C. Camilo Rodriguez Pena, "Compatibility Between the OECD's Hard-to-Value Intangibles Methodology and the Arm's Length Standard: What Is the Way Forward?," International Tax Studies, 8-2020, IBFD.

transferred, in particular if the intangible regards an HTVI.[33] As stated earlier, *ex post* results will always differ from *ex ante* projections since the *ex post* actual results mirror a single realization of all potential risk outcomes, whereas *ex ante* projections reflect the average of all potential risk outcomes. There is an inherent uncertainty when making projections.

- The *ex post* HTVI approach may very well ignore post-transfer DEMPE functions that (significantly) increase the value of the intangible.
- It is unclear whether the HTVI allows for a downward adjustment of the price agreed at the time of the HTVI transfer rather than solely an upward adjustment. Both the OECD Guidelines and the HTVI Guidance are silent on this matter.[34]

Importantly, in case the HTVI approach is inconsistent with the arm's-length principle, it should not be applied because of the existing tax treaties and domestic law.[35]

The governing principle in pricing a transaction involving HTVI or the rights to HTVI is the arm's-length principle. The HTVI approach was introduced as a "special measure" under the OECD BEPS project and operates as an anti-abuse measure. As a consequence, it should only be applied in exceptional circumstances when taxpayers do not provide appropriate valuation analyses for tax administrations to evaluate the arm's-length nature of the agreed pricing arrangements or evidence that there is no tax abuse.

3.3 Impact of Pillar One on HTVI Valuation and Approach

Another reason to reconsider if not recalibrate the application of the HTVI approach as currently in place is the potential impact of Pillar One. Under the agreed Pillar One solution to address the tax challenges arising from the digitalization of the economy, it is the intention that 25% of the residual profit (i.e., profit in excess of 10% of revenue of qualifying MNEs) will be allocated to market jurisdictions with nexus to qualifying MNEs. Furthermore, there is an amount B in relation to in-country baseline marketing and distribution activities under the Pillar One solution.

In general, it is considered that residual profits are attributable to unique and valuable intangibles. However, it would seem that application of the income-based method when taking into account the Pillar One measures will result in a lower value for IP transfer in case Amount A will be deducted from cash flows attributable to the transferred intangible in question. With that knowledge, unrelated parties may have wanted to renegotiate their licensing agreements. Whether associated enterprises would be allowed to do so is unclear.

33. *See* O. Fedusiv, "Transactions with Hard-to-Value Intangibles: Is BEPS Action 8 Based on the Arm's Length Principle?," International Transfer Pricing Journal, November / December 2016.
34. *See* C. Jie-A-Joen, L. Lu and F. bai, "INSIGHT: Transfer Pricing Valuation by Tax Authorities", Tax Management Transfer Pricing Report, 27 Transfer Pricing Report, August 9, 2018.
35. *See* J. Wittendorf, "BEPS Actions 8-10: Birth of a New Arm's Length Principle," Tax Notes International 87, 2016, pp. 331-358.

In addition, the question arises the extent to which Pillar One should be considered in valuing HTVI transfers at this moment in time prior to Pillar One being fully agreed to and implemented into domestic tax law. Is Pillar One a foreseeable event that should already be considered, while there is still political uncertainty whether all details included in Pillar One will be fully agreed to and implemented by all countries?

Amount B may impact the determination of routine profits to arrive at residual profits. The precise impact of Pillar One measures on the IP valuation should be analyzed since Amount A under Pillar One is calculated based on different parameters (e.g., the 10% threshold is based on profit before tax).

Note also that the value of IP owned by an MNE that is not subject to Pillar One would be relatively higher than the value of the same IP if owned by an MNE subject to Pillar One assuming everything else is the same.

For HTVI transfers that have already occurred and for which Pillar One is applicable in later years, will Pillar One be regarded as a reasonable unforeseeable event?

3.4 Accurate Delineation of Business Restructuring Transactions

As outlined in section 2, recent developments such as the COVID pandemic, the greater tolerance for (cross-border) remote working, the M&A activity and the digitalization of the economy invariably will lead to some sort of restructurings. For transfer pricing purposes, a key question is whether these restructurings lead to intragroup transfers of "something of value" or the termination/substantial renegotiation of existing arrangements resulting in a compensation payment, if any, to be paid to the restructured entities.

The transfer pricing definition of business restructurings is very broad. A key component to the transfer pricing analysis is to accurately delineate the business restructuring transaction, which will usually entail a functional analysis (including risks assumed and assets used) of the restructured entities before and after the business restructuring. Some challenges encountered in particular when accurately delineating a business restructuring may include the following:

- The application of the six-step risk allocation framework under Chapter I of the OECD Guidelines[36] to determine the economically significant risks assumed by the restructured entity before and after the alleged business restructuring. In case the economically significant risk is not transferred, the restructured entity should continue to be remunerated for this risk in the post-restructuring controlled transactions.[37] Based on the several years of experience we now have with the risk allocation framework, it is safe to say that a lot of time and effort goes into conducting and documenting the risk allocation analysis. An important step is to determine which party "controls the risk" which in turn is

36. *See* paragraph 1.60 OECD Guidelines.
37. The U.S. Announcement and Report Concerning Advance Pricing Agreements (dated March 23, 2021) explicitly states that a lot of time is spent on understanding the allocation of functions and risks between the associated enterprises when evaluating the APA request.

based on the capability to make decisions and the actual performance of decision-making function. This threshold test can lead to varying interpretations in practice. Collier and Dykes[38] maintain that there is disparity in the application of the risk allocation framework between tax authorities. One interpretation of the risk allocation framework is that the contractual assumption of a certain risk by a party should be respected if the party that is contractually assuming the risk has sufficient control over the risk through functional decision-making and has the financial capacity to assume the risk. In this interpretation, the contractual allocation of the specific risk between the related parties is evaluated / tested based on functional decision-making. The risk allocation analysis is conducted per economically significant risk. Another interpretation is that the profits of the MNE group should be divided based on a PSM between the parties conducting risk decision-making functions in the value chain, in particular the DEMPE functions. This interpretation relies largely on the location of functional decision-making by employees in the value chain of the MNE group. These different interpretations of the risk allocation framework are likely to lead to different outcomes. It would seem that the first interpretation of testing the contractual assumption of a risk is more appropriate and correct, but it would certainly help if the OECD would make that clear. If the contractual assumption of a risk is the starting point, the analysis serves to assure that the party that is contractually assuming the risks also performs (certain) key decision-making functions.

- Another element of the accurate delineation analysis regards identifying what has been transferred as a result of the business restructuring and whether that constitutes "something of value." Chapter IX of the OECD TPG refers to assets (transfers of tangible assets, of intangibles and rights in intangibles) or an ongoing concern as "something of value." In practice, there may be disagreement about what exactly has been transferred. Let us take the example of a local entity that performs certain functions independently and enjoys the full (economic) result of its efforts. A restructuring takes place after which the local entity performs these same functions but now for the risk and account of an associated entrepreneurial entity located in Switzerland. Based on the functional analysis, it becomes clear that certain assets, such as the inventory of final products, have been transferred. Upon audit, the local tax authorities argue that in addition to the transfer of identified assets, the local entity also transferred its right of conducting the business activities for its own account and risk and its relationships with third parties. Do these additional items constitute "something of value" that requires a compensation payment? Another example would be the conversion of a local full-fledged distributor (that distributes branded products) into a limited risk distributor. In such a case, the local tax authorities may take the position that local marketing intangibles have been transferred by the full-fledged distributor.

38. *See, e.g.*, R.S. Collier and I.F. Dykes, "On the Apparent Widespread Misapplication of the OECD Transfer Pricing Guidelines," Bulletin for International Taxation, January 2022.

- The determination of whether there is a transfer of something of value or a termination or substantial renegotiation of existing arrangements, which would be compensated between third parties in comparable circumstances. Paragraph 9.39 of the OECD Guidelines provides that the application of the arm's-length principle does not require a compensation payment for just a decrease in expected profits of the restructured entity. In practice, there is no doubt that a mere decrease in expected profits will trigger scrutiny by tax authorities. Taxpayers will need to be prepared to accurately delineate, explain and thoroughly document the facts of the case at hand. Emphasizing the commercial reasons for the business restructuring for the MNE group and for the restructured entity will be important in this respect.

3.5 Valuation of Compensation Payment, If Any, as a Result of Business Restructuring

MNEs are continuously restructuring their business. The 2008 discussion draft on the transfer pricing aspects of business restructurings provided tax administrations with the ammunition to tackle tax optimization structures related to business restructurings. More specifically, guidance was provided on risk allocation (i.e., whether risks have actually been transferred from the converted entity to the principal entity), the exceptional circumstances of not recognizing a transaction in the context of business restructuring and when a compensation payment may be due to the restructured entity. The OECD work resulted in Chapter IX of the OECD Guidelines.

Given the recent developments (e.g., the COVID pandemic, digitalization and economic developments) and all the BEPS measures, there are good arguments to say that Chapter IX should not be applied dogmatically by tax administrations and requires recalibration.

In the case of a business restructuring, it should be analyzed whether "something of value" (e.g., an asset or an ongoing concern) will be transferred and how that something of value should be valued. Not much guidance is provided in Chapter IX, other than that Chapter IX makes reference to the guidance provided in Chapter VI of the OECD Guidelines on the use of valuation techniques for transfers of intangibles or rights in intangibles. Chapter VI acknowledges in section D that (financial) valuation techniques, in particular income-based methods based on the calculation of the discounted value of projected future income streams or cash flows obtained from the exploitation of the intangible, if properly applied, may be used as part of the five OECD transfer pricing methods or as a useful tool in estimating the arm's-length price for the transfer of intangibles or rights in intangibles. However, these valuation techniques should be applied taking into account the arm's-length principle and the (other) principles in the OECD Guidelines. There is a cautionary note against the use of valuations of intangibles done for accounting purposes or in purchase price allocations, because of the use of "conservative" assumptions and differences between accounting and transfer pricing practices. Chapter VI provides that small changes in assumptions underlying the valuation model or in one or more valuation parameters when applying the income-based methods, such as accuracy of financial projections, growth rates, discount rates, useful life of intangibles and terminal values, taxes, and form of payment, can result in large differences in value calculated.

However, the guidance in Chapter VI on the use of valuation techniques specifically relates to transfers of intangibles or rights in intangibles. One methodology used in practice with respect to estimating the buyout compensation in connection with a business restructuring is to calculate the difference between the discounted cash flow (DCF) of the restructured entity prior to restructuring based on infinite life and the DCF of the same entity after restructuring based on infinite life. Discussions can arise on what the appropriate discount rate should be for the pre-restructuring and post-restructuring situations and the number of years to consider in calculating the DCF. There also are tax administrations that explicitly do not allow for DCF calculations based on infinite cash flows with respect to the routine functions performed by the restructured entity after restructuring, based on the argument that routine functions can easily be replaced in the market and contracts involving such routine functions have a relatively short term.[39] The determination of a compensation payment, if any, should also identify and value the ORAs to the parties, which can be challenging in practice. The ORAs should be assessed pragmatically and consider the business environment at the time of the business restructuring.[40]

Due to the lack of guidance, business restructurings have led and are leading to disputes. Tax administrations and taxpayers alike can benefit from more detailed guidance on the pricing of "something of value," specifically in the context of business restructurings based on experience gained since the publication of the initial Chapter IX in the 2010 OECD Guidelines.

4 CONCLUSIONS

While the HTVI analysis was included in the OECD Guidelines only in 2017, after the implementation of the 2015 BEPS Project initiatives, current developments merit a new look at the functioning of that exceptional mechanism. In real life, its application is turning out to be anything but exceptional. Similarly, renewed consideration or calibration of the business restructuring chapter would seem appropriate as well.

In addition to the requirement of accurate delineation, OECD BEPS Actions 8-10 and Chapter IX of the OECD Guidelines introduced several measures to limit tax avoidance, including requiring evidence on control over risk, (two) exceptional circumstances when tax administrations would be allowed to disregard or not recognize the actual transactions undertaken by taxpayers, an ORA test, analysis of where the DEMPE functions are performed, and in particular, in paragraphs 6.182-6.184, mechanisms to deal with the highly uncertain valuation that the tax administration can apply to determine the pricing of a transaction involving an intangible or rights in an intangible (on the basis that independent enterprises in comparable circumstances would have

39. Paragraph 5.4 of the Dutch Transfer Pricing decree of June 14, 2022, no. 2022-0000139020 published in the Gazette of July 1, 2022, No. 16685.
40. For example, the COVID pandemic may have affected the ORAs considered by the parties to the business restructuring.

agreed to the inclusion of such a mechanism to address the high uncertainty in valuing the intangible also). In addition to these measures, for exceptional circumstances, a special measure was introduced for transfers of HTVI, the HTVI approach.

Current developments have led that exceptional measure, with its exceptional consequences to be more applicable, without reasonable options for defense. Therefore, the exemptions from the HTVI approach require a new look and updating to be consistent with current practice and developments. Furthermore, considering that the HTVI approach functions as an anti-abuse rule, taxpayers should be granted the right to substantiate that there was no tax avoidance in play when transferring intangibles. Without reconsideration, inconsiderate and careless application of the HTVI approach carries the risk of becoming abusive.

CHAPTER 8

Recent Developments on Transfer Pricing and New Technologies

Marta Milewska & Carlos Mallen[*]

[*] This chapter is for general information only and is not a substitute for professional advice where the facts and circumstances warrant. The views and opinions expressed in this chapter are those of the authors and do not necessarily represent the views of PwC.

1 INTRODUCTION

Tax authorities in many jurisdictions are enhancing their digitization of the transfer pricing risk assessment and audit processes. They are implementing short deadlines for the multinational enterprises (MNEs) to respond to information requests during tax audits. Furthermore, they have begun imposing stricter requirements on MNEs to produce a trail from the accounting data extracted from the Enterprise Resource Planning (ERP) systems and automation system to the tax information presented in the documentation.[1] Failure of MNEs to recognize the importance of using information technology and automation relating to transfer pricing can lead to double taxation, complex audits, litigation processes and possible reputational damage. In the upcoming future, it will be difficult for MNEs to mitigate transfer pricing risk without technology.

Many MNEs consider some degree of automation for transfer pricing documentation process to assure a consistent and efficient framework (typically handled by the taxpayer with the support of an external consultant). However, technology budgets have decreased for nearly every business in recent years due to COVID-19 pandemic.[2] Likewise, tax departments, typically seen as cost centers within the organization, are showing reduced investments in innovation. Therefore, momentum is building with MNEs tax departments' technological solutions that allow to improve small- and medium-scale transfer pricing processes. Based on our experience, those solutions may be very successful from the cost-benefit ratio and many may pay off in the first year.[3]

Hemlinga et al.[4] propose to expand their research by understanding the perspectives of external tax consultants on transfer pricing technology. They suggest that the academic literature could benefit from insights into how external tax consultants—given their experience and expertise—perceive the ability to reduce the

1. Centro Interamericano de Administraciones Tributarias, Servicio de Impuestos Internos de Chile, Fondo Monetario Internacional, *Manual sobre Gestión de Riesgos de Incumplimiento para Administraciones Tributarias* (2020).
2. Deloitte, *2021 Mid-market Technology Trends Report. Survey of Middle-market Private Companies* (2021), https://www2.deloitte.com/us/en/pages/deloitte-private/articles/technology-trends-middle-market-companies-survey.html (accessed January 6, 2022).
3. PricewaterhouseCoopers, Llp., *TP Talks Podcast Series, Episode 67: TP Automation – efficiencies for projects of any size* (2021), https://www.pwc.com/gx/en/services/tax/transfer-pricing/podcasts/efficiencies-for-projects-of-any-size.html (accessed January 6, 2022).
4. Lars Hemlinga, Jacob Christian, Plesner Rossingb and Andreas Hoffjana, *The Use of Information Technology for International Transfer Pricing in Multinational Enterprises*, International Journal of Accounting Information Systems (2021), https://doi.org/10.1016/j.accinf.2021.100546 (accessed January 6, 2022).

barriers to technological tools in transfer pricing. Therefore, we seek to answer the following research question: What technological tools can be used for small-and medium-scale transfer pricing processes? The purpose of this chapter is to present a pragmatic approach to transfer pricing technology supported by real-life examples of its application by the MNEs.

Given the authors' expertise on transfer pricing in the jurisdictions where they provide services as transfer pricing consultants, this chapter focuses on technological solutions that can be applied to transfer pricing challenges of MNEs operating in Mexico. Nevertheless, the results of the analysis can be easily expanded to other jurisdictions, given the similarities of transfer pricing regulations across the world.

The remainder of this chapter is organized as follows: section 2 discusses existing research on technologies applied to transfer pricing. Section 3 summarizes existing transfer pricing obligations in Mexico and related challenges MNE tax departments face. Section 4 presents characteristics of the technological tools that should be considered to face the challenges described in the previous section. Section 5 proposes technological solutions applicable to the challenges described. Section 6 includes conclusions and suggestions for future research.

2 LITERATURE REVIEW

The Base Erosion and Profit Shifting (BEPS) project has significantly increased top management's attention on the activities of the tax department. That is the reason why external tax consultants and transfer pricing software developers have started offering software for transfer pricing automation,[5,6,7] pointing out the benefits of its implementation[8] as well as analyzing factors that help MNEs to automate transfer pricing.[9] Besides publications on automation in transfer pricing, some authors have been analyzing a possible application of data science in transfer pricing. Schoeneborn and Rastogi[10] discuss how the development of transfer pricing solutions is enhancing the

5. Deloitte, *Streamline: Transform Your International Transfer Pricing Operations* (2020), https://www2.deloitte.com/bd/en/pages/tax/solutions/automation-technologies.html (accessed January 6, 2022).
6. PricewaterhouseCoopers, Llp., *Transfer Pricing: Global Coordinated Documentation* (2015), https://www.pwc.com/gx/en/services/tax/transfer-pricing/global-core-documentation.html (accessed January 6, 2022).
7. KPMG International Limited, *KPMG Report: Automating Transfer Pricing Documentation* (2021), https://home.kpmg/us/en/home/insights/2021/11/tnf-kpmg-report-automating-transfer-pricing-documentation.html (accessed January 6, 2022).
8. Accenture plc., *Robotic Process Automation: The Future of Technology in Financial Services* (2017), https://www.accenture.com/no-en/insight-financial-services-robotic-process-automation (accessed January 6, 2022).
9. Thomson Reuters Co., *4 Factors to Help You Automate Operational Transfer Pricing* (2020), https://tax.thomsonreuters.com/blog/automate-transfer-pricing/ (accessed January 6, 2022).
10. Frank Schoeneborn and Divya Vir Rastogi, *Embracing the Automation of Transfer Pricing*, International Tax Review (2020), https://www.internationaltaxreview.com/article/b1l0frblzh0fdl/embracing-the-automation-of-transfer-pricing (accessed January 6, 2022).

day-to-day work of tax professionals. PwC[11] focuses on the exploitation of Big Data and emerging technologies in transfer pricing.

Notwithstanding the consulting firm's recognition of the inherent role of technology in transfer pricing risk management, few academic contributions have focused on the link between information technology (IT) and tax. Overall, academic research on technology in transfer pricing used by the MNEs remains surprisingly limited.[12,13] Hemlinga et al.[14] reviewed current academic research and noted that while there is an increasing importance of tax risk management in MNEs, which implies the need for a more direct interaction between the information technology experts and tax department professionals, research focuses mainly on technology in accounting.

Therefore, this chapter seeks to address gaps identified in existing literature in relation to different types of technologies that can be applied to transfer pricing by MNEs. We examine factors that should be taken into account when considering the technology application. We understand that budgets are currently tight due to COVID-19 circumstances, so special focus is placed on small and medium technological projects.

3 CURRENT TRANSFER PRICING OBLIGATIONS IN MEXICO

The following table summarizes transfer pricing obligations in Mexico:

11. PricewaterhouseCoopers, Llp., *Transfer Pricing Analytics: The Exploitation of Big Data and Emerging Technologies in Transfer Pricing* (2016), https://www.pwc.com/gx/en/tax/publications/transfer-pricing/perspectives/assets/tp-16-analytics.pdf (accessed January 6, 2022).
12. John Gallemore and Eva Labro, *The Importance of the Internal Information Environment for Tax Avoidance*, Journal of Accounting and Economics 60 (1), 149–167 (2015).
13. Robert Hamilton and James Stekelberg, *The Effect of High-Quality Information Technology on Corporate Tax Avoidance and Tax Risk*, Journal of Information Systems 31 (2), 83–106 (2017).
14. Lars Hemlinga, Jacob Christian, Plesner Rossingb and Andreas Hoffjana, *The Use of Information Technology for International Transfer Pricing in Multinational Enterprises*, International Journal of Accounting Information Systems (2021), https://doi.org/10.1016/j.accinf.2021.100546 (accessed January 6, 2022).

#	*Obligation*	*Content*	*Timing of Filing and Frequency*	*Typical Challenges Faced by MNEs*
1	Country-by-country annual informative tax return (CbC)	Financial and tax information of all entities, grouped by country	To be submitted annually by Mexican MNEs	Preparation of consistent information and extraction from the system Loading of information prepared in Excel spreadsheet into online application
2	Master annual informative tax return (Master File)	Predominantly qualitative information about the group, such as intangibles, chain value, financing, and service contracts	To be submitted annually	Challenges are not relevant for the purpose of this chapter
3	Local annual informative tax return (Local File)	Detailed information about each entity's transactions and the respective transfer pricing analyses. It also includes certain sections of the Master File and CbC information	To be submitted annually	Coordination of information provided by different areas, segmented financial information in line with the local Generally Accepted Accounting Principles (GAAP), tax transaction matrix

#	*Obligation*	*Content*	*Timing of Filing and Frequency*	*Typical Challenges Faced by MNEs*
4	Transfer pricing analysis (TP documentation)	Detailed information about each entity's transactions and the respective transfer pricing analyses	To be prepared annually and delivered to the tax authorities during an audit	Coordination of information provided by different areas, segmented financial information in line with local Generally Accepted Accounting Principles (GAAP), tax transaction matrix
5	Annex 9 to the multiple informative tax return (A9DIM)	List of transactions, segmented financial information of the tested party, and a summary of the transfer pricing analyses	To be submitted annually	Segmented financial information in line with local GAAP, tax transaction matrix Loading of information prepared in Excel spreadsheet into online application
6	Transfer pricing annexes to information about tax situation (ISSIF)	List of transactions, together with the transfer pricing method and a taxpayer's risk self-assessment questionnaire	To be submitted annually	Tax transaction matrix Loading of information prepared in Excel spreadsheet into online application
7	Transfer pricing annexes to statutory tax report (DF)	List of transactions, together with the transfer pricing method, a taxpayer's risk self-assessment questionnaire, and an auditor's risk assessment questionnaire	To be submitted annually	Tax transaction matrix Loading of information prepared in Excel spreadsheet into online application

#	*Obligation*	*Content*	*Timing of Filing and Frequency*	*Typical Challenges Faced by MNEs*
8	The Best Method Rule (BMR)	Identification and documentation of internal comparable transactions	To be applied annually; the tax authorities may request it be tested during a tax audit	Review, comparison, and analysis of individual invoices
9	Form 76	List of derivatives, transfer pricing adjustments, business restructurings, residual royalty payment and tax residence modifications, as well as capital participation changes	To be submitted quarterly	Monitoring of intercompany transaction amounts once they meet the established threshold
10	Audits and invitation letters from the tax authorities	Contents vary on a case-by-case basis, but in all cases, a high amount of information and documentation is requested	N/A	Gathering of requested information typically upon short deadlines

Source: Summary prepared by the authors.

From the above table, it can be observed that MNEs in Mexico have to comply with various requirements on an annual basis (in some cases it can be up to eight obligations),[15] in a timely manner, which may require significant resources. The CbC report has to be filed in Mexico only if the MNE is a Mexican corporation. The Master File is not relevant for the purposes of this article in view of its predominantly qualitative nature. For the purpose of transfer pricing documentation and Local File preparation, input information is provided by the local tax department. The remaining forms are typically filed by the taxpayer with the support of an external consultant. Similarly, invitation letters and audits are typically handled by the taxpayer with the support of an external consultant.

One of the major challenges while preparing transfer pricing documentation is the preparation of segmented financial information. If an accounting system has not been configured, the taxpayer usually needs to spend a considerable amount of time in doing so. Typically, ERP systems design is based on the prioritization of management reporting needs (business unit-level reporting), and it produces segmented financial information that is not based on legal entity-level reporting. In our experience, if segmentation methodology is not properly documented, the results may vary each year and be challenged during a transfer pricing audit.

The taxpayers are also required to identify and document internal comparables. Access to detailed information favors application of the Comparable Uncontrolled Price (CUP) method, which consists of a price comparison agreed between related and third parties. In Mexico, the best method rule applies to all transactions carried out between related parties, and the taxpayer may only use the other methods when the CUP method set is inappropriate for determining whether transactions were conducted at market prices/on an arm's-length basis. This effectively places the burden to prove and document the reasons for not applying this method on the taxpayer.

Taxpayers also spend significant time loading the annexes requested by the tax authorities into online applications. Given that the information presented in various returns may be overlapping, any discrepancies should be identified, and supporting tools should allow for agile intervention if deviations are detected.

Of note, based on our experience, many taxpayers spend most of their time obtaining tax transaction matrices and resolving differences in intercompany transaction amounts (the amount of the transactions for tax purposes may differ from the accounting records). Differences usually arise from: (i) different criteria used to group and/or classify transactions; (ii) absence of accounting records in one of the entities; and/or (iii) different criteria in currency translation policies. Although resolving differences may seem simple, it implies a significant amount of rework, especially if the transaction that has changed affects the documentation of various entities (and different tax personnel in charge), or if it is necessary to make an additional last-minute analysis.

Finally, during transfer pricing audit processes, the MNE-centralized transfer pricing area provides support to subsidiaries; nevertheless, information is typically required to

15. In Mexico, taxpayers can file either DF or ISSIF. The Local File and transfer pricing documentation are separate requirements, and there are slight differences in the content of each of them.

be provided by the local tax department. In practice, tax authorities are implementing short deadlines (within a few days) for MNEs to respond to information requests during tax audits. This adds tremendous pressure to the manual data processing approach and incentivizes MNEs to automate the transfer pricing documentation process.

4 SUGGESTED TECHNOLOGY CHARACTERISTICS

Following a review of the key transfer pricing compliance obligations in Mexico (points from 1 to 8 that described in table that summarizes transfer pricing obligations in Mexico), the main challenges are due and timely compliance with the deadlines set by the tax authorities and the use of reliable tax and accounting information. The following section briefly describes the characteristics that technology systems should have to allow MNEs to optimize transfer pricing compliance costs while leveraging their data.[16]

4.1 Data Extraction

First and foremost, we need reliable and consistent information for all entities in a group. There are two major factors required to achieve this:

(1) Information from accounting systems. It is key to know how to obtain and interpret information from accounting systems. To achieve this: (1) day-to-day urgencies should not limit a tax team's available time to learn how the accounting systems work, and (2) a team should have know-how transmission methods to prevent staff turnover from eroding its knowledge stock.
(2) Completion and integration methodologies. It is important to have robust methodologies to: (1) complete information that has not been recorded on accounting systems, and (2) integrate calculations from working papers outside accounting systems. A typical example in taxes is configuring accounting systems so that accounting records have a text field linking them to electronic invoices (tax records).

As of the data extraction for transfer pricing purposes, typically, transfer pricing practitioners would deal with financial data obtained from the ERP system, which may not be based on legal entity-level reporting. Furthermore, in certain cases, electronic invoices may need to be a direct source of obtaining tax transactions matrix (amount of transaction for tax purposes may differ from the accounting records).

16. Centro Interamericano de Administraciones Tributarias, Servicio de Impuestos Internos de Chile, Fondo Monetario Internacional, *Manual sobre Gestión de Riesgos de Incumplimiento para Administraciones Tributarias* (2020).

4.2 Availability and Adaptability

Taxpayers have tight deadlines to provide the information requested by the Mexican tax authorities. In addition to the above, we constantly face new obligations. Therefore, technology should easily adapt to meet new obligations, and systems should update their functions periodically to reflect new transfer pricing requirements while being available every time an action is required.

Bottom line, systems should be able to adapt to different scenarios and possible changes resulting from future tax obligations and process improvements. The latter should include improvements related to system interoperability (how different components interact with each other) and system integration (how different components work together).

As of transfer pricing obligations in Mexico, the taxpayers that file tax report need to provide transfer pricing report so the independent audit can file transfer pricing annexes, but at the same time, the transfer pricing advisors require tax report to finalize their transfer pricing study. That leads us to the chicken and egg problem and typically very short period for finalizing transfer pricing report and taking any action, if needed.

4.3 Profiling or Profiles

Systems are set up based on certain requirements to perform actions, and these actions are contingent upon those that will allow access to a type of user (e.g., levels of access to information, data recording, file extraction and graphic visualization, among others, are defined), depending on the needs of a user, area, or organization, always based on the maximum possible transparency and proper knowledge management.

In transfer pricing, profiles are important when sharing information within a group and with persons outside the group (e.g., advisors, tax authorities). For example, large groups typically have different business units that operate under different and independent administrations but under the same (or almost the same) board of directors. In this context, the information of one administration should not be shared with another administration. Typical items subject to this restriction are profit margins, agreements, etc.

4.4 Traceability and Comparability

Systems must allow for data traceability, from its origin to the modifications introduced, along with comparability. Traceability refers to accounting records that match tax records, in the understanding that this is not about tax reconciliation (e.g., nonaccounting taxable income, nontaxable accounting income). We refer to a tax function that keeps track of the costs and revenues of each entity and for each intercompany transaction.

It is worth noting that transfer pricing audits can happen many years after the transactions. Therefore, if the MNE has an ERP that does not have traceability for historic data, it could raise the risk of not being able to support results on audit.

4.5 Security and Access to Information

Systems must not only set restrictions for each profile but also have security tools or algorithms to manage highly sensitive information, for example, limiting which profiles may view and capture information and restricting access to and management of massive volumes of data.

Some examples of sensitive information in transfer pricing processes include data like individual compensation, intangible development costs and cost breakdowns that could be commercially confidential. Additional examples of sensitive information for many headquarters are: (1) complete shareholder structure, (2) tax and financial information of entities outside Mexico, and (3) workpapers backing up purchase price allocations and management fees.

5 WHAT TOOLS CAN WE USE TO FACE THESE CHALLENGES?

For the purposes of this chapter, technological tools are classified based on their functionality, as presented below:

- automation tools for saving time and also standardizing a process to reduce manual errors;
- data visualization for communicating data-driven messages;
- data science for making feasible complex analyses;
- cloud computing for managing large volumes of transactions or gaining insights from tons of data/large datasets.

Below, the authors describe each technological tool and give examples of their application to the transfer pricing obligations and challenges described above.

5.1 Automation

As described in section 3, many transfer pricing obligations for MNEs consist of manual and repetitive processes. Finance automation and robotics may allow to streamline MNEs' internal transfer pricing processes. The main benefits of robotics are presented below:[17]

- Reduced cost by 80%.
- Reduced time to perform tasks by 80%-90%.
- Increased quality by reducing human errors.
- Scalable solutions that fit into the current IT setup.
- Runs on top of existing IT infrastructure and requires no IT transformation project.

17. Accenture plc., *Robotic Process Automation: The Future of Technology in Financial Services* (2017), https://www.accenture.com/no-en/insight-financial-services-robotic-process-automation (accessed January 6, 2022).

- Keeps competences and control locally.

The transfer pricing-related activities and processes suitable for automation and robotics should not depend on human judgement. However, if processes require the sensitivity and decision mandate of a human, technology can help present the better options for a human to make the decision. Furthermore, the process for automation should be stable, initiated by a digital trigger, and supported by digital data. Finally, the bigger the volume of executions of the process, the major the benefit.[18]

Some examples of technologies used in automation fields include:

- Macros in Excel or Word.
- Software for data preparation and analysis.
- Software for Robotic Process Automation (RPA).
- Platforms for professional developers.

Programs can be developed to automate repetitive tasks ranging from the drafting of transfer pricing annexes to the massive generation and/or correction of intercompany agreements. It is worth noting that the tax authorities make full use of automation to generate invitation letters and/or requests addressed to taxpayers, asking them to correct minor errors in transfer pricing returns.

5.1.1 Automation to Submit A9DIM

Below is a description of a potential automation project for MNEs:

> *Problem statement.* Company X is obliged to submit A9DIM. The tax authorities provide a desktop application to prepare and submit A9DIM,[19] so Company X's tax team has to: (1) manually capture the transactions and a summary of the transfer pricing analyses, or (2) use a feature within the software to batch load this data. The latter is clearly the way to go. However, the A9DIM desktop application is very hard to work with, and the batch functionality is problematic as in case of errors, it is always difficult to identify the data point causing them.
>
> *Proposed technology.* Excel is a good option here, and it is the technology used to cope with the A9DIM desktop application. The proposed steps are: (1) concatenating data columns according to a layout provided by the application, (2) saving the concatenated data in a text file, and (3) loading it into the application.
>
> Another alternative is to develop formulas or macros that just concatenate data columns that have data validation steps included. We could also use Alteryx paired with the data validation and consistency routines for filing

18. Intercompany Software, *Eight Transfer Pricing Processes Suitable for Automation – and Seven Processes that are not* (2017), https://intercompany-software.com/articles/Eight_Transfer_Pricing_processes_suitable_for_automation_and_seven_that_are_not.pdf (accessed January 6, 2022).
19. Refer to Appendix A to see the content of A9DIM.

A9DIM. Data validation refers to features that help to meet the rules of the software, such as catalogues for transfer pricing methods, countries, transaction codes, while data consistency refers to using consistent names, tax identification numbers and addresses for entities, and reporting the same transactions for all entities. Failure to consider data validation and consistency results in programs that do produce a text file, but do not pass the validation checks of the A9DIM application, or in A9DIMs with different transactions, different tax identification numbers for the same entity and so on, even for groups with few entities.

Complexity. Complexity comes from the need to introduce data validation and consistency procedures.[20]

5.1.2 *Automation to Submit Information Online: ISSIF or DF*[21]

Below is a description of another potential automation project for MNEs:

Problem statement. Company X is obliged to file ISSIF and has to prepare the corresponding transfer pricing annexes, in particular the one covering intercompany transactions. The tax authorities provide an Excel template to capture the data that unfortunately prevents users from copy-pasting, so Company X's tax team has to do this manually. The Excel template is powered by a technology from Microsoft called Visual Studio Tools for Office (VSTO), which combines Excel with Microsoft NET Framework, Microsoft's platform for professional developers.

Proposed technology. RPA, Excel and Excel combined with VSTO are good options. Another good option is to acquire a license from vendors dedicated to the automation of ISSIF and DF. These vendors provide a plain Excel workbook without the copy-paste restriction that is then fed into their software.

Complexity. Complexity comes from the need to introduce data validation and consistency procedures.

5.1.3 *Automation to Submit the CbC Report*

Below is a description of other potential automation projects for MNEs:

Problem statement. Company X is obliged to file the CbC report for the group, which has more than two hundred entities worldwide. We are assuming that the company has a separate process to create the CbC. The tax authorities provide an online application to submit the CbC report, so Company X's tax team has to capture the financial and tax data of more than two hundred

20. As of the date of this chapter, tax authorities publish a desktop application that is installed into the taxpayers' computer to prepare and submit A9DIM.
21. Refer to Appendix B to see the content of ISSIF and DF.

entities manually. Please note that the CbC report asks for ten financial and tax data points per entity, so we might assume that a person capturing the CbC may get tired and possibly start making mistakes early in the data capture process.

Proposed technology. RPA is a good option since the tax authorities provide neither programs to automate its online application nor functionalities to batch upload data. RPA is software that replicates, for practical purposes, anything a person does with a computer, mainly mouse clicks and keyboard strokes. RPA programs are also known as robots or bots for short. RPA should be used only if the target applications do not provide programs to automate them.

Complexity. The IT department needs to authorize the use of bots. In the case of existence of CAPTCHA (Completely Automated Public Turing Test to Tell Computers and Humans Apart), RPA would have to be combined with human interaction to complete a "human" test. Finally, to take the most out of RPA software licenses, the bot would need to be trained in other activities, so it is busy most of the time. This means it is desirable to cover many activities in RPA projects.

5.1.4 Platform to Prepare TP Documentation

Below is a description of other potential automation projects for MNEs:

Problem statement. Company X needs to prepare its transfer pricing documentation and has twenty entities in Mexico. Company X's tax team considers that it is key to have consistent documents across entities and would like to minimize rework caused by changes to transfer pricing analyses and/or transactions that impact the documents of other entities.

Proposed technology. Believe it or not, Word has the infrastructure to handle this issue, albeit training will surely be needed. Another option is to acquire a license for specialized transfer pricing software equipped with text editor capabilities and integrated with comparable companies and/or transactions databases.

Complexity. The IT department needs to authorize the use of third-party applications for preparing transfer pricing documentation.

5.2 Data Visualization

By using visual components like charts, diagrams, and maps, data visualization tools provide an approachable way to recognize and explore trends, patterns, and outliers in data. Although descriptive analytics has been around for decades, new technological solutions - centered around data visualization tools as well as data computation tools and database management software - allow us to significantly expand the amount of data we analyze and efficiently grow data analytics to include a predictive and prescriptive angle.

Some examples of technologies in this field include:

- Spreadsheets and/or graphs in Excel.
- Software for data visualization (e.g., Tableau, MicroStrategy, QlikView, PowerBI, just to name a few).

A potential visualization project is monitoring the implementation of transfer pricing policies. Below is a description of such project:

> *Problem statement*. Company X needs to monitor the implementation of its transfer pricing policies. Since Company X pertains to a large group, monitoring its policy will be definitively challenging, as this entails huge amounts of information.
> *Proposed technology*. Assuming we have structured information, software visualization tools are a good option since they usually facilitate seeing information from a high-level perspective or simply seeing what matters most. In scenarios like these, it is important to have visualizations with actionable items. Regardless of the software for data visualization used, we should be able to give clear data-driven messages as well as calls for action, if needed.
> *Complexity*. The most complex issue here is the iterative nature of visualizations: once you have a draft, you or another team member may want to change something. It is very important that the team has a clear idea of the Key Performance Indicators (KPIs) to be shown, something that gets more complex if the team is large and there are no rules to reach consensus. Additionally, every change may have an effect on how the visualization software needs the data, consuming additional time.

5.3 Data Science

Data science is related to data mining, machine learning, time series analysis and Big Data. Data science uses scientific methods, processes, algorithms, and systems to extract knowledge and insights from noisy, structured, and unstructured data[22] and apply knowledge and actionable insights from data across a broad range of application domains[23] (Dhar 2013). Examples of structured data are tables in Excel workbooks, databases, XML and JSON files. Examples of unstructured data are agreements, filings to stock exchanges, annual reports, purchase orders, emails and media (e.g., pictures, audio, video).

Visualization tools, when dealing with significant amount of information, should be combined with data for storage and basic manipulation. Excel is effective but is often

22. Structured data is highly specific and is stored in a predefined format, where unstructured data is a conglomeration of many varied types of data that are stored in their native formats.
23. Vasant Dhar, *Data Science and Prediction*, Communications of the Association for Computing Machinery. 56 (12), 64–73 (2013).

time-consuming to maintain and review. Therefore, adding data and analytics solutions (e.g., SQL, Alteryx, PowerPivot) to the current Excel environment can reduce time and level of effort. The following graph shows a sample process flow leveraging data analytics and visualization technologies:[24]

ETL = Extract, transform and load, GL = General ledger, PBC = Prepared by client

We can apply data science to transfer pricing to classify intercompany transactions, identify internal comparables, segment financial information and forecast financial information. Forecasts can be useful in transfer pricing because: (1) current transfer pricing regulations put an administrative burden on transfer pricing adjustments that can be as high as having to ask for a ruling to tax authorities if the adjustment is made after filing the annual income tax return, and (2) current electronic invoice regulations state that taxpayers have until March of the following year to cancel any invoices. These restrictions combined with less time to comply can make the implementation of a transfer pricing policy difficult after year-end, especially in case of deviations and therefore the usefulness of forecasts.

Some examples of technologies in this field include:

- platforms for professional developers.
- programming languages with libraries specialized in data science.
- software specifically designed for mathematics, statistics, and data science.

5.3.1 *Identification of Comparable Transactions*

Below is a description of a potential data science tool project for MNEs.

> *Problem statement*. Company X is engaged in the manufacture and distribution of products. Company X sells its products to third parties and to Company Y, a related party. As part of its annual transfer pricing documentation process, Company X has to apply the best method rule and test if the sale of products to Company Y can be analyzed by using the CUP method through the application of internal comparables. Company X relies on current technologies to carry out this analysis as it has millions of transactions each year.
> *Proposed technology*. Assuming we have structured information, we may use Excel, Alteryx or data science programs to analyze the invoices issued by Company X. Company X can build a solution directly into its ERP in order to analyze its invoices and payment terms.
> *Complexity*. The most complex issue here is the availability of resources, both human and material, to carry out this analysis in case we need to go through

24. PricewaterhouseCoopers, Llp., *Transfer Pricing Analytics: The Exploitation of Big Data and Emerging Technologies in Transfer Pricing* (2016), https://www.pwc.com/gx/en/tax/publications/transfer-pricing/perspectives/assets/tp-16-analytics.pdf (accessed January 6, 2022).

millions of transactions for CUP analysis. In practice, we can go at a higher summary level like profit center, customer, product/brand or intercompany to get that information. The latter approach assumes the ERP is able to produce the information needed for the transfer pricing analysis (e.g., segmented COGS and profit center for the transaction under analysis), and the human resources are available to prepare a segmented financial statement.

5.3.2 Segmented Financial Information

Below is a description of another potential data science tool project for MNEs.

Problem statement. Company X is engaged in the manufacture and distribution of products. Company X sells its products to third parties and to XYZ Retail Operations, S.A. de C.V. (Company Y), a related party. Since the CUP method has not been applied, Company X needs to segment its financial statements in order to test its intercompany transactions.
Proposed technology. Excel may be sufficient for simpler cases of segmented financial information, while Alteryx can handle a medium complexity case. ERP systems can be configured to do segmentation right at the source, without the need for external software, but that could take significant resources, especially if the analysis requires information outside the ERP.
Complexity. The most complex issue here is the availability of resources, both human and material, to carry out this analysis.

Example of application of data science by tax authorities #1

Data science programming language for tax audit planning of tax fraud cases

Despite the main purpose of this chapter is to present a pragmatic approach to transfer pricing technology supported by real-life examples of its application by the MNEs, there are also interesting examples of application of data science by the Mexican tax authorities. Below is a description of potential data science project for the tax authorities.

The head of the Mexican tax authorities, Raquel Buenrostro Sánchez, gave a conference on June 23, 2020 (Presidential Conference 2020),[25] where she explained how data science is applied by the tax authorities. The tax authorities: (1) develop a model describing a typical taxpayer engaging in fraud transactions, (2) analyze available data, (3) identify patterns and relationships, (4) quantify damage, and (5) develop a remediation plan. As part of this analysis, the tax authorities identified 8,212 entities related to each other and analyzed about 22 million invoices.

25. Gobierno de México, Presidential Conference (June 23, 2020), https://www.youtube.com/watch?v=sJ-1NgAZSaA (accessed January 6, 2022). Raquel Buenrostro's presentation starts at 00:47:20.

Example of Application of data science by tax authorities #2

Data science programming language for tax audit planning due to noncompliance

Noncompliance can happen for a lot of reasons, such as lack of human and material resources, lack of training, and errors, and taxpayers who are knowingly deviating from what the law says. The core idea here is that noncompliers behave differently than compliers, so the goal would be to model the behavior of a hypothetical complier and compare it to actual taxpayers.

The following examples illustrate this idea: (1) a taxpayer that misses the deadline for its annual tax return, (2) a taxpayer with a lower effective tax rate than the benchmark calculated by the tax authorities, and (3) a comprehensive analysis of taxpayer tax returns and transactions that indicates a high probability of noncompliance.

5.4 Cloud Computing

Cloud computing offers customers a cost-effective alternative to purchasing and maintaining their own IT infrastructure. The cloud computing environment presents economies of scale since the cost of the consumer resources is generally shared among a broad user base. Cloud computing companies perform services over the internet, most often broken down into infrastructure as a service (IaaS), platform as a service (PaaS) and software as a service (SaaS).[26]

Cloud computing firms offer computing power and cognitive services, which are applications of artificial intelligence to certain tasks that formerly could only be done by people. In transfer pricing, we can use cognitive services to convert nonstructured sources of information (e.g., contracts, images, handwritten notes) into structured ones. An example includes:

- recognition of key data (e.g., names of companies, dates, amounts) on PDFs and images.

In general, vendors of this application have a desktop version of the software. However, the cloud-based versions are far superior in both capacity and speed. Lastly, cognitive services apply when we need to analyze thousands of documents.

A potential cloud computing project is a transfer pricing audit. Below is a description of such project:

> *Problem statement*. Continuing with Company X, let us assume the tax authorities are challenging the deduction of Company X's payments to Company Y, an entity providing management services to subsidiaries. As part

26. PricewaterhouseCoopers, Llp., *Transfer Pricing Perspectives: Fit for the Future* (2014), https://www.pwc.com/gx/en/tax/publications/transfer-pricing/perspectives/assets/tp-perspectives-ipad-oct-14.pdf (accessed January 6, 2022).

of the audit, Company X has to prove that it: (1) received a benefit related to services, (2) did not pay shareholder costs, and (3) did not pay for duplicate activities. For the purposes of this chapter, let us focus on the benefit test, which starts by being able to prove that services were actually provided.
Proposed technology. Cognitive services are a very good option here, assuming Company Y has digitized documentation showing it provided the services, such as photos of marketing team member visiting the subsidiary on a web camera. The strategy would be to apply cognitive services in order to recognize: (1) person and (2) handwritten names in roll call lists. If the pictures have geolocation, we could go even further and be able to prove the person provided the service. This approach is advisable if the digitized documentation has a bare minimum standard (e.g., certain resolution for scanned documents).
Complexity. The most complex issue here is the quality of the inputs and information security.

6 CONCLUSIONS

Transfer pricing discipline is at the core of the information collection process, including transactional data, legal entity company information, benchmarking data, legal settlements and other sources of information impacting intercompany pricing. These data sets exist across a variety of sources and systems. The ability to capture and analyze data is transforming every aspect of the transfer pricing life cycle, from strategy and planning to price setting, maintenance, documentation, and even dispute resolution.

In this chapter, we analyzed MNEs tax departments' possible use of information that allow to automate transfer pricing processes, visualize data for communicating data-driven messages, make feasible complex analyses, and cloud computing for managing a large volume of transactions or gaining insights from tons of data. There is a great variety of technological tools that can effectively manage intercompany activity to ensure that pricing can be defended, reporting compliance is achieved, and filing due dates are met. An application of technology is doable for small and large projects, and MNEs can utilize a range of solutions from simple to complex ones.

Based on our experience, transfer pricing technological journey can be initiated using the existing tools and licenses already available for MNEs. Definitively, it is worth continuing learning Word, Excel, and PowerPoint. Nussbaumer[27] does great storytelling with data using only Excel graphs. However, marketing and finance departments are often using data computation tools, database management software and visualization tools, and they may have extra license that can be used in tax department. It is also important to look for internal stakeholders for mutual benefit derived from technological tools that can be applied through various functional areas within MNEs.

27. Cole Nussbaumer Knaflic, *Storytelling with Data*. John Wiley & Sons, Inc. Honoken, New Jersey (2015).

What is absolutely clear is that the digitization of tax processes would also require other skills developed among existing tax personnel or imported into the tax department through new hires. In addition to transfer pricing and tax knowledge, the team would need to have or receive support from an external consultant with expertise in statistics, data science, programming, and artificial intelligence. Therefore, senior-level tax people should initiate more focused efforts to ensure IT agility within their departments. If tax departments are to successfully engage in organizational debates to promote transfer pricing technologies, they need to enhance their technological knowledge base.

Finally, we will outline some limitations of this research and provide suggestions for future research. First, our chapter focuses mainly on technological tools that are classified based on their functionality. Future research could conduct a more detailed study of ERP applications for transfer pricing. Second, our chapter focuses mainly on technological solutions available for MNEs. It would be interesting to understand the perspectives of the tax authorities and their technological needs. Third, this research focuses primarily on transfer pricing requirements in Mexico, so future research could explore transfer pricing regulations in other jurisdictions.

APPENDIX A ANNEX 9 TO THE MULTIPLE INFORMATIVE TAX RETURN (A9DIM)

Information presented below should be filed by each transaction and each related party:

#	*Concepts*
1	Name or denomination or company name (related party)
2	Resident's address abroad (street number, zip code, city, telephone)
3	Tax identification number
4	Key of residence country
5	Type of related party
6	Tested party
7	Transfer pricing method used
8	Transaction type
9	Indicate if you use internal comparables
10	Amount of the operation (pesos)
11	Transfer pricing adjustment (pesos)
12	"Percentage obtained from the operation: Profit"
13	"Percentage obtained from the operation: Loss"
14	Agreed rate or percentage (interest, royalties, commissions, among others)
15	Accumulated amount
16	Deducted amount
17	Amount of accrued operations
18	Amount of the payable operations
19	Amount paid
20	Amount of exempt operations
21	Indicate if tax rate established in tax treaty was used
22	Withhold rate
23	Income tax paid withheld
24	Net income or sales
25	COGS
26	Gross profit
27	Gross loss
28	Operating expenses
29	Operating profit
30	Operating loss
31	Average operating assets

#	*Concepts*
32	Specify range concept (total/interquartile)
33	Lower limit
34	Median
35	Upper limit
36	Number of comparables in the sample
37	SIC codes of the sample
38	Indicate if you made any comparability adjustments
39	Indicate the amount of the adjustment by which the transaction increased or decreased
40	Specify the type of transaction
41	Type of margin obtained from profit or loss
42	Describe client functions
43	Functions—Distribution
44	Specify
45	Functions—manufacture
46	Specify
47	Functions—Service provider
48	Specify
49	Leasing of goods
50	Specify
51	Others
52	Specify
53	Indicate if you have a transfer pricing study in place

APPENDIX B TRANSFER PRICING ANNEXES TO INFORMATION ABOUT TAX SITUATION (ISSIF)

Information presented below should be filed by each transaction and each related party:

#	*Concept*
1	Customer Name
2	Customer Tax ID
3	Transaction Name
4	Specify Other
5	Country
6	Amount
7	Method
8	Does the transaction involve unique and valuable contributions? (YES OR NO)
9	Is the transaction at arm's length? (YES OR NO)
10	Transfer pricing adjustment?
11	Modifications were made to VAT (YES OR NO)
12	Amount adjusted

Index

U

V

www.ingramcontent.com/pod-product-compliance
Ingram Content Group UK Ltd.
Pitfield, Milton Keynes, MK11 3LW, UK
UKHW020244290926
15470UKWH00002B/727

9 789403 546032